Morals, Ethics and Religions

Carl G. Schowengerdt

First Edition

Y-City Publishing, LLC

Published by:
Y-City Publishing, LLC
Post Office Box 2459
Zanesville, Ohio, U.S.A.
43702-2459
www.y-citypublishing.com
740-452-2931

Orders at www.y-citypublishing.com

ISBN 978-0-9767097-3-2

First printing, 2010

Library of Congress Control Number: 2010922125

Graphics provided by Digitalmighty Design
www.digitalmighty.com

CONTENTS

ACKNOWLEDGEMENTS

I am deeply grateful to those members of the family and close friends, who were willing to share of their time and effort, to wade through the initial versions of this manuscript, and provide their suggestions for improvement. You helped make sense of those sections that did not make sense. That list includes Eric Schowengerdt, Andrea Bell, David Schowengerdt, Bryan Ochalla, Jan Schowengerdt, Janet Ochalla, Carol Auchard and Shane Dement. Eric's knowledge of book formatting and layout has been a great blessing. Jan, as Editor-in-Chief, has been a tremendous source of support and resource throughout this entire effort. Her skills in graphic design have been superb. Carol, through her trenchant analyses, has allowed me to make sections rational, which were up to that point not easily understandable. My good friend, William Tanner Stewart, incited me to begin on this journey through long earnest discussions in Sunday school, and afterwards. All of you have taught me how to be reasonable and analytical, rather than preach. In this subject of morality, which is often imbued with great emotion and vested interest, combined with deeply set religious faiths, it is highly important to scrutinize only, and not proselytize. All of you have guided me to be a social scientist and not an evangelist.

For those contributions each of you has made, in your own way, I am truly grateful. This book has, indeed, been a group effort. Thanks to all of you.

INTRODUCTION

This book is about first, trying to provide better understanding of our morals, and then, using that clearer understanding, looking for those ways we can reform, or make better use of, our value systems. What reform is needed? You may ask. Morals are what they are. Just because we don't always observe them like we should doesn't mean that our value systems are flawed. Right is right, wrong is wrong, good is good and evil is evil. Our religions guide us, and tell us what our moral goals are, for which we should strive. Just because we are humans who often fail to do things correctly, and who err frequently, does not mean that our goals should change, or that our religions should change. Sure, we all keep trying to be good people, but just haven't been able to get there yet, except on occasion. There are times when we are witness to mercy and forgiveness that we find deeply warming, and know where we should direct our efforts: toward those types of goals. We should be more loving, and if we are more loving, then we are going to be better neighbors and citizens. We also have a lot of really bad guys out there, deviants in our societies, who keep cheating, lying, stealing, killing, and who drag us all down in our society. We are fighting all those who are evil, and are doing our best to either get rid of them or rehabilitate them in ways of justice. We don't need new understanding, or need to reform our morals. What we need to reform are those persons in our societies that don't obey those rules. We don't need to change our goals of goodness, we are prone to say. What we must do is change the behavior of those millions of people who are lawless, terrorists and murderers, by whatever force is necessary to achieve that goal.

This book begs to differ. It will ask each of us to understand that right, wrong, good, evil, morals, fairness, justice and ethics exist only in the value system of humans. It will attempt to lead each of us to the conclusion that, in spite of what we may have been taught in the past, there is no intrinsic divine Goodness in this universe. This book will ask each reader to accept that this universe does not care about humans. It will ask each reader to leave a land of religious opinion and enter a universe of relativity. This book will seek to loosen the tightly wrapped combination of morality and intense intolerance in our religions, which is all gnarled together in our heads. We have not yet understood that this combination of religious mercy and its opposite, religious intolerance, which exists prominently in our religions, is highly incompatible. The result of this unrecognized incompatibility is that we are encouraged to commit acts of great violence and cruelty, while feeling righteous. This complete incompatibility of religious morality, and religious hatred of other humans, has not fully registered in our heads, for reasons which are unclear. Our morals systems, if we look at them rationally, are a mess, and none of us seems to have squarely addressed that issue. We don't understand why our religions sometimes teach us hatred, more than they teach us compassion.

This discussion will hopefully give each reader a better vision of where morals derive, what they really mean, and what ethics should be. It will address the denial of our civil liberties by some who are quite religious, but who are greatly misdirected. It will prayerfully provide a clearer definition of what is moral, adding meaning and weight to those words we use to describe our values, sometimes tritely. The decisions we make in life are driven by fairly base human emotions. Those usual human motives of fear, greed, lust and egocentricity have driven our expressions of human cruelty. When those are sanctified by religious concepts, it is time to redefine what is right, what is wrong, what is moral, what is ethical, and how our religions are tied to our morals. We can't get rid of fear, lust and greed in our societies, at this time in our development. What we can do is to make it clear that when these base emotions become expressed as violent intolerance, that conduct is immoral, no matter what religious belief is used to justify those acts. That incompatible dichotomy of expression in our religions certainly deserves further discussion. The answers that come from these discussions will not be obtuse, and they will hopefully be different from those we have become used to hearing. I would fervently hope that each person who reads this book will, at the end, be able to say to him or herself, "That makes sense." I would hope that this discussion will contribute to a renewed understanding of how our value systems need to be defined, and how they need to be applied, without religious intolerance.

ISLAM MORAL REFORM

Examples of distorted value systems in current events highlight our need to redefine our existing morals. Our world currently contains multitudes of violent attacks which are broadcast as righteous, while they destroy our societies and deny millions the right to life, liberty and the pursuit of happiness. Using that golden standard of life, liberty and the pursuit of happiness, there is no more cogent example of distorted morals than the events of 9/11/01. The most fascinating aspect of that horror, and subsequent horrors that have followed, at least from a moral viewpoint, is why no one has asked, in depth, why both sides, to this day, continue to see this tragedy as black and white, good versus evil. There has been little understanding in the middle, from either Muslims or Christians. In general parlance, the only descriptions we have heard in the English language are that these were terrorist attacks. Many of the accounts that have been heard in Arabic describe this day as a glorious victory against the Great Satan. Why? Why does neither side understand the value system of the other side? Why do both sides continue to feel righteous while doing terrible things to other human beings?

We, as the American public and the American government, should have seen this coming for a full thirty years, but we did not. We were too involved in our personal lives, while we were watching Jimmy Carter, Ronald Reagan, George H. Bush, Bill Clinton, and fighting the Gulf War. We did not appreciate the hatred building in Arab communities around the world, directed toward the United States. When we experienced examples of that hatred, we simply passed them off, after a few weeks of attention, as other examples of jealousy of the

American way of life. Each of these attacks was like a wasp bite, hurting badly for a little while, and then going away. Certainly none of them, we thought, indicated any need on our part to think differently and act differently toward Muslim needs. We were so sadly mistaken.

We had been so secure in our way of life that, in 1979, we financed an Arab named Osama Bin Laden to recruit and arm a guerrilla force, to resist the Russian occupation of Afghanistan. After successfully resisting the Russians, that force continued to resist any invasion of Arab lands by foreign infidel governments. It became known as al Qaeda, and has continued to grow since that time, as hatred of the United States by Muslims has continued to grow. American meddling in the affairs of Arab lands in order to protect our oil interests has not set well with the Muslim nations. We further fostered that hatred, under recent administrations, by invading multiple other countries, giving billions in aid to Israel, but not a commensurate amount to Arab nations, and trying to control the economy of the entire world.

There has been a long past history over multiple centuries of Islam/Christian conflicts, and a rich recent history of that enmity. Muslim resistance to the favoritism and imperialism of America has rapidly accelerated over the last several decades. An early manifestation of that hatred occurred on November 4, l979. Iranian students, in support of the Islamic revolution, broke into the American Embassy in Iran. There were 53 diplomats in the building, who were held hostage for 444 days. President Jimmy Carter was urged to take some type of military action, but instead chose to hold prolonged negotiations with Iran. That siege was lifted by those students as the Islamic revolution was completed. Jimmy Carter was greatly criticized for his management of this crisis, and it played a significant role in his loss to Ronald Reagan, in the l980 election. Carter was felt to be too soft on extremists. No one seemed to care that his diplomacy had saved many lives, even though it took over a year to solve that crisis.

There was soon much more to follow. After the aggressive Israeli invasion of Lebanon in 1982, backed by the United States, an international peacekeeping force had been established in that country. A part of that contingent was an American marines barracks, situated at the Beirut International Airport. On October 23, 1983, a yellow Mercedes Benz truck driven by an Islamic suicide bomber arrived at the Beirut International Airport, at 6:20 a.m. The driver circled the barracks, then crashed through an outer retaining fence, between sentry posts, through the front gate, and arrived in the lobby of that building. He then set off his explosives, lifting the building up in a big fireball. As it settled, the entire building was destroyed. Three hundred American servicemen were killed. A few minutes later, a similar truck bomb was driven into the basement parking area of the French barracks, in West Beirut. It was detonated by another Islamic suicide bomber, leveling that building and killing 53 French soldiers. These blasts led to the withdrawal of peacekeeping forces from Lebanon, and greatly enhanced the cause of Islamic jihadists. There was no appreciable reprisal for these crimes.

On October 7, 1985, the cruise ship Achille Lauro was sailing from Alexandria to Port Said. Four men representing the Palestine Liberation Front commandeered the ship. They demanded the release of fifty Palestinian prisoners who were being held in Israeli jails. They were confronted by a wheelchair bound American, Leon Klinghoffer, who angered them. They killed him and dumped his body overboard. They negotiated with Egyptian authorities, who arranged transport for them on an Egyptian airliner, from Egypt to Tunisia, while negotiations were in progress. That flight was intercepted by American Tomahawk fighter planes, which forced the airliner to divert to Italy, where the captors were arrested. Egypt vociferously protested this invasion of their authority and their right to deal with their own crimes.

It was not as if we had not already received warning that Islamic extremists would use airplanes as giant destructive weapons. On December 21, 1988, Pan Am flight 103 left Heathrow airport at 1825 GMT. It was a Boeing 747, named Clipper Maid of the Seas, which reached an altitude of 31,000 feet over Scotland. At that point a bomb, placed in a suitcase which was situated in the forward hold, exploded. It had been placed there by two Libyan Muslim extremists who were not on that flight. The airplane disintegrated in mid air, pieces of the plane, luggage and passengers falling on and around the small town of Lockerbie, Scotland. The fuel laden wings formed huge fire balls on impact, tearing large craters in the ground. All 243 passengers, sixteen crew members, and eleven citizens on the ground were killed by the crash.

There was then the mysterious demise of an American airliner which took off from the east coast on a transatlantic flight, then inexplicably dove into the ocean, killing all passengers and crew aboard. Recovery of the flight recorder brought evidence that the pilot, once the flight had reached cruising altitude, had turned the flight over to the copilot, to go back in the cabin for some purpose relating to the crew and passengers. This copilot was an Arab of good reputation and work record. Once the dive began, there is no evidence that the pilot was able to get back in the cockpit to assume the controls. The last words issued by the copilot, before impact, were "May Allah be praised."

On February 26, 1993, a truck bomb was detonated in the parking garage beneath Tower I of the World Trade Center. Fifteen hundred pounds of urea nitrate-hydrogen were detonated, with the purpose of knocking the North Tower over onto the South Tower, thereby bringing both of them down. In spite of the blast, the building held without great structural damage, but did kill six and injured 1042. The plot was the work of a group of Arabic Islamic extremists, who had been financed by Khalid Sheikh Mohammed. This is the same Islamic true believer who later presented a different concept for bombing the World Trade Center Towers to Osama Bin Laden. Although his first attempt had been a failure, Mohammed's second attempt was a glorious success, if by success we mean accomplishing the goal of that mission.

On June 26, 1996, a fuel truck, unable to get through the gate, parked at the perimeter fence of a Saudi apartment complex housing American soldiers. Guards approached the truck to question the occupants as to their presence, but the drivers ran off to another vehicle parked nearby. A few minutes later the truck exploded, killing 23 soldiers and injuring 300 others. The perpetrators were not apprehended. This bombing took place less than a month after the Saudi government had beheaded four Muslim militants, who had been convicted of bombing an American military barracks in Riyadh, in November of 1995.

On October 12, 2000, the U.S.S. Cole, under the command of Kirk Lippold, moored at Aden harbor for a routine fuel stop. A small boat containing two passengers approached the ship from the port side. It appeared to the sailors to be a service craft, and they exchanged friendly greetings with the two men in the boat. A few minutes later, a great blast tore a huge hole in the side of the ship. It struck near the galley, where crew members were lining up for lunch. Seventeen sailors were killed and thirty nine were injured. Sailors were able to contain the flood by sealing off corridors and actuating pumps. The keel, fortunately, had not been damaged, and the ship remained afloat. It appeared that the blast had been accomplished by using plastic explosives, which had been molded onto the keel of the ship. Osama Bin Laden took credit, claiming this as another suicide victory for Islam against the foreign invaders.

Following his failure to bring down the World Trade Center Towers in 1993, Khalid Sheikh Mohammed was anxious to find redemption. He had not yet satisfied his hatred for the American infidels who denigrated the Islamic faith by supporting Israel and invading Arabic lands. Moreover, these Americans flaunted their wealth without caring for the poor, and flaunted their women as objects of sexual desire. The attitude of America toward the Muslim faith was, to Khalid Sheikh Mohammed, an apostasy. In his mind, America still needed to be taught a lesson. He initially presented his plan for using commercial airline flights to bring the World Trade Center Towers down to Bin Laden in 1996. While they were in discussion, Bin Laden was growing in Arabic influence and encouraging hatred of America. He issued a fatwa in 1996 calling for American soldiers to leave Saudi or suffer the consequences. He issued a second fatwa against the United States in 1998 for its support of Israel in the Israel/Palestine conflict. This religious war, fomenting for the last forty years, was heating up even further. Upon hearing no response to his demands, Osama felt that a major strike would be needed to get the attention of the imperious Americans and strike a blow against the Great Satan. He accepted Mohammed's plan, and began recruiting mujahedeen who would be willing to die for this cause. Although Mohammed was in charge of organizing this operation as soon as it could be done, it was Bin Laden who chose the participants.

Two of the initial recruits, Hazmi and Mihdhar, were selected because they were experienced jihadists from Bosnia. They came to the United States in 2000, where they took flying lessons in San Diego. They did not speak English well, and did not do well with those lessons. They still eventually participated in the attacks, but only as muscle enforcers. Recruits from Germany were added who spoke English well and who were accustomed to Western culture. They were sent to the United States where they took flying lessons in South Florida in the spring of 2001. Final selection of the sites, flights and assignments were completed in Spain, in July of 2001.

There were a total of 17,400 personnel in the World Trade Center Towers at the time the airplanes imploded into them. Most of those below the impact levels were able to escape. The South Tower burned for 56 minutes before collapsing and the North Tower burned for 102 minutes before collapsing. The intense heat above the levels of impact forced many to jump involuntarily out windows. Their bodies could be heard plopping on the pavement below. Those that climbed to the roof hoping for helicopter rescue were overcome by smoke, and probably died before the buildings fell. Of the 3300 known dead, 2603 were in the upper levels of the towers, 246 were on the airplanes, nineteen were hijackers, and 411 were emergency workers who responded to the call and were trapped when the buildings fell. There were 25 killed at the Pentagon. Twenty four remain missing to this day.

On Flight 93, which had been commandeered with the Capitol Building as the target, word got to the passengers by cell phone that other planes had crashed into the Trade Center Towers. Those passengers bravely attacked knife-slashing terrorists to take back the airplane. When it became apparent to the hijackers that they were going to lose control of the plane, the command to roll the plane over was given. A short time later, that plane plowed into the ground in a field near Shanksville, Pennsylvania, at 10:03 a.m., killing all on board.

Throughout all this terror, Osama Bin Laden remained consistent. Once he took up the battle to convert all people to Islam, and to drive all foreign invaders off Arab lands, he did not waver. In his 1998 fatwa against the United States, he quoted from the Koran, "Slay the infidels wherever ye find them." In his letter to the United States in 2002, he accepted responsibility for the 9/11/01 attacks, and made the following statement: "You are the worst civilization witnessed by the history of mankind. You are the nation who, rather than ruling by the Shariah of Allah in its Constitution and Laws, choose to invent your own laws as your policies, contradicting the pure nature which affirms Absolute Authority to the Lord and your Creator."

Although the United States has not been as easy to attack as previously, the work of al Qaeda has continued. There have been attacks on rail transportation systems in Spain and in London. Very few have any doubt that whenever there is an opportunity, there will be further attacks against Americans from Islamic true believers, wherever those Americans may be. Military and journalistic experts have labeled all these attacks as mostly political. That is probably true. That assessment misses the mark, however, that these vicious and cruel attacks are committed as part of religious fervor; they are commanded by the Koran. All it takes is a faithful Muslim, angered by some mistreatment, to carry them out, sacrificing his or her own life for this grand cause. The Koran commands him or her to do that act of violence against other humans, if those humans do not believe in Islam; it tells him or her that he or she will be glorified by their Islamic God for this explosive intolerance.

The audacity of these attacks, the financing necessary to carry them out, and the multiplicity of those involved indicate that there is indeed, an army of Muslim extremists who are committed to ending any life necessary in order to support their religion. Their number appears to be growing, as Western nations blindly attempt to deal with this threat militarily. The Bush administration could only see this as a conflict of good versus evil, that being terrorists (evil men) striking out against American imperialists (good people). The attempts of this administration to seek out militarily and kill those Muslims who have defended their land and their faith has resulted in an immense number of Iraqi and Afghan civilian deaths. The official death count for Iraqi civilians, as part of the Iraq war, was recently released, in newspaper accountings, as being 750,000. These, the military calls euphemistically, "collateral damage". According to a PBS special, morgue attendants say that only about one in five deaths is actually recorded. Those publicists for the interim government of Iraq apparently do not want it known how extensive the loss of human life has been. If this report is true, the actual civilian death toll is probably three million or more. These millions of dead have left behind them children without parents, burns, scars, loss of limbs and lifelong pain. We may have military victories, but we are losing the war of minds. We are most likely creating lifelong hatred of America. We have, it seems, so far failed to understand that this is a war of religious faith, and blinded morals, not a military battle.

Many questions remain. "Why have all these Muslims, over the last fourteen hundred years, consistently been willing to sacrifice their lives for this cause? Why have they consistently targeted others who do not share their particular faith? Why did the nineteen hijackers believe that this was the most gloriously righteous end to their lives, along with angry retribution against the 3000 others they took to death with them that day?" The castigation of these religious sui- cidists as being evil, as a part of an axis of evil, pitted against the forces of good in the world (primarily Christianity) was, in my opinion, greatly misguided. There is no doubt that this was a terrorist attack. There is also no doubt that those who carried out this act of horror did so with the deepest righteousness that exists in the human soul. They did so to become heroes to their families, their countries and their religions. If the reports that reach us are true, it would appear that they suc- ceeded rather spectacularly in that mission.

The Koran sheds great light on this moral conundrum. This book, when read in its entirety, is highly repetitive. The same themes and concepts are repeated over and over, in slightly different words. We are prone to throw in a phrase or two from the Koran that we have read somewhere, as if we understand this book. We can never under- stand it unless we can read it in its original language, and know the culture from which it came. The best we can do, as outsiders, is to col- lect all those quotes that clearly apply to the question at hand and see what they say, although perhaps poorly, through a veil of translation.

The literary form of the Koran is personal address. Although there are a few passages spoken by Angels or the Prophet Muhammad, all the others are spoken by the adjudged one true God of the entire uni- verse, Al-Lah (the God). Allah is variously referred to as I, We, He, My and Our. The Koran (or recitation) is not recorded in the exact sequence of those visions as received and spoken by Muhammad, then later recorded by scribes some thirty years later. The official version of the Koran rearranges them to place the longest Surahs (chapters) first, and the shortest, last. The major themes of this book, however, become repeated throughout these chapters.

Muhammad begins by demanding that all people believe in him as the last and greatest Prophet of all humankind, and as importantly, believe that he speaks the true words of the one and only true God in these recitations. In addition, Muhammad adds a terrible caveat. All those who do not believe in him deserve to be punished or killed for their infidelity. He then carries this punishment, in a moral sense, one awful step further. He equates belief in Islam as good, and disbelief in his vision as being evil. Now, in one fell swoop, we have the classic battle that comes to the fore in all religions. It is the battle of good versus evil, and only those who believe in Islam will be on the side of truth and justice. Those humans who are unfaithful (infidels) to this belief system deserve to be killed for their apostasy. The worst offenders in this system of good and evil are those who profess adherence to other faiths (primarily Judaism and Christianity), and especially those infidels who have wealth but do not share it with others. Such people as these, who appear to totally disagree with the tenets of Islam, deserve a violent end to their lives for their "evil" acts.

In my attempt to promote understanding of the depth of these messages, I include the following multiple quotes from the Koran, which say these things, and they are only representative. These will hopefully demonstrate the profundity of this message of distrust, exclusivity and punishment, which is contained in this Holy Book.

1:1. This book is not to be doubted.

1:6. As for the unbelievers, it is the same whether or not you forewarn them; they will not have faith. God has set a seal upon their hearts and ears; their sight is dimmed and grievous punishment awaits them.

3:18. The only true faith in God's sight is Islam.

5:33. Those that make war against God and His apostle and spread disorder in the land shall be slain or crucified or have their hands and feet cut off on alternate sides, or be banished from the land.

2:90. God's curse be upon the infidels! Evil is that for which they have bartered away their souls. To deny God's own revelation, grudging that He should reveal His bounty to whom He chooses from among His servants! They have incurred God's most inexorable wrath. Ignominious punishment awaits the unbelievers.

2:191. Slay them wherever you find them. Drive them out of the places from which they drove you. Idolatry is more grievous than bloodshed. But do not fight them within the precincts of the Holy Mosque unless they attack you there; if they attack you put them to the sword. Thus shall the unbelievers be rewarded; but if they desist, God is forgiving and merciful. Fight against them until idolatry is no more and God's religion reigns supreme.

4:17. God is all-knowing and wise. But He will not forgive those who do evil and, when death comes to them, say: "now we repent." Nor those who die unbelievers: for them We have prepared a woeful scourge.

7:40. For those who have denied and scorned Our revelations the gates of heaven shall not be opened; nor shall they enter Paradise until the camel shall pass through the eye of a needle. Thus shall We reward the guilty. Hell shall be their couch, and sheets of fire shall cover them. Thus shall We reward the evil-doer.

8:39. Tell the unbelievers that if they mend their ways their past shall be forgiven; but if they persist in sin, let them reflect upon the fate of bygone nations. Make war on them until idolatry shall cease and God's religion shall reign supreme.

9:73. Prophet, make war on the unbelievers and the hypocrites and deal rigorously with them. Hell shall be their home: an evil fate.

10:4. As for the unbelievers, scalding water shall they drink, and for their unbelief woeful punishment awaits them.

14:3. Woe betide the unbelievers, for they shall be sternly punished! Woe betide those who love this life more than the life to come; who debar others from the path of God and seek to make it crooked.

18:107. Hell is their reward: because they had no faith, and because they mocked My apostles and My revelation. As for those that have faith and do good works, they shall forever dwell in the gardens of Paradise, desiring no change.

29:68. And who is more wicked than the man who invents a falsehood about God and denies the truth when it is declared to Him? Is there not a home in Hell for the unbelievers?

2:113. The Jews say the Christians are misguided, and the Christians say it is the Jews who are misguided. Yet they both read the Scriptures. And the ignorant say the same of both. God will on the Day of Resurrection judge their disputes.

2:275. Those that live on usury shall rise up before God

like men whom Satan has demented by his touch; for they claim that trading is no different from usury. But God has permitted trading and made usury unlawful. He that has received an admonition from his Lord and mended his ways may keep his previous gains; God will be his judge. Those that turn back shall be the inmates of the Fire, wherein they shall abide forever.

4:160. Because of their iniquity, We forbade the Jews wholesome things which were formerly allowed them; because time after time they have debarred others from the path of God; because they practice usury – although they were forbidden it – and cheat others of their possessions. Woeful punishment have We prepared for those that disbelieve.

5:51. Believers, take neither the Jews nor the Christians for your friends.

5:72. Unbelievers are those that say: "God is the Messiah, the son of Mary."

5:73. Unbelievers are those that say: "God is one of three." There is but one God.

23:91. Never has God begotten a son, nor is there any other god beside Him.

47:3. When you meet the unbelievers in the battlefield strike off their heads and, when you have laid them low, bind your captives firmly. Then grant them their freedom or take a ransom from them, until War shall lay down her burdens. Thus will you do. Had God willed, He could Himself have punished them; (but He has ordained it thus) that He may test you, the one by the other. As for those who are slain in the cause of God, He will not allow their works to perish. He will vouchsafe them guidance and ennoble their state; He will admit them to the Paradise He has made known to them.

98:5. The unbelievers among the People of the Book [the Bible] and the pagans shall burn forever in the fire of Hell. They are the vilest of all creatures.

14:2. Woe betide the unbelievers, for they shall be sternly punished! Woe betide those who love this life more than the life to come; who debar others from the path of God and seek to make it crooked.

18:106. Hell is their reward: because they had no faith, and because they mocked My apostles and My revelations.

21:39. If only the unbelievers knew the day when they shall strive in vain to shield their faces and their backs from the fire of Hell; the day when none shall help them!

41:20. Forewarn them of the day when the enemies of God will be brought together and led into the Fire, so that when they enter it, their ears, their eyes, and their very skins will testify to their misdeeds.

69:15. Frail and tottering, the sky will be rent asunder on that day, and the angels will stand on all its sides with eight of them carrying the throne of your Lord above their heads. On that day you shall be utterly exposed, and all your secrets shall be brought to light. He who is given his book in his right hand will say: "Here it is, read my book! I knew I should come face to face with my account!" His shall be a blissful state in a lofty garden, with clusters of fruit within his reach. We shall say to him: "Eat and drink to your heart's content: your recompense for what you did in days gone by." But he who is given his book in his left hand will say: "Would that my book were not given me! Would that I knew nothing of my account! Would that my death had ended all! Nothing has my wealth availed me, and I am bereft of all my powers." We shall say: "Lay hold of him and blind him. Burn him in the fire of Hell, then fasten him with a chain seventy cubits long. For he did not believe in God the Most Great, nor did he care to feed the destitute."

That should be enough, although there is plenty more to draw from. The Prophet Muhammad demands that all people in the entire world believe in him as the greatest Prophet of all time. He demands that all people believe he has spoken from his mouth the true words of the only true God of the universe. He demands that all people swear allegiance to this God. He demands that no businessman charge interest on any loan. He demands that those who have wealth give freely to those who are in need. He demands that all the faithful Muslims consider all other men as their brothers. For some of this ideology, we can confess that we have great admiration. The prescribed punishments for those who do not share these particular beliefs, however, have become a horror factory in our current societies. Muslims are asked to maim or kill all those humans of any other faith, station, or nation who are infidels to the faith of Islam. Sin is disbelief in Islam, deserving of torture and death.

There is certainly far more to the religion of Islam than the above quotes. We cannot do the additional tenets of this religion justice throughout this particular discussion. There is belief in a Day of Judgment, when life on earth will end and all, living and dead, shall be punished or rewarded for their deeds while alive on this earth. This day is described in stark, graphic, vivid terms. There is a Heaven for those who are rewarded for their deeds, which is also described in glowing graphic terms. Those terms sound very much like a male Arab oasis, where there is plentiful fruit, food and drink, and most importantly, constant attendance by virgin women and young boys, catering to the every need of males who are granted access to this eternal paradise by their God, Allah. Women are specifically designated to a role subservient to their men, in the religion of Islam. Yet in spite of this male fantasy land, there is a strict command that all Muslims must give freely of their means to those who do not have as much. No Muslim will be granted access to their heaven unless he has cared for the lame, sick, poor, widow, orphan, and made the traveler welcome at his table.

Islam is a religion in which deep compassion is juxtaposed, adjacent to and wedded to, violent intolerance. Moral reform, it seems to me, cannot come too soon for this muscular, demanding, compassionate yet vehement religion. Until Islam can abandon its deeply embedded stance of punishment for all those who do not share that faith, this religion cannot in any way join our search for a moral code that encompasses all humans. It is, with this tenet of exclusivity, tearing us apart, rather than joining us together. This staunch belief that all humans who do not totally adhere to Islam are evil has created, it appears, great hatred and distrust amongst those true believers. If any Muslims fear loss or subjugation, Islam gives them a reason to strike out violently. An exploration of how this chilling intolerance has been fostered deserves our full examination. The beginning of that answer is found, strangely enough, in the Greek philosophies that existed prior to a fully recorded Bible, prior to Christianity, and prior to the origin of Islam.

JUDAISM MORAL REFORM

This gives us significant insight into the Muslim moral morass, but Islam is by no means the only example of misdirected rights and wrongs. In order to be unbiased, we must ask the same question about Judaism. Is Judaism not also in need of moral reform? The answer must be affirmative, if by morals we intend to mean equal respect for all other human beings. There is no doubt that all of human civilization owes a great debt to the Jewish emphasis on fairness and justice. Our civil laws have been patterned on the demands of this religion for equality of service. Our entire judicial system, designed to provide access for all people of all descriptions and faiths, carries a heavy flavor of Judaism. That flavor is to the great credit of this religion. Laws are formed to protect all citizens, regardless of special interest, color or creed. Our precious civil liberties stem from this same Jewish emphasis on equal advantage. The history of Judaism, so often persecuted, has made this religion especially empathetic towards others who also suffer from persecution. We are all deeply indebted to that great body of judicial thought which strives to give us all a level playing field. We cannot be thankful enough for these contributions to the betterment of our societies, given to us by Judaism.

Yet Judaism has a terribly dark side. Please understand that we all have parts of us that are pretty ugly. None of us is perfect, and most of us are far from it. Our religions are not perfect either. All of them have some terrible flaws. It is not the purpose of this book to be mean or angry, and certainly not the purpose to lay all the blame for our world conflicts at any one door. We can all share responsibility for this suicidal behavior we are now exhibiting. Please keep an open mind to the likelihood that there is some blame on all sides, which we all share. First, we have to understand why we are behaving so badly. That means that we have to understand our mistakes in social interaction that stem from all our misdirected moral systems. The tasks of this book are to define, as clearly as we can, where our right and wrong decisions do not make sense, and thereby cause us to make those mistakes. Once these problems are understood, then we can start dealing with them, and find ways to correct them. To that point, the best information we have, at this time, is that these misconceptions began with Judaism.

According to the Bible, there is an all powerful force, called God, who had formless material at hand, and decided to use it for a specific purpose. The questions we ask today about where that force came from and where that mass came from were beyond the thought concepts of those who wrote this story. It is childlike, as if to say, "My Dad built this house. This is what he did first and this is what he did last." There is poetic validity to the initial part of the sequence as described, and for that part we can admire those who wrote this mythology. According to this creation story, there was first the creation of light and dark, which correlates with what we know about this universe. Before additional events evolved in our universe, suns formed and galaxies began. Then God, the Bible says, separated the seas above (the sky) from the seas below. We understand that too. Our earth was formed only after our sun had been formed. God, this story says, then made the crust shift, forming earth and sea. That also coincides pretty well with our understanding of the gradual cooling of the earth's boiling seas and shifting of the cooling plates underneath to force up land masses and continents. Then, it says, God created life on the lands and in the seas. So far we are doing just great with this sequence. There is, however, at this point, one big bit of asynchrony. The generators of this fable say that at this time, God created the sun, moon and stars in order that we could know day and night, the seasons and the years. That doesn't fit. The best evidence we have is that the stars existed for some ten billion years before our sun and solar system came along.

The remainder of the first biblical creation story does pretty well with the sequence of evolution as we understand it. First there was the development of animal life in the seas. Then there was the development of animal life on land. Then, the Bible says, God created humans. This all can fit nicely with the understanding of a creationist or an evolutionist. Advanced life forms began in the seas and eventually shifted to reside on the land masses. Animal life (fauna) began in earnest sometime during the Cambrian explosion, seven hundred million years ago. There is one major error in this biblical sequence, as to when the stars in the sky began, and there is definite disagreement as to the time it took for these events to unfold. We can otherwise have nothing but respect for those who intuitively formed this story some three thousand years ago.

What immediately follows in this first biblical creation story has since caused us grave problems in our ability to figure out what is right and wrong. After the creation story, we already have one glaring misconception to deal with: The Bible makes it clear that this all powerful creative force is strictly a male. To that major conceptual deficit, the Bible now adds the following:

> *Genesis 1: 26–28. Then God said, "Let us make people" in our image, to be like ourselves. They will be masters over all life – the fish in the sea, the birds in the sky, and all the livestock, wild animals, and small animals.*
>
> *So God created people in his own image. God patterned them after himself; male and female he created them.*
>
> *God blessed them and told them, "Multiply and fill the earth and subdue it. Be masters over the fish and birds and all the animals."*

This is trouble. What we have so far is the conceptualization of a patriarchal nomadic tribe that has begun to question how the earth, sun, moon, stars, plant and animal life got here, how humans got here, and what relationship we have to whatever force began this creation. In their attempt to understand all this, they reached the conclusion that a giant father figure began it all, that he made us to look like him, and that he gave everything that exists to us to use in any way we want. Further, he did this with a purpose in mind, in which humans are a major player. Our interpretation of this accounting, up to this point in time, has been to believe that we are, since we are godlike, semi-divine; that we are highly important in the grand scheme of the universe; and that we are powerful, able to squander, pollute, and consume the resources of this planet to any degree that we wish. If this is the foundation we wish to use, we already have a miserable base on which to construct any rational system of right and wrong. These initial concepts are in themselves errant enough, but Judaism soon adds three additional distorted concepts of reality; their God is personally on their side; their God has formed a covenant with the Jewish people for a specific purpose; and those Jews who are faithful to that covenant will be established as the rulers over all other peoples for an eternity. With these beliefs, any chance we had to form a just system of morals that applies to all humans has been demolished.

The authors of the first words of the Bible are to be admired for figuring out the sequence they did without the benefit of any scientific instruments or discovery. If we can be broad minded enough to understand that this is a poetic conceptualization of our beginnings, we can all agree as to this beautiful account of our ancestry. If, on the other hand, these words are mistakenly taken for historical fact, we have terrible reconciliation problems. The Bible may be wandering, inconsistent, full of incest, female sexual slavery, jealousy, greed, slaughter, and all kinds of other base human traits, but it is good at one thing. Male descendancy is well documented. All the sons of all the sons are listed. For example, the male lineage from Adam to Noah (Genesis 5:1-30) is listed as through Seth, Enosh, Kenan, Mahalalel, Jared, Enoch, Methuselah and Lamech. The direct lineage from Noah to Abram is listed as Shem, Arphaxad, Shelah, Eber, Peleg, Reu, Serug, Nabor and Terah. Considering that the life expectancy at that time of life was about thirty years, and giving these the benefit of the doubt, each generation would account for about 25 years. In other words, if the Bible is believed word for word, it only took about 500 years from the beginning of human life for Abraham, the ancestor of Judaism, Christianity and Islam, to be born. This biblical account is, on a temporal basis, greatly inconsistent with what we know of our beginnings.

The rest of the Bible also does not leave much time from the beginning of all things here on Earth to our present civilization. We can pretty easily lay aside the biblical claims of certain men and women living for hundreds of years, since we have never known any human to do such. The lineage history of the tribes of Israel, as recorded in the Bible, if taken as fact and not as poetry, would indicate that only some additional 1500 years elapsed before the beginning of the Christian religion. Since some 2000 years have elapsed since the beginning of that religion, this leaves us with an estimate of 4000 years from the beginning of time to reach this age of relativity, gravity, space/time warps, e=mc^2, atomic bombs and trips to Mars. None of this biblical timeline can be reconciled in any way with what our astronomers, physicists, archeologists, and naturalists are telling us. They say that all of everything we know began in a massive explosion 14.5 billion years ago, and that life formed after 500 million years of constant asteroid strikes, boiling hot chemical seas and lightning strikes. They say that the first humanoids were seen four million years ago. They also say that this universe runs on physical laws which describe the interaction of large bodies, and chance/probability that describes the action of atomic particles. They do not find a guiding hand in this creation, and find no evidence of a power that is judgmental. The universe appears to be increasing in complexity, but beyond this development, no scientist has described planned value systems in the events of large and small objects. In plainer words, they do not see any good or evil in the evolution of this universe. They see a universe which began us by chance, allowed us to develop by a process of natural evolution, and will, in due time, through the natural events of the Universe, annihilate us completely, without concern or remorse.

There is not much point in belaboring this deep schism between those who are biblical creationists and those who believe in natural evolution, except that it bears directly on this discussion of morality. Those of our population who are deeply committed Israelites believe that the first five books of the Bible are the words of their God, forming the basis of this faith. Those who carry this religion as their faith should cherish it, if it provides them nurture and direction with their lives. That does not mean that all of it is correct, however. If followed fully, this religion asks its followers to believe that they are godlike, and here on earth for the specific purpose of becoming superior to all other human beings on earth, for all of time. The followers of Judaism must understand that these beliefs are incompatible with a system of morality which includes all human beings. We can't have a universal system of morals that applies to all humans if certain segments of the population are unalterably attached to delusions of superiority, punishment of those of other faiths, and eternal bliss only for those who adhere to this mythology.

The first few pages of the Bible do not waste any time giving us these mistaken concepts of human semi-divinity, a purposeful universe, human ownership of all the earth's resources, direct personal communication with the creator of all things, a covenant only with the Jews, and eventual superiority of Judaism over all other religions and peoples. The best way to demonstrate these Judaistic values, all of which I believe to be false, is to let the Bible speak for itself, as the history of the tribes of Israel develops. Watch for the rapid deployment of these ideas as we let this story unfold.

Abraham receives a direct message from his God to leave his father's house and go to the land of Canaan (which will be later defined). God tells Abraham the reason for this move is that He wants him to become the leader of a great nation. God tells him that this won't be easy, but that He will protect him. The concept of this tribe as the chosen tribe of the one and only true God is announced. The concept of a direct phone line between humans and God is magnified. The concept of certain humans being placed on earth for a specific purpose is clearly stated for the first time.

> *Genesis 12: 1–3. Then the Lord told Abram, "Leave your*
> *country, your relatives, and your father's house, and go to*
> *the land that I will show you. I will cause you to become*
> *the father of a great nation. I will bless you and make you*
> *famous, and I will make you a blessing to others. I will bless*
> *those who bless you and curse those who curse you. All the*
> *families of the earth will be blessed through you."*

Abraham leaves with his wife, Sarah, his flocks, his household, and is accompanied by his nephew Lot, who also takes his herds and household. They move to Canaan, but are forced to go to Egypt for a while because of famine. Abraham finds it necessary to become deceitful in order to save his own skin. He instructs Sarah to claim that she is his sister, not his wife, so that the Pharaoh won't kill him, in order that he may possess her. The pharaoh takes Sarah into his harem, and gives Abraham many gifts, pleased to have this beauty. When he later finds that Abraham and Sarah are married, he banishes them from Egypt. The concepts of male domination, women as property to be used for sexual gratification, and deceit for material gain are boldly articulated. Marriage vows have little meaning if you cannot only survive, but gain by prostituting your wife.

> *Genesis 12: 14–16. And sure enough, when they arrived in Egypt, everyone spoke of her beauty. When the palace officials saw her, they sang her praises to their king, the pharaoh, and she was taken into his harem. Then Pharaoh gave Abram many gifts because of her – sheep, cattle, donkeys, male and female servants, and camels.*

After being banished, Abraham and Lot arrive in Canaan to find that there is not enough grazing space for their cattle and sheep. After arguing about it for a while, they decide to split. Abraham stays in Canaan, and Lot goes to the fertile plains of the Jordan Valley, settling in a place near Sodom, where *the people of this area were unusually wicked and sinned greatly against the Lord*. After Lot leaves, their lord promises Abraham permanent possession of the land where he now resides. The Good versus Evil battle begins to take shape, Good, within the definitions of Judaism, being devotion to the customs of this Jewish tribe, and Evil being any other system of behavior or any other belief system. The concept that the Hebrew people have a divine right to this particular piece of the earth's surface is fully expressed.

> *Genesis 13: 13–18. After Lot was gone, the Lord said to Abram, "Look as far as you can see in every direction. I am going to give all this land to you and your offspring as a permanent possession. And I am going to give you so many descendants that, like dust, they cannot be counted! Take a walk in every direction and explore the new possessions I am giving you." Then Abram moved his camp to the oak grove owned by Mamre, which is at Hebron. There he built an altar to the Lord.*

Abraham and his household settle into this "promised land," but Abraham complains to the Lord that he does not have a son to be his heir. God mollifies this anxious man by telling him that he will have a son, and reiterates His permanent gift of all this land to the Jewish tribe, regardless of who is living there at that time. He also forecasts slavery for four hundred years. God promises this tribe great prosperity, but warns them that they will be displaced for a long time and enslaved before they can return to this land in prosperity. God also says that it does not matter who is living on this land. The Hebrew tribe has the right to take this land away from anyone else who resides here, because it belongs to them, as a gift from their God. After reading these passages, we can understand the fervent demand of Judaism to establish a state of Israel after World War I. That political maneuvering was simply, to them, a reincarnation of this imagined ancient divine right. The boundaries of this land grab are initially defined. Later clarification places those boundaries as from Egypt to the west, the Euphrates to the east, the Mediterranean to the north, and the deserts to the south.

> *Genesis 15: 13–14, and 18–19. Then the Lord told Abram, "You can be sure that your descendants will be strangers in a foreign land, and they will be oppressed as slaves for four hundred years. But I will punish the nation that enslaves them, and in the end they will come away with great wealth."...So the Lord made a covenant with Abram that day and said, "I have given this land to your descendants, all the way from the border of Egypt to the great Euphrates River – the land of the Kenits, Kenizzites, Kadmonites, Hittites, Perizzites, Rephaites, Amorites, Canaanites, Girgashites and Jebusites."*

Abraham continues to complain that he does not have a son. Sarah, perhaps reluctantly, gives him her Egyptian slave, Hagar, to use as sexual chattel. Abraham does so gladly, and the result is a pregnancy, which will result in the birth of Ishmael. Once this pregnancy occurs, however, Hagar's attitude changes toward Sarah. Sarah becomes extremely jealous, treats Hagar harshly, and drives her away. An angel of their Lord finds Hagar, advises her to return to the household of Abraham and Sarah, promising her that this son will have many descendants. He will also be a problem child, says the angel. Hagar claims her own direct communication with God. The stage is set for Ishmael to become the ancestor of Islam.

> *Genesis 16: 1–14. But Sarai, Abram's wife, had no children. So Sarai took her servant, an Egyptian woman named Hagar, and gave her to Abram so she could bear his children. "The Lord has kept me from having any children," Sarai said to Abram." "Go and sleep with my servant. Perhaps I can have*

*children through her." And Abram agreed. So Sarai, Abram's
wife, took Hagar the Egyptian servant and gave her to
Abram as a wife. (This happened ten years after Abram first
arrived in the land of Canaan.)*

*So Abram slept with Hagar, and she became pregnant.
When Hagar knew she was pregnant, she began to treat
her mistress Sarai with contempt. Then Sarai said to Abram,
"It's all your fault! Now this servant of mine is pregnant, and
she despises me, though I myself gave her the privilege of
sleeping with you. The Lord will make you pay for doing this
to me!"*

*Abram replied, "Since she is your servant you may deal with
her as you see fit." So Sarai treated her harshly and Hagar
ran away.*

*The angel of the Lord found Hagar beside a desert spring
along the road to Shur. The angel said to her, "Hagar,
Sarai's servant, where have you come from, and where are
you going?"*

"I am running away from my mistress," she replied.

*Then the angel of the Lord said, "Return to your mistress
and submit to her authority." The angel added, "I will give
you more descendants than you can count." And the angel
also said, "You are now pregnant and will give birth to a son.
You are to name him Ishmael, for the Lord has heard about
your misery. This son of yours will be a wild one- free and
untamed as a wild donkey! He will be against everyone, and
everyone will be against him. Yes, he will live at odds with
the rest of his brothers."*

*Thereafter, Hagar referred to the Lord, who had spoken to
her, as "The God who sees me," for she said, "I have seen
the One who sees me!"*

Immediately after this falling out, separating progeny, their God
reiterates his covenant with Abram. He renames him Abraham, states
that he will be the father of many nations and that this covenant
will last forever. There is a penalty to pay, however, to be the chosen
people. All males have to be circumcised, including servants and foreigners living in the household. If they do not get circumcised, they

will not be favored. You either get it cut off or get cut out. There are no rewards of greatness for those who are not circumcised. The eternity of this covenant is stressed. The permanence of this imagined land grant is stressed.

> *Genesis 17: 2–14. "I will make a covenant with you, by which I will guarantee to make you into a mighty nation." At this Abram fell face down in the dust. Then God said to him, "This is my covenant with you. I will make you the father of not just one nation, but a multitude of nations! What's more, I am changing your name. It will no longer be Abram, now you will be known as Abraham, for you will be the father of many nations. I will give you millions of descendants who will represent many nations. Kings will be among them!"*
>
> *"I will continue this everlasting covenant between us generation after generation. It will continue between me and your offspring forever. And I will always be your God and the God of your descendants after you. Yes, I will give all this land of Canaan to you and to your offspring forever and I will be their God."*
>
> *"Your part of the agreement," God told Abraham,"is to obey the terms of the covenant. You and all your descendants have this continual responsibility. This is the covenant that you and your descendants must keep: Each male among you must be circumcised, the flesh of his foreskin must be cut off. This will be a sign that you and they have accepted this covenant. Every male child must be circumcised on the eight day after his birth. This applies not only to members of your family, but also to the servants born in your household and the foreign-born servants whom you have purchased. All must be circumcised. Your bodies will thus bear the mark of my everlasting covenant. Anyone who refuses to be circumcised will be cut off from the covenant family for violating the covenant."*

This rather stringent caveat immediately follows. This covenant between them and their one and only God is only between this God and the descendants of Abraham and Sarah. They only are the favored and chosen people. The Lord promises greatness for Ishmael, but makes it clear that there is only one genetic line that will be above all other people, and it won't be his. The ideology that the Jewish people will always have to defend their chosen status, particularly against those who are descendants of Ishmael, becomes set in stone. The battle lines are drawn for generations to come, even though Ishmael is included in those circumcised.

> *Genesis 17: 19–21. But God replied, "Sarah, your wife, will bear you a son. You will name him Isaac, and I will confirm my everlasting covenant with him and his descendants. As for Ishmael, I will bless him also, just as you have asked. I will cause him to multiply and become a great nation. Twelve princes will be among his descendants. But my covenant is with Isaac, who will be born to you and Sarah about this time next year."*

An interesting aside comes next, which does not directly relate to the history of the Jewish tribe, but does directly relate to this discussion of the evolution of our morals. God has heard that Sodom is full of sin, and intends to destroy it. Abraham asks the philosophical questions as to how many good people have to be in Sodom to prevent their Lord from destroying the entire town. He begins with fifty, then goes down to forty five, forty, thirty, twenty and finally ten. On each occasion their Lord relents. It is a child-parent conversation, in which the son knows better than the father. This story emphasizes two beliefs. One is that humans communicate freely and directly with the God of all, and can frequently convince this God to act as they advise or request. The second, often missed, but clear implication, is that humans are sometimes more compassionate than their Old Testament God, who frequently strikes out in great anger, before He has thought everything through.

> *Genesis 18: 17–26 and 32–33. "Should I hide my plan from Abraham?" the Lord asked. "For Abraham will become a great and mighty nation, and all the nations of the earth will be blessed through him. I have singled him out so that he will direct his sons and their families to keep the way*

of the Lord and do what is right and just. Then I will do for him all that I have promised. So the Lord told Abraham, "'I have heard that the people of Sodom and Gomorrah are extremely evil, and that everything they do is wicked. I am going down to see whether or not these reports are true. Then I will know."

The two other men went on toward Sodom, but the Lord remained with Abraham for a while. Abraham approached him and said, "Will you destroy both innocent and guilty alike? Suppose you find fifty innocent people there within the city – will you still destroy it, and not spare it for their sakes? Surely you wouldn't do such a thing, destroying the innocent with the guilty. Why, you would be treating the innocent and the guilty exactly the same! Surely you wouldn't do that! Should not the Judge of all the earth do what is right?"

And the Lord replied, "If I find fifty innocent people in Sodom, I will spare the entire city for their sake....."

Finally, Abraham said, "Lord, please do not get angry. I will speak but once more. Suppose only ten are found there?"

And the Lord said, "Then, for the sake of the ten, I will not destroy it."

The Lord went on his way when he had finished his conversation with Abraham, and Abraham returned to his tent.

When Isaac is weaned, Abraham declares a party to celebrate. It is obvious that Sarah is still jealous of this other woman and other son of her husband. When she sees Ishmael taunting Isaac, she angrily banishes Hagar and her son from the camp. Abraham gives them a bottle of water and sends them out into the wilderness. Hagar, in despair and out of water, abandons her son under a bush. Their Lord hears her crying and sends an angel to comfort her and guide her to water. Greatness is again promised for Ishmael, although he is not one of the chosen people.

Genesis 21: 8–21. As time went by and Isaac grew and was weaned, Abraham gave a big party to celebrate the happy occasion. But Sarah saw Ishmael – The son of Abraham and her Egyptian servant Hagar – making fun of Isaac. So she turned to Abraham and demanded, "Get rid of that servant and her son. He is not going to share the family inheritance with my son, Isaac. I won't have it!"

This upset Abraham very much because Ishmael was his son. But God told Abraham, "Do not be upset over the boy and your servant wife. Do just as Sarah says, for Isaac is the son through whom your descendants will be counted. But I will make a nation of the descendants of Hagar's son because he also is your son."

So Abraham got up early the next morning, prepared food for the journey, and strapped a container of water to Hagar's shoulders. He sent her away with their son, and she walked out into the wilderness of Beersheba, wandering aimlessly. When the water was gone, she left the boy in the shade of a bush. Then she went and sat down by herself about a hundred yards away. "I don't want to watch the boy die," she said as she burst into tears.

Then God heard the boy's cries, and the angel of God called to Hagar from the sky. "Hagar, what's wrong! Do not be afraid. God has heard the boy's cries from the place where you laid him. Go to him and comfort him, for I will make a great nation from his descendants."

Then God opened Hagar's eyes, and she saw a well. She immediately filled her water container and gave the boy a drink. And God was with the boy as he grew up in the wilderness of Paran. He became an expert archer, and his mother arranged a marriage for him with a young woman from Egypt.

God decides to test the obedience of Abraham. He tells him to take his only son by Sarah, his pride, designated heir to the family and designated ancestor of the Hebrew nation, to the top of Mount Moriah, murder him and burn him as a sacrifice to this God. This is a contradiction to all the previous prophecy of a great nation through Isaac, so this God has either lied or is being totally devious. Abraham, however, decides to do as he has been told by his God. Just as he is about to commit this horrible act, his God tells him it was just a test. Abraham sacrifices a ram instead, apparently thinking he has to kill something to appease his Lord. Although the official pronouncement of this story is a test of obedience, it is something far more than that. Tribal custom at that time, in many tribes, was to sacrifice your first child and your first crops in order to appease whatever gods controlled things, and guarantee healthy crops, healthy children for the rest of the year. A person of our generation might liken it to a big Mafia scam, paying for protection up front, in order to survive. The fact that this primitive practice was a terrible waste of human resource, as well as a terrible waste of food supply, had not yet struck home to these wandering tribes. More importantly, this practice fostered brutality, rather than compassion. This story is, for the above reasons, more cogently an accounting of moral evolution. God, whoever and whatever that might be, did not want human sacrifice. What He wanted most was morality. The further realization that this God also did not want animal sacrifice had not yet occurred in the minds of these nomads. The end of this piece again stresses the obstructive concept that ultimately their nation will be superior to all other nations.

> *Genesis 22: 1–19. Later on God tested Abraham's faith and obedience. "Abraham!" God said.*

> *"Yes," he replied."Here I am."*

> *"Take your son, your only son – yes, Isaac, whom you love so much – and go to the land of Moriah. Sacrifice him there as a burnt offering on one of the mountains, which I will point out to you."*

> *The next morning Abraham got up early. He saddled his donkey and took two of his servants with him, along with his son Isaac. Then he chopped wood to build a fire for a burnt offering and set out for the place where God had him to go. On the third day of the journey, Abraham saw the place in the distance. "Stay here with the donkey," Abraham told the young men. "The boy and I will travel a little farther. We will worship there, and then we will come right back."*

> *Abraham placed the wood for the burnt offering on Isaac's shoulders, while he himself carried the knife and the fire. As the two of them went on together, Isaac said, "Father?"*

> *"Yes, my son," Abraham replied.*

> *"We have the wood and the fire," said the boy, "but where is the lamb for the sacrifice?" "God will provide a lamb, my*

son," Abraham answered. And they both went on together.

When they arrived at the place where God had told
Abraham to go, he built an altar and placed the wood on
it. Then he tied Isaac up and laid him on the altar over
the wood. And Abraham took the knife and lifted it up to
kill his son as a sacrifice to the Lord. At that moment the
angel of the Lord shouted to him from heaven, "Abraham!
Abraham!"

"Yes," he answered. "I'm listening."

"Lay down the knife," the angel said. "Do not hurt the boy in
any way, for now I know that you truly fear God. You have
not withheld even your beloved son from me."

Then Abraham looked up and saw a ram caught by its horns
in a bush. So he took the ram and sacrificed it as a burnt
offering on the altar in place of his son. Abraham named the
place "The Lord will provide." This name has now become a
proverb. "On the mountain of the Lord it will be provided."

Then the angel of the Lord called again to Abraham from
heaven. "This is what the Lord says. Because you hove
obeyed me and have not withheld even your beloved son,
I swear by my own self that I will bless you richly. I will
multiply your descendants into countless millions, like the
stars of the sky and the sand on the seashore. They will
conquer their enemies, and through your descendants,
all the notions of the earth will be blessed – all because
you have obeyed me." Then they returned to Abraham's
young men and traveled home again to Beersheba, where
Abraham lived for quite some time.

Isaac is not the direct progenitor of the twelve tribes of Israel.
His son, Jacob, is the one given that status. Jacob, if judged by the
criterion of prosperity, is a good choice for this lofty appellation. He
is also value driven. He works for an extra seven years to get the wife
he wants, and gets two of them in the deal, Leah and Rachel. On the
other hand, he is a quite poor choice as the father of all Hebrew tribes,
if judged by the criterion of morality. He has quite a few despicable
traits, which include most notably deceit, theft and infidelity. He steals
his fraternal twin, Esau's birthright, or share of the family property, by

a calculated piece of coercion. By a significant bit of trickery, he steals his father's blessing from Esau, at a time when Isaac is old, blind and ill. He has many children by several women other than his wives, Leah and Rachel. He steals sheep from his employer, Laban, through an ingenious piece of subterfuge, culling out those that are streaked and spotted. When all of this thievery starts to catch up with Jacob, and he is afraid for his life, he sends all his wives, concubines and children away. He stays in the camp alone until God appears in the form of a man. Jacob "wrestles with God" overnight, and receives a new name in the process.

> *Genesis 32: 22–26. But during the night Jacob got up and sent his two wives, two concubines and eleven sons across the Jabbok River.*
>
> *After they were on the other side, he sent over all his possessions. This left Jacob all alone in the camp, and a man came and wrestled with him until dawn. When the man saw that he couldn't win the match, he struck Jacob's hip and knocked it out of joint at the socket. Then the man said, "Let me go, for it is dawn."*
>
> *But Jacob panted, "I will not let your go unless you bless me."*
>
> *"What is your name?" the man asked.*
>
> *He replied, "Jacob."*
>
> *"Your name will no longer be Jacob," the man told him. "It is now Israel, because you have struggled with both God and men and have won."*

The Israelites are again forced to migrate to Egypt because of a famine in their land. There, they are enslaved and ruthlessly driven to hard labor. In spite of this hard life, they prosper too much. The Pharaoh becomes alarmed at the growth of this subpopulation, and orders all newborn Hebrew males to be killed. When this doesn't work, he orders all male Hebrew children to be thrown into the Nile. A man and a woman from the priestly clan have a child whom they hide for three months. Then, hoping for the best, they place the baby in a tar pitch reed basket, at the site where the Egyptian princess bathes. When the princess finds the baby, is touched by his cries, and wants to keep him, she needs someone else to nurse him. Asking for suggestions, she is guided to the Jewish woman who had the baby. Mom gets her baby back to nurse until he is weaned, and the life of Moses is spared. Other than this exception, the rest of this story is gruesome. There is slavery, oppression, widespread murder, and absence of sanctity for human life.

> *Genesis 2:1–10. During this time, a man and a woman from the tribe of Levi got married. The woman became pregnant and gave birth to a son. She saw what a beautiful baby he was and kept him hidden for three months. But when she could no longer hide him she got a little basket made of papyrus reeds and waterproofed it with tar and pitch. Then she put the baby in the basket and laid it among the reeds along the edge of the Nile River. The baby's sister then stood at a distance, watching to see what would happen to him.*

> *Soon after this, one of Pharaoh's daughters came down to bathe in the river, and her servant girls walked along the riverbank. When the princess saw the little basket among the reeds, she told one of her servant girls to get it for her. As the princess opened it, she found the baby boy. His helpless cries touched her heart. "He must be one of the Hebrew children," she said.*

> *Then the baby's sister approached the princess. "Should I go and find one of the Hebrew women to nurse the baby for you?" she asked.*

> *"Yes, do!" The princess replied. So the girl rushed home and called the baby's mother.*

> *"Take this child home and nurse him for me," the princess told her. "I will pay you for your help." So the baby's mother took her baby home and nursed him.*

> *Later, when he was older, the child's mother brought him back to the princess, who adopted him as her son. The princess named him Moses, for she said, "I drew him out of the water."*

After Moses has become an adult, he has to run away from Egypt with a price on his head for killing an Egyptian supervisor, who was beating a Hebrew slave. God tells Moses to go back and bring his tribe back to their homeland. Moses is mightily afraid to return to Egypt.

Even though his God gives him miraculous signs to use, in making this request to free the Israelites, Moses pleads to not be selected for this dangerous job, expecting death if he appears again in Egypt. God becomes angry with him. This is not the god of total Goodness we hear about later in the Bible. This is a demanding and jealous tribal God, quick to anger, and willing to kill anything or anybody who gets in his way.

> *Exodus 4: 1–14. But Moses protested again, "Look, they won't believe me! They won't do what I tell them. They'll just say, 'The Lord never appeared to you.'"*

> *Then the Lord asked him, "What do you have there in your hand?"*

> *"A shepherd's staff," Moses replied.*

> *"Throw it down on the ground," the Lord told him. So Moses threw it down, and it became a snake! Moses was terrified, so he turned and ran away.*

> *"Perform this sign, and they will believe you," the Lord told him. "Then they will realize that the Lord, the God of their ancestors – the God of Abraham, the God of Isaac, and the God of Jacob – really has appeared to you."*

> *Then the Lord said to Moses, "Put your hand inside your robe." Moses did so and when he took it our again, his hand was white as snow with leprosy. "Now put your hand back into your robe again," the Lord said. Moses did, and when he took it out this time, it was as healthy as the rest of his body.*

> *"If they do not believe the first miraculous sign, they will believe the second," the Lord said. "And if they do not believe you even after these two signs, then take some water from the Nile River and pour it out on the dry ground. When you do, it will turn into blood."*

> *But Moses pleaded with the Lord, "O Lord, I'm just not a good speaker. I never have been, and I'm not now, even after you have spoken to me. I'm clumsy with words."*

> *"Who makes mouths?" the Lord asked him. "Who makes people so they can speak or not speak, hear or not hear, see or not see? Is it not I, the Lord? Now go and do as I have told you. I will help you speak well, and I will tell you what to say."*

But Moses again pleaded, "Lord, please! Send someone else."

Then the Lord became angry with Moses......

The plagues that their Lord has promised, if the Pharaoh does not believe the signs he has sent, now begin. They are announced as a demonstration of the power of the Lord to do whatever it takes to help his chosen people. He does not care what torment He causes for other people as long as what he does helps those who are Israelites. This is, in other words, still a vengeful, provincial, tribal god. Israelite thought process does not yet include a God of all peoples. Moreover, the sequential evolution of the plagues as recorded are exactly what one would expect if there were a viral, bacterial or chemical poisoning of the Nile. According to a PBS special, these events occurred because of a geographic fault, which caused contamination of the Nile, prob-ably with iron. The Nile first turns red, then produces a massive fish kill. There is then wide spread death of frogs, followed by swarms of gnats, swarms of flies, followed by death of livestock, boils, and then widespread human deaths. Hail and locusts are thrown in for good measure. There is nothing here to make us believe this wide spread devastation was a series of "miracles" done to favor a certain group of people. The Pharaoh, however, believes maybe the Israelites are to blame, and angrily lets them go. The 430 year Egyptian servitude comes to an end, and the Exodus begins for 600,000 men, as many women and children, their flocks, and whatever hurried plunder they have confiscated as they flee.

> *Exodus 10: 24–29. Then Pharaoh called for Moses. "Go and worship the Lord," he said. "But let your flocks and herds stay here. You can even take your children with you."*
>
> *"No," Moses said, "we must take our flocks and herds for sacrifices and burnt offerings to the Lord our God. All our property must go with us, not a hoof can be left behind. We will have to choose our sacrifices for the Lord our God from among these animals. And we won't know which sacrifices he will require until we get there."*
>
> *"....Get out of here!" Pharaoh shouted at Moses."'Don't ever let me see you again! The day you do you will die!"*
>
> *"Very well," Moses replied. "I will never see you again."*

The Hebrew tribe has a multitude of hardships ahead of them before they are to settle in their "promised land." Yet they are grateful to have escaped their long period of slavery in Egypt, and wish to commemorate this monumental event in their history by converting it into a yearly several day festival. More germane to this discussion, they have evolved somewhat in their morals. A part of the ceremony involves preparing their food as they did in preparation for their journey, without leavening, and part of it is finding a way to say thanks to their Lord. The traditional manner in which they have expressed their deepest gratitude to their Lord, in the past, has been the gruesome primitive custom of killing and burning on the altar their first born male children, first born male animals, and their first crops. This moral horror is still a major part of their lives, but at least for the human first born males, it has now become a pretend ceremony. The animals are not so lucky. For just being born first, they get the knife, a bleating gasping death, and then the fire — or else the agony of having their necks broken. There is a lot of depraved morality remaining to correct.

> *Exodus 13: 1–7 and 10–16. Then the Lord said to Moses. "Dedicate to me all the firstborn sons of Israel and every firstborn male animal. They are mine."*
>
> *So Moses said to the people, "This is a day to remember forever - the day you left Egypt, the place of your slavery. For the Lord has brought you out by his mighty power. (Remember, you are not to use any yeast.) This day in early spring will be the anniversary of your exodus. You must celebrate this day when the Lord brings you into the land of the Canaanites, Hittites, Amorites, Hivites, and Jebusites. This is the land he swore to give your ancestors — a land flowing with milk and honey. For seven days you will eat only bread without yeast. Then on the seventh day, you will celebrate a great feast to the Lord. Eat only bread without yeast during those seven days; In fact, there must be no yeast in your homes or anywhere with the borders of your land during this time."*
>
> *"So celebrate this festival at the appointed time each year. And remember these instructions when the Lord brings you into the land where the Canaanites are now living. All firstborn sons and firstborn male animals must be presented*

*to the Lord. A firstborn male donkey may be redeemed from
the Lord by presenting a lamb in its place. But if you decide
not to make the exchange, the donkey must be killed by
breaking its neck. However, you must redeem [that is to say,
kill an animal in place of] every firstborn son."*

*"And in the future, your children will ask you, 'What does
all this mean?' Then you will tell them, 'With mighty power
the Lord brought us out of Egypt from our slavery. Pharaoh
refused to let us go, so the Lord killed all the firstborn males
throughout the land of Egypt, both people and animals.
That is why we now offer all the firstborn males to the Lord
– except the firstborn sons are always redeemed.' Again I say,
this ceremony will be like a mark branded on your hands or
your forehead. It is a visible reminder that it was the Lord
who brought you out of Egypt with great power'"*

The Israelites escape through the Red (or the reed) Sea, and
then wander in the wilderness, looking for adequate food and water,
barely finding subsistence. There is one advance in civil order. Moses'
father-in-law sees his son-in-law spend all day taking care of personal
disputes. He convinces Moses to appoint "some capable, honest
men who fear God and hate bribes" as judges, each overseeing several hundred people. The judicial system in Judaism is born. Then,
as they reach the base of Mount Sinai and camp there, Moses has
another mountain top experience with his Lord, just before creating
the Ten Commandments. The promise that their God has selected
the Israelite tribes as his chosen people, above all other people of
all other nations, is again repeated with emphasis. It is clear that this
recurring theme is the primary cherished base for this religion.

*Exodus 19: 3–6. Then Moses climbed the mountain to
appear before God. The Lord called out to him from
the mountain and said, "Give these instructions to the
descendants of Jacob. The people of Israel: you have seen
what I did to the Egyptians. You know how I brought you
to myself and carried you on eagle' wings. Now if you will
obey me and keep my covenant, you will be my own special
treasure from among all the nations of the earth. For all the
earth belongs to me. And you will be to me a kingdom of
priests, my holy nation. Give this message to the Israelites."*

Now there is that monumental passage in the Bible of Judaism, when their Lord gives the people of Israel his Ten Commandments. The first four statements demand allegiance to a colloquial, jealous, vengeful, primitive tribal God who will be living in a wooden box, 3 ¾ x 2 ¼ x 2 ¼ feet in dimension. He promises to carry hatred with him for centuries, guaranteeing he will afflict the innocents of following generations with suffering and death, for anyone who has displeased him. The last six commandments do have significant moral value, but are immediately overridden by the massacre carried out at the command of Moses, as soon as he comes down from the mountain. There is, in other words, no practice of these morals as they are preached. The one who preaches them with such vehemence, Moses, immediately desecrates his own commandments.

Exodus 20: 2–17. I am the Lord your God, who rescued you from slavery in Egypt.

Do not worship any Gods besides me.

Do not make idols of any kind, whether in the shape of birds or animals or fish. You must never worship or bow down to them, for I, the Lord your God, am a jealous God who will not share your affection with any other god! I do not leave unpunished the sins of those who hate me, but I punish the children for the sins of their parents to the third and fourth generations. But I lavish my love on those who love me and obey my commands, even for a thousand generations.

Do not misuse the name of the Lord your God. The Lord will not let you go unpunished if you misuse his name.

Remember to observe the Sabbath day by keeping it holy. Six days a week are set apart for your daily duties and regular work, but the seventh day is a day of rest dedicated to the Lord your God. On that day no one in your household may do any kind of work. This includes you, your sons and daughters, your male and female servants, your livestock and any foreigners living among you. For in six days the Lord made the heavens, the earth, the sea, and everything in them, then he rested on the seventh day. That is why the Lord blessed the Sabbath day and set it apart as holy.

Honor your father and mother. Then you will love a long full life in the land the Lord your God will give you.

Do not murder.

Do not commit adultery.

Do not steal.

Do not testify falsely against your neighbor.

Do not covet your neighbor's house. Do not covet your neighbor's wife, male or female servant, ox or donkey, or anything else your neighbor owns.

The Ten Commandments do carry significant moral value. Six of these statements are solid moral guides for us to follow. They are a notable advance in the evolution of human morality, at least in part. The bylaws, however, which immediately follow in the subsequent passages of Exodus, said to be given to Moses by his God, contain some rather primitive and draconian moral advice.

Exodus 21 and 22. If his master gave him a wife while he was a slave, and they had sons or daughters, then the man will be free in the seventh year, but his wife and children will still belong to his master.

When a man sells his daughter as a slave, she will not be freed at the end of six years as the men are.

Anyone who strikes father or mother must be put to death.

Anyone who curses father or mother must be put to death.

Kidnappers must be killed.

If an eye is injured, injure the eye of the person who did it. If a tooth gets knocked out, knock out the tooth of the person who did it. Similarly, the payment must be hand for hand, foot for foot, burn for burn, wound for wound, bruise for bruise.

If this is true and if the bull kills someone, it must be stoned, and the owner must also be killed.

Yes, keep the Sabbath day, for it is holy. Anyone who desecrates it must die.

A sorceress must not be allowed to live

Anyone who has sexual relations with an animal must

be executed.

Anyone who sacrifices to any god other than the Lord must be destroyed.

In keeping with these severe punishments for not following the customs of this tribe, the massacres of his own people at the explicit direction of Moses will soon follow. The people of Israel are afraid of their Lord, and ask Moses to go to the mountain top alone to receive instructions as to their covenant. Moses leaves his brother, Aaron, in charge. When Moses does not come down for 40 days, the people become restless. In order to placate them, Aaron asks them to donate their gold, melts it down, forms a golden calf, and tells the people to worship it until Moses returns. When Moses returns and finds a wild party going in worship of this hunk of gold, he goes into an immediate rage. He throws the stone tablets down that contain the inscribed Ten Commandments, smashing them. He calls for those loyal to this imagined covenant between their God and the tribe of Israel to step forward. His priests and judges do so. He commands all others to be killed. Three thousand brothers, sisters and children are massacred. Moses, obviously, has no idea how to apply his newly demanded morality, making a mockery of his own laws. Not only were the Ten Commandments written in stone, but the nation-state of Israel has now been born, written in political stone. You either adhere to the beliefs and customs of this tribe, or you are killed. A glaring example has been set for the inquisitions, crusade massacres, witch hunts, burning and torture of infidels and cruel Taliban punishments, to follow in later centuries. There is now a central religious law which is enforced by the judicial system and police. All who do not follow that religious law are either tortured or killed.

Exodus 32: 25–29. When Moses saw that Aaron had let the people get completely out of control – and much to the amusement of their enemies – he stood at the entrance to the camp and shouted, "All of you who are on the Lord's side, come over here and join me." And all the Levites came.

He told them, "This is what the Lord, the God of Israel, says; strap on your swords! Go back and forth from one end of the camp to the other, killing even your brothers, friends and neighbors." The Levites obeyed Moses, and about three thousand people died that day.

*Then Moses told the Levites, "Today you have been ordained
for the service of the Lord, for you obeyed him even though
it meant killing your own sons and brothers. Because of this,
he will now give you a great blessing."*

The remaining Israelites who have not been massacred by the
Moses military accept the covenant that has been submitted to them,
including the stringent bylaws, rather gladly. They are happy to still be
alive. Then their God makes some additional promises and demands.
He promises to throw out those who are living on the land that he has
guaranteed for the Israelites. It does not matter that there are other
people living there now who consider this land their home. The evic-
tion notices and bulldozers are going out, so to speak. These "other
people" are to be despised and avoided, or killed. This is still a primitive God who is teaching violent aggrandizement, isolationism, hatred,
and disrespect. Moreover, wasteful animal sacrifice is still a prominent
part of the tribal morals.

*Exodus 34: 10–16 and 19. The Lord replied, "All right. This
is the covenant I am going to make with you. I will perform
wonders that have never been done before anywhere in all
the earth or in any nation. And all the people around you
will see the power of the Lord – the awesome power I will
display through you. Your responsibility is to obey all the
commands I am giving you today. Then I will surely drive out
all those who stand in your way – the Amorites, Canaanites,
Hittites, Perizzites, Hivites and Jebusites."*

*"Be very careful never to make treaties with the people in
the land where you are going. If you do, you soon will be
following their evil ways. Instead, you must break down
their pagan altars, smash the sacred pillars they worship
and cut down their carved images. You must worship
no other gods, but only the Lord, for he is a God who is
passionate about his relationship with you."*

*"Do not make treaties of any kind with the people living in
the land. They are spiritual prostitutes, committing adultery
against me by sacrificing to their gods. If you make peace
with them, they will invite you to go with them to worship
their gods, and you are likely to do it. And you will accept*

*their daughters, who worship other gods, as wives for your
sons. Then they will cause your sons to commit adultery
against me by worshiping other gods."*

*"Every firstborn male belongs to me – of both cattle and
sheep. A firstborn male donkey may be redeemed from the
Lord by presenting a lamb in its place. But if you decide not
to make the exchange, you must kill the donkey by breaking
its neck. However, you must redeem every firstborn son. No
one is allowed to appear before me without a gift."*

Specific instructions follow for building the tabernacle, ark, table,
lamp stand, altars, washbasin, courtyard, chest piece. There is specific
clothing and conduct demanded of the priests. There is still at this
point, no doubt. This Hebrew God is still a genie in a bottle, confined to
a small box, primitive, demanding, jealous, quick to anger, destructive,
bigoted, and totally amoral as far as the rest of the world is concerned.

*Genesis 37: 1–9. Next Bezalel made the Ark out of acacia
wood. It was 3 ¼ feet long, 2 ¼ feet wide, and 2 ¼ feet high.
It was overlaid with pure gold inside and out, and it had a
molding of gold all the way around. Four gold rings were
fastened to its four feet, two rings at each side. Then he
made poles from acacia wood and overlaid them with gold.
He put the poles into the rings at the sides of the Ark to
carry it.*

*Then, from pure gold, he made the Ark's cover – the place of
atonement. It was 3 ¼ feet long and 2 ¼ feet wide. He made
two figures of cherubim out of hammered gold and placed
them at the two ends of the atonement cover. They were
made so they were actually a part of the atonement cover –
it was all one piece. The cherubim faced each other as they
looked down on the atonement cover, and their wings were
stretched out above the atonement cover to protect it.*

When the Israelites leave Sinai to go to the land they believe
their Lord has promised them, they find advanced civilizations there.
Their scouts tell them that this is indeed a rich land of milk and honey,
but those who now inhabit that land are quite powerful and well
entrenched. The Hebrew tribes spend forty years getting up their
courage to invade this "promised land." They go through periods of
starvation and drought, and at one point, a plague that takes 24,000

lives. All of this they blame upon their failure to follow the strict isolationist laws that Moses has established. Anyone who consorts with the enemy, meaning any different faith, deserves to be killed. The Israelites believe they are the chosen people of their one and only true God. Their blood (genes) cannot be defiled by any other human blood.

> *Numbers 25: 1–9. While the Israelites were camped at Acacia, some of the men defiled themselves by sleeping with the local Moabite women. These women invited them to attend sacrifices to their gods, and soon the Israelites were feasting with them and worshiping the gods of Moab. Before long Israel was joining in the worship of Baal of Peor, causing the Lord's anger to blaze against his people.*

> *The Lord issued the following command to Moses. "Seize all the ringleaders and execute them before the Lord in broad daylight, so his fierce anger will turn away from the people of Israel." So Moses ordered Israel's judges to execute everyone who had joined in worshiping Baal of Peor.*

> *Just then one of the Israelite men brought a Midianite woman into the camp right before the eyes of Moses and all the people, as they were weeping at the entrance of the Tabernacle. When Phinehas son of Eleazar and grandson of Aaron the priest saw this, he jumped up and left the assembly. Then he took a spear and rushed after the man into his tent. Phinehas thrust the spear all the way through the man's body and into the woman's stomach. So the plague against the Israelites was stopped, but not before 24,000 had died.*

After the death of Moses, his assistant, Joshua, believes it is time to fulfill this self-aggrandizing prophecy, invade this imagined promised land, and conquer all the inhabitants who are now there. Joshua follows Moses' example of executing anyone who does not follow the Israelite tribal faith, down to the letter. It was nice to hear the story in Sunday school about the Israelites winning a battle. It was pleasant to sing that song, "Joshua fit the battle of Jericho, Jericho, Jericho. Joshua fit the battle of Jericho, and the walls came a' tumblin' down." This euphemism does nothing for the described horror of those battles. The modus operandi is the same for each of them. Lay siege to the cities, then kill all the inhabitants, plunder at will, then destroy it completely. Progressively, those kings to the East, West, North and South of the Jordan are killed and their cities destroyed. In all, 31 kings, their armies, their people, children and animals are murdered, their cities are burned to the ground, and their cultures are destroyed. This self-appointed promised land now belongs to the Israelites, taken through a deeply destructive process of greed, genocide and vicious intolerance. Then the land is plundered, and divided amongst the twelve tribes of Israel. Judged by any value standard, these are primal, vicious immoral acts.

> *Joshua 6:20–21. When the people heard the sound of the horns, they shouted as loud as they could. Suddenly, the walls of Jericho collapsed, and the Israelites charged straight in to the city from every side and captured it. They completely destroyed everything in it – men and women, young and old, cattle, sheep, donkeys – everything.*

> *Joshua 8: 21–29. When Joshua and the other Israelites saw that the ambush had succeeded and that smoke was rising from the city, they turned and attacked the men of Ai. Then the Israelites who were inside the city came out and started killing the enemy from the rear. So the men of Ai were caught in a trap, and all of them died. Not a single person survived or escaped. Only the king of Ai was taken alive and brought to Joshua.*

> *When the Israelite army finished killing all the men outside the city, they went back and finished off everyone inside. So the entire population of Ai was wiped out that day – 12,000 in all. For Joshua kept holding out his spear until everyone who had lived in Ai was completely destroyed. Only the cattle and the treasure of the city were not destroyed, for the Israelites kept these for themselves, as the Lord had commanded Joshua. So Ai became a permanent mound of ruins, desolate to this very day.*

> *Joshua hung the king of Ai on a tree and left him there until evening. At sunset the Israelites took down the body and threw it in front of the city gate. They piled a great heap of stones over him that can still be seen today.*

There is no other way to call it. These Israelite conquests were brutal, amoral and primitive. These massacres, with total destruction of all life and all property are hard to explain, even in that ancient time. In one sense it seems petty to question the vicious and callous nature of these attacks, since that was common practice at that time in human history. And perhaps that is the point, in this discussion of moral evolution. The Israelites have perceived that significant moral improvement is needed in their culture. They have expressed some of those as part of their covenant with their God, in their Ten Commandments, as authored by Moses. What they haven't learned yet is that this morality applies to them at all times, not just when it is convenient. They also have not learned yet that their God is the God of all people, and that this God wants all people to lead a compassionate life. They haven't yet learned to practice what they preach. The conclusion arises that these battles were so vicious because their faith told them this land was theirs. Other people who were living there had no right to do so, according to their faith, because their tribal God had given it all to them. It is particularly disturbing to see the faith of Judaism yet today celebrate these ancient malicious land grabs as if they were great moral victories. As judged by any reasonable moral standard, they were the opposite. Instead of being proud, the faith of Israel, as all other faiths, should be contrite and humble about the vicious and amoral behavior of their ancestors.

This realization that their God is not just a tribal God, but the God of all people, finally arrives in the preaching of the prophets. The prophets forecast punishment and misery for the Israelites, because the people of these tribes continue their immoral ways. None of these is more enlightened than Isaiah. He understands that his God also is the God of the Babylonians, and believes that his God will use the Babylonians to punish the immoral Israelites, destroying their temple, and placing them again in exile. He understands that animal sacrifice is abhorrent. He understands, in eloquent words, that what their God wants is not victories, sacrifices or rituals, but compassionate human behavior. He has a dream, like Martin Luther King, Jr., of a time when the Lord of all humans will bring peace to all people of the world. This is a remarkable Prophet, whose vision is to be greatly admired. Built upon the Wisdom of Solomon and the Songs of David, this man's vision is a beacon for us all. This vividly expressed morality is a quantum leap above that primitive morality of Abraham, Moses and Joshua.

Isaiah 1: 5–17 and 2: 1–5. "Why do you continue to

invite punishment? Must you rebel forever? Your head is injured, and your heart is sick. You are sick from head to foot – covered with bruises, welts, and infected wounds – without any ointments or bandages. Your country lies in ruins, and your cities are burned. As you watch, foreigners plunder your fields and destroy everything they see. Jerusalem stands abandoned like a watchman's shelter in a vineyard or field after the harvest is over. It is as helpless as a city under siege. If the Lord Almighty had not spared a few of us, we would have been wiped out as completely as Sodom and Gomorrah."

"Listen to the Lord, you leaders of Israel! Listen to the law of our God, people of Israel. You act just like the rulers and people of Sodom and Gomorrah. 'I am sick of your sacrifices,' says the Lord. 'Don't bring me any more burnt offerings! I don't want the fat from your rams or other animals. I don't want to see the blood from your offerings of bulls and rams and goats. Why do you keep parading through my courts with your worthless sacrifices? The incense you bring me is a stench in my nostrils! Your celebration of the new moon and the Sabbath day, and your special days for fasting – even your most pious meetings – are all sinful and false. I want nothing more to do with them. I hate all your festivals and sacrifices. I cannot stand the sight of them. From now on, when you lift up your hands in prayer, I will refuse to look. Even though you offer many prayers, I will not listen, for your hands are covered with the blood of your innocent victims. Wash yourselves and be clean! Let me no longer see your evil deeds. Give up your wicked ways. Learn to do good. Seek justice. Help the oppressed. Defend the orphan. Fight for the rights of widows.'"

This is another vision that Isaiah, son of Amoz, saw concerning Judah and Jerusalem:

"In the last days, the Temple of the Lord in Jerusalem will become the most important place on earth. People from all over the world will go there to worship. Many nations will come and say, 'Come, let us go up to the mountain of the Lord, in the Temple of the God of Israel. There he will teach

us his ways, so that we may obey him.' For in those days, the
Lord's teaching and his word will go out from Jerusalem."

"The Lord will settle international disputes. All the nations
will beat their swords into plowshares and their spears into
pruning hooks. All wars will stop, and military training will
come to an end. Come, people of Israel, let us walk in the
light of the Lord!"

Isaiah was a prophet for all ages, as were Mahatma Gandhi and
Martin Luther King, Jr., to follow in later years. They all had significant flaws, many of which are mentioned in this book. They also all
had one great enduring message they gave to the human race, at
least in part: you must respect all other humans. Until you treat all
others as you would like to be treated, there will not be peace on
this planet. We all know that we are not following this sage advice.
We still, at this age of human development, allow our major religions
to freely express their poles of intolerance, rather than emphasizing
their poles of compassion. Each of these religions has, as an essential piece of their faith, the belief that all those who do not share
their mythology will be subjugated for an eternity, or be tortured in
Hell for an eternity.

Perhaps this is why Israel has not yet learned the lessons taught
by their prophet, Isaiah. The actions of this nation, now the center of
Judaism, since its creation early last century, would lead us to believe
that it still lives in the morality of an eye for an eye and a tooth for
a tooth. Understandably, the people of any nation have the right to
protect themselves and defend themselves if others threaten their
survival. They certainly have the right to their faith. The problem
is that Judaism has not as yet accepted any other faith as containing equal value. The followers of Judaism are firmly convinced that
they are the superior people over all other people on the face of
our planet. If there is anyone who believes otherwise, that person
cannot be considered to have as much human value. It appears that
this faith has much yet to learn in moral equality.

After the inception of Islam in 621 BC, that religion dominated
the entire Arab world, including the lands of Palestine. The crusades,
five centuries later, put an abrupt end to this period of prosperity and
enlightenment in those lands. Not only did the Christians massacre all

Muslims they encountered, but they also slaughtered the Jewish population in large numbers. Jews were also expelled from England at that
time. There was a large immigration to colonies in Europe and Russia.
They did not fare well in those lands, at assorted times during the following centuries. In 1492, while Spain was bankrolling Columbus to
sail the ocean blue, they were expelling the Jew. Portugal followed
suit in 1497, expelling all known Jews from their country. During the
Khmelnytsky rebellion in the Ukraine from 1648 to 1654, over 10,000
Jews were massacred. Widespread anti-Semitism smoldered in Europe
and Russia throughout all these centuries, and throughout all these
centuries, there was a slow return of Jews back to Palestine. By the
19th century, the majority of Jerusalem inhabitants were Jewish, and
the lands of Palestine were ten percent Jewish.

The first Zionist congress was held in 1897, "to establish a home
in Palestine for the Jewish people…" This home could not be, in their
opinion, in some other land that no one else wanted. It had to be in
Palestine, the land that, according to their belief system, had been given
to them by divine right. It did not matter that other people were living
there, had homes, families and jobs there. This land, they believed in
the bottom of their hearts, was only theirs, given to them by their God.
It took about a century of political maneuvering and planning for that
fervent desire to bear, at least by moral standards, fetid fruit. During
World War I, the British sought Jewish emotional support and financing for their war against Germany. Zionists used that support to obtain
a reciprocal agreement. Lord Balfour declared in 1917 that the British
government "viewed with favor the establishment in Palestine of a
national home for the Jewish people." Sensing that their Zionist movement was gaining support, there was further migration of those with
Jewish faith to Palestine from 1920 through 1940. This migration now
threatened disruption of the fabric of Palestine society. Militia groups
formed amongst the native Palestinians, attacking Jewish settlements,
the inhabitants of which the Palestinians considered invaders. This
hostility simmered as World War II brewed, but World War II additionally changed the dynamic of political alignment.

The British controlled Transjordan, Sudan, Kuwait, the Arab
Emigrates, Bahrain and Yemen. They needed all this Arab support
for the coming storm of a world war, and were no longer supportive of the Jewish cause. In protest, Jewish militias bombed the British

Military Headquarters in Palestine in 1946. Britain, in response, jailed all Jewish immigrants who could be declared as illegal. Many nations protested both these acts, including the United States of America. Britain, now wanting to wash its hands of this entire volatile region, referred this dispute to the United Nations. Reinforced by the wide spread revulsion of the rest of the world toward the Nazi Holocaust, the United Nations, on November 29, 1947, passed a resolution to partition Palestine into two states, one for Palestinians, and the other for former Palestinians, those of the Jewish faith.

The other nations of the world did not really care, in the sense that they simply wished to get rid of this problem. No one wanted to intercede and get in the middle of this miserable mess. The result was a Palestinian religious civil war, Jew against Muslim. It has not stopped since. Palestinians, rightfully so, did their best to defend their homes and their land against these vicious invaders. They were unfortunately, no match for the Israeli forces, who had been planning this assault for the last century. They were better organized and better armed. Beginning at Tel Aviv, the Jewish militias cut a swath through Palestinian land on their way to Jerusalem. Fighting was particularly heavy along this corridor, reminiscent of the first Hebrew invasion of this land of Canaan. All of the villages and settlements on the way to Jerusalem were completely destroyed. More than 10,000 Palestinians were killed while defending their homeland, and 6,000 Jews died during this invasion, taking this land which, to their way of thinking, had been usurped from them. To them, this land had been given to them by their God; no one else had a right to live here. This re-enacted Hebrew invasion of Palestine with complete destruction on their way had come full circle. The cause of perceived divine right had trumped anything that was ethical or moral about this civil war.

On May 14, 1948, the last British forces left Haifa. The Jewish agency declared creation of the state of Israel. This new state was immediately recognized by the United States of America and by Russia, who doubtless were deeply hopeful that this recognition would put an end to the incessant fighting in this religious cesspool. They had no idea what was yet to come. Muslim and Jewish battles continued heavily for the next year. The weary combatants finally agreed to boundaries which would establish the state of Israel. Egypt still, at that time, held the Gaza strip, and Jordan controlled both East Jerusalem and the West Bank. Rather than a settlement, it was simply a respite, as both Muslims and Jews gathered their breath before going to battle again over this land they both considered theirs.

In 1956, enmities between Egypt and Israel elevated. Egypt closed the Suez Canal and nationalized it. Israel, backed by French and British military, took back the canal and the Gaza strip. Their reward was a nuclear plant, built by the French, allowing Israel to develop nuclear weapons by 1968. Israel did not believe any other Arab power should have the same capability, though. They wanted no one else to have what they had. Israel protected its interests by assassinating German scientists who were developing missile systems in Egypt, then by aerial bombardment, destroying a nuclear plant the French were building for Iraq. When the invasion of Lebanon by Israel in l982 deteriorated into a tri-holy war between Jews, Christians and Muslims, Christian forces, abetted by the Israelis, invaded Palestinian refugee camps and massacred 400,000 of those Muslim inhabitants.

It seems we may never see the end of this Muslim-Jew-Christian conflict. Rather than abating, it has exploded into the world at large. The inability to find some resolution of the differences between the Muslim, Jewish and Christian faiths has allowed this poison to infect the rest of the world. Muslims are now known as the violent ter- rorists of the entire world, with the express intent of tearing down all other societies but their own. Christians are known as American imperialist invaders, who will use military might to protect their exalted standard of living in any way they have to do that. Jews are known as supreme egotists, who will use any devious or overt vio- lence necessary to protect their self appointed status as the superior people of the entire world, given to them by presumed divine right. They believe, without insight, that their personal God, who favors them over all other people, gave them the right to take this land of Canaan away from those others who called it their home.

It is often quite difficult to know how much of these murderous conflicts are due to self-centered human fear, greed and jealousy, presented under the disguise of religious rectitude, and how much is fervent devotion to religious dogma. It is probably, for the most part, the former. We let our fears dictate when we act violently toward others, then try to find justification for our actions. To use an example close to home, George W. Bush, after 9/11/01, had given the CIA explicit directions to find weapons of mass destruction in Iraq. When they came back with negative answers, they were told to look further. Those findings they then presented were apparently magnified in the minds of Mr. Bush and his advisors, to the point that, to them, they were evidence of immediate danger. This was a time of great anguish for Mr. Bush. America was under attack, and it was under his watch. He was tremendously fearful that, if he did not act, other Muslims would be encouraged to further terrorize America. He was also rightfully fearful that, if other Muslim nations joined, America might well lose its access to Middle East oil, a commodity upon which the economy of this country was dependent. In his soul-searching over these imminent threats to the United States of America, Mr. Bush reached out to one great source of inspiration in his life, his religion. His religion told him that there was a great deal of evil out there in the world, and it was the duty of good Christians to fight that evil. Using that philosophy as his guide to action, Mr. Bush declared that certain other nations were totally evil, and on that basis felt justified in ordering our invasion of another sovereign nation, Iraq.

I do not intend this to be derogatory. Mr. Bush was faced with very real threats to the United States of America. He had to act, and act rapidly. He did the best that he could, based on that information available to him, and based on the greatest sources of strength in his life that he knew. Unfortunately, some of those sources were the mistaken philosophies of his religion, which led him, and us, badly astray. I believe that the invasion of Iraq was a fear-driven mistake, which was justified, in the minds of those who made that mistake, by the faulty morals of the Christian religion.

Likewise, the violent disruptive actions of Muslims and Jews seem to carry the same potent mixture of fear, violence, and religious justification. In the case of Judaism, that justification is fed by concepts of superiority, domination, and punishment, so vividly expressed in this religion. In my opinion, Judaism is deeply in need of moral reform. Until the faith of Judaism can accept all other humans as their equals, their moral system will remain primitive. This religion is not close to being ethical, a behavior that requires an equal respect for all other humans, all other beliefs and all other life. Judaism cannot achieve high morality, until it sheds that self-appointed superiority. Judaism must, in other words, abandon its most cherished tenet, before it can become part of our search for a universal ethic.

In a moral sense, the only contract that should exist between the God of creation and Judaism, is a command to teach all the rest of us compassion. That covenant should not be this biblical contract, which has so far set a glaring example of bigotry and violent aggression toward the rest of the human species.

CHRISTIANITY MORAL REFORM

Nor, in this discussion of the religious misdirection of our morals, is Christianity without fault. This religion has also shown blindness to its own moral flaws. I hasten to immediately add that there was, coming from the mind of its prophet, Jesus, a remarkable understanding of what it takes to become fully ethical. This begins with the underlying concept of treating others as you would want them to treat you. This seminal understanding has found expression in multiple religions, and was also articulated by Isaiah. Jesus took that understanding of Isaiah, and added one crucial element to it, in a few words which have since glowed throughout the centuries. Let's take our first look at it, and then we will come back to it a bit later, with more to say.

> *Matthew 22: 34–40. But when the Pharisees heard that he had silenced the Sadducees with his reply, they thought up a fresh question of their own to ask him. One of them, an expert in religious law, tried to trap him with this question.*
>
> *"Teacher, which is the most important commandment in the law of Moses?"*
>
> *Jesus replied, "You must love the Lord your God with all your heart, all your soul, and all your mind. This is the first and greatest commandment. A second is equally important. Love your neighbor as yourself. All the other commandments and all the demands of the prophets are based on these two commandments."*

I am particularly fond of that last sentence. If these concepts are fully applied by each of us, in practical manners, there is nothing else we need in the way of laws, rules, or priestly monitors to become fully moral. If we follow these few words, we will have a morality which can extend to a system of ethics applying to everyone. I could possibly stop writing here and say that's all that needed to be said. Unfortunately, as in all other matters, the devil is in the details. Having eloquently expressed these remarkable leaps of morality, Jesus was himself unable to apply them to everyone, everywhere, including himself. He was a saintly savant who expressed human morals better than anyone one else had in the human species, up to that point in time. He not only understood that each of us has to be deeply reverent toward that force which created us and gave each of us this beautiful life. He also understood that this deep respect had to apply to all those other humans around us. Beyond this, he eventually understood what no Prophet before him had fully articulated: this respect must also extend even to our enemies. No one else had clearly voiced that leap of appreciation that we are all in this together.

Unfortunately, he was also, if we are to judge by the New Testament as it is recorded, egotistical, controlling and demanding. Although he may well have said something much different, this recorded account states that his way was the only way. No one could get to his false promise of eternal life except through the belief that he, Jesus, was a part of the only God of the universe, a divinity on earth. He demanded that those who wished this fabulous prize give up everything precious, including their mothers, fathers, brothers and sisters, before they could enter this promised paradise. He believed that he existed before Abraham. He believed that he was invincible, and would return, after his death, in great glory, ruling and judging all people forever. Most of all, he fell prey to that same demon which has ruined any religion: exclusivity. He believed that his only mission was to extend these morals to the Jews. He had achieved the remarkable understanding that "to love your neighbor" also included your enemies. Yet he believed that his only mission was to apply this system of conduct to Jewish enemies. Jesus was, in other words, still a prisoner in the immoral jail of exclusivity.

There is no question about Jesus' orientation. He was thoroughly a Jew, deeply believed in the Jewish faith, and only wished to make the Jewish faith better. Jesus was well aware of the preceding evolution of morality in Judaism. These concepts were the background for all his thoughts. He knew all these stories and all these legends of his faith. He knew the teaching of all the prophets before him and all the deeds of his ancestors. He was keenly aware of the belief their God had made a contract with the Jewish people, and expected all of them to adhere to that covenant. He did more. He carried the concept of a personal God to its ultimate level. To him, his God was not distant. His God was with him every minute of every day, guided every step that he took, and had a plan for his whole life. We are told that, if the biblical words are correctly interpreted, he referred to his God affectionately as *Daddy*. His only desire was to serve the wishes of his heavenly father, whether that meant pain or adulation. His only aim was to somehow bring the others he taught to that same personal relationship with their God.

I know of no better way to present both these flawed and prescient concepts in his brilliant mind, than to use the only record that exists of his teaching, the gospels of Matthew, Mark, Luke and John. That being my intent, several apologies are immediately in order. The first is that I must confess to having been a practicing Christian for most of my life. I understand this religion more than any other, and will be prone to use it more as examples in this exploration of moral evolution. I hope you will understand that I favor no one religion over another in this discussion. Each religion has it blessings and its curses. This discussion of morality in Christianity, however, will be lengthier and more detailed than that of Judaism and Islam, simply because it is a history with which I spent most of my life. I would hope that whatever major conclusions are drawn will apply also to all other religions.

In like manner, I hope you will understand that none of this discussion is done in anger. I am simply trying to look at the record of Christianity rationally. This has been different than the way I looked at it for most of my life, and I suspect, the way the majority of those in the United States of America look at this record today. Even though there were many conflicting statements in the gospels, I used to accept them as each a separate valuable lesson in morality or belief. For example, Jesus on one hand says we should love our enemies, and in another passage, says that all those who are not with him are against him, and will burn in Hell forever. He curses the priests and curses a fig tree, causing it to die, but then says we should all love one another. Accepting all of these contradictory directives as all moral, as all part of a perfect document recording the life of a perfect human, is to me no longer an acceptable plan of action. The only way this record makes any sense to me is to understand that we all say contradictory things in our lives. We all make stupid mistakes in our lives. My outright and overt attempt in these pages is to claim that Jesus was not a perfect divinity, but a human who did contradictory things and made stupid mistakes, as we all do. This record, to me, does not otherwise make any sense. My job is to separate the wheat from the chaff, by direct explanation and quotation. I need to do my best to separate out those pronouncements and directives that are false and misleading, leaving those which can serve as a solid guide for our lives. And I need to do this without favoring one directive over another, judging each precept simply for what it says. Whatever is said critically is only an attempt to be rational, rather than biased.

I will also apologize for spending most of this discussion going over the gospel of Matthew in detail, more so than the other gospels. There is a reason for doing so. According to most biblical scholars, Matthew was the first recorded gospel, and was known to the writers of the other three accepted biblical texts before they were written. This analysis is intended to only study the moral pronouncements in these gospels, and those pronouncements are, with one major exception, all contained in Matthew. This will allow us to examine each of those precepts in full detail, using those quotes in Matthew which apply to each, and not repeating that process in each of the other gospels. Each gospel will receive its due, deservedly so, because each is written from a unique perspective. Those unique perspectives all bear directly on how these life directives are presented, and those differences need to be expressed for us to understand them the best.

Perhaps the most cogent caveat, as far as this discussion is concerned, is that we simply don't know exactly what Jesus said. Matthew, Mark and Luke, using historical records in each, are estimated to have been written about thirty years after Jesus' death. John is estimated to have been written about sixty years after Jesus' death. That means about thirty years of story-telling and arguments occurred between various sects before any word was placed on papyrus. Identical sounding but different words are misinterpreted, and stories altered to fit the need of the person telling the story. None of the original documents was preserved. The earliest known manuscripts on vellum were written some 250 years after Jesus' death. They are not in the original Aramaic, but translated to Greek, most certainly containing multiple misinterpretations in that translation. Greek, as written at that time, was a continuous line of letters, without spaces, periods, punctuation, accents or chapters. Many abbreviations were present, which the reader was supposed to understand. Scribes made frequent errors, whether accidental, hearing, copying or intentional. All of these errors occurred in the documents as preserved. Considering these multiple opportunities for contamination and alteration, it is highly unlikely that any of the original sentences of this remarkable, charismatic teacher have been fully preserved.

We have to understand that the Christian community in the first two centuries after Jesus' death was a boiling sea of controversy. There were multiple sects, each claiming to have correct, but different interpretations of their Prophet's life. Some said the Jews were responsible for his death. Others said that the Romans were the guilty party. Some said that this was a Jewish reformation religion, others that it was entirely a religion of the gentiles. Some thought that Jesus was a divinity on earth, and others said that he was a human who became divine by his actions on earth. Some said that there was a divine Holy Spirit, and others disputed that claim. Some worshipped Mother Mary and Mary Magdalene more than they worshipped Jesus or his God. Some said that the God of Jesus could be contacted by mystical communion, so that each person had direct access to this God for comfort and guidance. Others said that only those who believed in Jesus as their savior and intermediary could reach their God. Some said that there was a life eternal, and others retorted that this claim of life after death was ridiculous. Each of these sects bent the reported words of Jesus to fit their own cause.

The emperor Constantine, who mistakenly attributed one of his victories in battle to the Christian religion, had experienced quite enough of this religious squabbling. He directed the bishops of the Christian church to get together and make up their minds about exactly what the church believed about Jesus' life. The result was the Council of Nicea in 325. The bishops knew they were under the sword. Constantine was not a very nice guy. He murdered his brother-in-law, his wives, his sons or anyone else whom he considered a threat to his power. They knew that if they did not reach some kind of consensus, they might pay with their necks, even though Constantine was enthusiastic about the Christian religion. As it was, those who disagreed with the final doctrines of the Nicean Council were exiled and excommunicated. After that council, the early Christian Church, which had accepted anybody and allowed multiple points of spirituality and worship, now became a male priest, intermediary dominated religion. The official doctrines that Jesus was a God on earth, that access to Heaven could only be obtained through Jesus, and that there was a tripartite divine entity of God-Jesus-Holy Spirit, had to be accepted by everyone. These doctrines found their way into the sayings of Jesus, as has been recorded in the gospels.

More importantly, these supposed beliefs of Jesus were altered for him in another very dramatic way before any word of his life was written. As if these other distortions of the words coming out of Jesus' mouth were not enough, the Christian church in the first three centuries had to withstand the threat of Mithraism. Mithraism, an ancient religion dating back to at least the fifteenth century BC, was more dominant than Christianity in those first centuries AD of the Roman Empire. Mithra was the Persian god of kings, the God of mutual obligation between the king and his warriors, the God of war, the God of contract and the God of justice. When kings or rulers of surrounding territories pledged allegiance to the burgeoning Roman Empire, they did so in Mithraic ceremonies. In the second century, hundreds of inscriptions citing Mithra appeared in the Roman Empire, many of them along the military boundaries in Britain, along the Danube, Rhine and Euphrates rivers. Mithra was declared the protector of the Roman Empire by the Emperor Diocletian in 307 AD.

Mithra, according to the mythology of this religion, was born on December 25. His mother was a virgin female, fertilized by the Heavenly Father. His birth was witnessed by shepherds and by Magi, who brought gifts to his sacred birth place. As an adult he performed many miracles, raising the dead, healing the sick, making the lame walk, helping the blind to see and casting out devils. He carried the keys to the Kingdom of Heaven. After his early death, he was placed in a tomb covered by a rock. After his death, the rock was rolled away and he was withdrawn from the tomb. He miraculously came back to life, and ascended to Heaven. Before his triumphant ascension, he held a last supper with his Twelve Disciples. His ascension to Heaven was celebrated at Easter.

The early Christian Church, faced with a fight for survival against this dominant other religion in the Roman Empire, immediately adopted all this mythology for its hero, Jesus. Christianity is truly the copycat religion. Since the mythology of Christianity is identical to that of Mithraism, and since Mithraism preceded Christianity by centuries, there is only one reasonable conclusion. Christians claimed the same wondrous and magical feats for their hero, in an effort to make Jesus look just as great as Mithra. Fortunately for Christianity and unfortunately for Mithraism, this ploy was extremely successful. Constantine is quoted as saying that he did not know whether he was worshipping Mithraism or Christianity, because they had identical beliefs. When Constantine attributed one of his battle victories to Christianity and became a convert, however, the twin religions rapidly split, to the great detriment of Mithraism. Constantine declared Christianity a protected religion by the Roman Empire. Following his death, all the Roman emperors were Christian, save for Julian, "the apostate." Julian paid dearly for his dissension; he was killed at an early age. The Christian Church, blessed by the power of Rome, viciously eliminated all "pagans" (translation, mostly Mithraists) who disagreed with their faith. All Mithraic shrines were burned and looted, their gold, treasure and religious relics carried off to Constantinople. This veil of terror reached its peak when the shrine of Mithra, on the Vatican hill, was seized by Christian priests. They not only looted and stole the temple; they also stole the title for their High Priest. The High Priest for Mithraism was the Pater Patrum, or Pope. The Pope was now Christian, not Mithraic, and the site he had lived no longer belonged to Mithra, but belonged to Jesus, the Pope and the priests of Christianity. The Christians had totally usurped Mithraism in this vicious political power struggle.

The whole point of this discussion is to make the case that all this Mithraic mythology was added to the Christian religion after Jesus' death, and before the gospels were first written. Every subsequent relation, translation, copy and interpretation further corrupted whatever original words were uttered. Every quote that we read in the Bible has all this extra stuff thrown in on top of it, as if we started with a piece of meat at the bottom of the pot and then kept adding ingredients, vegetables, stock, seasonings, water, salt and pepper, until we have an aromatic stew, only 5% of which is the essential ingredient that was the start. I use this analogy for a specific purpose. Although the message of the gospels has been twisted, distorted, misinterpreted, mispronounced, plagiarized, misspelled, misheard, mistranslated and misrelated, there is still a marvelous message that shines through. Although I firmly believe that what we read in the Bible is so degraded and so buried in mythology that we do not have any reliable words from the mouth of Jesus, and even though I believe that this overwhelming corruption of his words leaves us without any clear knowledge of what he actually believed or said, we do have two reasonable facts left on which to analyze these documents. One is that Jesus made a deep and life-changing impression on those who knew him. The other is that we have what we have, and we are where we are. The gospels as they now exist are what all Christians refer to when they make their most momentous decisions in their lives. For these reasons, I have chosen to analyze this biblical record as it now exists, rather than conjecture as to what Jesus may or may not have said. Incorrect as it may be, this is the record upon which we have to pass judgment as to what parts of it we should avoid, and what parts to follow as guides to our lives.

THE GOSPEL OF MATTHEW

The intent of Matthew is evident from the very first sentence. This account of the life of Jesus was written to establish this man as the long awaited Messiah of the Jewish religion. It is pretty clear that there is doubt in the mind of many people as to whether Jesus is the chosen savior of the chosen people. Matthew considers it his job to present all the evidence he can muster that Jesus is that Messiah for the Jews. All this evidence involves only the people of Israel; any extension of his message to those other than Jews is incidental and accidental. Matthew begins with a male lineage list which purportedly gives Jesus direct descendancy from Abraham through the house of David. He immediately labels him as the Messiah, throws in the Mithraic miracle of virgin birth and promptly combines these with Old Testament prophecy.

1: 22–23. All of this happened to fulfill the Lord's message through his prophet.

Look! The virgin will conceive a child!

She will give birth to a son.

And he will be called Immanuel

(meaning God is with us)

The stage is set for what is to follow. We are off and running, not to stop until Jesus' disciples have been instructed to go into the world and teach everyone else that he was that savior for the Jews. On the way, these pages in Matthew are packed full of miracles, old and new prophecies, and highly conflicting moral advice. This mixed morality is what we need to look at carefully, to determine as best we can, what part of it makes sense, and what does not. We cannot look at any of it as if this is purely holy word, which cannot be challenged in any way. We have been accustomed to doing so, and in fact, have been encouraged to do so, as if these stories, parables and teachings have been transcribed exactly as they happened, all of them fitting together perfectly without conflict. We have been taught that this collection is a smooth, golden scheme which teaches us how we should live. On the contrary, when we look at these gospels carefully, we find that each Testament of the Bible is a conglomerate of manipulated and distorted tales, all grouped together in a fashion that suits the social purpose of that author. Those contain a plethora of conflicting good and bad advice, conflicts which we have largely ignored, thinking that we just don't understand all of them yet.

Well, we can understand them. The only thing we have to do is to look at Matthew asking what part of it is rational, and in particular, ask if whatever morality is taught or implied will realistically guide us to lead better lives. As we do so, we are immediately struck that there is a frightful mixture of awful morality combined with bad advice, which is compounded by great leaps in moral understanding, never before adequately expressed. There are illusions of grandeur, which are a tragic misdirection of our moral compass. There is an emphasis on violent punishment for those who are infidels, which is also highly immoral. There is emphasis on an apocalyptic end to the earth, which may well be true, but leads us far astray from concentrating on our behavior while we are here on earth. There is an entire crowd of teaching which is best delineated as really bad advice. Pacifism can be and is carried too far. The exclusion of all those who are not Jews, from access to the divine, must be described as immature, at best, and if taken in full context, immoral.

Then, leaping out from this pool of poison fish, there are three startling revelations which are glorious leaps of high morality, never before emphasized by any religion or prophet. (1) Love of God must be combined with love of neighbor. (2) Neighbor includes those of different faith and different race. (3) Neighbor also includes your enemies. Now we have finally achieved an initial understanding of what human ethics should be. The only problem is in knowing how to apply these principles in our lives. Even Jesus was not able to bring himself to behave that way. Let's have at it.

ILLUSIONS OF GRANDEUR

There are two aspects of Jesus' conceptualization, as is recorded, which I consider major moral failures. If we are to pass judgment on this record as it now exists, the first of those we are obliged to address concerns his egomania. There have been millions of people throughout history who have believed, somewhere in their soul, that they have had direct communication with the God of all creation, or that all their actions are directed, down to the most minute twitch, by their personal God, or that they are a God of some type, living here on earth. They have believed that they have immense power and can command all other people how to lead their lives. Some of them, such as Jim Jones and David Koresh, acting on their egotism, have been responsible for major human disasters. There have been societies and times in our history when such people have been readily accepted as a normal part of their life. There were hundreds of messiahs existing around the time of Jesus, each of whom had his following, was reported to perform miracles, and each of whom had his own recipe for obtaining rewards in heaven. Judging by the deep impression on all those who came to know Jesus, we will have to assume none of these others had his charisma, or his understanding of what moves humans. Having said as much, this still does not excuse Jesus' grandiose assessment of himself. Supreme egotism does not allow us to give others good advice. If Jesus came before a judge in this country, at this time, stating that he heard voices from his God, was himself a God on earth, would come back to life after death, and would then rule in glory over all others for an eternity, it is certain that he would be locked up in a psychiatric institution and placed on drugs to attempt suppression of his schizophrenic mind. I beg forgiveness for saying so, but believe that this decision would be quite correct. There is no doubt that he had a brilliant mind, a deeply caring soul, and gave us glorious moral precepts never before fully expressed. There is also no doubt, to me, that this biblical record describes a person who believed that he was a God in training, who had to serve this preceptorship on this earth before he could rule over everyone else for an eternity in his Heaven. As it is described, this egomania constitutes one of the major moral flaws in the remarkable teachings of this major Prophet.

> *4: 19–20. Jesus called out to them, "Come, be my disciples, and I will show you how to fish for People!" And they left their nets at once and went with him.*

Jesus tells his disciples, on multiple occasions, that if they follow him, they will learn how to control and command other people, and achieve greatness.

> *8:21–23. "Not all people who sound religious are really godly. They may refer to me as 'Lord,' but they still won't enter the Kingdom of Heaven. The decisive issue is whether they obey my Father in heaven. On Judgment day many will tell me, 'Lord, Lord, we prophesied in your name and cast out demons in your name and performed many miracles in your name.' But I will reply, 'I never knew you. Go away, the things you did were unauthorized.' "*

Only those who believe that Jesus is the great Messiah will, in his opinion, be able to perform miracles; only those who believe in his Lordship will survive the devastating apocalypse, which he believes is imminent.

> *8:21–22. Another of his disciples said, "Lord, first let me return home and bury my father." But Jesus told him,*

"Follow me now. Let those who are spiritually dead care for their own dead."

Probably one of our more sacrosanct morals is that each of us must take care of our own family, and in particular, our own mother and father. Jesus, rather disgustingly, says that this familial duty is unimportant to him. All he cares about is whether or not this disciple will belong completely to him and no one else.

10: 5–8. Jesus sent the twelve disciples out with these instructions: "Don't go to the Gentiles or the Samaritans, but only to the people of Israel – God's lost sheep. Go and announce to them that the Kingdom of Heaven is near. Heal the sick, raise the dead, cure those with leprosy, and cast out demons. Give as freely as you have received!"

Jesus is so convinced he has superpowers, he believes he can transfer these miracle powers to his disciples, so that they too can overcome natural events and physical laws. And make no mistake about it – this misdirection is intended only for Jews. No one else matters.

10: 34–37. "Don't imagine that I came to bring peace to the earth! No, I came to bring a sword. I have come to set a man against his father, and a daughter against her mother, and a daughter-in-law against her mother-in-law. Your enemies will be right in your own household! If you love your father or mother more than you love me, you are not worthy of being mine; or if you love your son or daughter more than me, you are not worthy of being mine."

This is pretty awful. If the purpose of our religion is to teach us family values, this is the opposite. Jesus advocates violence against all family members who do not wish to participate in his particular egocentricity.

12: 30. "Anyone who isn't helping me opposes me and anyone who isn't working with me is actually working against me."

Egomania demands total allegiance. Everyone else is the enemy. This is not kindness, graciousness and empathy.

12:41–42. "The people of Nineveh will rise up against this generation on judgment day and condemn it, because they repented at the preaching of Jonah. And now someone greater than Jonah is here - and you refuse to repent. The queen of Sheba will also rise up against this generation on judgment day and condemn it, because she came from a distant land to hear the wisdom of Solomon. And now someone greater than Solomon is here – and you refuse to listen to him."

Jesus believes he is a greater prophet than Jonah and Solomon. They do not even come close to his preaching and wisdom, in his opinion. Like Muhammad Ali, he is the greatest.

12: 46–49. As Jesus was speaking to the crowd, his mother and brothers were outside waiting to talk with him. Someone told Jesus, "Your mother and your brothers are outside, and they want to speak to you." Jesus asked, "Who is my mother? Who are my brothers?" Then he pointed to his disciples and said, "Those are my mother and brothers. Anyone who does the will of my father in heaven is my brother and sister and mother!"

"Anyone who does the will of my father in heaven" may be interpreted as "Anyone who does whatever I tell them to do." The only people important to Jesus are his sycophants. Those who should be most important to him, his family, no longer matter in his distorted philosophy.

16: 13–16. When Jesus came to the region of Caesarea Phillipi, he asked his disciples, "Who do people say that the Son of Man is?" "Well," they replied, "some say John the Baptist, some say Elijah, and others say Jeremiah or one of the other prophets." Then he asked them, "Who do you say I am?" Simon Peter answered, "You are the Messiah, the Son of the Living God."

Having his disciples follow him everywhere and do whatever he says is not enough. He also demands that his disciples believe he is the greatest person that has ever lived on the face of the Earth.

25:33–43. "But when the Son of Man comes in his glory, and all the angels with him then he will sit upon his glorious throne. All the nations will be gathered in his presence, and he will separate them as a shepherd separates the sheep from the goats. He will place the sheep at his right hand and the goats at his left. Then the King will say to those on the right, 'Come, you who are blessed by my Father, inherit the Kingdom prepared for you from the foundation of the world. For I was hungry, and you fed me. I was thirsty, and you gave me a drink. I was a stranger, and you invited me into your home. I was naked and you gave me clothing. I was sick, and you cared for me. I was in prison, and you visited me.'

"Then these righteous ones will reply, 'Lord, when did we ever see you hungry and feed you? Or thirsty and give your something to drink? Or a stranger and show you hospitality? Or naked and give you clothing? When did we ever see you sick or in prison, and visit you?' And the King will tell them 'I assure you, when you did it to one of the least of these my brothers and sisters, you were doing it to me!'"

"Then the King will turn to those on his left and say, 'Away with you, cursed ones, into the eternal fire prepared for the Devil and his demons. For I was hungry, and you didn't feed me. I was thirsty and you didn't give me anything to drink. I was a stranger, and you didn't invite me into your home. I was naked, and you gave me no clothing. I was sick and in prison, and you didn't visit me.'"

"Then they will reply, 'Lord, when did we ever see you hungry or thirsty or a stranger or naked or sick or in prison, and not help you?' And he will answer, 'I assure you, when you refused to help the least of these, my brothers and sisters, you were refusing to help me.' And they will go away into eternal punishment, but the righteous will go into eternal life."

This is a wonderful lesson which each of us should carry with us all our lives. Whatever good thing we do for another human, we do for all humans, because we are all in this together. Any time we fail to help someone else in need, we fail all other humans. We are so struck by this marvelous moral lesson that we usually fail to see what else this message contains. Jesus believes he will be the Almighty God, sitting on a regal throne somewhere in the sky, commanding all the angels and passing judgment on all humans. He is pointedly vindictive toward all those who do not do those things he tells them to do. They will be tortured for an eternity. This beautiful moral precept of overall compassion is buried under megalomania. Jesus emphasizes his self-appointed regal power for an eternity, more than his moral lesson. Why he has such anger against goats remains unexplained.

> 26:64. *"Yes, it is as you say. And in the future you will see me, the Son of Man, sitting at God's right hand in the place of power and coming back on the clouds of heaven."*

Standing before the High Priest Caiaphas, Jesus again asserts his belief that he is a God on earth, who will rule in all power over all humans, for all time.

VICIOUS PUNISHMENT

The second major moral deficiency I see in the teachings of Jesus is his great anger at all those who do not accept him as a divinity on earth. The punishments he forecasts for those who have other beliefs are extremely harsh. This degree of harshness can only come from someone who cannot tolerate diversity, other beliefs, other religions, other cultures. I find this intolerance deeply offensive. It is the anger of an egomaniac. It is either his way or the fiery furnaces of Hell for an eternity. He apparently, if the recorded gospel is correct, cannot bring himself to practice what he preaches. One of the great pillars of morality is tolerance. If another person has a belief system which gives them sustenance and guidance in life, they should by all means be allowed to keep that set of beliefs. We are all individuals. We all have separate belief systems. Allowing that diversity of belief and building on the strengths of those various beliefs is how we all grow and prosper. When the demand is made that all of us have to believe in a certain way or be tortured, then we are all in deep trouble. We can never achieve a state of ethics if torture is accepted as the treatment for someone who believes differently. This is a hateful, depraved philosophy.

Again, this discussion is, so far, still only in the book of Matthew. We will later address these same issues to some degree in the other gospels.

> *3: 11–12. "I baptize with water those who turn from their sin and turn to God. But someone is coming soon who is far greater than I am – so much greater that I am not even worthy to be his slave. He will baptize you with the Holy Spirit and with fire. He is ready to separate the chaff from the grain with his winnowing fork. Then he will clean up the threshing area, storing the grain in his barn but burning the chaff with never-ending fire."*

John the Baptist predicts the coming of Jesus, who will do wonderful things for those who are willing to accept him. The emphasis in this passage, however, is upon the fiery punishment that awaits those who choose to follow some other leader.

> *13: 40–43. "Just as the weeds are separated out and burned, so it will be at the end of the world. I, the Son of Man, will send my angels, and they will remove from my Kingdom everything that causes sin and all who do evil, and they will throw them into the furnace and burn them. There will be weeping and gnashing of teeth. Then the godly will shine like the sun in their Father's Kingdom. Anyone who is willing to hear should listen and understand!"*

Jesus makes it clear he plans to send his henchmen to ferret out all those who are not willing to show obeisance to him as the true Messiah. The Gestapo and the torture chambers are coming.

> *18: 2–6. Jesus called a small child over to him and put the child among them. Then he said, "I assure you, unless you turn from your sins and become as little children, you will never get into the Kingdom of Heaven. Therefore, anyone who becomes as humble as this little child is the greatest in the Kingdom of Heaven. And anyone who welcomes a little child like this on my behalf is welcoming me. But if anyone causes one of these little ones who trusts in me to lose faith, it would be better for that person to be thrown into the sea with a large millstone tied around the neck."*

What a wonderful lesson this is. We all should remain deeply humble throughout our lives. We all need to keep a childlike enthusiasm for life. We all should never tear away a nurturing faith that sustains others. The punishment phase of these moral lessons, however, is intense. Reform and education would be a humane choice. Murder by drowning for someone who needs further moral training is simply callosity.

> *18: 7–9. "How terrible it will be for anyone who causes others to sin. Temptation to do wrong is inevitable, but how terrible it will be for the person who does the tempting. So if your hand or foot cause you to sin, cut it off and throw it away. It is better to enter heaven crippled or lame that to be thrown into the unquenchable fire with both of your hands and feet. And if your eye causes you to sin, gouge it out and throw it away. It is better to enter heaven half blind than to have two eyes and be thrown into hell."*

It would be difficult to become more primitive than this. If Jesus followed this, his own advice, he would have met his own death without hands, feet or eyes. His anger, bigotry and violent predictions for those who did not share his egomania would have warranted at least these body losses, if not the loss of additional appurtenances and appendages.

> *24: 15–22. The time will come when you will see what Daniel the prophet spoke about: the sacrilegious object that causes desecration, standing in the Holy Place – reader, pay attention! Then those in Judea must flee to the hills. A person outside the house must not go inside to pack. A person in the field must not return even to get a coat. How terrible it will be for pregnant women and for mothers nursing their babies in those days. And pray that your flight will not be in winter or on the Sabbath. For that will be a time of greater horror than anything the world has ever seen or will ever see again. In fact, unless that time of calamity is shortened, the entire human race will be destroyed. But it will be shortened for the sake of God's chosen ones.*

According to Jesus, as Matthew speaks for him, all people on the face of the earth have only a few months or years to accept him as the great and glorious Messiah. If they happen to think otherwise, they will all be destroyed, and all will suffer a horrible death.

> *25: 41–43. Then the King will turn to those on the left and say, "Away with you, you cursed ones, into the eternal fire prepared for the Devil and his Demons. For I was hungry, and didn't feed me. I was thirsty, and you didn't give me anything to drink. I was a stranger and you didn't invite me into your house. I was naked and you gave me no clothing. I was sick and in prison, and you didn't visit me."*

The sentiments of compassion that are hereby expressed are laudable. The punishment for those who do not behave is vindictive: those unbelievers are cursed and tortured for an eternity.

DAY OF JUDGMENT

Perhaps this eschatological fault is not as immoral as illusions of grandeur and vicious punishment for those who do not believe Jesus is grand and glorious, but it is troubling enough. Jesus makes multiple references to a Judgment Day. That will also be an apocalypse, when all of the world and its inhabitants will be destroyed. At that time, the dead will, according to Jesus, come back to life, defying all laws of physics and nature. All humans will, living or dead, be judged by him from his glorious throne of power over all humans. Exactly what qualifies one to be selected to go to Heaven is never fully defined, except for one requirement. The one clear qualification necessary to enter this eternal pleasure zone is to believe in Jesus as the Jewish Messiah. Long prophesied by the Jewish prophets, this concept is also, if we take this gospel at face value, a core in the teachings of Jesus. Matthew is determined to prove to the world, through this gospel, that Jesus is that long awaited Messiah, who will imminently accomplish the final goals of that prophecy of centuries. It is not just giving eternal pleasure to all those who accept Jesus as that Messiah, and torturing or killing all those who have some other faith. It is also a fervent belief that at the time of his apocalyptic return, Jesus will become the king of all people everywhere, and the nation of Israel will dominate over all other nations for the remainder of eternity. It is these superiority and exclusivity concepts for Judaism that makes the Day of Judgment such an immoral swamp.

Jesus makes multiple references to this final tragic event occurring within his lifetime, or at least within the lifetime of the disciples. Obviously, this dire prediction was false. From our vantage point today, we understand that at some point our species will disappear. The earth will take a direct hit from an asteroid that will eliminate us or all life, or the sun will in its final throes, engulf the earth, reducing all that is here to atoms. What we also understand is that none of this will happen at hand of a vindictive personal God. We particularly understand that there is no one particular genetic human group that is favored by any imaginary deity. The only question that remains is whether this day of apocalypse was a literary motif taken from Mithraism by Matthew, or whether it was indeed the megalomania of Jesus. Yet it becomes a moot point. Regardless of how you cut it, this is a false moral pathway. Concentration on some imagined life after death, rather than on doing whatever we can for each other while we are here, is a tragic misdirection of our energies and mutual moral obligations. We are only here for the blink of the eye, in universe time, and as best we can tell, don't go anyplace else when we die, other than into atoms (or perhaps other universes). We do not get any other chance, in this life, to be kind and compassionate.

> *5: 11–12. "God blesses you when you are mocked and persecuted and lied about because you are my followers. Be happy about it! Be very glad! For a great reward awaits you in heaven. And remember, the ancient prophets were persecuted, too."*

This advice to his disciples occurs at the end of the Sermon on the Mount. Those great words of comfort are followed by this wayward misdirection, encouraging his followers to seek punishment. The justification for this really bad advice is that they will be given great pleasure after they die. It is a terrible false promise. No one, in the history of mankind, has enjoyed being derided and tortured. This kind of stupidity is the result of concentrating on an imaginary life, rather than this one and only life.

> *10: 21–23. "Brother will betray brother to death, fathers will betray their own children, and children will rise against their*

parents and cause them to be killed. And everyone will hate
you because of your allegiance to me. But those who endure
to the end will be saved. When you are persecuted in one
town, flee to the next. I assure you that I, the Son of Man,
will return before you have reached all the towns of Israel."

At the time of the apocalypse, Jesus predicts that both the Inquisition and the Gestapo will be operating simultaneously. As if that promise is not morally distasteful enough, he then compounds that error by saying that this overwhelming catastrophe will occur within the next few months or years. It appears that he got both of these concepts quite wrong.

22: 10–14. So the servants brought in everyone they could
find, good and bad alike, and the banquet hall was filled
with guests. But when the king came in to meet the guests,
he noticed a man who wasn't wearing the proper clothes
for a wedding. "Friend," he asked, "how is it that you are
here without wedding clothes!" And the man had no reply.
Then the king said to his aides, "Bind him hand and foot
and throw him out into the outer darkness, where there is
weeping and gnashing of teeth." For many are called, but
few are chosen.

This accounting of a wedding feast where none of the original invitees wished to attend, and street guests are recruited to fill the hall, was intended to make the point that although many are invited to the life eternal, only a few are chosen. There are even some who get there, but then got thrown out for improper social attire. It's a great story. The claim, however, that there is an exclusive, elite club of people who get to survive after death is, as far as we can tell, false. As importantly, the claim that we should concentrate our efforts on becoming a member of this elite club is a grave misuse of our talents while we are here on earth.

24: 26–29. "So if someone tells you, 'Look the Messiah is out
in the desert,' don't bother to go and look. Or 'Look, he is
hiding here,' don't believe it! For as the lightning lights up
the entire sky, so it will be when the Son of Man comes. Just
as the gathering of vultures shows there is a carcass nearby,
so these signs indicate that the end is near.

Immediately after those horrible days end,

the sun will be darkened,

the moon will not give light,

the stars will fall from the sky,

and the powers of heaven will be shaken."

This graphic description of the end of the earth and all life is intended to frighten all who listen, into accepting Jesus as the great Messiah now, rather than when it is too late to obtain this false promise of eternal life. This is not just a bait and switch; it is hard sell advertising tactics. Unfortunately, the promised purchase product of a life eternal does not, as best we can tell, exist. Those who give of their time and energy to achieve this goal waste their resources. It is better that we spend our time on Earth trying to be good people, than cowering in fear we won't get to an imagined futuristic clubhouse door in time.

The next two deficits in the morality of Jesus I do not find quite as trying, but they are bad enough. Both lead us in the opposite direction from human behavior which will benefit us all.

FULFILLING THE SELECTIVE PROPHECY

The base Matthew uses as a literary plan are those prophecies from the sages of the Old Testament, who uniformly and repeatedly express the belief that there will someday appear a great Jewish savior, who will free all the Israelites from their centuries of oppression and suppression. This champion of their causes will make them all become moral and honest, but more importantly, will be victorious in all armed conflict that may occur at that time, defeating all military and civil forces arrayed against Israel. This savior then becomes a Messiah, who will be an overpowering military ruler, enabling Israel to become dominant over all other nations for all time. In this sense, the gospel of Matthew is not about morality as much as it is a literary apology for military dominance. It seeks to establish this particular Prophet as the king predicted in the Bible by the Jewish prophets. Matthew not only uses multiple references to this biblical prophecy, but also has Jesus say it himself. If this is accepted at face value, both Jesus and Matthew consider Jesus to have existed to deliver the Israelites from bondage, and not anyone else. Any morality which is limited to only a select race or nation, as superior to all others, is indeed highly deficient. It is nowhere close to rising to the level of morality we can call ethics.

13: 13–15. "That is why I tell these stories, because people see what I do, but they don't really see. They hear what I say, but they don't really hear, and they don't understand. This fulfills the prophecy of Isaiah, which says:

You will hear my word,

but you will not understand;

you will see what I do,

but you will not perceive its meaning.

For the hearts of these people are hardened,

and their ears cannot hear,

and they have closed their eyes –

so their eyes cannot see,

and their ears cannot hear,

and their hearts cannot understand,

and they cannot turn to me

and let me heal them."

Even the oral narrative techniques Jesus uses, as described by Matthew, are done in order to fulfill biblical prophecy.

15: 21–26. Jesus then left Galilee and went north to the region of Tyre and Sidon. A Gentile woman who lived there came to him, pleading, "Have mercy on me, O Lord, Son of David! For my daughter has a demon in her, and it is severely tormenting her."

But Jesus gave her no reply – not even a word. Then his disciples urged him to send her away. "Tell her to leave." They said. "She is bothering us with all her begging."

Then he said to the woman, "I was sent only to help the people of Israel – God's lost sheep – not the Gentiles."

But she came and worshiped him and pleaded again, "Lord, help me!"

"It isn't right to take food from the children and throw it to the dogs," he said.

This is a rather terse little ditty. Jesus' disciples don't believe this woman has any business bothering him, because he came only to save the Jews. Jesus states in his own words that he does not wish to deal with any other group, race or nation. Only the Jews deserve to be saved. The obvious corollary is that gentiles or any other group do not count in this quest. Morality, for Jesus, only extends to the Jews. As such, the teachings of this purported Messiah of the Jews come nowhere close to universal morality.

17: 1–9. Six days later Jesus took Peter and the two brothers, James and John, and led them up a high mountain. As the men watched, Jesus' appearance changed so that his face shone like the sun, and his clothing became dazzling white. Suddenly, Moses and Elijah appeared and began talking with Jesus. Peter blurted out, "Lord, this is wonderful! If you want me to, I'll make three shrines, one for you, one for Moses, and one for Elijah."

But even as he said it, a bright cloud came over them, and a voice from the cloud said, "This is my beloved Son, and I am fully pleased with him. Listen to him." The disciples were terrified and fell face down on the ground.

Jesus came over and touched them. "Get up," he said. "Don't be afraid." And when they looked they saw only Jesus with them. As they descended the mountain, Jesus commanded them, "Don't tell anyone what you have seen until I, the Son of Man, have been raised from the dead."

His disciples asked, "Why do the teachers of religious law insist that Elijah must return before the Messiah comes?"

Jesus replied, "Elijah is indeed coming first to set everything in order. But I tell you, he has already come, and he wasn't recognized, and he was badly mistreated. And soon the Son of Man will also suffer at their hands."

This intense mini-drama is a minor fait accompli. Matthew has craftily constructed a theatrical scene which illuminates four of his themes all in one fell swoop. Jesus is claimed as the Son of God, meaning that he is the long sought Messiah. Jesus is intimately associated with the founder of the Israeli nation-state, Moses. Elijah appears, and it is explained that this appearance is necessary before the Jewish Messiah can appear. John the Baptist is recognized as the immediate predecessor of the Messiah. We have to admire Matthew for creating this adroit, brief, but potent, literary ploy. Unfortunately, there is little moral value in this terse little drama, if it applies only to an isolated Hebrew tribe.

> *20: 17–19. As Jesus was on the way to Jerusalem, he took the twelve disciples aside privately and told them what was going to happen to him. "When we get to Jerusalem," he said, "the Son of Man will be betrayed to the leading priests and the teachers of religious law. They will sentence him to die. Then they will hand him over to the Romans to be mocked, whipped, and crucified. But on the third day he will be raised from the dead."*

Although this conversation is attributed to Jesus, it is given in third person. It appears likely that Matthew is talking, describing retroactively the accepted accounting of those events. He wants to make it appear that Jesus knew exactly what he was doing, in order to fulfill the prophecies of this rebellion within the Jewish religion.

> *21: 1–5. As Jesus and the disciples approached Jerusalem, they came to the town of Bethphage on the Mount of Olives. Jesus sent two of them on ahead. "Go into the village over there," he said, "and you will see a donkey tied there, with its colt beside it. Untie them and bring them here. If anyone asks what you are doing, just say, 'The Lord needs them, and he will immediately send them.'" This was done to fulfill the prophecy,*
>
> *Tell the people of Israel,*
>
> *Look, your King is coming to you.*
>
> *He is humble, riding on a donkey –*
>
> *Even on a donkey's colt.*

Even the stage setting has to be appropriately arranged for this grand entry, to coincide with words contained in previous books of the Bible.

26: 52–54. "Put away your sword," Jesus told him, "Those who use the sword will be killed by the sword. Don't you realize that I could ask my Father for thousands of angels to protect us, and he would send them instantly? But if I did, how would the Scriptures be fulfilled that describe what must happen now?"

These words fulfill all the other prophecies of death and resurrection needed to produce a Messiah, but they ring hollow. Not only can we not swallow the premise that Jesus can produce thousands of military angels on a moment's notice, but we also find it rather incredulous that all of this was planned in advance.

27: 50–53. Then Jesus shouted out again, and he gave up his spirit. At that moment the curtain in the Temple was torn in two, from top to bottom. The earth shook, rocks split apart, and tombs opened. The bodies of many godly men and women who had died were raised from the dead after Jesus' resurrection. They left the cemetery, went into the holy city of Jerusalem, and appeared to many people.

The Roman officer and the other soldiers at the crucifixion were terrified by the earthquake and all that had happened. They said. "Truly, this was the Son of God."

This is a nice finishing touch. Like the ending of a great play, the drama is great. Matthew does it well. He has accomplished his task of presenting a magnificent drama showing Jesus as the long expected Messiah of the Hebrews. We note, parenthetically, that only the curtain in the national shrine of the Jews was torn. No other drapery in any other shrine or temple matters. The problem we are left with is that all this emphasis on Jewish prophecy, apocalypse, a Day of Judgment, and messianic fulfillment leaves us without rational moral guides for our lives. Any morality which applies to only a small segment of the human population, with dire punishments predicted for all who do not share that faith, is a at best colloquial, and at worst, immoral for the rest of the human population on the face of the earth.

EXTREME PACIFISM

I have found this subject difficult to discuss in the past. What works in one human situation is not sure to work in another situation. The problem of knowing when to trust another person and when to distrust that person is eternal. In this search to define better moral behavior, about all we are pretty sure of is that neither of the extremes will create stable societies. We all know that a total lack of resistance to complete selfishness will not teach anyone any lessons. On the other hand, as has been quoted above, all of us are pretty clear that those who live by the sword will die by the sword. If we choose violent retaliation for any physical or emotional hurt we sustain, we can expect that we will receive like payment. Violence begets violence, and war begets war. If every time we have a grievance against another human we strike, kill, or maim, the entire society falls apart in revenge, murder, destruction of property, loss of sustenance, instability of families, loss of accumulated knowledge, and immense human suffering. If our goal is life, liberty, and the pursuit of happiness, violent reprisals and selfish self-interests don't get it. There has to be a degree of trust for any society to grow and progress, in comfort and knowledge. Those of us who have had the opportunity to live in societies that strive for trust and justice are deeply grateful for that sustaining cocoon.

Most of this book so far has been an examination of how human society has gradually progressed from groups that were extremely violent to those where some form of compromise is demanded to settle disputes. How to settle those inevitable and constant human disputes with the least instability of each society is part of what we call morals. These codes of conduct are rules we have adopted for each of us to follow, in order to give the greatest good for the greatest number. We have, for example, described some of the tribal laws of the Hebrews as being primitive and savage. We have to understand, however, that these were a great advance over what existed before these laws were created. An eye for an eye and a tooth for a tooth, a hand for a hand and a cow for a cow were a great improvement over the lawlessness that preceded it. We have traced through this history, the gradual reduction in draconian punishment for misdeeds, and noted that our religions have championed that cause. We are deeply indebted to those parts of Judaism, Christianity and Islam that have emphasized compassion and empathy.

It would seem that what we have been headed for all along during this moral progression is exactly what is contained in Matthew and the other gospels of the New Testament. Jesus, although he does not practice it himself, advocates extreme pacifism. One should not resist at all, he states. If struck, offer to be struck again. If demanded to carry someone else's load, carry it further than demanded. If asked to forgive, forgive endlessly. Now, this is beautiful stuff. We have spent our lives reading it in Sunday school and hearing it from the pulpit, with great admiration that one person could be so perfect. We are exhorted to also behave with great passivity toward assaults on our person and character, thinking that this is the ultimate goal of a peaceful society. Aye, there's the rub.

The rub is that passively accepting violent aggression simply encourages those perpetrators to be more brutal in their aggression. The only reason the meek will inherit the earth is because they have been ground into the dirt by the heels of those who have pushed them down and walked all over them. Extreme pacifism, as is preached by Jesus, is amoral, if we may call it that. If we define morality as that system of human behavior that gives us all the greatest chance of fulfillment in our lives, extreme pacifism is a dismal failure. Appeasement of selfish transgression only fosters that transgression to continue with greater force. Not only is this terrible advice, but Jesus himself is quite incapable of leading his life completely passively. He curses a fig tree, willing it to death. He curses the High Priests, calling them vipers, snakes, and probably much more vituperative words if we had the correct translation. He explodes in anger in the temple, assuring himself of being targeted as a troublemaker that must be eliminated.

Extreme pacifism is a complete disaster, but controlled pacifism is a winner. There is no other scheme of social interaction that comes anywhere close. In the language of social theorists, it is called tit for tat. This plan of dealing with the actions of other humans or groups simplifies that process into a few simple rules, that work better than any other, whether seeking cooperation or facing evil. It has been amply studied in societies and computer games. It always proves to be the most "moral" of any plan of social interaction, better than great aggression, and better than extreme pacifism. These are the rules by which tit for tat operates.

1. When you encounter another individual or group, always offer cooperation and friendship first. If you receive a like response, then you can work together to the great benefit of both of you.

2. If your offer of help and friendship is met with a hostile or treacherous response, immediately withdraw. Do not offer again. It is up to the other person or group to show you they have learned their lesson and are now willing to work with you.

3. If the initial act of another person or group is hostile and violent, immediately respond with vigor and force. Your response must be enough to convince that other party that they cannot behave in this way without paying a very dear price.

4. Your response should always seek the least violent and destructive means of resisting transgression and teaching your transgressor a lesson, but it must be enough to achieve those goals

5. Avoid anger and jealousy. There will always be someone else who has gotten more with less effort. Accept the cards you were given, make the best of them that you can, and move ahead with life.

6. Everyone deserves a second chance, if situations seem to have changed. It is then important for you to offer one more chance for that person or group to cooperate with you.

7. Two chances are enough. If both of your offers of generosity and cooperation are met with treachery, offer no more.

If the members of any society learn to work with each other, that society will prosper. If the members of any society all act in deceitful and selfish ways, that society will suffer. Those who are violent and aggressive will kill each other. On the other hand, even if there are only a few members of a society who are willing to cooperate, they will prosper while others fail, and there is the impetus for that society to become more caring. Tit for tat wins, big time, and complete passivity, or complete aggression, are bad losers. These particular teachings of Jesus, encouraging us to be totally passive at all times, lead us badly astray.

> *5:22. "But I say, if you are angry with someone, you are subject to judgment. If you call someone an idiot, you are in danger of being brought before the high council. And if you curse someone, you are in danger of the fires of hell."*

It is certainly easier said than done, is it not? If this pronouncement is true, Jesus is in danger of the fires of Hell. He is like the politician running for office, He promises wonderful things during the election, but once in office, behaves much differently.

> *5: 38–42. "You have heard that the law of Moses says, 'If an eye is injured, injure the eye of the person who did it. If a tooth gets knocked out, knock out the tooth of the person who did it.' But I say, don't resist an evil person! If you are slapped on the right cheek, turn the other, too. If you are ordered to court and your shirt is taken from you, give your coat, too. If a soldier demands that you carry his gear for a mile, carry it two miles. Give to those who ask, and don't turn away from those who want to borrow."*

The command to not resist an evil person is made with emphasis. Every truth is tempted to expand until it becomes a falsehood, and we have certainly reached that point with this utterance. A completely passive response to violence simply encourages further violence.

> *18: 21–22. Then Peter came to him and asked, "Lord, how often should I forgive someone who sins against me? Seven times?"*

> *"No!" Jesus replied, "seventy times seven!"*

The implication is that each of us should forgive forever. If by that, the intent is to say that we should allow sinful acts to continue forever, without resisting them, then this teaching is terribly wrong. We might forgive forever, but we shouldn't forget, and we should not let bad behavior continue without immediately resisting that bad behavior.

> *21: 12–13. Jesus entered the temple and began to drive out the merchants and their customers. He knocked over the tables of the money changers and the stalls of those*

*selling doves. He said, "The Scriptures declare, 'My Temple
will be called a place of prayer,' but you have turned it into
a den of thieves."*

It is easy to understand Jesus' anger against the moneychangers,
who were gouging the prayerful as they came to purchase animals
for sacrifice. Judged by current standards, we can particularly find
the practice of animal sacrifice to be primitive, and agree that this
practice was detestable. We understand that these practices were
a religious racket, far removed from our personal relationship with
our God. That anger that Jesus has is completely understandable, in
these senses. He finds his religion has been reduced to primitive rituals and monetary gain, and he is right to express his complete distaste
for these practices. This anger, however, is the anger he says no one
should have, and it consumes him. He preaches an inept philosophy
of extreme pacifism, and moreover, finds it quite impossible to live by
his own advice.

DEFICIENT MORAL ADVICE

These remaining items I found personally to be poor social advice,
but did not see that they were egregious examples of moral misdirection. We can quibble about them, but I did not want to leave them
without comment. Most of these are well embedded in our memories, and carry nice moral lessons, if we interpret them properly. They
all, however, can be easily misinterpreted, and have been frequently
quoted as directives for poor behavior we have been exhorted to
follow. Each needs a few words of clarification, in order for them to
make sense. Again, we are still just in the gospel of Matthew.

*6: 1–6. "Take care! Don't do your good deeds publicly, to
be admired, because then you will lose the reward from
your Father in heaven. When you give a gift to someone in
need, don't shout about it as the hypocrites do – blowing
trumpets in the synagogues and streets to call attention to
their acts of charity! I assure you, they have received all the
reward they will ever get. But when you give to someone,
don't tell your left hand what your right hand is doing. Give
your gifts in secret, and your Father, who knows all secrets,*

will reward you."

"And now about prayer. When you pray, don't be like the hypocrites who love to pray publicly on street corners and in the synagogues where everyone can see them. I assure you, that is all the reward they will ever get. But when you pray, go away by yourself, shut the door behind you, and pray to your Father secretly. Then your Father, who knows all secrets, will reward you."

The obvious lesson is that we should always remain humble in our devotion to our deity. No one likes a braggart, and no one enjoys listening to those who publicly display their conceit. These points are well taken. On the other hand, insisting that all devotion to our creator should be entirely private is not correct. When we pray together, we gain a sense of community commitment which we share together. Those societies that stress empathy, and formally recognize those that are empathetic towards their fellow humans, are healthy societies. Those societies that stress both private and public compassion will prosper.

6: 25–33. "So I tell you, don't worry about everyday life – whether you have enough food, drink, and clothes. Doesn't life consist of more than food and clothing? Look at the birds. They don't need to plant or harvest or put food in barns because your heavenly Father feeds them. And you are far more valuable to him than they are. Can all your worries add a single moment to your life? Of course not."

"And why worry about your clothes! Look at the lilies and how they grow. They don't work or make their clothing, yet Solomon in all his glory was not dressed as beautifully as they are. And if God cares so wonderfully for flowers that are here today and gone tomorrow, won't he more surely care for you? You have so little faith!"

"So don't worry about having enough food or drink or clothing. Why be like the pagans who are so deeply concerned about these things? Your heavenly Father already knows all your needs, and he will give you all you need from day to day if you live for him and make the Kingdom of God your primary concern."

Our understanding of all this has been to stress that happiness or fulfillment is not achieved by hoarding possessions. As far as we can tell, that is certainly true. Many of the most rewarding lives spent on this earth have not been encumbered by a large volume of possessions that must be protected at all times. These passages say more, however; they say we should aim for being destitute. Whoever thought up these words must live on a different planet. We do need to put crops in the field, care for them, harvest them and store them for later use. We do need to worry about having food, shelter and clothing. Life becomes an interlude of suffering without those basics. In this sense, the pagans have it right; Jesus does not.

> 7: 18–19. "A good tree can't produce bad fruit, and a bad tree can't produce good fruit. So every tree that does not produce good fruit is chopped down and thrown into the fire. Yes, the way to identify a tree or a person is by the kind of fruit that is produced."

We accept this thought pretty well, such as saying that you can judge parents by their children or you can judge a company by its products. On the other hand, I have in my yard an ugly twenty year old plum tree that has a rotten trunk and mold on all its branches. It only has two good limbs left, and they have some beautiful plums growing on them this year. A few yards away, there is a mature healthy apple tree which has never produced anything but gnarly, wormy fruit. Comprehensive judgments of good and evil lose their meaning in a fluid human society. Even the most perfect human will do some evil things in his or her life; and even the most immoral of humans will show acts of compassion in some compartment of their lives.

> 15:16–20. "Don't you understand?" Jesus asked him. "Anything you eat passes through the stomach and then goes out of the body. But evil words come from an evil heart and defile the person who says them. For from the heart come evil thoughts, murder, adultery, all other sexual immorality, theft, lying and slander. These are what defile you. Eating with unwashed hands could never defile you and make you unacceptable to God!"

Jesus has been criticized by the priests because he and his disciples do not wash their hands before eating, as do observant Jews.

This is his angry reply. The concept that cleanliness of spirit must come from the inside seems to make sense, until we realize that much of that cleanliness has to have been instilled there from the outside by our mentors. And furthermore, we are not talking about matters of the spirit here. We are talking about personal hygiene in a world that is full of germs and pathogens. If Jesus comes to my house, he will be asked to wash his hands before he comes to the supper table.

> *17: 17–21. Jesus replied, "You stubborn, faithless people! How long must I be with you until you believe? How long must I put up with you? Bring the boy to me." Then Jesus rebuked the demon in the boy, and it left him. From that moment the boy was well.*
>
> *Afterward the disciples asked Jesus privately, "Why couldn't we cast out the demon?"*
>
> *"You didn't have enough faith," Jesus told them "I assure you, even if you had faith as small as a mustard seed you could say to this mountain, 'Move from here to there,' and it would move. Nothing would be impossible."*
>
> *21: 21–22. Then Jesus told them, "I assure you, if you have faith and don't doubt, you can do things like this and much more. You can even say to this mountain, 'May God lift you up and throw you into the sea,' and it will happen. If you believe, you will receive whatever you ask for in prayer."*

Sure, we all have to have faith. We all have to believe when we start any project that we can carry it through. Things that initially seem impossible finally get done, if we continue to apply ourselves to that task. That is not exactly what this passage says, however. It says that if you have great faith in your cause, you will achieve your goal like magic. That's not the way the world works. There is an additional vital piece of advice that is missing: it takes effort. If you believe strongly enough in something, you will find a way to get it done, through perseverance. It will not happen just by wishing it were so. Additionally, we have to understand very clearly that even if we want something deep in our soul, it may or may not happen.

> *18: 12–14. "If a shepherd has one hundred sheep, and one wanders away and is lost, what will he do? Won't he leave*

the ninety-nine others and go out into the hills to search for the lost one? And if he finds it, he will surely rejoice over it more than over the ninety-nine that didn't wander away! In the same way, it is not my heavenly Father's will that even one of these little ones should perish."

Jesus advises that a shepherd should leave 99 sheep unprotected in order to save just one. If this makes sense to anyone, I don't believe that person is thinking straight. It would be appropriate if this lesson said that as soon as the shepherd could get someone else to guard his flock, he would spend every effort to find the lost sheep. If it said that he would sorrow greatly over the lost sheep and keep calling for it, that explanation we could also understand. If it said that he would grieve forever over the one that was lost, and realize he had to do a better job guarding those that were left, that too would make sense. As it stands, this lesson is another piece of bad advice from Jesus. We all need to cut our losses in life, and move ahead with what we have left. There is no other reasonable choice we can make.

19: 27–30. Then Peter said to him, "We've given up everything to follow you. What will we get out of it?"

And Jesus replied, "I assure you that when I, the Son of Man, sit upon my glorious throne in the Kingdom, you who have been my followers will also sit on twelve thrones, judging the twelve tribes of Israel. And everyone who has given up houses or brothers or sisters or father or mother or children or property, for my sake, will receive a hundred times as much in return and will have eternal life. But many who seem to be important now will be the least important then, and those who are considered least here will be the greatest then."

How many times have we heard these false promises in our storied past: free land, Ponzi schemes, communes of love and peace, gold in the hills, paradise across the ocean, glory and power? There is a sucker born every minute, and there are myriads of slick salesmen out there willing to promise the moon and the sun in order to take what we have away from us. There are multiple errors in this passage. Jesus, showing his egocentricity, demands that his disciples possess nothing else and have no devotion to anyone else. They must be exclusively his. He compounds that by giving them the false prom-ise of great glory, wealth and power, to make up for their destitution in this life. He adds to that with the irrational promise that they will live forever, for going through this life hungry and poor. This tells us a lot about his sanity. The only saving grace of this passage is the recogni-tion that all each of us can do is lead the most moral life that we can, and leave the judgment of how great we were for someone else to decide, after we are dead.

> *26: 6–13. Meanwhile, Jesus was in Bethany at the home of Simon, a man who had leprosy. During supper, a woman came in with a beautiful jar of expensive perfume and poured it over his head. The disciples were indignant when they saw this. "What a waste of money," they said. "She could have sold it for a fortune and given the money to the poor."*

> *But Jesus replied, "Why berate her for doing such a good thing to me? You will always have the poor among you, but I will not be here with you much longer. She has poured this perfume on me to prepare my body for burial. I assure you, wherever the Good News is preached throughout the world, this woman's deed will be talked about in her memory."*

If this is not hypocrisy, it is difficult to know what is. Jesus has been preaching incessantly to his disciples and listeners that they should give up all their possessions, give everything they have to the poor, and follow him. Now when a smitten woman wastes a whole jar of expensive perfume on him, he likes it a lot. He is singing one song, but traveling his own egocentric path. The poor don't matter at all if it is Jesus that is going to benefit.

MAJOR MORAL ADVANCES

I beg your indulgence for having spent this much time on these misshapen directives in the gospel of Matthew. My defense is that if you look at all these admonitions rationally, they do not make sense. Sunday school discussions of these inconsistencies always came to naught, when I tried to point out to my beloved friends that these passages were not good moral guides. The most wonderful and lovely people on the face of the earth, when challenged, always fell back to that unassailable position of humility. "These teachings are all correct. We just haven't studied them long enough to fully understand their message." Since these teachings have seemed puzzling to others, but clearly false to me, I have felt obliged to explain fully why these particular gospel lessons are so misleading. Perhaps this is all a matter of message contamination over time. The gospels come to us after multiple transfers by word of mouth, multiple translations, and multiple social agendas in the intent of their writers. On the other hand, they are what they are. This is the record we have to help guide our lives, and is one of the reasons, in my opinion, why we have not found our moral compass. Unless we understand that the New Testament is full of bad moral advice, we will not be able to comprehend those principles of human behavior that will allow all of us to reach our fulfillment. I promise to not flog these same points over and over again for the gospels of Mark, Luke and John. If the points made here have no meaning for anyone else, so be it. To me, these false directives have been a basis for the reasons we have used to excuse the treatment of other humans with disgust and cruelty. When our friends or our country have committed immoral acts, we have simply looked the other way, believing that there was justification for those odious acts. I believed it was time to set the record straight, as to how greatly misguided many of the teachings in the New Testament are.

Fortunately, after having spent all this time complaining about moral malfeasance in the New Testament, we are ready for the Good News. What comes next is glorious. There are three themes found in the New Testament gospels which are fully emphasized nowhere else, in no other religion, each of which is a quantum leap in moral enlightenment. Each is like an electron expansion to a new outer orbit, with immensely greater energy, sphere and influence. They begin with two themes which are common to just about all religions.

The first theme, which all religions teach, is that of great humility before their God. Each of us has to understand that we are nothing in comparison to the great forces that have created this universe and seem to be a part of all events, human and otherwise, for all time. This deep reverence for whatever began all things is highly just and appropriate. We will never understand how best to deal with each other, if we approach life with egotism. We always have to be humble, and truly grateful for this one beautiful life we are given. Passages in Buddhist, Hindu, Confucian, Jewish, Christian and Islamic literature, all describe this awe and wonderment in majestic, hair-raising and deeply reverent terms.

> *Proverbs 19: 1–6. The heavens tell of the glory of God.*
> > *The skies display his marvelous craftsmanship.*
> > *Day after day they continue to speak;*
> > *Night after night they make him known.*
> > *They speak without a sound or word;*
> > *Their voice is silent in the skies,*
> > *Yet their message has gone out to all the earth,*
> > *And their words to the world.*
> > *The sun lives in the heavens*
> > *Where God placed it.*
> > *It bursts forth like a radiant bridegroom*
> > *After his wedding.*
> > *It rejoices like a great athlete*
> > *Eager to run the race.*
> > *The sun rises at one end of the heavens*
> > *And follows to its course to the other end.*
> > *Nothing can hide from its heat.*
>
> *Proverbs 148: 1–5. Praise the Lord!*
> > *Praise the Lord from the heavens!*
> > *Praise him from the skies!*
> > *Praise him, all his angels!*
> > *Praise him sun and moon!*
> > *Praise him, all you twinkling stars!*
> > *Praise him, skies above!*
> > *Praise him, vapors high above the clouds!*
> > *Let every created thing give praise to the Lord,*

For he issued his command, and they came into being.

Also present in all religions is a simple command, which has been phrased in different words and terms, with the intent identical in all religions. It is often prefaced by some really good advice about not judging others until you have taken stock of your own deficiencies.

Matthew 7: 1–5. "Stop judging others, and you will not be judged. For others will treat you as you treat them. Whatever measure you use in judging others, it will be used to measure how you are judged. And why worry about a speck in your friend's eye when you have a log in your own? How can you think of saying, 'Let me help you get rid of that speck in your eye,' when you can't see past the log in your own eye? Hypocrite! First get rid of the log from your own eye, then perhaps you will see well enough to deal with the speck in your friend's eye."

This admonishment is then often followed by this universal basic moral law, timeless and shining.

Matthew 7: 12. "Do for others what you would like them to do for you. This is a summary of all that is taught in the law and the prophets"

This is where we usually stop, thinking this is all that needs to be said about morals. Yet these two basic marvelous teachings are not nearly enough. There are four more great advances in human morality which are needed to reach a stage of universal ethics, three of which are found in the New Testament, not as clearly expressed previously in any other religious literature. Embedded in all these other misdirected morals we have addressed above, are these three jewels, which, as best we can tell, come most purely from the mind of Jesus. These are not new moral jewels. They are the necessary bylaws, the specifics that explain exactly what it means in our relationships with each other, if we have reverence for our creator, and treat others as we would like to be treated.

COMBINATION LOVE

The first remarkable contribution of Jesus was to recognize that neither love of our God nor love of neighbor can stand alone. You can't have one without the other, and be a moral person. This concept deviates somewhat from Eastern religions, which all emphasize individual illumination. Buddhism and Hinduism, both remarkable religions for their emphasis on purification of the human soul, seek mystic depths of understanding which are life-changing, but can remain foreign to all those of us who do not partake in those beliefs. These religions are all about reconnection with the whole of the universe. The aura of peace in their souls which they find as they transcend through these stages in their religions must be magnificent. These are religions of deep mysticism and individual enlightenment, which serve those devoted to them marvelously well. This depth of communion with their divine and communion with all of life is often greatly missing in the religions of Abraham. We all need to experience that numbing, hair-raising identity with all things everywhere, that transcendence above earthly problems. This emphasis on individual purification resides par excellence in these religions.

There is no religion, organization, or philosophy that does not have its flaws, however. The one flaw I see in our Eastern religions is that morality becomes, in part, secondary. If we define morality as those codes of conduct between humans that allows us all to prosper, this is not a major emphasis of these religions, which emphasize individual enlightenment. To be fair, if one achieves enlightenment, one then becomes more moral and loving. It is also true that each of these religions does speak at length about each individual entering life fully. The Buddhist who has achieved Nirvana is then obliged to return to the market place and teach his or her methods of transcendence to those who have not yet achieved lofty status. The Hindu, during his or her worldly cycle, is expected to conform fully to social and ritual duties, and traditional rules of conduct for his or her caste, family and profession. Yet the major emphasis in each of these religions is that each individual shall not find peace in their soul until they have identified fully with the cosmic force, whatever that may be.

That emphasis on transcendence may be, in many ways, the most correct. The overwhelming peace, openness and excitement of the soul that happens at those times, in itself, transcends words, and I am at the moment having trouble expressing that feeling in words. Our marketplace Abrahamic religions would benefit greatly by placing more emphasis on purification of the soul, and less on belief in a certain mythology. Yet there is, in our more Western religions, an emphasis on human interaction and empathy, not clearly found anywhere else. This concentration on how we should behave reaches a new height of understanding in the words of Jesus. Absolute devotion to the creator, or creation, is the greatest commandment; but there is another commandment that is just as great: love your neighbor as yourself. You must have the two together. Neither can stand fulfilled without the other. This, then, becomes an entirely new ball game. Love of our God and striving for communion with our God must always coexist with loving our neighbor, or else neither is fulfilled. Let's look at it one more time now, in its full context. This is a great advancement in human morality. I have to immediately add, however, that this new concept is not an end-all in itself. We still have to define exactly what "neighbor" means, and do so in two additional stages. We also have to include in that heightened morality, life other than human life, if we are to reach a universal ethic. All of these statements will require a great deal more explanation, but let us take this combination step first.

> *Matthew 22: 34–40. But when the Pharisees heard that he had silenced the Sadducees with his reply, they thought up a fresh question of their own to ask him. One of them, an expert in religious law, tried to trap him with this question: "Teacher, which is the most important commandment in the law of Moses?"*
>
> *Jesus replied, "You must love the Lord your God with all your heart, all your soul, and all your mind. This is the first and greatest commandment. A second is equally important: Love your neighbor as yourself. All the other commandments and all the demands of the prophets are based on these two commandments."*

The point to be made is that none of us is just an individual. Each of us is certainly unique, and each of us needs to defend that uniqueness. Each of us needs to find our own peace with our God. Each of us needs to feel both humility and gratitude for this remarkable world and this remarkable life. Beyond our relationship with our God, however, none of us stands alone. We are a part of our family, our community, our nation, our earth, and just one part of all other life. We are social animals who do not survive and prosper without the assistance, guidance and cooperation of all those who surround us. Even the solitary explorer needs other life in order to survive. Deep and full communion with our God means also deep and full communion with all other life. Human fulfillment does not exist without there being both our God and other life in the equation. How astonishing. No one else saw this clearly before, and Jesus sees it with utter clarity. This is a stunning increase in understanding of the human condition.

WHO IS YOUR NEIGHBOR?

This is the one part of this discussion on morality which is not contained in Matthew. I have the temerity to include this section, which is found only in the gospel of Luke, at this point in this flow of thought, because it fits entirely with the other teachings of Jesus. It appears that Jesus, as all of us do, learned as he taught. His first utterance as to compassion for others, which has already been quoted, is followed by a statement that this is all you need to know.

Matthew 7: 12. "Do for others what you would like them to do for you. This is a summary of all that is taught in the law and the prophets."

This may be a summary of all that is taught in the Jewish law and the teachings of all the Hebrew prophets, but Jesus, himself, later recognizes that this simple command is not nearly enough. He justly expands that teaching to include the love of god, combined with the love of your neighbor, as is quoted above. When he knew better, he did better. Now he understands that any just morality must include both the spiritual and social aspects of our individual selves. His perceptive social mind, as it has expanded its horizons, has now understood, in succinct and brilliantly phrased language, a union of moral self that no one anywhere, in any religion, expressed clearly before. This is a remarkable advancement of morality in human society.

Ah, but he has even more to learn. He finds his new sphere of morality immediately challenged. His disciples are puzzled. They ask the same question that has been asked throughout the history of the

Jewish religion. They are perhaps puzzled, because Jesus himself has told them he is only there to reform the Jewish religion, not other religions or peoples. This raises a serious question in their minds. Who is my neighbor? Is it my friends and family? Is it also the Sadducees and Pharisees? Is it someone who has no religious faith? Is it possibly someone who is not a Jew? They find that this new horizon in their morality is impossible to follow unless they know exactly where the fence is set. How far should they go in expressing love for their neighbors?

Jesus, to his credit, immediately knows that he did not say enough. He almost effortlessly takes another quantum leap in human morality, never before expressed fully by any prophet of any religion, with this story. It is not corroborated by other accountings in any of the other gospels, but is completely consistent with this rapid growth of Jesus' personal morality, and fits completely between the concept above and the concept to follow. There seems little doubt that it does express his quickly expanding morality, accurately. This story is also timeless, just as the quote above it is timeless. It is beautifully expressed, and immediately follows, in Luke, his pronouncement of the newly formed most important, combination commandments.

> *Luke 10: 30–37. Jesus replied with an illustration: "A Jewish man was traveling on a trip from Jerusalem to Jericho and he was attacked by bandits. They stripped him of his clothes and money, beat him up, and left him half dead beside the road.*

> *By chance a Jewish priest came along: but when he saw the man lying there, he crossed to the other side of the road and passed him by. A Temple assistant walked over and looked at him lying there, but he also passed by on the other side.*

> *Then a despised Samaritan came along, and when he saw the man, he felt deep pity. Kneeling beside him, the Samaritan soothed his wounds with medicine and bandaged them. Then he put the man on his own donkey and took him to an inn, where he took care of him. The next day he handed the innkeeper two pieces of silver and told him to take care of the man. 'If his bill runs higher than that,' he said, 'I'll pay the difference the next time I am here.'*

> *Now which of these three would you say was a neighbor to*

the man who was attacked by bandits?" Jesus asked.

The man replied, "The one who showed him mercy."

Then Jesus said, "Yes, now go and do the same."

This marvelous lesson was not lost on the early Christians. They did go and do likewise. Although they could have perhaps carried this valuable teaching even further, they nevertheless felt deep respect for each other. Within each Christian community, love of neighbor was freely expressed in the form of personal pastoral care, social welfare, and immediate assistance from others in the community, when any individual was overcome with the vicissitudes of life. One of the great drawing forces for others to become converts to this new religious movement was its communal empathy. "Look, how they love one another." They were ecumenical. Women, slaves, poor and dispossessed were all welcomed into the community. This produced a vitality in the early Christian communities that was not found in any other social group at that time. They flourished, because their prophet and seer had seen a way for them to live that was better than any other previous guides for social interaction. Love of neighbor was love for all neighbors everywhere, regardless of sex, class, race, color or belief. How remarkable.

Ah, but Jesus grew even further. He saw one additional lesson that no one else before him had clearly expressed. He finally achieved the standard of an ethic that can be applied to all humans everywhere. The question of "Who is my neighbor" got carried one giant leap further, to an extreme that we all still have trouble stomaching today, and to an extreme even he, Jesus, was not personally able to achieve. The fact that this seer was not able to practice what he preached, and the fact that we routinely today flout this teaching with abandon, does not make it any less correct.

LOVE YOUR ENEMIES

This lesson did not come out of a clear blue sky. Not only is it an obvious accurate extension of the "Who is my neighbor question," but it is also deeply rooted in Jewish thought. The Old Testament is mostly several hundred pages of exhortation addressed to the Israelites, demanding that they show obedience to their God. The Israelites are told in no uncertain terms that the laws expressed in these pages are to be followed explicitly, or else there will be dire consequences. Famines, exiles, thousands of deaths in battles, destruction of their temple and other natural disasters are all attributed to the failure of the Israelites to follow the laws of their God and their priests. They are also, in no uncertain terms, told exactly how they are to live in relationship to one another. There are temple rites, priestly rites, sacrifice rites, cleanliness rites, crop guides, animal husbandry laws. There are pages upon pages of sexual admonitions, legislating when you have sex, who you have it with, how you clean yourself afterwards, and what your obligations are to the products of that sex. This is not to be disparaging. Most of these copious laws were written in an attempt to bring order to the community. Enforcement of these arcane laws was an honest attempt to provide justice and fairness in the community. These people were not concerned with expressions of compassion as much as the very necessary task of bringing order to the community.

As such, there is no direct command to love one another, or much less, show affection for the tribe in the next valley that would love to take your crops, your land, your animals and your women, if they had the opportunity. The Israelites did have to protect one another, however, and there are scattered in these pages of history and religious law, snippets of concern not only about other members of the family, but also other humans that are not members of the family or of the tribe.

Leviticus 25: 35–38. If any of your Israelite relatives fall into poverty and cannot support themselves, support them as you would a resident foreigner and allow them to live with you. Do not demand an advance or charge interest on the money you lend them. Instead, show your fear of God by letting them live with you as your relatives. Remember, do not charge your relatives interest on anything you lend them, whether money or food. I, the Lord, am your God, who brought you out of Egypt to give you the land of Canaan and to be your God.

Deuteronomy 10: 17–19. The Lord your God is the God of gods and Lord of lords. He is the great God, mighty and awesome, who shows no partiality and takes no bribes. He gives justice to orphans and widows. He shows love to

the foreigners living among you and gives them food and
clothing. You, too, must show love to foreigners, for you
yourselves were once foreigners in the land of Egypt.

This advice, we might say, pretty much went in one ear and out
the other. The Israelites were a closed community. They had appointed
themselves as the one and only chosen people of the one and only
great God, selected to become dominant over all other nations both
by example and power. This mystique was maintained with the rite of
male circumcision and male dominance, careful to record its history
in male lineage. The various feats of these males was recorded by
word of mouth for centuries, before being committed to papyrus page.
These self-appointed righteous tribes were in a fight for survival. They
did not have time to worry about humans from far-off lands. They had
their hands full trying to maintain their unique status in a semi-arid
land with limited resources, and neighbors who were not shy about
taking whatever they could away from the Jews. These were not centuries in which anyone could contemplate an ethic which would serve
for all people for all time. Yet in spite of that rather desperate struggle
for survival, these ancient people recognized that there was need to
have compassion for the disadvantaged and foreigner in need.

There are great rules of conduct in Buddhism and Hinduism. There
are these glimmers of understanding in the history of Judaism, in spite
of that struggle for survival. The compassion in the Islamic community for those who are other than their family is immense. They are
commanded by their Prophet to take care of all those who do not
have as much. Yet each of these religions follows rules of exclusivity,
practiced with aplomb in all of these religions. The unfortunate aspect
of each of these religions is to believe that only they hold the keys to
the truth and the direct line to the one and only God. Unfortunately,
each of them also has the belief that those who hold different beliefs
should be punished in some minor or major way for their infidelity.
That leaves us with a rather drastic moral impasse. No religion can
embrace exclusivity and punishment of others who hold other beliefs
in one hand, and on the other hand show love for its enemies. The
two are incompatible. The maddening thing is that this is precisely
the situation in the dominant religions of our world today. This final
leap, coming from the mind of Jesus, achieving a universal ethic, is
not practiced by us at all. We mouth it; we don't do it, which makes

hypocrites of us all.

This remarkable moral mountain was described in only two of the gospels. It is first iterated in Matthew, then more floridly expressed in Luke, as was his style. It is not found in Mark or John. The two accounts we have, however, are very similar, and the message is gloriously unmistakable.

Matthew 5: 43–48. "You have heard that the law of Moses says, 'Love your neighbor' and hate your enemy. But I say, love your enemies! Pray for those who persecute you! In that way, you will be acting as true children of your Father in heaven. For he gives his sunlight to both the evil and the good, and he sends rain on the just and on the unjust, too. If you love only those who love you, what good is that? Even corrupt tax collectors do that much. If you are kind only to your friends, how are you different from anyone else? Even pagans do that. But you are to be perfect, even as your Father in heaven is perfect."

Luke 6: 27–36. "But if you are willing to listen, I say, love your enemies. Do good to those who hate you. Pray for the happiness of those who curse you. Pray for those who hurt you. If someone slaps you on one cheek, turn the other cheek. If someone demands your coat, offer your shirt also. Give what you have to anyone who asks you for it, and when things are taken away from you, don't try to get them back. Do for others as you would like them to do for you."

"Do you think you deserve credit merely for loving those who love you? Even the sinners do that! And if you do good only to those who do good to you, is that so wonderful? Even sinners do that much! And if you lend money only to those who can repay you, what good is that? Even sinners will lend to their own kind for a full return."

"Love your enemies! Do good to them! Lend to them! And don't be concerned that they might not repay. Then your reward from heaven will be very great, and you will truly be acting as children of the Most High, for he is kind to the unthankful and to those who are wicked. You must be compassionate, just as your Father is compassionate."

There is a lot not to like in the above passages, and I have already addressed those issues in the material on Matthew. I take great exception to the command to always turn the other cheek, or, in other words, take great exception to the command to become totally passive in the face of aggression. Those commands are not inductive to a healthy society. Aggression has to be met with resistance, and sometimes very great resistance, in order to teach that aggressor a lesson which will lead to a healthier society. As is often seen in these gospels, a really good concept can be carried too far. It then becomes very bad moral advice, if not immoral. Literal acceptance of these passages, which command extreme pacifism, leaves us all lying in the dust.

If properly interpreted, however, there is even more to like in these passages, if not outright admire. It is absolutely true that the sun and the rain fall on the just and on the unjust. Our solar system and our universe do not care. Good things happen to evil people and bad things happen to good people. We cannot expect some spirit in the sky to rectify all the moral wrongs that we encounter in our lives. It is up to us to correct those inadequacies in our behavior and the behavior of others, and make them right, while we are here. It seems true that the best touchstone of how we should behave in any encounter with another human is to ask this simple question, "How would I want to be treated in this situation." It seems true that we should pray for our enemies. That does not mean that we give them whatever they want, but it does mean that we approach our every move with them, attempting to understand why they act the way they act. Everything we do with someone who harms us should be an attempt to get them to rectify their ways. Retribution in anger serves no good for our society. Rehabilitation and expressions of concern establish wonders, for those who have lost their moral compass. As far as we can tell, we should love our enemies with all fibers of our soul; but we should do it with tough love.

THE GOSPEL OF MARK

There is no moral pronouncement in Mark that is not already contained in Matthew. The intent of this gospel is clear from the beginning. It is constructed to give the strongest possible account affirming that Jesus was the Messiah of the Jews. Mark is unconcerned about lineage

and childhood events, as were present in Matthew. He begins not with
lists of ancestors or accounts of magical birth events but concentrates
on the ministry of Jesus. This gospel at frequent turns contains the statement that a certain event in the life of Jesus, as described, occurred
to fulfill a prophecy made in the Old Testament. It begins immediately
with John the Baptist, whose major purpose is to predict the coming of
this Messiah for the Jews.

*1: 1–11. Here begins the Good News about Jesus the
Messiah, the Son of God.*

In the book of the prophet Isaiah, God said,

"Look, I am sending my messenger before you,

And he will prepare your way.

He is a voice shouting in the wilderness.

Prepare a pathway for the Lord's coming!

Make a straight road for him."

*This messenger was John the Baptist. He lived in the
wilderness and was preaching that people should be
baptized to show that they had turned from their sins and
turned to God to be forgiven. People from Jerusalem and
from all over Judea traveled out into the wilderness to
see and hear John. And when they confessed their sins, he
baptized them in the Jordan River. His clothes were woven
from camel hair, and he wore a leather belt; his food was
locusts and wild honey. He announced; "Someone is coming
soon who is far greater than I am – so much greater that I
am not even worthy to be his slave. I baptize you with water,
but he will baptize you with the Holy Spirit."*

*One day Jesus came from Nazareth in Galilee, and he was
baptized by John in the Jordan River. And when Jesus came
up out of the water, he saw the heavens split open and the
Holy Spirit descending like a dove on him. And a voice came
from heaven saying, "You are my beloved Son, and I am
fully pleased with you."*

This dramatic opening scene completely sets the stage for the
accounts that follow.

9: 11–13. Now they [the disciples] began asking him, "Why

do the teachers of religious law insist that Elijah must return before the Messiah comes?"

Jesus responded, "Elijah is indeed coming first to set everything in order. Why then is it written in the Scriptures that the Son of Man must suffer and be treated with utter contempt? But I tell you, Elijah has already come, and he was badly mistreated, just as the Scriptures predicted."

This is the conversation reported after Jesus was seen by his disciples as transfigured, on the top of the mountain, talking to both Moses and Elijah. Mark further solidifies his claim for Jesus as the Jewish Messiah, by making him appear godlike, then associating him with Moses, and Elijah.

The gospel of Mark highlights the miracles performed by Jesus, as if driven to demonstrate that this candidate for the position of the great Messiah had greater power than all others who might want to claim that position for themselves. The techniques Mark uses to make the case for Jesus, as opposed to all other candidates, are a great emphasis on prophecy fulfillment and this constant stream of miracle stories. Neither of these techniques helps us in our search for moral enlightenment. Both, if anything, are steps backwards. Mark, apparently, did not believe that the prescient teaching of Jesus to love your enemies had any value in his gospel. It just didn't fit into this constant flow of supernatural events and Old Testament fulfillment. Even the greatest commandment story, which is included in Mark, loses its power against this towering backdrop of magic, mythology and prophecies. Mark does not see fit to relate the Good Samaritan story for the same reasons. Unless the question of "Who is my neighbor" is defined as all people of all races, colors, creeds, stations and other beliefs, these great commandments lose much of their punch. That did not matter to Mark. He was on a mission to convince the world that Jesus was the savior of the Jews.

The end point of this collection of miraculous events is when the whole world ends, described in stark, graphic terms, at which time only those who believe that Jesus was the Messiah will go to Heaven, while all others will be condemned for an eternity.

13: 23–27. Watch out! I have warned you!

> *At the time, after those horrible days end,*

The sun will be darkened,

The moon will not give light,

The stars will fall from the sky,

And the powers of heaven will be shaken.

Then everyone will see the Son of Man arrive on the clouds with great power and glory. And he will send forth his angels to gather together his chosen ones from all over the world – from the farthest ends of the earth and heaven.

This apocalyptic end to the world as we know it is often described in this gospel as the "Good News." We can hardly call this destructive end to the earth and solar system "good news." It is more accurately described as a demand that all people accept Jesus as the Messiah of the Jews, or suffer forever. This is not good news. This is isolationism and bigotry. We do not make the world a better place by punishment for all those who do not believe in this certain myth. We will have to presume that this pronouncement condemns the vast majority of all humankind to suffer eternally, since "only a few will be chosen."

The emphasis in Mark on an afterlife is also a moral step backward in this gospel. When some other pretend existence is stressed as more important than the one life we know on this earth, we have then lost our moral compass.

The gospel of Mark is beautifully written. It is colorful, and flows well until the extra ending. In the assessment of scholars, it seems obvious that this additional piece, 16: 9–19, was added by some other author at a later time. Otherwise, this gospel tells the story Mark wishes to convey with style and flourish. In the search for higher morality, however, this pied piper leads us down from the mountain that was achieved in Matthew. We will not create a better human society by believing that some other life is more important than this life, that diseases are cured in a second just by saying so, that death is easily overcome, that poison can't hurt us, and that an exclusive religious club is superior to all other people for all time.

THE GOSPEL OF LUKE

Luke behaves like an investigative journalist who has a hot story. Luke was reported to have had personal contact with several eyewitnesses to events in the life of Jesus. His friend, Theophilus, who was a Gentile, asked Luke to tell him all he knows about these stories of Jesus. The reason for his keen interest is that he also wants eternal life, if that is what you get from becoming a believer in Jesus as the Messiah. Like an enthusiastic new convert, Theophilus wants all the promises he can garner that this exciting prediction will come true. Luke is happy to accommodate his friend with style. Not only are the previous themes of Matthew and Mark repeated, they are embellished and polished until each shines like a jewel. The gospel of Luke is a theatrical production formed in a staged setting guaranteed to please his good friend, Theophilus.

The prophecies of Jesus about his death and resurrection are repeated on multiple occasions. The apocalypse, Jesus predicts, will come within the lifetime of some of the disciples. Theophilus can expect to get his prize soon. Miracles occur with a flourish. The blind see instantly, the dead return to life instantly, and the lepers are cured instantly. The comment is frequently made as to how impressed the people were with the miracles they saw.

> 5: 21–26. "Who does this man think he is?" the Pharisees and teachers of religious law said to each other. "This is blasphemy! Who but God can forgive sins?"
>
> Jesus knew what they were thinking, so he asked them, "Why do you think this is blasphemy? Is it easier to say, 'Your sins are forgiven' or 'Get up and walk?' I will prove that I, the Son of Man, have the authority on earth to forgive sins." Then Jesus turned to the paralyzed man and said, "Stand up, take your mat, and go on home, because you are healed!"
>
> And immediately, as everyone watched, the man jumped to his feet, picked up his mat, and went home praising God. Everyone was gripped with great wonder and awe. And they praised God, saying over and over again, "We have seen amazing things today."

The resurrection story and the after death sightings of Jesus are enlarged. Jesus magically appears and also disappears in an instant on multiple occasions. The grand finale of this theatrical production is the beautiful ascension of Jesus into heaven, as directly witnessed by his disciples, after they have been blessed. They are filled with joy, and spend the rest of their days praising God. Luke gave his friend, Theophilus, exactly what he wanted. Here was a story that would thrill anyone who wished to escape from this world of inexorable disease, oppression and inevitable death. Luke's story promises a full escape from the confines of this difficult life, and does so with a flourish.

As in Matthew and Mark, the morality lessons in this gospel range from the ridiculous to the sublime, but, with credit to Luke, are always given with flair. The first of these is quite primitive. When Jesus is eight days old, he is circumcised, and taken to the temple for purification. Two doves lose their lives in this ancient rite. These creatures are, as we have previously discussed, a substitute for the savage earlier Jewish custom of killing your first born son as a sacrifice of obeisance to their demanding and jealous God. Mary and Joseph are not far removed from savagery, and the temple priests who condone this onerous practice are routinely practicing immoral human behavior, if judged by our standards today.

> *2: 21–24. Eight days later, when the baby was circumcised, he was named Jesus, the name given him by the angel even before he was conceived.*
>
> *Then it was time for the purification offering, as required by the law of Moses after the birth of a child, so his parents took him to Jerusalem to present him to the Lord. The law of the Lord says, "If a woman's first child is a boy, he must be dedicated to the Lord." So they offered a sacrifice according to what was required in the law of the land – either a pair of turtledoves or two young pigeons.*

This rather base event is followed by those themes developed in Matthew and Mark, some of which are odious, and others of which are terrific. Our objections to those moral directives which have seemed particularly misleading have already been expounded in the section on Matthew. There are a good many of them which do not make moral sense. Luke's gospel places great emphasis on an afterlife, a false promise which deludes us into thinking we should devote our effort to some cause other than behaving the most correctly we can while we are on this planet in living form. There is significant emphasis on an apocalypse, when the great majority of humans will supposedly be killed or tortured eternally for not believing that Jesus was the Messiah of the Jews. There is great emphasis on Jesus' great power and glory when he returns for the apocalypse to judge the living and dead, rather than emphasis on his moral teachings. The egotism of Jesus is overbearing, in this gospel account. He believes he commands the Sabbath, all people, all mountains, streams and valleys, and the heavens above as well. Pacifism is pushed to the point of incredulity. I do not mean to imply that any of this moral misdirection was done with evil intent. It is perhaps most appropriate to say that we forgive Luke for being too eager to please.

Yet in spite of this moral morass, which is found in all the gospels, Luke attains a depth in moral understanding not seen in any of the other New Testament accounts. A universal human ethic, if we may rephrase it this way, has to have four solid pillars in order to have a stable base which will serve as a guide of conduct for all people everywhere. There has to be love of God, or in other words, a deep and abiding reverence for that force which gave us this beautiful life. There must be love of neighbor, that is to say, an understanding that we all prosper only if we all work together in mutual respect. There must be love of all neighbors everywhere, a realization that we are all as humans in the same struggle for survival on this same planet. That love of neighbor must even extend to those humans who harm us, even though our responses may only be expressed as tough love. All of these four elements are found in Luke, and are not fully expressed in any other gospel or religious record, up to that time. The greatest commandment story attaches love of god and love of neighbor to this table base, together for the first time. The Good Samaritan story extends that love of neighbor to all races, creeds, beliefs and colors of humans, adding a third leg. The directive to love your enemy provides the fourth pillar – and now the base is stable. Human ethics have arrived; If only we could bring ourselves to use them properly.

There is an additional section in Luke which does not relate to our discussion on morality, but which deserves at least a passing comment. It is not found as completely anywhere else in the Bible. Luke lists 77 ancestors for Jesus, beginning with Adam, in an effort to establish Jesus' dynastical claim to be the messiah of the Jews. That means an estimated 1925 biblical years passed from the time of the first human to the time of Jesus' birth. If we add 2010 years to that figure, this gives us a fairly exact estimate that, according to Jewish tradition, it has only been 3935 years since our solar system, earth moon, sky, stars, fish, animals and humans were created. Although all the scientific evidence we have says that this estimate is off by about four billion years, it is still a wonderful myth. It fits in perfectly with all the other mythology which is contained in this delightful and colorful gospel, written to please a friend.

THE GOSPEL OF JOHN

The gospel John is said to have been written by the apostle John, "the apostle Jesus loved." It is dated much later than the other gospels, however, the accepted time being about 90 AD. This means that this gospel, if we accept the above assignments, was written some sixty years after Jesus' death. By this time, John, if it was he that wrote this account, feels no compulsion to prove to anyone else that Jesus was the Messiah of the Jews. He has no need to recount miracle birth events or list long lines of male lineage. None of those are necessary. John knows, in his own mind, exactly how this story began and exactly how it ends. He is personally convinced that Jesus was the Messiah of the Jews, and does not feel compelled to prove these points to anyone. John has a different agenda to pursue. In his mind, the only important message he has to impart is that Jesus was the God on earth, as well as the God in the heavens. To that purpose, he begins this gospel with a bold and remarkable flourish.

> *1:1–5. In the beginning, the Word already existed. He was*
> *with God, and he was God. He was in the beginning with*
> *God. He created everything there is. Nothing exists that he*
> *didn't make. Life itself was in him, and this life gives light*
> *to everyone. The light shines through the darkness, and the*
> *darkness can never extinguish it.*

This message, now brazenly announced, is illuminated with passion in the pages that follow. This same theme is unvarying, presented in compelling and vivid manner. These miracles and stories of Jesus are used, not to convince others that these fantastic acts of healing and power over death occurred. That is not the question to John. These miracles are accepted as fact to this true believer, former disciple. These stories of power over disease and death are used to make the same claim, over and over, using different names to say the same thing. This gospel asks that you believe in Jesus as a part of the one and only God, using many different names. He is called the gate, the good shepherd, the bread of life, the blood of life, the way, the truth, the light and the resurrection.

This is not a collection of stories wondering how it will turn out, as in other gospels. The outcome is already known, as far as John is concerned. The only conflict we have, which is greatly stressed in this gospel, is the confrontations Jesus has with Jewish leaders. The priests take great offense at Jesus' statements that only he can grant access to heaven, that he will live forever after death, and that only those who believe in him as the Messiah will also live forever. There are multiple statements that, because of these megalomaniac beliefs, the Jewish leaders believe that Jesus is demented, and plan to kill him. There are several statements that Jesus escapes all these planned murders at the hands of the Jewish elite because "his time has not yet come."

> *7: 6–8. Jesus replied, "Now is not the right time for me to go. But you can go anytime, and it will make no difference. The world can't hate you, but it does hate me because I accuse it of sin and evil. You go on. I am not yet ready to go to this festival, because my time has not yet come." So Jesus remained in Galilee.*

> *8: 19–20. "Where is your father," they asked.*

> *Jesus answered, "Since you don't know who I am, you don't know who my Father is. If you knew me, then you would know my Father, too." Jesus made these statements while he was teaching in the section of the Temple known as the Treasury. But he was not arrested, because his time had not yet come.*

> *8: 57–59. The people said, "You aren't even fifty years old. How can you say you have seen Abraham?"*

> *Jesus answered, "The truth is, I existed before Abraham was even born!" At that point they picked up stones to kill him,*

but Jesus hid himself from them and left the Temple.

There are multiple predictions, reportedly coming from the mouth of Jesus, stating that he is here on earth for only this purpose; to die and come back to life, as proof of his divinity and power over death. There is no guesswork involved in this gospel. These same themes are repeated page after page. According to John, Jesus is a divinity on earth, who promises that all those who believe he is the God, will live forever.

> *John 3: 16–17. For God so loved the world that he gave*
> *his only Son, so that everyone who believes in him will not*
> *perish but have eternal life. God did not send his Son into*
> *the world to condemn it, but to save it.*

These fantastic claims, followed by these futuristic false promises, present major moral sinkholes. It may be that Jesus was not such an insane egotist, and that these words were placed in his mouth, making these magnificent claims, in a concerted attempt to sell this hero and this religion to other people. We have what we have, however. This message is so consistent throughout all the gospels, we have to accept that Jesus, as presented, was an egocentric human with the demented belief that he was divine. Charisma aside, he believed that he had power over life and death. This emphasis on magical powers is an absolute misdirection of reality. If we keep waiting for someone else to perform miracles for us, we will not devote our effort to solving human problems and making our own miracles. None of us gets an easy fix, as is promised by this account. We all have to work really hard to accomplish something of value while we are here on this planet.

Which brings us to the most immoral lesson in the gospel of John, in my opinion: the fantastic promise that all who accept the myth of Jesus as the God on earth will live forever. One of the worst facets of all religions is this sordid promise of an eternity of pleasure for all those who accept a certain mythology. It is nowhere more emphatically stated in the New Testament than it is in this gospel. The tragedy of this belief is its denial that we have only one life, and that we have only this one chance to create something that will benefit those who follow us. Any misdirection away from doing the best we can, while we are here, is immoral. Yet that is precisely the message of this gospel. Those who treasure this life will lose it, we are told. Well, John got both those parts right. We should deeply treasure this life, and we will lose it. The statement that those who despise this life will keep it for an eternity, I find to be absolute moral garbage. Worse, when disdain for this precious life is compounded by punishment for those who carry a different faith, we pile dead bodies on top of that garbage.

The Gospel of John does not at all stress those moral pillars that are necessary to form a solid base for a universal ethic. It does have, however, one passage of saving grace. Jesus washes the feet of his disciples, an act of great servility in that society. His disciples are stunned at this act of humility. Then he tells them to go and do likewise. This is, in a sense, an extension of the Good Samaritan story. One finds great morality only in service to others. What a wonderful lesson. He or she who is the greatest master, is, by that status, also obliged to be the greatest servant. The Gospel of John, which is full of moral misdirection, produces at least this one glowing winner.

> *13: 32–37. After washing their feet, he put on his robe again and sat down and asked, "Do you understand what I was doing? You call me 'Teacher' and 'Lord,' and you are right, because it is true, And since I, the Lord and Teacher, have washed your feet, you ought to wash each other's feet. I have given you an example to follow. Do as I have done to you. How true it is that a servant is not greater than the master. Nor are messengers more important that the one who sends them. You know these things – now do them! That is the path of blessing."*

COMMENT ON THE GOSPELS

Are practicing Christians still mixed up about their morals, and unsure of exactly what their religion is telling them? Of that, there seems little doubt. Our local newspaper, which is often no more that twelve pages, still has frequent articles about religious belief and practice, and may have pages of such articles in the Sunday edition. Frequently those stories document atrocities that sects of Buddhism, Hinduism or Islam are committing on other people of other faiths. Most of them, however, deal with the various struggles Christian denominations are going through trying to understand how they should lead their lives. This article, for example, appeared this week in our small paper.

> *Friday, May 15, 2009. "Torture debate prompts evangelical soul-searching", by Eric Gorski, AP Religion Writer.*

> *Among evangelical leaders, debate over the use of harsh interrogation techniques against suspected terrorists has prompted introspection about faith, ethics, the Golden Rule, just wars, Jack Bauer and Jesus.*

> *A number of evangelical leaders have made opposition to torture without exceptions a moral cause over the past three years, part of a broadening of the movement's agenda beyond traditional culture war issues. Others in the movement, including many Christian right leaders, have largely resisted or stayed silent.*

> *Now, President Barack Obama's release of Bush administration memos justifying harsh interrogation techniques and a new poll showing white evangelicals more sympathetic to torture have leaders taking stock of whether evangelical opinion has shifted on the topic.*

> *"I have said before that torture is like a bone caught in our throat – we can't swallow it and we can't spit it out," said David Gushee, a professor of Christian ethics at Mercer University in Atlanta and president of Evangelicals for Human Rights. "I think we're still there."*

> *The poll data from a survey of 742 U.S. adults released April 29 by the Pew Forum on Religion and Public Life found 62 percent of white evangelical Protestants said torture of a suspected terrorist could be often or sometimes justified to obtain important information....*

> *Those who attend religious services at least once a week were more likely than those who rarely or never attend to say torture is sometime or often justified in that scenario – 54 percent to 42 percent.*

This article goes on to quote various religious authorities on their opinions as to the use of torture in terrorist suspects, and quotes their reasons why they think this practice is acceptable or not. Those quotes demonstrate considerable waffling on this subject. The remaining discussion in this article concentrates on conjecture as to why such a disparity of opinion exists on this subject within the Christian community. It does make the point that political and ideological affiliations are better predictors of opinions on torture, but leaves with the supposition that religious faith strongly plays on those opinions.

This article seems to be a rational analysis of this lack of unanimity on the subject of how one human treats another in time of conflict. It is at least an open window on the fact that practicing Christians, who know very well what the New Testament says, and what their Prophet has directed them to do, don't quite make sense of those teachings. Perhaps this inability to see great harm in torture comes mostly from basic human drives. We make the decisions we make based on survival instincts. We are looking for comfort, sex and pleasure in our lives, and we are driven by the fear that we will lose one of these moieties we find so precious. If we think that another human threatens to take away something that gives meaning to our lives, we do whatever it takes to defend ourselves. At this point, the end begins to justify the means. Torture is okay if it will protect us from harm and death. The long term ramifications of that torture are lost in the immediate drive to survive. I have no doubt that these motives play an important role in leading each individual to his or her own conclusions about how cruel they should be towards another human.

What bothers me the most about this article is the last paragraph, which indicates that those who attend church the most often are more accepting of torture. I understand that this is a crazy world, and that there are threats to our lives everywhere. I understand that each of us is searching for the best way we can get through this life. I understand that all of us struggle at times knowing how to deal with those who threaten us and injure us. Perhaps there are other demographics we could ferret out that would indicate why churchgoers are more inclined to torture other humans, than those who do not go to church. My belief, however, and reason for writing this book, is that our religions, specifically Christianity in this instance, are giving us mixed messages about what is right and what is wrong. Our churches are giving us some really screwy morals, which range from complete passivity to vicious retaliation, and we are, as a result, having a lot of trouble figuring out just exactly what our attitude should be toward our fellow humans. We appear to be failing in our attempts to find solid moral guidance from our religions. The reason we fail is because our religions have not yet come to grips with the fact that many of their most sacred texts are filled with truly awful moral advice. It would seem that it is time to redefine which of our sacred teachings has value, and which should be avoided.

This is probably too much to ask of any Christians who are deeply wedded to their Bibles as the word of God. I do not wish to engage in a contentious argument with anyone about whether or not the Bible is Holy. It is improper for me or anyone else to interfere with the cherished religious beliefs of other persons, as long as those beliefs give them sustenance and direction in their lives. We will have to resolve our conflicts by some means of explanation, assurance and dialogue, although those who wish to use their beliefs as an excuse for cruelty will find mighty opposition from me. For those as Christians who are not chained to the Bible as infallible literature, I beg your great indulgence. I plead with you to consider that Jesus was human, and that he made big mistakes, as all of us do. I ask you to consider that he learned as he taught, as all the rest of us do. I beg you to consider that Jesus, although he articulated three moral advances never done fully before him, and first gave us a basis for human ethics, was not able to adhere to his own standards, as happens to all of us. I ask you to consider that he was a megalomaniac, who at times had a violent temper. I mostly implore you to understand that in most of the New Testament, the reported teachings of Jesus contain strong elements of immorality, rather than pure and timeless straight arrows into the future.

It is no wonder that Christians can't decide whether torture is moral or immoral. They are awash in mixed messages as to how they should guide their lives. Every intersection that every dutiful Christian comes to has signs pointing in all directions. Some of those arrows lead us in very good directions, many lead in very bad directions, and the remainder of those directional signals are simply waving in the breeze. Until the Christian faith can understand that some of the Jesus teachings in the New Testament are terrible advice, this religion will not develop the morality their Prophet brought them. It may be difficult for many to consider that Jesus was wrong about a lot of things, but that, in my considered opinion, he certainly was. He was wrong about the selective superiority of the Jewish tribes, his disdain of familial piety and devotion, his imagined power over the physical laws of the universe, the myth of resurrection from death, his personal godliness, a selective Heaven only for those who ascribed to a certain faith, and abject pacifism, just to name a few. He was, in fact, wrong about most things he uttered or taught. By offering these criticisms, I do not mean to denigrate the marvelous moral directives of Jesus that do make sense. For those, we will always be grateful.

Christians face three massive impediments to figuring out exactly how they should deal with the rest of the world population. One is that Christianity has not yet realized that it cannot deal effectively with the real world as long as it accepts its mythology as fact. Demanding unquestioning credulity for a perfect human on earth, virgin birth, magical supernatural cures over disease, coming back to life after a full and complete coagulated death, power over all humans, power over the entire universe, a personal human figure God who is on their side, and an eternal life full of pleasure, leaves this religion unable to relate to the market place. This religion is off in a magical cloud somewhere, while the rest of us are trying to figure out how to relate to one another, particularly during hard times and conflict.

The second massive problem that Christianity needs to solve, if it is to exist as a solid source of moral strength for us, is its exclusivity. Perhaps all of us gravitate to a cause that promises good things just for us and not anyone else. As we have seen above, most vociferously announced in the gospel of John, Christianity demands that its followers accept Jesus as a divinity on earth, and the Messiah of the Jews. Only if each of us makes a public announcement that we believe Jesus was divine, so says Christianity, will we be given rights to that exclusive club in the sky, where everyone lives forever in great pleasure. Only these few, who pronounce this belief, are chosen. We would have to say that any religious dogma which does not show equal concern for the needs of all human beings, cannot be considered moral.

The third massive impediment for Christianity to reach morality is the emphasis of this religion on horrendous punishment for all humans, for all time, who do not believe that Jesus was a God on earth. According to this religion, all other humanity which does not share that belief, representing ninety percent or more of all who have lived, will be tortured in pain for an eternity. We should all cringe at that cruel philosophy of this religion, but have not seen any awakening realization of the immense damage this concept carries, for more than two millennia.

There are these three imperatives for Christianity to become a vibrant, pulsating, sustaining force in human society, teaching us how to lead our lives with strength and compassion. Christianity needs to realize that its myths are myths. These magical stories about Jesus can be told and retold with color and enthusiasm, as long as everyone understands that these are marvelous pieces of mythology, which still have soulful meaning when interpreted poetically, but only poetically. Christianity must also understand that it is only one of many religions which give its followers direction in life, and that all humans can reach the heaven of a beautiful life, regardless of their faith. It has to give up being exclusive, and become inclusive, regardless of mythical faith. And it must understand that any demand of punishment for other believers, is highly immoral.

Most of all, Christianity has this lodestone of gold, which it has left buried under this trinitarian pile of snakes for the last two millennia. Christianity is the first religion to produce, all together, the four moral pillars of a universal human ethic. When Christianity can come to the realization it must not only preach, but must also, in all practical ways, follow these marvelous morals, then it can become a religion for all people, for all time.

The jury is still out. Christianity may or may not come to its senses. It may, or may not, eventually, become ethical, rather than mythological, elitist and punitive. Until this religion is able to accept these redirections, it will remain highly immoral. If we may use a familiar phrase, their time has not yet come.

HUMAN VALUE DEFINITIONS

This book has so far been written with a prolonged introduction to the problems addressed. I thought it most important to state the case for moral reform in our religions, and most specifically, in the religions of Abraham, before spending time on definitions. At this point we should pause and do just that. We should not go further until it is made clear just what is meant by the words we have been using so far to give grades of value to the actions we make, most particularly in relationship to each other. You may have noticed that these value words have been used to refer to some situations and not to others. You may have also noticed that the word ethics has been used only in a narrowly defined manner. There have been reasons to do so.

The words humans use to describe value are many, but mostly include good, evil, right, wrong, fairness, justice, morals and ethics. These are often thrown together interchangeably in descriptions of events and in conversation, as if there were little difference between them. I always chafe at these, what are to me, misuses of these words. I think each of them has a specific meaning and derivation, and should be used only in those more narrow definitions. I particularly favor a narrow use of the word ethics, and that just isn't the way you see it in print. Very scholarly authors, such as in the encyclopedias, freely describe a religious ethic or a Jewish, Christian, Muslim ethic. This liberal use of the word ethics creeps into newspaper articles and general population use, so that it is used to describe any human value system. This word is often used when describing unresolved religious conflicts, and that to me is also a misunderstanding of what ethics are all about. I would hope that, in this discussion, there will be more enlightened definitions and uses of these words, ethics in particular, and also a clearly expressed reason for those more precise definitions.

I sat twice in our hospital system as chairman of the Ethics Committee, and often thought it was a significant misnomer. The matters we dealt with were often economic, as much as value assessments of behavior. Some of it related to individual arrogance, disrespect, laziness and indifference, attitudes which were unacceptable in the care of patients who were dependent on us to give them the best we had to give. Those cases simply became matters of deciding how to change that behavior in the most effective manner, without causing a big brouhaha. Far too many of the cases we were asked to decipher, unfortunately, related to the rational use of limited resources, as opposed to the needs of patients. Should you deplete your blood bank to attempt to save one person, even though the chance of success is low? Are you not depriving several dozen other people from benefit, if there is no blood available when they need it? Should you keep a deathly ill person on a ventilator in the ICU for weeks, even though the chance of survival is extremely low? Should you keep a person alive on a ventilator for years, even though that person will not ever have a meaningful life in human terms? Should we spend several hundred thousand dollars putting a patient in the ICU on ventilator support, repeatedly, even though that patient refuses to stop smoking? Should we give terminal cancer patients very expensive medicines, do procedures on them, in an effort to prolong their lives by three or six months, when their inexorable death is expected? Should we offer a patient major surgery, when the risk of death or life long disability from that surgery is thirty percent? Should we be doing lung transplants, with several million dollars of expense, when the average length of survival after that transplant is five years? Should we spend about one fourth of our total health care resources taking care of people during the last few months of their lives? When what can be done comes up against the financial resources available to provide that care, conflict arises. The pseudonym for the intensive care unit, in hospital jargon, is the expensive care unit.

I do not mean to imply that each of these situations does not demand due respect and tough decisions. They are all difficult to resolve, particularly when we are struggling to find ways of providing adequate health care for the entire population. What is moral, at current practice, often ends up on the desk of an uncaring insurance bureaucrat. That bureaucrat has been instructed to cut costs, so the company can pay its investors, look good in the stock market, and provide multimillion dollar bonuses for its CEO's. The result, as we are acutely aware, has been a violation of the health care system, and a burgeoning percent of the population that is totally uninsured. Not only are insurers welshing on their promises, but entire hospital corporations are formed, in order to profit from health care. They do so by taking only the insured, and refusing the uninsured. That money which has been stolen from the total health care dollars, because these insurers and for profits are not doing their part, then means that resources are limited. Hospitals which still provide for the needy are under the budget sword, and have to cut waste in all ways that they can. They merge, eliminate duplications, and put off adding new services. Once all that is done, what is left winds up in budget committees and ethics committees. Was too much done, or was not enough done, using the limited resources available?

I also do not mean to imply that this dilemma is any different than those decisions we face throughout life. We are always confronted with that problem. These are the resources we have, and these are the things we would like to get done. Which of those alternatives we choose depends on our priorities. What our priorities are depends on our unique situation, and whether we consider that particular decision as a short term goal or a long term goal. Most of those very trying patient decisions I saw daily were solvable by simply facing these facts. Every patient needed to be told what their situation was, what resources were available to treat that problem, what the chance of success would be using those resources, and what failure would be like if those treatments were unsuccessful. Once each of them possessed knowledge as to what lay on both sides of the scale, each of them could make their own decision as what risks they wished to take to reach a certain goal. It was never up to me, after that patient had been fully informed. It was always up to them.

The part of informed consent I saw the most neglected was making sure each patient understood, in terms of their own language use, what could be expected if a certain treatment choice failed. Most patients got a fairly good description of what to expect if a certain treatment, procedure or operation succeeded. That was appropriately followed by a relatively accurate assessment of what the chance of failure would be, expressed as a certain percentage point. The explanation usually stopped at that point, expecting that each patient would make their decision based on that information. It was understood that the physician or surgeon favored this particular medical treatment, at least in a statistical sense, or else it would have not been offered. What was often very important to patients, however, and often swayed their ultimate decision, was the details of failure. Here is what you can expect if this surgery fails to achieve the expected result. When this information was also made clear to them, patients sometimes changed their decisions. Whatever it was at that point, both patient and provider could live with their conscience afterwards. A cavalier attitude, always expecting the best results, was inevitably a recipe for disaster, both on the part of the patient and the provider.

Perhaps this is a bit too far afield. If the above approach holds true for all situations, it would appear that making right and wrong decisions is nothing more than combining honesty and a full assessment. If this is so, morality does not require a lot of definitions and a lot of convoluted thought. The implication is that decisions as to what to do are easy as long as you just use common sense. Although I have great respect for this position, I also find it very troubling. When presenting a family with the current terminal state of disease of their loved one, the expected chances of survival and expected chances of death, and then asking them to make a decision as to whether they were ready to pull the plug, or not, the response was many times animated and diverse. Some said yes, and others wanted to wait a while. Family members who were not there for that soul-searching session would call in to say that they were completely opposed to letting their father, mother, brother or sister die, and would be suing hospital, doctors, and other family members if such action were taken. All five stages in the face of death, including denial, anger, bargaining, depression and acceptance were sometimes present at once. Usually, every family member had a somewhat different answer to that question, depending on their position in the family and emotional attachment to the dying patient. It was a deeply troubling decision for each of them, and none of them saw it exactly the same way. What was right for one was wrong for another. Some saw such an action as an immediate evil, and others saw ending that life as the good and humane long-range thing to do, although a painful decision. What we often had to do was wait a few days, continue to answer all their questions, let them talk to each other, cry with them when our emotions were also overcome, and let them reach their own consensus. We seldom had to ask that one of them be appointed power of attorney to make those decisions, but that was sometimes the only remaining solution for providing family decisions, when the patient could not make those decisions for him or herself.

Please believe, I do not by any means think that death of a loved one is ever easy, and believe that it is always a time for tears. There is always sorrow and grief, something that is an omnipresent part of our lives. How long we stay in sorrow and pain, and how long it takes us to reach acceptance for this loss in our lives, however, is greatly dependent on whether we understand adequately what good and evil are, what is fair, and what is just. If all we can sense is the pain, and not understand how or why this is happening, it becomes a great deal more prolonged, and a great deal deeper. With understanding, comes peace and acceptance. To that end, I believe it is inadequate to use all these value words of our lives interchangeably. We have to understand whether this good and evil that throws us all around in our lives is an innate force in the universe, or something we have created. We have to understand why five members of a family, when faced with a terrible loss, make five different decisions as to what is right. Clear definitions are in order, followed by some understanding as to what different definitions are being used by our religions, and how they came to be established. In particular, we have to understand how these mistaken definitions are leading us astray, as currently promoted by our religions.

GOOD AND EVIL

The word good has a whole paragraph in the dictionary which defines various uses of this letter combination as an adjective, most all of which relate to material evaluations. Those definitions of this word as a noun are less wordy. The first of those hardly says anything: "something that is good." The second is quite problematic: "something conforming to the moral order of the universe." These shades of Socrates are our first order of business in discussing good and evil. Although this definition is quite correct in that it conforms to the usual use of this word, I find this definition to be, nevertheless, quite wrong, and need to explain why in detail. In brief, the reason for this objection is that we have no evidence there is a moral order in the universe. We have no business ascribing a human value system to the universe, which doesn't know good or evil, and doesn't care.

The word evil has a much more limited set of definitions in the dictionary, when used as an adjective or a noun. Apparently the human population finds it much more difficult to describe how things are good, rather than to flatly declare them evil. The reasons for that disparity are worthy of conjecture. As a noun, the first definitions of evil are fairly clear: "something that brings sorrow, distress or calamity," and "the fact of suffering, misfortune and wrongdoing." The second definition is again, that description which is greatly troubling: "a cosmic evil force." It is quite apparent that Webster, or his designees, emphasized the teachings of Socrates, rather than those more accurate teachings of Protagoras, when choosing their definitions of both good and evil. This requires a prolonged clarification and discussion, exploring exactly what each of these august gentlemen believed.

A UNIVERSAL GOOD?

Socrates was the second of several great Greek minds that influenced all of philosophy, scientific endeavor and social conduct that followed them, throughout the world. Socrates lived from 470–399 BC. He eschewed physical pleasure, and often denied himself ordinary comforts. He preferred the company of younger men, because he felt they had greater inquisitiveness and energy. He often talked to artists, poets and politicians, quizzing them about the details of their work. He was particularly interested in what they considered to be right or wrong, and why they reached those conclusions. Periods of total involvement in human effort were often followed by deeply mystical daydreaming trances. He might spend hours or even days listening to the voices in his head argue different points of philosophy. After each of these sessions, he felt it his obligation to teach this knowledge he had gained during those trances, to all those around him. He wanted to share his enlightenment, and declared it his godly mission to alleviate ignorance and bring knowledge to all other humans. As with the later trances of Muhammad, none of those mystical revelations which Socrates experienced were recorded by him. Our only record of his teachings comes from the writings of his disciples, primarily those of Plato.

Socrates believed that there was a God, who was the ruler of the world, and that the soul of each man (perhaps also woman) was a part of this great divinity. That meant that the soul of man was also immortal. Immortality of the soul, however, did not to Socrates make one good or moral. That could only be achieved by increasing one's knowledge, so that eventually each individual, as they knew more, would become more like his omniscient and all-good God. Socrates equated knowledge and goodness, his God being the ultimate of those qualities. He felt that if any one human had knowledge of that goodness, they would always choose that action over one that was not good. He believed that this universal goodness or morality could be reached with the accrual of knowledge. He believed that the national good could never be achieved until all citizens had knowledge of this absolute Good in the universe. It was, to him, every person's responsibility to tend to one's soul until this state of knowledge and goodness was reached. He felt that it was the duty of politicians to promote this spiritual health of the community, rather than give people what they wanted.

The reasons for the persecution of Socrates remain somewhat obscure. In 399, he was indicted for "impiety." The accusations against him were "corruption of the young," and "neglect of the gods whom the city worships and the practice of religious novelties." Whether Aristophanes' use of Socrates in *The Clouds* to discuss atheism, as part of a burlesque scene, is part of the inducement for these false charges, is unclear. It appears to have been for the most part, a political struggle. Socrates favored an oligarchy, rather than democratic rule, and the democrats were now in power as the result of a counterrevolution. They feared that Socrates was teaching otherwise, and wished him to change that pressure against them. The death penalty, it seems, was inserted in those charges against him simply as a means of guaranteeing that he would change his position and support them. Socrates obstinately refused to do so, asked to be excused from these charges as a benefactor of the republic, and forced their hand. The vote for the death penalty was 280 to 220 by the incensed politicos. After a month's delay, and even though he was offered opportunities to escape, Socrates drank the poison Hemlock, unwavering to the end in defense of his principles.

The obstinacy of Socrates in defending his philosophy, and his willingness to die in defense of those principles, seems to have made a deep impression on all those who followed him. This concept of a God of all the universe who possesses all knowledge and is totally good has now survived beyond Socrates, through a succession of disciples, for the last 2400 years. Unfortunately, those errant concepts have also led us deeply and tragically astray for the last 2400 years.

Plato lived from 428 to 348 BC. He was the product of an aristocratic family, and was initially drawn to politics. He considered Socrates an older friend, whom he deeply admired. Plato is responsible for documenting the thoughts and philosophies of Socrates in multiple discourses, most all of which survived. Following the death of Socrates, Plato withdrew from political life, for the most part, and established the Academy, thought of as the first university. It was an institute of philosophical and scientific research. Friends and pupils of Plato produced works on history, botanical classification, law, and important mathematical contributions in solid geometry and curvilinear volumes. Plato, in his own literary efforts, showed his greatest concern as to what their God was, how easily this God could be reached, and trying to determine the value of the human soul. Each of those subjects shows the great influence of Socrates on his personal philosophies.

Plato believed that there were three morally fatal false beliefs; atheism, denial of moral government, and belief that divine judgment could be bought by offerings. He moved the concept of a Supreme Force to a more distant realm. This supreme Good, he believed, was the source of all reality and order in the universe, as well as the light by which all things are seen and understood. This form was the source of all things and responsible for all things in the world. This supreme Good could be approached and appreciated only by prolonged study. In later Platonism, this Supreme Force was described as "the light of the world." Not only does Plato conceive of their God as very distant, he further promotes the mistaken concept that the universe contains an intrinsic value system. As far as we can tell at this time, he was wrong on both counts.

Plato's entire discourse, The Phaedo, was an attempt to justify the immortality of the human soul. In this discussion, he expresses three concepts concerning the human soul. One, he says that the soul is divine, and is for that reason immortal. Second, he believes that the soul is cyclical, (reminiscent of Hindu concept) recurring in many lives, and simply relearns things it previously learned. Third, he says, the human soul is immutable. It does not change over time. The kindest thing to say about all this philosophizing concerning the human psyche is to say that Plato had a brilliant mind, and was doing the best he could to understand why humans seemed to understand so much more than all other life, using the tools he had at his disposal to figure out where humans belonged in the universe. Perhaps he was correct, in some ways. Quantum physicists tell us that there are other "you's" in other universes. DNA can be extracted from animals that have been dead for millions of years, with the hope that it can be used to reconstruct that animal. Certainly, whatever we have done during our lives that affects others after us, has some degree of immortality. The best evidence we have at the present time, however, is that our individual selves do not survive beyond this one and only precious life.

Aristotle, 384–322 BC, had three major periods in his life. Initially he studied at the Academy in Athens under Plato for twenty years. Upon Plato's death in 347, his nephew, Speusippes, was named as head of the Academy. Aristotle left, in apparent disgust at not being named to that position, and went into an interlude of travel with friends for twelve years, eventually settling in Mytilene. There he married the king's daughter, founded the Assus Academy, and was the tutor for the future Alexander the Great. He returned to Athens at age 50, where he founded his own school, the Lyceum. He is said to be responsible for the scientific principle of conclusion based on study and observation of objects.

Aristotle believed in the immortality of the soul, an ultimate reality termed God, and a moral life. He got all these concepts from his teacher, Plato, who, in turn, got most of his concepts from Socrates. Aristotle's early concepts of the soul agreed also with those of Plato, that the soul was a separate being in an unnatural relationship with the body. Aristotle modified this unnatural concept later in life. He came to believe that the soul was a vital principle which united with the body to form the individual person, a concept which seems more rational and less contrived. He also had a different concept of their deity from that of Plato. Aristotle believed that their God was an unmoved Mover, who was the first cause of all things, all beings and all motion, but after that first cause, not involved with any of the natural events of the universe or the machinations of humans. This, in a certain sense, agrees in general with what our greatest scientific minds are now telling us about our universe. All of this began, and it is still working, but we have no evidence that there has been any planned manipulation by any driving forces, in any of the subsequent events of the universe, including life.

There was another great Greek mind, who preceded these famous three, and whose concepts were far more rational than those of Socrates, Plato and Aristotle. Protagoras lived from circa 490–420 BC, but has unfortunately never received the amount of press that was given to the other great minds that followed him. The major reason may be that very few of his writings have survived, simply because his concepts of God and morality were far too advanced for his countrymen to accept. The only major account of the thoughts of Protagoras that survived is a dialogue of Plato, named Protagoras. In this contrived exchange of ideas, Plato argues against the concept of Protagoras that goodness is a teachable human virtue. For Plato, human virtue is external and godly, reachable only by prolonged study.

Protagoras was labeled as a sophist, in the most complimentary meaning of that word. This word derives from the Greek goddess of wisdom, Sophia. In that sense, he was indeed a great sophist, a wise man who taught knowledge to those who came to him. Although sophistry has come to be known, in usual language, as philosophizing using specious reasoning, that would be a great misuse of that term for this precocious man. The only quotes which have survived him still carry great impact: "Man is the measure of all things: of things which are, that they are, and of things which are not, that they are not." In his lost work, *On the Gods*, he is quoted as saying: "Concerning the gods, I have no means of knowing whether they exist or not or of what sort they may be, because of the obscurity of the subject and the brevity of human life." For this agnosticism, he was accused of impiety, his books were publicly burned, and he was exiled from Athens circa

415 BC for the rest of his life. He paid very dearly for being right on both counts. He was completely correct, as far as we can tell, in that morality is a value system which relates only to humans; and he was completely correct that we have so far found no proof of creator gods who meddle in human affairs.

Protagoras has not been entirely alone. Most every era, it seems, has had one or more humans who understand human thought and our place in the universe, far beyond the understanding of their peers. We see that, for example, in the book of Job. The author of this story, man or woman, understood that life is not fair, that good things happen to bad people, and bad things happen to good people. The author disguises this understanding as an allegory, an argument between the God of Goodness and the God of Evil. Job gets caught in the middle, and is put to the test. Previously greatly prosperous and virtuous, every bad thing that can happen to a person, happens to him, including loss of family, loss of crops and animals, as well as disfiguring diseases. All of Job's friends come to him in beautifully drawn dialogues, to tell him in various ways that he must have lied, cheated, or done something else to displease his God, otherwise these terrible things would not be happening to him. Job maintains his trust in his Lord, whom he believes is totally good, in spite of this barrage of accusations and sophistry from his friends. At the end, however, Job cracks, starts through the first phase of death and dying, and gets angry with his God. Why me, Lord? What did I ever do to deserve this? What follows in the book of Job is this marvelous tumbling poetry which proclaims the greatness of the God of creation.

Job 38: 1–41. Then the Lord answered Job from the whirlwind.

"Who is this that questions my wisdom with such ignorant words? Brace yourself, because I have some questions for you, and you must answer them.

Where were you when I laid the foundation of the earth? Tell me, if you know so much. Do you know how its dimensions were determined and who did the surveying? What supports its foundations, and who laid its cornerstone as the morning stars sang together and all the angels shouted for joy?

Who defined the boundaries of the sea as it burst from the

womb, and as I clothed it with clouds and thick darkness?
For I locked it behind barred gates, limiting its shores. I
said, this far and not farther will you come. Here your proud
waves must stop!

Have you ever commanded the morning to appear and
caused the dawn to rise in the east? Have you ever told the
daylight to spread to the ends of the earth, to bring an end
to the night's wickedness? For the features of the earth take
shape as the light disturbs the haunts of the wicked, and it
stops the arm that is raised in violence.

Have you explored the springs from which the seas come?
Have you walked about and explored their depths? Do you
know where the gates of death are located? Have you seen
the gates of utter doom? Do you realize the extent of the
earth? Tell me about it if you know!

Where does the light come from and where does the
darkness go? Can you take it to its home? Do you know
how to get there? But of course you know all this! For you
were born before it was all created, and you are so very
experienced! (This God is really sarcastic!)

Have you visited the treasuries of the snow? Have you
seen where the hail is made and stored? I have reserved
it for the time of trouble, for the day of battle and war.
Where is the path to the origin of light? Where is the home
of the east wind?

Who created a channel for the torrents of rain? Who laid
out the path for the lightning? Who makes the rain fall on
barren land, in a desert where no one lives? Who sends the
rain that satisfies the parched ground and makes the tender
grass spring up?

Does the rain have a father? Where does dew come from?
Who is the mother of the ice? Who gives birth to the frost
from heavens? For the water turns to ice as hard as rock,
and the surface of the water freezes.

Can you hold back the movements of the stars? Are you
able to restrain the Pleiades or Orion? Can you ensure the
proper sequence of the seasons or guide the constellation
of the Bear with her cubs across the heavens? Do you know

the laws of the universe and how God rules the earth?

Can you shout to the clouds and make it rain? Can you make lightning appear and cause it to strike as you direct it? Who gives intuition and instinct? Who is wise enough to count all the clouds? Who can tilt the water jars of heaven, turning the dry dust to clumps of mud?"

What wonderful stuff. There is about a page more, before Job's God ceases telling him to stop being a fool. At that point, Job finally understands. We, as humans, are miniscule parts of the universe. Good and bad things happen to all of us without rhyme or reason. The universe is capricious, and life is precarious. All we can do is to, each time we meet disaster, pick up the pieces and move on with life; or, when it has come to be our time, give up gracefully.

Job 42: 5. "I had heard about you before, but now I have seen you with my own eyes. I take back everything I said, and I sit in dust and ashes to show my repentance."

Job and his author understood, several millennia ago, that this universe is far more vast than we can possibly understand, that humans are insignificant in the grand scheme of the universe, that there is not a personal God always directing us to a good and lofty goal. What is valuable to us as humans is meaningless for the rest of the universe. What a pleasure it is to see that understanding come to the surface several millennia ago. We are just now beginning to catch up, and reach the same understanding.

Whether or not Protagoras had access to the Book of Job, it is clear that he understood these things too. When Protagoras says that "man is the measure of all things," what he is saying is this: there is not intrinsic goodness or badness in the universe. Statements as to whether something is good or bad, moral or immoral, are purely humanly derived value judgements. Protagoras states an opinion entirely different than the lofty claims of Socrates and Plato, who state that virtue and morality are intrinsic parts of a God of the entire universe. For Protagoras, he correctly perceives that these values exist only for human consumption. Good and evil, right and wrong, justice and injustice, morality and immorality do not exist in the rest of the universe. The universe does not have an intrinsic value system. Protagoras also sees clearly that there is no evidence for gods that are interested in and control human lives for their own purposes. For being so right as to agnosticism and as to values being humanly derived, he was shunned and his books were burned. Human minds were not ready yet for his concepts. Instead, they took avidly to the other Greek philosophies of a great and totally good, distant God. These were the concepts that were rampant when the books of Judaism and Christianity were translated into Greek. These were the concepts that became an intrinsic part of Judaism, Christianity and Islam, all to our great misfortune since that time.

These were precisely the schisms that boiled incessantly in the first three centuries of Christianity, and that the Council of Nicea faced, when commanded by Constantine to reach a consensus as to what the doctrines of Christianity should be. The Christian community had gone through some discussion about the Mithraic miracles, but for the most part, avidly swallowed this mythology hook, line and sinker, fully adopting it into their own religion, in their attempt to become dominant. The rest of it was not so easy. The most vehement disagreements centered around how good their God was, how far away He was, how reachable He was, how personable He was, and as to when and how much Jesus was divine. Socrates said that his God was omniscient, omnibeneficent, and omnipotent, and that the human soul was an immortal part of this grand entity. God was in all humans, he said, but this did not necessarily make humans virtuous. Only with the accrual of knowledge would each individual achieve godlike goodness and morality. Plato said that his God was a supreme Good, who was the light of the world, and who could be approached with prolonged study. Aristotle said that his God was an Unmoved Mover, who began all things, but who did not interfere in any way with the events of the universe or humans. Judaism said that their God was the God of all people, but had specifically contracted with the tribes of Israel to be His chosen people, dominant over all other people. This God was personally involved with the life of the Jewish people, punishing them when they did not follow his law. Jesus said that his God was a personal father, always a part of every action he took in his life.

The Nicean Council members apparently thought that all of these god concepts were correct, or else felt obliged to include all of them in their official version of their god. Whether or not they were aware of the teachings of Protagoras, they certainly chose not to listen to that line of thought. This concept of goodness as only a human value system did not please or entice them at all. They had no truck with the possibility there might not be a grand God who manipulated human lives. They wanted their God to be all things to all people, in order to entice all other creeds to their religion. The result was a remarkable geometric contraption called the Trinity. According to this doctrine, their one and only God was not only distant and supreme, but this God was also all-powerful, all-knowing and responsible for all events of the universe. In addition, and in particular, this God was totally good. God was in all things and all pathways, including humans. A part of God was very personal, temporarily on Earth, in the form of Jesus. The early Christian priests parceled out these various concepts to a tripartite entity which had enough space for all of these incompatible concepts. God, in their official version, now consisted of an all powerful Near Figure, an all powerful Far Figure, a generalized Holy Spirit, and was also intensely personal. Since these are quite incompatible beliefs, adopting them required, of necessity, a God with multiple parts. The God that was constructed at the Nicean Council was declared to be all of these things all at once, and they called it the Trinity. It was, in modern parlance, a committee job.

A UNIVERSAL EVIL?

There was one residual theological piece that this triangular contraption did not solve for Christianity, however, and even more so for Islam to follow. The total goodness part presented an additional challenge. It has not been a problem for Judaism, because that faith has always believed that, even though their God does very destructive things, these are all done with a purpose in mind. For the followers of Judaism, every natural disaster is an act of their God, planned to teach them a lesson. Every disaster affecting other people is a planned act of their God to punish those other people for indiscretions that do not match with what Judaism considers right, or else indirectly teach the children of Israel a lesson. All events in the universe, no matter where those events occur, are done by their God, in their opinion, who always has the future of Israel in His mind. Their God is a pretty bad actor at times, but always because he is working to protect and nurture his favorite nation and contracted people, the Israelites. This contorted logic, however, does not work at all for Christianity and Islam.

If their God is totally good, as the Christians now claim, none of this rationalization applies. A totally good God will not be capable of doing all the terrible things that happen to humans. That necessitates the literary creation of another powerful force in the universe, the Devil, or the great Satan. If their totally good God is all-powerful, that means that He is stronger than this Devil, but not by much. There is a great deal of evil out there in the world, at least by religious standards. Now we have an entirely new scenario developing. Since the totally good God will have to eventually win this battle over human souls, against this great Satan, the final battle will have to be a monumental cataclysm. Now we have created a predicted apocalypse which will destroy all the earth and all its inhabitants, as these great powers fight over human souls. All of the world and possibly the universe will be destroyed, according to these beliefs, in a furious fight over who is good, who is evil, what is right, what is wrong, which ones are moral and which ones are immoral. If this conjecture be so, most of us are faced with a grim end, and endless torture to follow, all at the hands of a totally good God.

Our astronomers, physicists, naturalists, geologists, archeologists and mathematicians all tell us that these religious interpretations of human life carry no resemblance to what they have observed. They say that all events occurring at atomic and subatomic levels occur by random action. The only appropriate word to describe the activity of the smallest measurable particles is chaos. All interactions occur by chance and not by purpose or design. They tell us that random action does produce patterns, however, and that these patterns are measurable in the interaction of large objects. These laws are so reliable, they allow terribly precise calculations. We can, using these physical laws of the universe, guide a space craft through millions of miles to land on a specific site on another planet. That absolutely remarkable feat, however, does not to them contradict the fact that we live in a universe of chance occurrence without plan or purpose.

If what our scientists are telling us is true, and we have no reason to believe otherwise, it seems time for us to grow beyond this archaic concept of some mysterious fixed Goodness in the universe, and far beyond the concept that there is a fixed intrinsic Evil Force in the universe. We have so far found no evidence of any discernible force anywhere in the universe that cares about human life in any way. We can find no value system that exists for all the rest of the universe. The only value system that exists, pertains only to life, and in particular, human life. Good and evil, to the best of our knowledge, exist only in the minds of Homo sapiens. This understanding is crucial to developing a reasonable human morality system.

HUMAN GOOD AND EVIL

The rest of this particular discussion then becomes more straightforward. Good and evil come into existence as soon as there is one person on the face of the earth. We are complex creatures with multiple needs. We certainly crave the basics of shelter, sustenance and sexual gratification. We also need more than that. We have intellects that crave knowledge and crave expression. There are not too many joys greater than learning something that we did not understand before, opening up an entire new world of comprehension to us. There are fewer long term pleasures than expressing ourselves fully, to the point of giving someone else understanding that they did not have before. Some scenes, some pieces of music, some observations of human tenderness give us goose bumps from the sheer pleasure of that illumination. We live for moments like that when the whole world takes on a different hue. I am not sure what else to call this additional human need, other than fulfillment. We all crave this extra dimension, which extends beyond our basic needs.

Whatever substance or event helps us achieve our basic needs, and our fulfillment, we call good. Whatever takes away our basic needs, or stifles our fulfillment, we call evil. These are purely human terms which, struggle though we might, we cannot find anywhere else in our universe. It has been nice to call up some other force or power, give it fancy names like God or Supreme Good, and glorify this marvelous force that makes life meaningful for us. That's pretty much the way the human mind works. We externalize all of our thoughts, emotions and values, bestow them on some imaginary creature or animal, and have them talk for us. Our cartoons, movies and television shows are full of talking bears, possums, cats, dogs, spiders, rabbits, ducks, birds, coyotes and other assorted creatures, who express very human values, using human language. We are led to believe that the marvelous piece of art on the ceiling of the Sistine chapel is pretty much what the God of the universe looks like. The truth is, if there is a God, this has to be a grotesque cartoon characterization, at the best. The fact is, no animal speaks human language, other than a few primates who have learned how to sign. We can anthropomorphize till kingdom come, but it doesn't wash. Good and evil are purely and only human values. Protagoras was absolutely right, but they didn't listen then, and we still aren't listening now.

On January 29, 2002, President George W. Bush gave his State of the Union message to the United States of America. As previously cited, he had been struggling knowing what to do about the terrorist attacks on the United States of America. If he did not act, we were all in deep trouble. In his torment, he appears to have reached for his great source of strength, his religion, to tell him what to do. This good/evil concept of his religion immediately came to the fore. It declared that the good forces of Christianity should declare war against the forces of evil in this world. This, to him, seemed to be the way he could convince the American public that attacking other nations was the moral thing to do. He began by citing the government of North Korea as a regime that was developing weapons of mass destruction, while starving its citizens. He accused the Iranian regime of also developing weapons of mass destruction, exporting terror, and suppressing the hope of the Iranian people for freedom. He concentrated his comments on Iraq, which he accused of developing anthrax, nerve gas and nuclear capability for over a decade. He said that this regime had already used poison gas to kill thousands of rebellious Kurds, its own citizens. "States like these, and their terrorist allies, constitute an *axis of evil*, arming to threaten the peace of the world. By seeking weapons of mass destruction, these regimes pose a grave and growing danger. They could provide these arms to terrorists, giving them the means to match their hatred. They could attack our allies or attempt to blackmail the United States. In any of these cases, the price of indifference would be catastrophic."

On May 6, 2002, the future United States UN Ambassador, John R. Bolton, gave a speech entitled "Beyond the Axis of Evil." In that speech, he added three more nations to this list of supposed totally evil entities: Libya, Syria, and Cuba. His reasons for doing so were that these were "state sponsors of terrorism and are pursuing, or who have the potential to pursue, weapons of mass destruction, or have the capability to do so in violation of their treaty obligations." In January of 2005, the incoming Secretary of State, Condoleezza Rice, added four more states to this list, deeming them "outposts of tyranny," naming Cuba, Belarus, Zimbabwe and Myanmar.

This decision of Mr. Bush does not make any sense unless we understand it in the context of the good/evil conflict which is an intrinsic part of his religion. During this period of our nation, our administration dealt in paranoia and distrust. If we were to listen to these administrators, there was a great body of menacing and scheming evil in the world, which was growing daily, adding converts and nations, all of whom were bent on doing hateful acts against the United States of America. Some of that fear was well justified. There was hatred against the United States coming from many quarters. This hatred had been building for centuries, as Muslims suffered at the hands of Christians and Jews. It was certainly time to examine that hatred on both sides, to determine what fueled it, and what could be done to alleviate that anger and distrust. Finding a way to defuse this simmering hostility would not be easy, however. The problem was that it was a two way street.

There was the same kind of fear within the Muslim nations. They saw the United States as the "Great Satan," which was bent on destroying their way of life and their religion. They had ample evidence of this disrespect and outright disdain, as Christianity and imperialists repeatedly invaded their countries. They saw the same cycle coming again, as it had in the thirteenth century, when Christian invaders entered their peaceful lands, slaughtering men women and children with vicious zeal. They had suffered, in the twentieth century, with the rapacious land grab by Jews, wresting their land from them in a sudden invasion, backed by the military might of Christian nations. They had since that time sustained repeated attacks on their home lands from the newly created state of Israel, again fully backed by the military might of the United States. And now the United States had again shown its antipathy toward Muslim nations by invading Afghanistan and Iraq. It was almost as if the United States was purposefully asking angry young Muslims to hate them and hurt this nation in any way possible.

This understanding of why there was such Muslim extremist anger directed against the United States was woefully lacking in the Bush administration. Mr. Bush and his advisors instead chose to attach a different interpretation to these sad events. They apparently did not see that the Muslim terrorists flew airplanes into the world trade center towers because they each believed that this was the most moral and glorious act they could commit with their lives, and the greatest blow they could deliver against the "Great Satan," who threatened their nations and their precious religion. They instead chose to believe that these Muslim extremists did so because they had tapped into some inexorable evil force that was basic for the entire universe. This reasoning was, in my opinion, a grave error, for which the rest of the world is still paying. The same mistake, however, was made by the Muslims who plotted and then carried out this horrendous act. They also made the same mistake of thinking that they were combating some universal evil force, which had surfaced in the United States of America.

These concepts of a Universal Good and conversely, a Universal Evil, are purely Socratic. These Socratic doctrines have become embedded in our religions and accepted by all our true believers as universal truths. None of the Israeli, Christian and Islamic faithful doubt that there is a great good God who is on their side, who is constantly fighting the Evil Force in the world, and who constantly calls for his faithful to carry his cause for Him, to fight for their religion, to overcome this terrible evil that plagues the human race and prevents their particular religion from becoming dominant.

The voice of God is calling

His summons unto men

As once he spake in Zion

So now he speaks again

Whom shall I send to succor

My people in their need

Whom shall I send to loosen

Their bonds of shame and greed

It becomes so easy, if you believe this concept of a Universal Good,

or a completely good God, to embrace the fervor of fighting and killing those who are in the army of evil. The true and blind believers of
our religions are completely captured by that fervor. That willingness
to sacrifice their own lives and take the lives of others, in a cause
which to them is greater than any of them, becomes to them a glorious martyrdom. How deeply tragic these cruel actions are. These
doctrines of a universal Good, and a universal Evil, encourage us to
rapaciously take that most precious gift of all, human life, treating it
with utter disdain.

These shadows of Socrates still hover over us, darkening our skies
and our horizons, leading us to commit great acts of cruelty against
each other in the name of an imagined great good God, or a great
Satan. To the best of our knowledge, there is no intrinsic good or evil
in the universe. The universe cares not one whit about humans or
what happens to them. Good and evil are purely human values, which
do not deserve any elevation beyond each person's judgment of what
is good or bad for them. We would be best served by keeping good
and evil as individual judgments of value. These values have no business being extended to other universal realms, where they are used in
ways that are destructive of human society. The Bush administration
values were most well intended, but also were deeply Socratic, and by
that means, deeply misguided. It is as if Protagoras has placed a curse
over us for not listening to his keenly perceptive mind, and burning his
books. It appears that this curse will not be lifted until we can accept
that good and evil are purely human individual judgments. Until we
understand that Protagoras was right, and Socrates was wrong, we are
in a heap of trouble.

> *Man is the measure of all things: of things which are, that
> they are, and of things which are not, that they are not.*

RIGHT AND WRONG

The jury of twelve men and women listen intently, trying to catch
every word, as the staid prosecuting attorney presents her opening
statement, accusing the defendant of crimes that must demand a
guilty verdict. The reasons she states seem clear and persuasive, and
the minds of the jury members soon drift to the early conclusion that

this man must surely be guilty of his alleged terrible crimes. Then the flamboyant attorney for the defense begins his opening statement, and within minutes has cast great doubt as to whether any of the accusations of the prosecutor are true or not. There is now great doubt as to whether it is right or wrong to convict this defendant. Then the first witness is called, and gives evidence that seems to clearly indicate it is right to convict. Upon cross questioning, however, there is doubt as to the validity of that witness' statements, and a number of minds on the jury switch back to that doubt. There is no longer a right or wrong majority on the jury. As the trial proceeds, and bits of evidence or testimony build, right and wrong shift back and forth multiple times. The final closing statements of the attorneys, powerfully driven with emotion, again sway jury minds one way or the other. After the court trial, another trial begins in the jury room. Members are divided as to a guilty or not guilty verdict, and some cannot decide either way. What is right and what is wrong in this monumental event in the life of this defendant, hangs in the balance. After animated discussion lasting hours, the most silver tongued and/or emotional members of the jury get their way, and a verdict is reached. It has not been reached without right and wrong changing position multiple times during that trial.

If you read any magazine catering to the legal profession, you will find pages and pages in the back of that magazine that are devoted to advertisements for those who offer their services as experts in any field, for a price. There are ads for jury experts, who will advise what jury members to choose, by age, sex, financial status, marital status and profession, that will be likely to give a verdict for that lawyer for that particular trial. There are brilliant attorneys for hire, who have never lost a case, because they know just how to trigger human minds to decide in their favor. There are private investigators who specialize in digging for dirt that will cast doubt on anyone's testimony. In addition to this vast army of experts for hire, regardless of who is right or wrong, there are judges who have their own agenda. Some of them are lenient, some are harsh, and some of them advise juries falsely. Our legal system of trial by a jury of peers is fraught with vagaries of right and wrong, so that if you have enough money, you can probably get a verdict in your favor. A jury decision does not necessarily mean that the correct decision was made.

We are, of course, fortunate to have a system of justice which does use a jury of peers, in general terms, to decide what is right and what is wrong. In spite of the most persuasive and skillfully crafted arguments attorneys can offer, those who have lived in the marketplace are aware of how cunning some humans can be. They look skeptically at grandiose claims, imagined schemes, and stretched descriptions of normal human behavior. They have not survived in life without being taken many times, and have learned by those sad experiences every time. Once they begin talking with each other honestly and openly, they are able to answer their own questions and doubts, reaching a decision which is, most of the time, correct, based on the evidence submitted to them. This does not mean to say that other evidence, had it been presented to them, would not have resulted in a different verdict. It does say that they made the best right or wrong decision they could make, at that time, against that person, using the knowledge that they possessed.

Right and wrong judgments in human life vary from moment to moment and group to group, time to time. Throw in another variable in the equation, and what was wrong the minute before, now becomes right. The worst of enemies at one time become the best of friends at other times. German and American soldiers of the Second World War stand together at the beach in Normandy and reminisce in friendship. What is right for George Bush is wrong for Osama Bin Laden. What is right for Israel is not right for Palestine. What is right for Protestants in Ireland is not right for Catholics. What is right for an American soldier is wrong for an Iraqi freedom fighter. What is right for a Sunni is not right for a Shiite. What is right for China is not what is right for America, a chilling fact lost on those politicians who give us an astronomical debt. Our most precious possessions are being sold to Chinese, German and Arabic bankers, who may at any time exercise their power to make different right and wrong decisions.

There is no certain right and no certain wrong. These values shift like the changing sands in a windstorm, depending on the variables of the moment. We like to think of our values as absolute, and would like to think that, as we have all heard the saying, "what is right is right, and what is wrong is wrong." The exact opposite, in fact, is what is true. Right and wrong are our generalist values of a particular moment, under particular circumstances, applying to a particular group, and have no lasting value beyond that moment. Good and evil are entirely individual human judgments, and right and wrong are entirely momentary human judgments. We get in a lot of trouble when we make more of these human valuations than those made within the limited spheres of a particular person or persons, time, place and circumstances. Each right and wrong is individual, and does not in any way extend to the world at large.

MORALITY AND IMMORALITY

We go to church in order to learn how to be moral. We seek throughout all our lives to find ways in which we can become better persons. We punish our children by lecturing them or withdrawing privileges when they do something we consider unkind or disrespectful. We believe that the only stable society is a moral society. We send our young children to camps to teach them how to get along with other children while at play, as well as while at school. We think that a measure of other parents is how well they have taught their children about their manners. Young boys and girls are sent to become Boy Scouts and Girl Scouts, so they can not only learn home-making skills, but also learn proper behavior. A good scout is always trustworthy, loyal, helpful, friendly, courteous, kind, cheerful, thrifty, brave, clean and reverent. These values look pretty solid to us. It looks to us as if these are morals all children should learn everywhere. If they did, we would have cooperative, industrious and prosperous societies. It seems that these are also rather permanent values, which are fairly immutable. Our only failure, we think, is that we quite often don't practice what we preach.

The first definition of morals in the dictionary is *principles of right and wrong behavior; ETHICAL*. It lists as synonyms, *ETHICAL, VIRTUOUS, RIGHTEOUS, NOBLE*. These definitions and synonyms are no doubt quite correct, in the sense that they reflect the common usage of these terms in our society, but I have great problems with all of it. We get the immediate concepts that, not only are morals fixed values toward which humans strive, but that morals, ethics and goodness are the same thing, just expressed by different words. The concept of Socrates, that there is a fixed Goodness in the universe, finds due expression in Webster's. The Socratic concept that the more knowledge one has of this fixed Goodness, the more moral one becomes, seems alive and well in this dictionary. We tend to speak of a certain group or religion as having ethics and morals, as if the two words were one and the same. We speak, in our religions, of trying to emulate the perfect morality of our God, and by that means becoming personally more moral. As far as definitions go, I find all of this hugely wanting. Morality, to the best of my knowledge, has nothing fixed about it. Morality has all the solidity of loose statistics, varying greatly from one group to another, one situation to another and one time to another. Morality is variously applied according to the needs of that particular group at that particular time, in those particular circumstances. I also object greatly to the equation of morals and ethics. These two concepts are entirely different entities, each of which deserves a greatly clearer definition.

There are outstanding examples of the great variability of our morals, in any society one wishes to examine. Traditional Chinese culture, for example, was heavily influenced by Confucian concepts of morality. Confucian philosophy emphasized family loyalty, industriousness, and further learning that would support the family. The practical application of these values became a bit autocratic. All of the authority in the family was centered in the patriarch, who controlled completely all of the family's production, income and expenditure. The mother in the family had no authority and no independence. Sons and daughters were expected to be completely obedient to the father or older brother. No other values in Chinese life were more important than this family structure.

That all changed with the communist cultural revolution, culminating in The People's Republic of China, established in 1949. By decree and propaganda, the absolute authority of the family guardian no longer existed. The idea that children received sustenance from their parents, so that they could in turn support their parents at a later age, was considered highly inappropriate. Not only did this standard of behavior change, but a marriage law passed in 1950 established the equality of men and women. Marriages were no longer arranged by parents. Nurseries, kindergartens and nursing homes were established, enabling women to get an education and hold a job. The number of women students in universities increased by a factor of five. There were soon as many women scientists and technicians as there were men. The morals of Chinese society had suddenly changed. What was right and what was wrong for women to do was dramatically different, within a few years. Solidarity of the family unit lost, but the entire female population of China gained immensely in personal freedom.

The morality of Hindu society is another case in point. The structure of Hindu society was solidly based on the Hindu religion for millennia. Although that religion is so complex it is impossible to describe in a few words, there are a few central beliefs which served as a basis for that structure of Indian society. There is belief in an all-embracing Power which is the cause, source, foundation and eternal carrier of all creation. There is also the belief that there is a noble class of Brahmins, who achieve their status by birth, and who are supposed to represent the greatest sanctity, purity and social prestige a human can possess. In addition, Hindu belief contains the concept that life is a series of rebirths. According to this religion, each of those rebirths can occur at different stations in life. No person can change their station during that particular rebirth cycle, but the stage at which they are born the next time around is determined by good deeds or misdeeds each of them performs during their current life.

The practical application of this belief system resulted in a fatalism in Indian society. Whatever good or bad things happened to any one person were felt to be the result of good or bad deeds (karma) performed in a different life. There was no opportunity to change status and rise to a different level of education, pleasure or comfort during that life. This led easily to a caste system, consisting of some 3,000 castes and subcastes, the members of each of which felt themselves to be superior to certain other castes. Even the untouchables had their own system of subcastes, so that they could feel superior to some other group of people.

While I was serving part of my surgical residency at the VA Hospital in Cincinnati, in the 1960s, we had a group of Indian students come in for a period of time, to learn surgical techniques. One of them was a Brahmin, who looked quite stylish and handsome with a curled moustache, brown skin, colorful turban and clothing. That group had not been there for more than a few days, however, before a pile of nicely curled, pyramid-shaped brown soft stool appeared on the floor of the men's toilet stall, rather neatly covered in part with a paper towel. It appears that the toilet, since it was used by persons of lower class, could not be used by someone of his status. He did the only thing which, to him, was morally correct. Needless to say, as soon as our department chairman visualized and smelled the effect of this moral behavior, he found it necessary to request that this student go elsewhere for the remainder of his training. A different standard of moral behavior applied in our institution.

When India became a sovereign democratic republic, establishing a constitution in 1950, democratic ideals were incorporated into that lengthy legal document. This caused a cataclysmic change in at least the approach to the caste system. Fundamental rights were guaranteed to the citizens of India, including possession of property, freedom of speech, freedom of expression and freedom of conscience. Preventive detention for expression of beliefs was forbidden. Untouchability was constitutionally abolished. There were to some degree, quota programs established for citizens of lower class to attend universities, similar to those affirmative action programs which were established in the United States in an attempt to overcome racial prejudice. This attempt to eliminate the caste system in India has not been without turmoil. While the legal morality of the society may have changed, the *de facto* practice of distinct social classes still exists. Nevertheless, what was considered moral just a few years ago in India now had an entirely different face.

Following the communist revolution in Russia, in 1917, there was major political unrest as various political ideologies fought for control. A March revolution was succeeded by a November revolution, at which time conservative elements took control of Russian government. Some liberal policies adopted after overthrow of the Czar were abolished. Private property was not allowed; land was distributed to those who worked on the land. Workers were given no control over industry, banks were nationalized, courts and police were abandoned. Revolutionary tribunals were established as a system of justice, and a worker's militia was formed. Class privilege, titles and inheritance were abolished. Church and state were separated and the sexes declared equal. The calendar was altered to coincide with that used by Western nations.

Under these social changes, the economy did not prosper. There was sporadic civil war until 1921, when Lenin declared that the goal of a fully communist state was momentarily not achievable. The market system and market economy were partially restored. Farmers were allowed to sell their produce freely after they had paid their taxes. Small industries were allowed to operate freely, although large industry, transportation, public utilities and the banking system remained nationalized. Primary and secondary school systems were expanded, with the marvelous result of eliminating illiteracy among the youngest Soviets within ten years. As part of this new economic policy, morality codes were changed substantially. The family unit was no longer considered valuable. Free love was praised, abortion was legalized and divorce made as easy as requesting it. Children were encouraged to inform the authorities about parents who expressed anti-Soviet views. In spite of that rather draconian measure, resulting in parental internments, the economy finally prospered with this greater freedom of movement.

Further stringent changes in the moral codes of Russian society were soon to occur, however. Joseph Stalin seized central power in 1928, through a series of deft political moves. All lenience came to an abrupt end. Trade unions were abolished and all industry renationalized. Quality was traded for productivity as five year plans were developed, using unattainable goals. Technical skills were emphasized rather than academic knowledge. All artists, musicians, writers and philosophers were carefully monitored to make sure whatever they produced met party approval. All farms were organized into collectives, which were under tight central governmental control. Any citizens who protested any of these measures were tried, convicted, and either killed or deported. Several purges of more than a million Soviet alleged dissidents occurred, most of those being executed or dying in Siberian exile. It was not a good time to be a Russian. This puritanical state banned abortion, made divorce nearly impossible, and gave severe punishment for the crimes of juveniles and the insane. Any worker who did not display punctuality and complete obeisance was also severely punished. Shades of this deeply restrictive morality, during which no one trusted anyone else, still exist in Russia today.

Native cultures have shown morality codes even more deviant from those we consider to be usually normal, in our current societies. The history of the Australian continent is another case in point. In some estimates, the first humans arrived in Australia out of Southeast Asia some 250,000 years ago. These aboriginal cultures had a population of about 300,000 at the time the first European explorers found this continent. This native population consisted of about 500 tribes and sub-tribes, all of whom were semi-nomadic hunters and gatherers. Cooperation among members of each tribe was essential for survival, and religion was an essential part of their world. They believed in a mythical dream-like state which was the source of all creation, including humans, animals and all life. They were a part of the whole world, and the whole world was part of them. Life and death were both part of this same mythical continuum. They never feared death, and never felt isolated. The land on which they lived was jointly owned by all creatures, as part of this mythical state, which included both reality and dreams.

Patriarchal lineage was used as a means of identifying who belonged to what clan. There was no barrier to any man becoming a leader in his society, but women were excluded from learning the sacred rituals. Those were passed on exclusively to boys as they reached puberty. This ritual passage was not just learning religious practices and customs, but also consisted of significant body intrusions. Circumcision was the most important, and in most tribes was also accompanied by urethral meatotomy. There was bloodletting, piercing of the nasal septum, hair removal, scarring from fire, tearing out fingernails and gashing of the head, all proclaimed morally necessary by their mythology. For girls, there was also mutilation at the time of puberty, supported by the aboriginal mythology. For most, that consisted only of hymenotomy, but in some tribes, excision of the labia majora was also done.

Although the marriage of a sister and brother was taboo, as well as marriage of a man to his mother or mother-in-law, all marriages were arranged within the clan. Many of those were completed in infancy, and all marriages were pre-arranged for girls before puberty. Polygamy for men was considered both legitimate and good. Frequently men had two or three wives, and the most influential members of the tribe might have ten or twelve wives. There was no judicial system. All disputes were settled by the elder men, who had full authority in that clan. All of these practices were fully accepted by the members of the tribe as being moral and correct.

This strange to us but stable morality for several hundred thousand years came to an end rather abruptly as European explorers and colonists reached Australian shores. A Spanish expedition out of Peru landed at the New Hebrides Islands in 1605, naming that land Australia del Espiritu Santo. Dutch ships coming around the Cape of Good Hope headed for Java went too far east, landing on Australia in 1611. Further Dutch explorations found Tasmania and New Zealand. The voyages of James Cook in the 1770s led to British colonization. The British had lost the American colonies as a dumping ground, and needed someplace to relieve its crowded prisons. Australia served that purpose for British unwanted. These aboriginal customs and morals faded gradually as these cultures mingled, although not without strife between those natives trying to defend their several hundred thousand year old way of life, against the strange rules of these new invaders.

Down at the bottom of the paragraph in the dictionary which defines the various uses of the word morality, is this statement: *MORAL implies conformity to established sanctioned codes or accepted notions of right and wrong.* This definition, which is down near the last, is the definition which should be, in my opinion, first. Morality is never the same. It varies dramatically from group to group, time to time, place to place, and environment to environment. There has never been, to my knowledge, any fixed morality or immorality in the history of the human species. What works for us today, in our efforts to get along with each other in a peaceable manner, will not necessarily work for us ten years from now. I would hate to think, for example, that we were tied to bigoted racial prejudice forever because it was what our society thought was right, and that this right was fixed in stone. As we grow in our understanding of each other, and those things we need to do so that we can all survive, we should change our conduct, or in other words, our morals, accordingly.

My fear is that we are still too tied to Socrates. We still think that there is some universal morality or goodness in the universe that we can tie into by adopting certain religious customs, and feel that if someone else does not accept those same religious beliefs, they are tied to some universal evil in the universe. The result of that misology is the sanctioned forced death of several thousand innocent souls in the World Trade Center Towers. The result of that misology is the sanctioned misdirected blunders of the Bush administration, committed by a president and his advisors who may have meant well, but who were locked into the misdirected hatred of an archaic value system. The result of that sanctioned misology is the attacks of Israel on its neighbors. The result of that sanctioned misology is suicide bombing of Sunnis against Shiites. The result of that sanctioned misology is the hatred of the Iranian elite directed toward Israel.

Yes, we all do evil things to each other. Yes, we need to do whatever we can to redirect those acts of cruelty to some form of cooperation. As an intrinsic part of that redirection, we particularly need to give up our ignorant and immature concept of fixed values. There is no fixed good or evil, right or wrong, morality or immorality in the universe. These are judgments which have value only for humans, all of which are relative. We are still shackled to the chains of Socrates, and have been unwilling to break free from that prison.

Protagoras, where are you when we need you?

•

MORES, FAIRNESS AND JUSTICE

Mores refer to those collected folkways expressed by any certain society at any certain time in its existence. Mores change over time, as well as show variable expression from one group to another. These are the collective customs that are accepted behavior in that society. This word should not be confused with morals, although it often is used in that manner. Folkways are customs of any society that do not carry heavy value. There are frequently many different ways of doing the same thing, and folkways are those particular ways a certain society chooses to function, as opposed to other choices they have. Getting out of a waiting line to forge in up front, for example, is a violation of a particular folkway, but that violation does not usually deserve appearance before a judge, or jail time. Mores are those collections of behavior patterns which any particular society considers important, but not necessarily punishable by law. Perhaps it should be added, for consistency, that mores certainly have no connection to any fixed value system in any universe, anywhere that we know.

Fairness is such a nebulous entity. What is fair for an owl is not fair for a mouse. What is fair for a frog is not fair for a fly. What is fair for a human is not fair for a pig. What is fair for a shark is not fair for a human. Fairness depends entirely on our own personal point of view, does it not? Whenever we perceive that there is some impediment to our basic needs and fulfillment, while others do not have that same impediment, we consider ourselves to be unfairly singled out for punishment. When we face the odds in the game of chance, we want our odds to be just the same as those that face everyone else. What we are unwilling to accept, sometimes, is that the game of life is indeed a game of chance, and that this game of chance will not always turn our way. There will always be someone else who has gotten more with less effort than that we have expended. There will always be someone else who is richer, smarter, faster, prettier, sexier and/or more successful in life. Life, in that sense, is never completely fair. The sooner we accept the fact that we will always lose to the odds in certain parts of our life, the better off we will be, and the better we will make use of those odds that did turn out in our favor.

Having said as much about fairness, and our need to work with what we have in life, rather than think we have not been treated fairly because someone else got more, with less effort, does not mean that we should be fatalistic about our lives. This is not to say that we should not, at all times, do our very best to provide a level playing field, and present even-handed odds to all of us who are pursuing our dreams. That is one of the basic tenets of democracy. All members of a democratic society should have the same opportunities, as much as is in our power to provide, for their own pursuit of happiness. Although we recognize the importance of equal opportunity, we have many times in the past been blind to exactly what that means. Racial bigotry still persists; the rich are getting richer and poor getting poorer in our current business schemes. Vested interests pay lobbyists big bucks to get legislation passed that will benefit them and put money in their own pockets, as opposed to legislation that would benefit all the people. Legislators, who wish to get re-elected, do what the lobbyists tell them to do, rather than what their constituents need. These constituents are the people that elected those legislators to represent them and their needs, but that is not what is happening. Our elected officials are helping those who pay them money and are not helping us. The great middle class is shrinking, leaving more and more citizens without opportunities for higher education and personal advancement. That is what is not fair. We may not get what we want, and we may not achieve our goals, while others are able to do so, but each of us should at least have the opportunity to reach for those goals. Fairness does not mean equality. Those who believe that because someone else has more than them, they are owed extra largess, have it all wrong, although this seems to be the attitude that prevails in our welfare system. Fairness should mean only this: we should all have the same chance to play the game of odds, and show how hard we are willing to work to achieve our goals.

Justice has that certain ring to it, does it not? "Let Justice be served." We all have the feeling that justice is a necessary part of any stable society, as if it is an underlying basic or impermeable principle of human society. Some of this concept comes through in the dictionary, where one of the synonyms given is RIGHTEOUSNESS. It would certainly be easier for us if this definition were true, and we could depend on the same justice everywhere there is a stable society. Unfortunately, that proves to not be the case. What is justice for the Taliban is not justice for the Pakistani government. What is justice in India is not justice in China. What is justice in Alaska is not necessarily justice in Alabama. Justice is the punishment phase for those violations of values which any society holds dear. It is the way each society seeks to provide conformity, whether that conformity is the same as other societies or not. Justice is the way we enforce our morals. Since our morals vary remarkably from one society to another, so does justice.

Perhaps some will find this stance a bit too much. Certainly the argument has been raised by moralists that there are certain admonitions which are standard in most societies. Warnings against murder, theft and infidelity, such as are in the Ten Commandments, are common to most societies, as well as some form of punishment (or justice) for those who do not follow these rules. Unfortunately, activists for these commandments regularly violate them in their own lives. Killing is considered normal during a war, even worse when given euphemisms such as "collateral damage." Most of these activists approve of capital punishment, whereas killing another human, regardless of their heinous crimes, does not make the rest of us better people. Stealing from someone you hate may be considered a righteous thing to do. The rate of infidelity amongst the stationed in life seems to be about the same as with those who are less fortunate. Perhaps we should set our own house in order, before declaring that these are rules that everyone else should follow.

In addition, there are other deviations from these "norms" in our society, as well as in many other societies. Abortion is the law of the land, even though it means murdering an unborn life. Female infanticide is regularly practiced sub rosa in those societies where a premium is placed on male babies. Honor killing is considered by some to be cleansing when one group or family has wronged another. Having mistresses or many wives is still considered normal in some societies. Taking money and possessions from a drug dealer is considered a good thing to do. I speak not to condone or promote all these practices, but simply to make the point that every society establishes what works for them, no matter how deviant those practices may be from those of other societies. After having figured out what works the best for them, each society places a rating scale on its values, declaring some of them so important to them, they are considered "morals." That morality, and the justice system used to enforce that morality, varies tremendously from group to group, time to time, place to place, and circumstance to circumstance.

ETHICS

Has all this discussion about the impermanence of our value systems left us wanting? Perhaps we can find something more solid in whatever ethics are. I hope so. It is clear to me that we should not think of ethics and morals in the same breath. I do not agree with the definitions as listed in the dictionaries, or as discussed by ethicists in our encyclopedias. To reiterate my previous complaint, I think we will be much better served if we are able to differentiate the immense variability of morals from the standards of ethics. I have used the word ethics sparingly in this book so far, when describing the value systems of human society. That has been done purposefully, in order to separate the two concepts. Ethical basics, in my opinion, do represent generalities that can be used as solid guides of human conduct. I would prefer that we think of ethics as principles of human conduct which apply to all humans in all situations, and as such, represent a higher level of conduct than that found in our variable morals. I do not think that we should define ethics, as is commonly done, as a study of morals. That definition simply reduces ethics to the vagaries of human morals, which change like the weather, and are never the same. I find the discussions of ethics in our encyclopedias deeply esoteric and greatly wanting in substance. I would hope we can understand that human ethics are not just human morals, are not part of some mysterious Goodness which resides somewhere in the universe, and are not an obtuse philosophy filled with long esoteric words, the meaning of which is unclear to everyone.

Try on some of these terms for size: *meta-ethics, normative ethics, deontological ethics, teleological ethics, naturalistic cognitivism, non-cognitisism, commendatory invariance argument.* I fully confess my inability to understand what these terms mean, even after reading the material that describes them, and abjectly confess that I am unable to explain any of these theories to anyone else. Any attempt on my part to explain any of this would result in further confusion. Perhaps it is just as well to leave all of those terms alone. Most of those discussions of these terms seem to have a cyclical question, which we have already addressed. They all dwell repeatedly on the question as to whether there is an intrinsic Goodness in the universe or not, and what this means to human values. If one can accept, as this discussion has previously emphasized, that there is no intrinsic good or evil in the universe, and that all values are human values, then most of the above discussions, using the above terms, become moot.

If we think of ethics as not just a study of morality systems, not a part of some mysterious basic goodness, and not some esoteric philosophy, then we are obliged to say exactly what ethics are, rather than just describe what they are not. Actually, that is a pretty simple answer, because we have already been there in this book. A comprehensive human ethic has to contain four elements, each of which has to be present for those principles to form that ethic. There has to be love of your God with all your heart, soul and mind. There has to be love of your near neighbor as yourself. There has to be love of all distant neighbors as yourself. There has to be love of your enemies as yourself. Until all these loves are in place, as pillars, we are incapable of doing unto others as we would have them do unto us.

It may seem incongruous to you to include love of God as one of the pillars of human ethics, or overriding values. What we are talking about, after all, is the relationship each of us has with other humans, and how we should best get along with each other. What point is it to be discussing some far off entity, when what we really need to know is how humans should react to other humans? Actually, this pillar is the cornerstone of human ethics, as defined above, but it will need some explaining. None of the respect we show for other humans, constituting the other pillars of our house of ethics, comes into play unless we have gotten our own pillar constructed first. Once we realize what our own position is, in relationship to everything else in this universe, then we can figure out where we belong in relationship to other life. And there is a big caveat. This love of God, of which I speak, is not the same as that which most everyone else forms in their mind when they think of this term and its meanings.

Love of God is certainly a common perception of the human mind. Every seer, every prophet, every primitive tribe, every religion contains voluminous praise for the creator of all things and the guide for human life, whatever or whoever that may be. Those in these religions who have attempted to express their appreciation for this world and this life have struggled to find words which carry enough descriptive emotion to convey their humble feelings. Some of this has resulted in magnificent poetry and singing prose, some of which we have already quoted from the Book of Job and the Book of Psalms, in the section on good and evil. Buddhism describes the greatness of Heaven, or complete Enlightenment. The Koran is full of praise for the great one God, Allah.

THE EXORDIUM

IN THE NAME OF GOD

THE COMPASSIONATE

THE MERCIFUL

Praise be to God, Lord of the Universe,

The Compassionate, the Merciful,

Sovereign of the Day of Judgement!

You alone we worship, and to You alone

We turn for help.

Guide us to the straight path,

The path of those whom You have favored,

Not of those who have incurred Your wrath,

Nor of those who have gone astray.

2: 28. How can you deny God? Did He not give you life when you were dead, and will He not cause you to die and then restore you to life? Will you not return to Him at last? He created for you all that the earth contains; then, ascending to the sky, He fashioned it into seven heavens. He has Knowledge of all things.

2: 106. Did you not know that God has power over all things? Did you not know that it is God who has sovereignty over the heavens and the earth, and that there is none besides God to protect or help you?

This is, indeed, the crux of this matter. Love of God does not mean love of some mysterious goodness, which inhabits some mysterious nether realm of the universe. It does not mean love of some mysterious loving father figure, who is up there somewhere, directing everything that we do and everything that all others do. It does not mean love of some distant bureaucrat chief, who can be reached if we are sufficiently fervent in our requests, and who will then grant favors in our behalf. It does not mean love of a great boss, who will, if we have been good enough employees, grant us a paid retirement for an eternity. It does not mean love for the director of this major drama, who already has the plot formed in his mind and who knows exactly how all of this play on a great stage will end. It does mean bone-deep, gut-wrenching, soaring of the mind, abjectly on the knees respect for the vastness, complexity, and totality of this universe and its myriad mysteries. We should at all times be awestruck by this indescribable greatness of our universe, and our infinitesimal unimportance in the grand scheme of this universe, whatever that might be. We should be crawlingly humble at this opportunity to spend the brief times of our lives in this grand universe, and should treasure absolutely every minute of life. That means we should treasure, down to the deepest of our nerves, every minute of our lives – as well as the lives of all others, who have also received this most precious gift. This is the love of God, of which I speak, and which, if we have, sets the cornerstone pillar for the house of human ethics.

Praise be to Jesus for what comes next. Although he had many deeply serious flaws, he saw and understood, for the first time in human expression, all collected together, what the other pillars should be to build a house of ethics. That is not to say that the Buddha or Confucius did not also understand these concepts, and taught them to their students. None of that literature contains these concepts in such a startling manner, however, as that we find in the teaching of Jesus. He made three giant steps in understanding of what it takes for us to all live together peaceably, steps that no one else had articulated before so clearly. The first of those was an equation no one else had quite mastered. You can't just love your God with all your heart, soul and mind. If you truly do that, you have to also love your neighbor as yourself. The two have to both be present, combined in substance and strength, for this house to be built. This is the foundation for all ethics.

The biblical record indicates that Jesus had awe for the great power that created the universe, but in his thinking, personalized that awe so deeply that to him this great Creator was a loving father figure who he believed would guide him and protect him at every turn of his life. He lived his whole life with this faith that he would be cared for at every turn, and believed that this personal direction would, if he bowed to his gracious father's heavenly will, lead him to victory in his personal aims. He also believed that all others, who were his followers, were also being led to the goals of that great power. He intuitively recognized that all humans had to work together to achieve that unity with his heavenly father. He understood well that if there was not both this reverence for the Creator as well as respect of one human for another, better lives could not be achieved. For that vision, we are deeply indebted.

What Jesus saw intuitively, for perhaps the wrong reasons, we are now able to see with knowledge as to our place in the universe and understand with greater clarity. The deal is, it is us against the universe. This entity which has allowed us to exist and also sustains us, is also indifferent as to whether we are here or not. There is no God who cares, no planned goal for our existence, and no known existence after our deaths. Our species will be unceremoniously eliminated in due time, as are all species that exist. We are a species given a precious life for a limited time, in a limited space. In order for our species to survive the longest time, in the most productive manner, we have to understand that we are at the mercy of a universe which does not care whether we are here or not, and have to understand that if we do not develop the capacity to work together for our mutual advantage, neither we individually, nor our species, will last very long.

The other reason for that necessary combination of love for our God as well as love for neighbor, for us to survive most fully for the longest time, is the other deal. We are social animals. It certainly is possible for any of us, with great effort, to survive in this world, all by ourselves, for long periods of time. We can find edible food and/or grow it. We can erect shelter. We can, with preparation, withstand the ravages of nature. None of us, however, living a life singly, would be able to find complete fulfillment, and certainly would not continue our species while living in that confinement. Most all of what any of us has in our lives has been afforded to us by others who cared. This includes not only the love and direction of parents; it includes a community that cares enough about all its inhabitants to set rules and laws, to enforce them, to allow us to keep our possessions, whatever they may be. It depends on workmen who care enough about the products of their labor to do quality work, which will stand over time. It includes people who are willing to work together in concert and tandem to build homes which form a nest for shelter and nourishment. It depends on traditions of the past which teach us lessons about life and the contributions toward our welfare of those who have preceded us. It includes our mythology, which brings color and excitement to our lives. It includes community celebrations, where everyone can let go a bit more freely in revelry. It includes our blessed teachers, who bring us knowledge and wisdom to create order in our empty cluttered minds.

This combination of knowing that we are at the mercy of the whims of this vast, powerful universe, and that we need each other to survive the most fully, is precisely what should drive us to behave better. Saying it so simply may take all of the beautiful poetry out of those phrases, and leave us wanting to put the flowers back in our hair, but it certainly, to my mind, gives us a better understanding of what our ethics should be. While we laud these passages in the Bible, and are thrilled at the leap in understanding which they represent, I believe that they lose much of their meaning in everyday life. How in the world we translate those ethereal phrases into everyday action in our lives becomes an enigma to us, and fails to make any difference in our everyday behavior. Well here it is, in plain black and white. Know that we have no value in our immense universe. Know that we need all other humans working together for each of us to reach his or her fulfillment, and to make the best use of all our precious resources, so that we can all survive the most fully, the longest period of time. Know that there is a document, formed at the beginning of this country, which places these values in glowing, practical terms. That is human ethics. Perhaps if we understand them in these plain and simple terms, we will start working harder at them.

> *Matthew 22: 35–40. Then one of them, which was a lawyer, asked him a question, tempting him and saying,*
>
> *"Master, which is the great commandment in the law?"*
>
> *Jesus said unto him, "Thou shalt love the Lord thy God with all thy heart, and with all they soul, and with all thy mind.*
>
> *This is the first and great commandment.*
>
> *And the second is like unto it. Thou shalt love thy neighbor as thyself.*
>
> *On these two commandments hang all the law and the prophets."*

That is, indeed, all we need to know. Yet it was a bit more than his disciples could handle all at once. Jesus had scarcely caught his breath, before being asked to express the next leap of ethical understanding, in a telling parable. His disciples, still puzzling over the command to love their neighbors as much as their God, had to know just how far this neighbor thing was going to go. It took a story, using a neighbor they usually shunned, a Samaritan, and self-righteous pillars of their faith, a priest and a temple assistant, to bring the point home. Admittedly, we are on a bit of thin ice, using just this one story, to stabilize a house of ethics. It is a story found only in the gospel of Luke. Why the other gospel authors found this story too unimportant to include in their dictums is not clear. But it fits perfectly with the concept fully expressed above, and leads directly to the command to also love your enemies.

The command to love your enemies is found both in Matthew and in Luke, and, as such, appears to be a valid teaching of this prophet. It is the fourth pillar needed to build a house of ethics. Your neighbor is not just your next door neighbor, or your close friends. Your neighbor is your near neighbor, and your far neighbor, as well as the far neighbor who wants to kill you or do you harm. The implied extensions of those teachings have been fully addressed in the section on the moral advances of Jesus, and need not be repeated here. Love of God, love of your near neighbor, love of your far neighbor, and love of your enemy are the four moral pillars, which, when combined, are sufficient to build an encompassing fold of human ethics. Ethics, in my minority opinion, does not exist until all four of these elements are fully expressed by the human species. The practical ways these four elements can be expressed will require prolonged further discussion in later chapters. We do not need to struggle to find those practical ways, however. They find full expression in a document which is familiar to all of us, called the Declaration of Independence of the United States of America – and in the action of those remarkable individuals who showed us exactly what this Declaration meant.

HUMAN ETHICS

It follows that we are not there yet. We may at times get close, with certain acts of great compassion for other humans who have suffered great disaster, but who are otherwise unknown by us. We have many examples of heroic action taken by an observer, without regard for his or her own safety, trying to save another human who is in peril. We see devoted parents who give of all their strength and resources so that their children may survive, and do better than they have done. We see deeply empathetic individuals donate one of their kidneys for transplant, sometimes even to strangers, when that donor is moved by compassion for another human's need. We see sorrow for the loss of others, and loving assistance given to those who are trying to find a stable life again. We see remarkable acts of courage by firefighters, police, EMT's and soldiers. We see selfless devotion to the needs of other humans by health care workers. We see family units that stick together through thick and thin. We have major religions which emphasize compassion and mercy. All in all, we have a lot to work with. The foundation is there to produce an ethical society. We surely have not found a way, however, to make that ethical society happen yet with any consistency.

Some of what we have called ethical human behavior in the past, thinking that we have reached a plane above ordinary morals, appears to be a pretty bad joke, or significant naiveté on our part. Our war crimes trials seem to fall in this category. The victors congratulate themselves on having brought the losers to justice for those crimes they committed against other humans during that conflict. Learned judges are assembled from several countries, as if all that combined trial wisdom will bring an impartial correct decision. There is some sort of farce, speaking unkindly, that goes on trying to decide exactly who will defend these evil persons, so that this major social event has the semblance of a real trial. Witnesses are called to testify for the prosecution, and even a few witnesses are called to speak for the defendants. The defendants are sometimes asked to speak on their own behalf, in a somewhat forced weak attempt to justify these terrible things they have done. After this play is run on this international stage, sentence is passed on the accused. The sentences passed are usually drastic. All those who participated in creating this evidence and forming these sentences for these criminals then falsely congratulate themselves on having been highly ethical, and having brought civilization back to moral behavior.

These critical comments probably do not do the Nuremburg trials justice. These trials appear to have been an honest attempt by caring, intelligent people to make the world a better place, and prevent the horror of World War II from happening again. They felt that, if those who had committed these atrocities were called to answer for their cruelty, the world might be spared of seeing such depravity again. We have to agree that this feeling was shared by most all of us at that time. We believed that we were doing civilization a great favor by this attempt to put a halt to such destructive antisocial behavior. Little did we know that, in spite of these attempts to obtain justice, there were other atrocities waiting for us around the corner, in a seemingly endlessly cycle of cruelty expressed by one human toward another. We are supposed to learn from our history. Unfortunately, it seems, there are always young ones who are hormone driven, and who have not read these history books. All they know is their own particular needs or grievances.

At the end of that global conflict, the United States, Britain and USSR formed a military tribunal, which was later accepted by nineteen other nations. The focus of this tribunal was not Italy or Japan, but aimed squarely at those remaining Germans who had been most instrumental in carrying out that war. Twenty Four of the German high command were indicted on four counts: 1) crimes against peace, defined as the planning and execution of wars of aggression in violation of international treaties, 2) crimes against humanity, defined as exterminations, deportations and genocide, 3) war crimes, defined as violations of the laws of war, and 4) a common conspiracy to commit these above criminal acts. The defendants were given a copy of the charges made against them, were allowed to respond to those charges, were allowed to have legal counsel, and allowed to cross examine witnesses against them. During these trials the defendants presented two major defenses to those charges against them. One was that only the state could be found guilty of war crimes, since each person on both sides was just doing what the state asked of them. The tribunal replied that crimes of the state were performed by individuals, each of whom had to answer for his or her own actions. The second defense, that these were charges manufactured after the hostilities ceased, and not known by anyone during that conflict, was also rejected by the tribunal. Their response was that these acts were known to be criminal acts before the war began, and had not been created just for this occasion. The trials lasted ten months, ending in 1946. Twelve of the defendants were executed by hanging, three sentenced to life imprisonment, four to prison sentences of ten to twenty years, and three were acquitted.

There seems little doubt that the Nazis demonstrated unwarranted aggression toward the rest of the world, and that this degree of antisocial behavior had to be addressed. It would be just the same as if a man killed one of his neighbors, just because of that person's race or religion, was caught, charged with that crime, and then had to stand in front of jury and judge to answer to that unacceptable violent act. Our society falls apart unless those who try to tear it apart are not brought to answer for their bad behavior. In this sense, it was absolutely right to hold these war crimes trials against these wayward defendants, and seems appropriate that they were found guilty of these crimes. That part of these trials is not the part that raises moral questions, in my mind. The tribunal responses to the defense arguments also seem correct. Each of us has to answer for our own actions, regardless of what someone else is telling us to do. None of us can hide behind someone else's decision, if that direction is obviously, to us, going to be deeply harmful to society. We are pretty sure that war is a crime against humanity. It is very difficult to justify initiating a war on the basis of grandiose schemes and megalomania. About the only time war is justified is if we are defending ourselves against someone else's aggression.

The rest of this pageantry is open to serious question, I believe, for several reasons: 1) All war is a crime against humanity. To single out only this particular war as bad enough to warrant that label seems quite facetious. 2) War is war. You do whatever you have to do to win. To demand that both sides play by certain rules, reduces war to a game played by hormonal testosterone driven men, as if it were a game of football with referees on the sidelines. 3) Everyone conspires during a war. That is also what each side does in order to win. It is difficult to think that the losers behaved much differently than the winners, in this regard. 4) Most importantly, there was no attempt or intent to hold any of the Allies accountable for the atrocities that they committed during that war. They were without doubt, not blameless. Any kind of civilian death that would help the Allies win that war was, to them, fair game. After the Germans had been convicted, there was no corresponding trial for the Allied commanders. 5) The issue of capital punishment was not even considered. Regardless of the great atrocities that the Nazis committed, it is difficult to believe that adding additional murders to those millions of murders already committed, made the world a better place.

The first three of these objections I raise probably fit best in the category of realizing that these judges were simply trying to find charges that would stick, after the crimes had been committed. Although these charges were patently false, if held to the crucible of time, they were not amoral, as far as we can tell, or done with malevolent thought. Those war theorists who made them up were doing the best that they could do, with what they had, at that time. It will serve no particular value to worry about whether they were right or wrong in doing so. The fourth objection, however, raises a serious moral question. Until such time as the victors in a war are held accountable for their crimes against humanity, as well as holding the losers accountable for their bad behavior, we do not have a system of ethics. I have little doubt that holding this trial by tribunal was a moral act. It was an honest attempt to rectify what appeared to be a world that had lost its moral direction. It had to be made clear that such total disregard for human rights had to be addressed in the most vigorous legal way possible. Without the additional examination of the acts of the victors, however, these war crimes trials cannot be labeled as ethical. The fifth objection, as listed above, is likewise a significant moral question. We cannot consider capital punishment ethical, if we understand that ethics is about treating even our enemies with respect, and about deeply respecting the sanctity of life.

The Kosovo War Crimes trials in 2003, as another example, were quite a bit messier. Those provinces which comprised the Yugoslav nation had been the site of continued ethnic unrest through the Balkan wars, World War I, and World War II. The only power that held them together was that of the socialist dictator, Marhall Josip Broz Tito. All of the provinces, including Slovenia, Croatia, Bosnia, Herzegovina, Montenegro, Kosovo, Macedonia and Serbia, had some separatist activity. Of those, the worst agitation for independence was found in Kosovo. This province was situated south of Serbia and adjacent to Albania to the southeast, and had a large population of Albanian citizens. Their language, culture and education were chiefly Albanian. According to the Yugoslavian constitution, established in 1945, Kosovo was supposed to be an autonomous region, but that meant little in fact. Albanian separatists in Kosovo were brought to trial for subversive activity and jailed for their efforts. Tito did allow some degree of separate identity. He allowed the University of Pristina to become separate from Belgrade University, and allowed Albanian language education. Otherwise, all provinces, including Serbia itself, remained under the strict central control of that dictatorship.

That unity all fell apart with the death of Tito in 1980. There was almost immediately, in 1981, student unrest, and gradually increasing enmity between Serbia and Kosovo. Some 500,000 Kosovo citizens were arrested over the next 10 years over various charges of rebellion. That citizen unrest was fueled, in large part, by an economic crisis, and further fueled by the Serbian Orthodox church. The bishopric of that church was greatly concerned about the treatment of Serbian members of its church who lived in Kosovo, and continued to criticize the government for not being more proactive in the protection of its members. There was also some justified cause for concern about the lawlessness in Kosovo society. The Albanian mafia, seizing the opportunity afforded by economic depression, had become dominant in some communities. There were various reports of destruction and arson. The economy of Kosovo collapsed. Several hundred thousand Serbian residents immigrated back to Serbia, and several hundred thousand Albanian residents immigrated back to Albania. Kosovo fell under the strict control of the Serbian secret police.

This critically unstable political situation reached a boiling point in 1990, when Slobodan Milosevic, believing it was time to act more stringently to quell this rebellious province, canceled the autonomy of Kosovo. Albanian was no longer the official language, the professors at the University of Pristina were fired, and some 22,000 students expelled. Kosovo held a referendum, in which 98% of the population voted for independence, and elected a president. Serbia declared that both the referendum and the presidential election were invalid. Kosovo became radicalized, and there was soon the formation of a guerilla force called the Kosovo Liberation Army (KLA). It was funded in large part by the Albanian diaspora. Raids on Serbian arms depots yielded weaponry, and there was soon a full scale guerilla war. The KLA was labeled by Serbia as a terrorist organization, with ties to the Albanian mafia. Most of the international community agreed with that label, including the United States, but there was no action by the nations of the world to interfere in any way, during the initial phases of this conflict.

By 1999, it became impossible to ignore this festering conflict any longer. Some 250,000 displaced persons had faced winter hardships without shelter, and there was discovery of mass graves, where massacres had occurred. Neither side was blameless. Their hatred of each other led to large scale killing of civilians as well as soldiers. Attempts at diplomacy failed. Kosovo continued to claim its independence. Serbia, backed by Russia, believed that Kosovo should be part of the Yugoslav nation, and that this terrorist rebellion had to be squashed. The United Nations failed to act, but NATO did. According to the Rambouillet accord, formed by NATO in l999, Kosovo was to become an autonomous region, with the capability to hold free democratic elections. That accord was rejected by Serbia and Russia, and

Milosevic, as head of the Yugoslav nation, did not personally attend that conference. Without resolution of this internal war, NATO soon informed Milosevic that Serbia would be bombed into submission, until such time as it agreed to these terms.

The NATO bombing campaign began in March of 1999. The earliest targets were military objects, but those did not seem to make much change in the war. Targets progressively switched to the infrastructure of Serbia, including bridges and power stations. The most controversial target was the Serbian television broadcast station, which NATO claimed was being used for Serbian propaganda, but was nevertheless accompanied by the death of all in that building when those bombs fell. There was international protest at this tactic of the NATO commanders, but by that time, it didn't matter too much what other bombs fell. Milosevic had experienced enough trauma. He agreed to the withdrawal of Serbian forces from Kosovo, and the entry of NATO ground troops as a peace keeping army. By its end, the estimates varied greatly as to how many lives had been lost during this civil war. By some figures, more than 500,000 people could no longer be accounted for, and additional mass graves were encountered after the major conflict ceased. Even without overt war, sporadic ethnic cleansing continued long after an uneasy truce had been established.

There was afterwards, plenty of war crimes material to go around, involving all participants in that conflict. Slobodan Milosevic was indicted for crimes against humanity, violation of the rules of war, violation of the Geneva accords, and genocide. These charges were made not only for his decisions during the conflict in Kosovo, but also for the previous conflicts in Bosnia and Croatia. Cabinet members of the Yugoslav government were also indicted on similar charges. The Prime Minister of Kosovo was indicted for crimes against humanity, but later acquitted of those charges. Four of the KLA commanders were charged with war crimes, but later acquitted of those charges. NATO was severely criticized for its choice of bombing targets, as well the use of depleted uranium ammunition and cluster bombs. The International Criminal Tribunal, however, elected to not indict NATO for these particular war crimes. As for Milosevic, he was found dead in his cell while awaiting trial in the Hague.

In one sense, it seems improper to be hypercritical of the International Tribunal in these war crimes trials. There were egregious acts of inhumanity on both sides. Both combatants and their supporters needed to answer for their disrespect for human life. If we do not call attention to those wanton murders, even in time of war, we are not doing our job as responsible citizens. Only if those who show that disrespect are called to answer for their callosity, can we demonstrate that this type of behavior is unacceptable to the world community. Only if there is some penalty for this depraved behavior, can we hope that others will not be so tempted to behave in similar fashion. Certainly, there was a degree of international horror at the sight of mass execution graves, and a hope that we would not see that type of human behavior again. Unfortunately, as we know now, that hope proved to be vain. There have since then been killing fields around the world, including Ireland, Rwanda, Darfur, Palestine, Afghanistan and Iraq.

While it may be appropriate to call these war crimes trials an attempt at morality, they certainly were not ethical. Ethics demands that all combatants answer for their inhumane actions. That did not happen in this case. The KLA commanders were indicted, but had no penalty assessed for their actions during this war. Accounts of Serbian soldiers being bound with barb wire and dragged behind cars, and of women being repeatedly raped, were not investigated further. Three of the witnesses against Ramush Haradinaj, the former prime minister of Kosovo, were killed. Two were shot to death, and a third died in an automobile accident. The NATO command was not asked to answer for their use of depleted uranium and cluster bomb artillery, which was guaranteed to produce civilian casualties. It was obvious that those most influential countries in the International tribune did not want Kosovo to pay for its bad behavior, wanted only Serbia to be punished, and were unwilling to confess guilt for their own wrongful actions in this conflict.

A valid human ethic, which provides a level playing field for all combatants in any conflict, asks that each treat the other with respect, with every attempt to compromise rather than resort to violence, has not happened very often during national disputes. Whichever side does not get its way has immediately resorted to the killing of those who hold different needs and different beliefs. We are certainly a far cry from the full application of human ethics. That's understandable in the sense that we are still evolving as a human species, and still have not yet learned how to be compassionate at all times. We have just now been thrown together as a world community, and are only slowly coming to the realization that unless we learn to cooperate with each other, we will all suffer. How we achieve that cooperation, to achieve a human ethic, has so far escaped us.

Unfortunately, some of our most influential modern moralists have not yet bothered to make that necessary distinction between morals and ethics. Richard Taylor, for example, in his book, *Good and Evil*, does not at any time bother to make a distinction between the two, even though the remainder of his discussions about human values are exceedingly astute and germane. Peter Singer, Professor of Ethics at Columbia University and the University of Melbourne, is the author of several outstanding books on human value systems. Professor Singer blandly states that he uses the two words, morals and ethics, interchangeably, finding it unnecessary to define one as separate from the other. In spite of my admiration for these two gentlemen and their works, I find this lack of definition rather trying. Perhaps being so concerned about semantics and dictionary definitions does not have a great deal of value, and I would be better off to leave these definitions as they are. On the other hand, most of communication consists of understanding what the other person is talking about. If we do not define morals as those human actions which are accepted within each group as what, for that group, gives them the best chance of success and long term survival; and do not accept ethics as those human actions which are based on the overriding principles of love of god, love of near neighbor, love of far neighbor and love of enemy, then we are not on the same page. Ethics, in my opinion, should only be conceived as those guiding principles of human conduct which are above any moral system, and apply equally to all humans in every situation. Moreover, I believe that we have so far only been discussing human ethics. If we wish to use the phrase, a universal ethic, then we have to realize that this ethic applies to all of life, and not just to humans. I offer my apologies, but will continue to shake my head, until such time as those who discuss human values, even in the most erudite, thorough and intelligent manner, realize that they are discussing two entirely different entities, depending on whether they speak of morals or ethics. I will also shudder, if anyone speaks about a universal ethic, and does not include all other life as a part of that discussion.

A UNIVERSAL ETHIC

The house of a universal ethic has to be built on a rock foundation, if it is to survive through mental earthquakes, floods, tornados
and hurricanes. Our choices are rather limited. The only rock formation that will not allow our house to shudder and fall through all those
challenges is the knowledge that all our values are human derived.
Any attempt at a universal ethic which uses a fixed Goodness somewhere in the universe, a universal lodestone of love somewhere in
the universe, a universal father figure telling us what to do, a bureaucrat in the sky who answers requests and takes sides, or any other
external figure of imagination, is doomed to fail. We have to begin
building our house by knowing that all good, evil, right, wrong, fairness and justice are only human derived. The universe does not care.
The only thing the universe knows is that stuff happens. The only
reaction of the universe to any human situation is to allow those
organisms which adapt to their particular environment to survive,
while it unceremoniously kills those who do not adapt to their environment. The universe is not, as best we can tell, carrying us to some
grand and glorious goal, other than allowing us to evolve. It's quite
the opposite, as a matter of fact. The universe, according to everything that we know about it, will kill us all at that time it may happen,
whenever that may be. It will not, at that time it eliminates us, have
any feeling of sorrow or pleasure. It will be just the same to it as
moving a boulder from a mountain top to a valley, or exploding a
dying sun. The universe has no morals or ethics; only humans worry
about such things.

Protagoras certainly understood this foundation, and tried to
tell us this is the only way we can understand the different values
different people attach to the same problem, depending on their
particular position. We didn't listen then, and still aren't listening
very well now. Richard Taylor understands this part of morality, as he
discusses Protagorean theory, but we aren't listening to him.

> Laws and practices vary from one time and place to
> another, and none is objectively true or false….the
> thoughts, feelings, and opinions of human beings are the
> measure of everything.

Peter Singer understands the great defects of our value systems all too well, but we are not listening to him either.

> *The crucial moral questions of our day are not about homosexuality or abortion. Instead moralists should be asking: what are the obligations of all of us in the affluent world when people are slowly starving in Somalia? What is to be done about the racist hatred that prevents people living together in Bosnia, in Azerbaijan, and in Los Angeles? Are we entitled to continue to confine billions of non-human animals in factory farms, treating them as mere things to serve the pleasures of our palate? And how can we change our behavior so as to preserve the ecological system on which the entire planet depends?*
>
> *Ethics is no part of the structure of the universe, in the way that atoms are.*

We have been led badly astray by Socratic philosophy, as fostered by our religions, because those concepts are what humans find most comforting. Everyone likes to think that there is a grand reason for us to be here, and at some time, a glorious future. We all would like to think that there is some source of infinite love and strength in our universe, which, if we can convince it to be on our side, will guide us through any confrontation, and lead us to victory. We would like to think that no matter how difficult life is, we will, at the time of our death, be allowed to live in comfort and pleasure for an eternity. The pervasive quality of this wishful thinking in human society fogs our brains, leading us to make really bad decisions about how we relate to other humans. Rather than make the very best of the life we have, we leave it up to some distant power, or other life, to make society better.

We need some powerfully strong morals to serve as the four pillars we insert into this rock foundation for our house of ethics. We already know what they are, and no others will do. For an enclosure of ethics that can survive all punishment, there has to be love of our God, love of our near neighbor, love of our far neighbor, and love of our enemy. When these pillars are in place, other moral I-beams fit securely on them to carry our flooring, and support the frame for our walls and roof. The implications of this ethics system are not vacuous. Love of God does not mean love of some ethereal mysterious father figure. It means awe and humility at the vastness of our universe, and abject gratitude for this magnificent opportunity to live, to love, to think, to learn, to grow, to understand. Love of neighbor is not just the matter of liking someone who lives next to you. It is the deepest respect for all humans everywhere, whether they are your friend or foe. Most importantly, this overwhelming respect for our own life, and all other humans, cannot be just confined to humans. If there is this gut-filling respect for life, it has to extend to all life. If our value system does not include all life, it is not a universal ethic.

Why should we worry, you may say, if our future is so bleak? If we are not here on this earth as part of a grand plan, what value is there in being alive, you may say? During my radio station interviews, if they continue long enough, I can be pretty sure that at least one of the callers will express great dismay at being told they have only this one brief knowing existence, regardless of how many other universes may exist, and no great force in this universe that cares about them. They feel abandoned, unwanted, unnerved, and aimless. My attempts to tell them that what this really means is the great necessity to live every moment to the fullest, make absolutely the most contributions to the human race we can while we are here, and treasure every moment of this beautiful life, do not satisfy them. They are not consoled unless they can believe that a great good God loves them and will let them live forever. I personally find those concepts appalling. They take away the urgency each of us should feel at obtaining the greatest fulfillment of our minds and making the greatest contributions towards the lives of others while we are here. We should worry about our ethics because that is the way we can, as a human species, survive the longest time with the greatest fulfillment.

Those ethics, to be universal, must include the deepest respect for all life. Even animal rights activists do not sometimes carry this concept far enough. Their concentration on the cruelties of animal farms is well deserved and badly needed, but it should not stop there. All of life is interrelated. All of life is interdependent. All of life is dependent on the same resources existing on this single planet. If we do not understand that what affects one species affects all other species, then we do not understand enough to survive very long on this planet. We cannot poison our streams, lakes and oceans with industrial and animal waste, and not also poison all those creatures that live in that environment. If we poison our environment, then we have poisoned the food sources for all of life. We cannot deny that animals also have emotions. Animal mothers grieve abjectly in pain if their children are killed or lost. We cannot deny that, since all of life is interrelated and interconnected, all other life has just as much right to exist as the human race. Consider this: the planet earth, if humans were suddenly eliminated, and only other animals remained, would have a much greater chance of surviving in a stable state for the next million years. We are the cancer of this earth, and we are turning it into a contaminated dump. The only way we are going to survive for any length of time will be to adopt that universal ethic, which shows humility before our God, humility before all other humans, and humility before all other life.

This deep and abiding respect for all life, which considers all other life as essential for survival, does not mean that we can be irrational about the human situation. Although we often choose to not think about it very much, none of us survives without something that lives being killed on our behalf every day. Killing, unfortunately, is a part of life. All the food that we eat in order to exist, has been alive at some point before it enters our mouths. To us, maybe we just consider that material on our plates a source of protein, fats, carbohydrates and minerals to be enjoyed by our palates and processed by our body factories into energy sources, vitamins, enzymes, hormones and salt solutions that support our remarkably complex inner society. Without that sustenance, we would not be able to move, communicate, love, have pleasure, or think grand thoughts. We euphemistically refer to this constant killing for survival as the "circle of life." It is not a nice little circle in a colorful diagram, or something we can shove in a storage bin, so we don't have to think about it for years. It is what is necessary for animal life to continue; all animal life dines on other life in order to survive.

While we are obliged to accept that all animal life kills other life, this does not mean that it should, at any time, be callous. It means exactly the opposite. That means we understand that all life is interdependent, and whatever killing we do should be the least disruptive of other life as we can manage, at all times. This has far-reaching implications. It means that sport fishing and hunting, while those may a great source of pleasure for those that do so, is not ethical. It must be a real thrill to catch a swordfish in the ocean with a reel and line that can barely take the strain, fight with it and play with it for hours, then land that monster beautiful fish. How satisfying it must be to have our pictures taken adjacent to that fish and demonstrate our power over something so strong, and our masterful finesse at pulling it out of the sea. That's something to show the rest of the world with pride. Unless that fish was filleted and placed in that fisherman's freezer, however, because he needed that food to survive, or unless it was given to the poor, who had no other meal for that day, that catch was unethical. Expedition hunting, in order to shoot a moose and hang its head on a wall, is unethical. Going out in the field with trained dogs, straining with your eyes, ears, soft breath and quiet tread, waiting for that rush that comes when the quail take off to the sky in fear, to see how many you can bag, is unethical, unless those birds were needed for the sustenance of that hunter. Going on a safari to get the thrill of danger and the thrill of power that comes with killing something so big or so fierce, is unethical, if the only purpose is to hang a trophy on a wall, or have a story which inflates our personal egos. If we only kill that which we must have in order to survive, and do so in the manner which is least disruptive of other life, then we are ethical.

This deep respect for all life has many other implications, as well. We do not at this time, unfortunately, live in a world where other animals and humans live in mutual respect. The Australian aborigines did, until the colonists came from Europe. The American Indians did, until the Europeans landed. They worshiped the game that they hunted, because they understood that, without that game, they would not survive. They understood that their game, they, and their environment were all part of one entity, and that they had to deeply respect all parts of that world, because all parts of that world were interrelated. The Great Spirit was in the land, in the water, in them, and in all other animals. They were right. That respect has vanished, as humans have populated all lands, and developed megacities, where all food is shipped in. Animals have become objects, to be manipulated as protein sources, without regard for their pain or discomfort. This devaluation of other life devalues us too. We are using other animals for the convenience of their taste, in megafarms which waste our grain resources and contaminate our lands, streams and oceans. If we look at our survival with understanding, the only animal products we should eat are those which we must have for survival. All other foods should be fruits and vegetables. Any other way of nutritionally sustaining ourselves is unethical.

This deep respect for all life also has significant meaning for the manner in which we treat our own kind. There has always been a controversy about how we manage the weakest and most vulnerable members of our species. Is it moral to take the tube feedings away from a woman who was once beautiful and vibrant, but who is now, after an automobile accident, no longer able to communicate in any appreciable way with her loved ones, has frequent seizures, and often grimaces as if in pain? Is it moral to no longer feed an elderly person who is incontinent of stool and urine, who can no longer recognize her family, and whose Alzheimer's disease has progressed to the point of vegetation? Is it moral to consider infanticide for a baby that is born deformed and ill, with a loud heart murmur, a baby that obviously will lead a short life of pain and vegetation? Is it moral for a woman who has been raped to have an abortion, even though the fetus is now at 7 months gestation? These questions and others of equal difficulty puzzle our minds and challenge our intellects. We search in our souls for the right answers to these and similar questions.

Peter Singer, a world recognized moralist who has thought deeply about these subjects, preaches a morality of utilitarianism. He understands with great clarity that our morals are not derived from some super being God, or some mysterious Good source in the universe, but are derived from us. He understands that morals are an accumulation of those behaviors which are acceptable in various societies. What works is what is moral for a utilitarian. Singer, however, in spite of the depth of his understanding in other areas, leaves me greatly wanting. He never clarifies whether he is talking about morals or ethics, which leaves me believing that he does not fully understand either of those categories. His theory of usefulness leads him to believe that infanticide is acceptable up to eighteen weeks of age, and that euthanasia is acceptable if that is what the patient wants, for good reason. While he takes those stands uncomfortably, he feels obliged to do so because they fit with his other utilitarian morality schemes.

Singer has also paid a bit dearly for those pronouncements. A lecture at Saarbrucken, Germany was intercepted by angry protestors, who were incensed at his stance that infanticide may at times be justified for handicapped babies. His lecture at the University of Zurich was interrupted by protestors, who greatly objected to his support of euthanasia, when that was the patients wish, for some good reason. Singer felt obliged to answer to those angry outbursts by adding an additional chapter on those topics in the second edition of his book, *Practical Ethics*, and also discussing those protests in the preface to that edition. He appears to be quite correct that his views on both these subjects were misinterpreted by those unruly crowds, and certainly is correct to object to the censorship of his free speech, particularly on a topic of this nature, so germane to the events occurring during the Nazi purges and mass murders. What Professor Singer fails to understand, however, in my opinion, is that there is a good reason to raise strong objection to infanticide and euthanasia, other than a visceral and emotional outburst against any treatment of human subjects that smells anything like the treatment of Nazis against Jews.

Singer is correct to make the point that Greeks allowed infants whom they considered to not have an adequate chance for a normal life, to die by exposure and starvation. He is correct that many societies in the past have believed that those elderly members who are no longer able to make significant contribution to that community should be encouraged to go off and die, or else have their death ritualistically hastened. This is not ancient civilization, however, and we have to make those decisions which give all of us who live at this time the opportunity for the longest and most successful life. He is most certainly, in my opinion, not correct that there is no slippery slope when human killing is condoned in certain categories that are not connected to self-defense.

> There is, anyway, little historical evidence to suggest that a permissive attitude towards the killing of one category of human beings leads to a breakdown of restrictions against killing other humans.

I am not sure exactly what books Professor Singer has read that lead him to make this statement, but my readings of all books, throughout all my life, my interpretation of the world news, and my personal experiences in life, have taught me exactly the opposite. Once you condone human killing in any category, for any reason, it becomes easier to condone that murder in other categories. There are always going to be vested interest groups, who, for various reasons of fear, greed, envy and egotism, will want to stretch that allowance a bit further, to satisfy their own particular selfish needs. Utilitarianism may theoretically justify voluntary human killing in certain categories, but if it does, it is not a universal ethic that applies equally to all living things. Singer should know that, particularly in Germany, there is ample evidence that a doctrine which condones human killing in any category can be carried to the point of societal suicide. Contempt breeds contempt, and callosity breeds callosity. Killing breeds more killing. I simply don't know how many more examples any of us need, to convince us that infanticide and euthanasia are not ethical practices in a humane society. Perhaps those actions can be labeled as moral practices, if they are fully accepted in those communities that use them. There is no way, however, this can be considered ethical. A universal ethic demands a deep and abiding respect for and effort to preserve all life. Killing can only be condoned when it is needed to preserve other life.

I have spent my entire career fighting death, and trying to make the most moral decisions I could, on a daily basis. I have hundreds of times said, when we had tried everything, and the patient had not responded, "Okay, let's call the code." I then had to deal with the grief of family members who were not yet ready to accept that death, and deal with their sorrow in ways that were as compassionate and understanding as I could muster. I have dealt with cancer on a daily basis, particularly those who were not curable, and who were dying slowly by degrees, in pain. I have had to deal daily with severe pain issues, requiring large doses of narcotics, administered in any way that they can be administered, until those patients obtained relief of pain. I had to suffer, when they suffered. I dealt daily with the needs of patients who were going through the stages of death and dying, as well as deal with those same issues in their loving family members. I had to look for unclosed circles, and help them tie those ends, to obtain closure, so they could go peacefully. I have personally struggled thousands of time with the statistics, trying to interpret for patients what their chances are of success with surgery, and what can happen if that surgery fails. Every time I have opened a chest to take out a lung tumor, I have marveled at the magnificent intricacy of the human heart and lungs, and determined, at each time, that I should do whatever I can do to preserve that godly magnificence. I have hundreds of times counseled families for days about their loved one on a ventilator, and what the chances are that that particular patient will ever be able to come off, and breath on their own again. I have gently tried to lead them to their own conclusions, whenever that was to be, as to when it was moral to pull the plug, and let their father or mother go. I have had to ask very gently, many times, if they wish to keep their loved father, mother, brother or sister alive to satisfy or own needs, or if it would not be kinder and more loving to let them go peacefully. I have had to make rending decisions daily in the operating room, in the ICU and on the cancer unit. Through it all, I kept looking for an ethic that would apply for all patients, in all situations. I did not find that ethic clearly expressed in my religion or my surgical journals. I found it mostly in the courage of my patients, the steadfast love of their families, and the devotion to the needs of others in compassionate nurses. These are the things that I have learned in the past 48 years, from that practice.

1. Life is an exceedingly precious one time gift.

2. Few of us understand that we have only one chance to live this one life right.

3. Few of us treasure our health, until it is gone.

4. As a result, few of us make the most we can of this one precious gift of life.

5. None of us is fully prepared for death.

6. There is no eternity of each unique life. It comes by chance and leaves by chance, permanently.

7. Good things happen to bad people, and bad things happen to good people.

8. There is always a way to relieve pain and suffering.

9. Every death is unique, occurring in its own special circumstances.

10. None of us is entirely ethical; some are almost never ethical.

I do not believe there is any justifiable philosophy that can condone taking any life, other than from the necessity to continue other life with meaning and potential. I believe that the only universal ethic is one which includes humility before the grand mysteries of our universe, humility before all our neighbors, including our enemies, and humility before all other life. I believe that all life can end without pain and/or suffering. I believe that if an infant is so deformed, that life would be a misery, it may be kinder to let that infant go. I believe that such a death can be allowed without pain and/or suffering, and should not arrive by killing. I believe that terminally ill patients should be allowed to die when their time has come, and should be given relief of their pain and/or suffering, until that death occurs. I do not believe that infanticide or euthanasia can be justified in a universal ethic. I believe that any category of moral killing, other than that necessary to sustain life, is, in fact, immoral, and will beget other killing on false moral grounds. I believe that each death is an individual event, and that there is no set moral rule that covers each of those deaths. I believe that each of us who is faced with making moral decisions at that time of someone's death should ask ourselves one question; "What would I want done for me, if that were me in this position?" I think at those times each of us needs to reach into our souls, make the best empathetic decision we can make, based on the information we have, then move on with life.

Sometimes it seems as if we are light-years away from this universal ethic that applies to all of life. We know what it should be, but so far have been miserable failures at knowing how to make it happen. That ethic seems, for one, to be covered by a dense, dark shroud of religious beliefs that will not let that ethic become visible to us. It seems many times as if our religions are doing whatever they can to keep us from becoming an ethical species. Our religions have, on one hand, given us some marvelous moral guides to good behavior. At the other pole of their belief systems, however, they preach very immoral behavior. They tell us to treat with disdain, shun, punish, or kill those who do not share their particular faith. These same religions, with their wonderful morals, also preach some awful concepts of human behavior. They tell us very strange things, such as that there is a God of the entire universe that takes sides in human conflicts, or that there is some other mysterious life that is more important than this life. These misleading beliefs delude us, and lead us into deviant, harmful human behavior. We need to understand that how these dark religious shrouds have stymied our every effort to be ethical.

We also find, at every turn, we are dealing with a species that still runs a great deal on fear, egotism and greed. We are having a whole lot of trouble switching from a species that found itself in isolated groups, each trying to defend itself against the invasion of natural disasters, other animals, and other humans. Each of us seems to still be in that mode of "our group against all other groups." We believe that we must fight to get what we want and need, or we will not survive. There was certainly good reason for this attitude and practice for the last four million years of human history. Now, for the first time, however, things are different. We are no longer isolated human groups. There is no longer any one group, nation, race, color, religion or genetics that deserves priority over other humans. We are one world, where all peoples interact and interrelate. We are not only one world for human beings, we are one world for all of life. Unless the human species can find a way to humbly respect all other humans, and all other life, we are not going to survive much longer. How many nations have to develop atomic bombs before some hot head pushes his or her button, and the whole earth becomes hotly radioactive? We need rather desperately to examine what we can do to guide these base human emotions into ethical, rather than self-destructive, behavior.

Just because we are not there yet, does not mean that we should not continue to reach for the stars of a universal ethic. The reasons for doing so have become rather compelling.

THE SEVEN SINS OF ABRAHAM

This discussion so far has tried to make the point that the morals of Judaism, Christianity and Islam are, in part, greatly misdirected. A good segment of what each of these religions is telling us to do gives us wonderful guidelines for our behavior. Unfortunately, other major parts of these religions encourage us to be miserably destructive of our societies. The examples given in the preceding chapters on these religions have, I would hope, demonstrated these points. This discussion has also tried to clarify just exactly what our value terms mean, and how we should use them in our interactions with each other. How to correct these grievous moral errors becomes the next question. We can't correct our attitudes toward each other, and learn how to become compassionate, supportive communities, unless we understand the basis for our wayward and self-destructive morals. Perhaps this is oversimplification, but I believe that these immoral directions of our religions all began with the rationalizations of those ancient Israeli tribes. Their self-centered ideation served as the ground substrate for those false concepts which were basic to Judaism. Those concepts were added to, in part, by Christianity and Islam, at the inception of those religions. The sum total of that anthropomorphic thinking forms a group of seven errant perceptions, which are differently emphasized, but shared by these religions. I believe this group of seven hypotheses to have been such grievously false guides, I have taken the liberty of labeling them as the seven sins of Abraham.

I would immediately add the disclaimer that it is not these religious beliefs, in and of themselves, which are the root cause of human misbehavior. The root cause of human immorality is fear, greed, jeal-

ousy and anger. Whether or not we encourage the expression of these
destructive attitudes, and how accepting we are of the excuses made
for these antisocial expressions, are the problems. If we have religious
beliefs that foster this destructive behavior, it becomes terribly convenient to use our religions as those excuses for our species suicidal
behavior. It is simply the way we have allowed these concepts to be
used that has been so deadly.

Okay, so maybe Abraham had a whole lot more than seven sins.
Maybe all of us have quite a few more sins than that. It is, of course,
a play on words, following the example of St. Gregory the Great, who
in the sixth century classified the seven deadly sins of Christendom as
pride, covetousness, lust, envy, gluttony, anger and sloth. According to
the thirteenth century religious philosopher, Thomas Aquinas, these
were the seven deadliest sins because these particular sins were
sure to give rise to other sins. These are, no doubt, traits which all of
us have to some degree, and need to de-emphasize as much as we
can. Abraham was, probably, little different than the rest of us in this
regard. These human traits, however, are not the ones of which we
speak at this time. Both the Bible and the Koran trace the patriarchal
origins of Judaism, Christianity and Islam back to Abraham, through
his sons, Isaac and Ishmael. The basic ideology of these three religions traces back to those religious concepts that existed at the time
of Abraham. That shared ideology, although it has altered somewhat
over time, was nevertheless well expressed in Genesis, at the time
of Abraham, and now, with its later additions, falls easily into these
seven categories; this ideology has plagued the human species since
that time. I would submit that these seven religious concepts have
repeatedly served as the rationale for all those self-destructive sins as
listed by St. Gregory, and a whole lot more. These seven sins of human
behavior have not lain without these religions. They have lain within
them. Although each of the three religions attributed to Abraham,
Judaism, Christianity and Islam, have their own beliefs that they add
on to these basic concepts, demanding that their followers accept that
particular interpretation, the commonality of these religious concepts
is striking. The expressions of these shared beliefs have far-reaching
consequences for human behavior, however, much of them not good.
These are the major shared beliefs of our Abrahamic religions, each of
which misleads us from reaching a universal human ethic.

1. There is an all-powerful grand Creator, who began the universe with a design and a purpose. This Creator is still creating, and controls all events in the universe at all times, including all events in the lives of humans.

2. The human species is an integral part of this grand plan. As major players in this grand scheme, we not only have a purpose for being here on earth, but also have a grand destiny.

3. Humans were made in the image of the Grand Creator, who was male. We look like Him and He looks like us.

4. We, as humans, can communicate with our Grand Creator. If we are sufficiently fervent in our requests, and our need is sufficiently great, our requests (prayers) will be answered, with outcomes in our particular favor, as opposed to other humans, life, or inanimate objects.

5. All objects and life which exists on this planet earth were given to humans by this Grand Creator, to use as we see fit, for both pleasure and sustenance.

6. The Grand Creator and sustainer of the universe is totally good.

7. All those who adhere to a certain combination of mythology, which includes these basic concepts and a few others, will be granted an eternal life of pleasure, free of pain and distress. Those who do not adhere to these particular concepts will be shunned or tortured for an eternity.

On top of these common myths, Judaism demands that all humans everywhere accept their contention that the Jewish people, and only the Jews, have an exclusive contract with this one and only Grand Creator. They are the chosen people above all other people. They demand that all other nations accept their eventual superiority over all other nations, or else be punished. On top of these common myths, Christianity demands that all humans accept Jesus as a divinity on earth, or else undergo torture for an eternity. On top of these common myths, Islam demands that all humans accept that Muhammad was the last and greatest Prophet, who spoke the true words of the one and only

God of the universe, or else be killed. Unfortunately, each of these religions has been true to their word, demanding total adherence to their wayward mythology. For all those humans who do not agree with this mythology, these religions demand punishment. For these reasons, each of these common myths deserves examination, each serving as a primary religious pardon for immoral human behavior.

A PURPOSEFUL CREATOR

We cannot deny that this universe was created. We are here and this planet is here. We see magnificent snow covered shaggy peak mountains, beautiful blue lakes, lush green meadows, vibrantly gorgeous colors, violent storms and erupting volcanoes. We see an abundance of life in myriad forms and species, all of it in a dynamic, pulsing cycle of interaction. We look to the heavens and see stars. We have instruments that tell us some of these stars are galaxies, consisting of billions of other stars. We are told that there are billions of these galaxies, and that the extent of the universe has not yet been measured. We are amazed that our sun is a star, consisting of a constant nuclear explosion which is 93 million miles away. We are surprised to learn that this particular planet, where we live, has a hot rotating liquid iron core, producing a magnetic shield. If this planet did not have this shield, we and all life on this planet would not exist. The nuclear electromagnetic storm from our sun would have stripped all life away, were we not in this protective cocoon. We keep searching for life on other planets in our universe, but so far only know of this one special planet which has the conditions just right for us to exist. We are in awe of the vastness and strangeness of this universe, and grateful for our lives. It seems to many of us as if everything we learn about our universe simply reinforces our opinion that this universe was created for some grand purpose, which specifically includes us, particularly on this special planet.

We really struggle with the concept that maybe something simply happened. Everything that we do in our lives, we think, is done for some reason. There is no one muscle twitch or stray thought, as far as we know, that did not occur for some reason. We search for food, comfort, security, love, shelter, and fight off bugs, critters, other human scum that tries to take away from us whatever we have been able to garner. Every blessed little thing that we do, as we attempt to survive, has a reason behind it, we think. Physicists tell us that we live in a world of complete balance, to the extent that for every positive, there has to be a negative. They even say some really far out things, such as that whatever happens in this universe, in order to have balance, must be happening in an opposite way in an opposing universe. What? Some of this is more than our weak minds can comprehend. We are doing well to even understand that every little thing that we do has an effect somewhere else, in some way.

God concepts have been with us since the beginning of humans. We understood that everything else seemed to have its place, and that there had to be something or some force which caused the events around us, leading to food or famine. We had no knowledge of any physics, astronomy, archeology, electromagnetic fields, gravity laws, nuclear particles, back when these God concepts were formed. It just did not, at that time, make any sense to think that the world we saw around us was not here for a purpose. We find it easy to understand why ancient nomadic Arabic tribes believed that some great power had begun our universe, and did so for a purpose. Now our brightest scientific minds tell us that this is not so. They tell us that there is cause and effect in that part of the universe we can observe, but that there is no design or purpose in any of the underlying natural events in the universe.

Our physicists tell us that this order we see in the interaction of large objects does not apply at all in the basic building blocks of our universe, subatomic particles. Everything there is chaos and random. There is no design or purpose in any of the basic energy fields which make up everything else that exists. Our astronomers tell us that the universe is exploding and has no discernible borders. There is no detectable progression toward a determined end that they can see. Our archeologists tell us that life began 14 billion years ago on this planet, but remained primitive, confined to the seas, until the Cambrian explosion some 600 million years ago. There is some evidence that this rapid change in life forms was preceded by meteoric and volcanic activity. Our naturalists tell us that there is no design in the gradual evolution of more complex forms of life. They say it is blind and purposeless. Those organisms that adapt to their environment, through natural genetic variation, are selected to survive, whereas those that do not adapt to changes in the environment are summarily disposed. Our socialists tell us that Homo sapiens didn't go anywhere for 400,000 years, then suddenly colonized the earth's surface about 40,000 years ago, without discernible plan, simply looking for a sustaining environment. As opposed to the understandable primitive beliefs of the ancient Jewish tribes, no one who now studies our universe and our solar system sees any plan for any of it, and sees no external manipulation of these random events.

The obvious question to ask is "Why should it matter?" If there is not a Supreme Creator who is still manipulating events in human affairs, for a grand purpose, why does this make a difference in human behavior? The great problem that I see with this belief in a Grand Manipulator, is that it makes us inactive fatalists. We become immoral by default. If we believe that everything that happens in this universe, and everything that happens in our lives, is the result of various manipulations carried out by a Grand Creator, we simply accept them as necessary, regardless as to how cruel or immoral those events may be. We simply say that "the Lord moves in strange and mysterious ways," and make no effort to correct those wrongs. The glaring fault in believing that everything in our lives happens with a purpose in mind, in my opinion, is to leave us pathetically actionless. If we believe that everything terrible that happens to humans occurs at the wish of a Master Manipulator, according to His complete direction, we do not immediately see that any catastrophe or cruel act involving another human is an immediate call to action, for each of us to do whatever we can to alleviate that suffering. If we do not act, thinking that everything in the world happens because it is the wish of a Grand Creator, we do not prevent that cruelty from happening again.

HUMAN PURPOSE

A simple and charming hymn, taken from the Books of Psalms and Chronicles, attached to a pleasing melody, and frequently used in church services, has these words. *I love you Lord, and I lift my voice, to worship you. O my soul, rejoice! Take joy, my King, in what you hear: May it be a sweet, sweet sound in your ear.* The instructions say that this hymn is to be sung with feeling. On the opposite side of the same page is this hymn, used for that same worship service, the words and music composed by Michael W. Smith. *O Lord, our Lord, how majestic is your name in all the earth! O Lord, our Lord, how majestic is your name in all the earth! O Lord, we praise your name! O Lord, we magnify your name. Prince of Peace, Mighty God, O Lord God Almighty.* The Lord words are to be stretched out for two bars as this hymn is sung. These hymns do not stand alone. Much of our hymnals are devoted to songs of varying intensity and tempo, praising the Lord. Some drag, some are beautiful, some are militant, and all are to be sung with great feeling.

One has to wonder exactly what Lord those who sing these hymns so lustily are addressing. What picture is forming in their minds as they profess their enthusiastic love for their Lord? Is it the glorious picture that is painted on the ceiling of the Sistine Chapel? Is it a shimmering force field out somewhere in space? Is it a kindly father figure who has shown benevolence toward them in their lives? According to Gallup poll numbers obtained in February, 2001, only twelve percent of the American population believe that humans came to exist without the direction of a God. Virtually all who are worshiping in this manner believe that their God looks like them, created the universe, is still creating, is in total control of their lives, does whatever He wants with their lives, is a male, and has a plan for each of them, as well as a grand plan for the human species. There is great emotion involved in this singing. These songs are sung fervently, with loud voices, expressing the deep feeling that there is some great force in the universe to which they should pay their deepest homage, because that force knows exactly where they are headed, and when they will get there.

There are many good reasons for these concepts in the human mind. For one, we are highly anthropomorphic creatures. We imagine that everything else looks like us and behaves like us. We let possums, bears, cats, dogs, birds, mice, spiders, rabbits and all kind of other creatures do our talking for us in the cartoons. We picture Mother Nature as wearing a white robe, having a halo, and waving a wand. We think of the Tooth Fairy as looking like Peter Pan. We pictorialize the Christmas spirit of giving as a jolly bearded fat man wearing a red suit. And we give the controlling forces of the universe the appearance of a regal, robed elderly man. We can't help it; it's just the way we are.

Secondly, we see everything else run by cause and effect. So should we; surely there is someone or something that knows why this began and where it is headed. Thirdly, we find that this is often a life of great travail. If we could not believe that there is some goal to be reached, it would be difficult to tolerate the suffering that exists. We find it greatly comforting to think that there is a reason for all the frustrations of our lives.

There is exceeding comfort in believing that this life is being guided to a grand purpose. Yet all the natural evidence we have is otherwise. Everything that we have been able to learn about our universe, and our place in it, tells us that this solar system began by chance, this planet formed by chance, life began on this planet by chance, the human species evolved by chance, all interactions in this universe occur by chance, and our future will be determined by random events in the universe. As far as we can tell, there was no purpose in our beginning, and will be no purpose in our end. Yet rather than throw our hands up in despair, we should rejoice. We should fall to our knees in homage that we have been given this magnificent gift of life for this short period of time. We should shout our praises for this opportunity to learn and create, grow in knowledge, sense beauty and share love. For all these things we extend our utmost praise and soulful devotion. We love this chance opportunity to have these marvelous lives for our short period of time on this earth. That reverence remains unchanged, even though we are here, as best we can tell, without design and without purpose aforethought.

The great problem with this concept of constant external manipulation, grand human purpose, and a glorious future, in my opinion, is that we become lazy beasts. We think that all we have to do is survive day to day in the easiest way possible, and human destiny will happen anyway. It is not up to us to make things better, according to this belief. That, I believe, is a terrible error. When any one of us sees some aspect of deprivation, pain or sorrow, it is completely up to one of us to alleviate that suffering, and prevent that pain from going on further. Each of us has only one life and one chance to make this a better society. Human society does not provide life, liberty, equal opportunity and freedom from pain unless one or more of us takes the effort to make it so.

IN THE IMAGE OF GOD

It would be inappropriate to think of our unwillingness to understand our world around us, unless we place those things in human terms, as a flaw of the human character. It is a bit strange, if you look at our propensity to think of all things as human oriented, since we are so insignificant in the totality of the universe. On the other hand, it's just the way life is. It is probable that all animal life sees the world only in its own terms. As far my cats are concerned, the whole world revolves around them. Dogs think that this is a dog's world, and cows, most likely, only see the world in cow terms. The raccoon that comes up on my back porch at night to finish off whatever cat food is left, it is likely, sees the entire world only through raccoon eyes. She is raccoonomorphic in just about the same way as we are anthropomorphic. All of life sees the rest of the world in the terms that it can understand, in order to survive. There is nothing wrong with that, unless, of course, you happen to believe that any one of those individual species perceptions is the only true perception. Because, make no mistake about it, our God was formed in the image of humans; it was not the other way around. We formed an image of the underlying force of the universe to fit our limited knowledge, at that particular time in our nomadic history.

And there are certainly great flaws in the grandiose thought that we have an appearance similar to the all-powerful force that began this vast universe, if that is how it began. If we look like the Grand Creator, we think, there must be more than just a resemblance there. Two creatures who look alike must share more traits between them than just looks. If the Grand Creator is all-powerful, then we must possess some degree of that power also. If we look like the Grand Creator, who has command over the entire universe, then we must have some degree of control over that universe also. If we look like the primary force of all things, we must be getting close to our ultimate goal of being like that God. If we resemble the genesis of all things, which exists forever, we would think that we, through devotion to cause, may also achieve eternal life. If we look like our God, there is a reason why we should to be able to communicate directly with that powerful force through our prayer, and be granted favors or rewards, just for us, from our look-alike. We do indeed, derive great comfort from thinking that we look like the great force that began and sustains the entire universe. We also, unfortunately, derive great delusions from this concept of likeness. Those delusions lead us to make some pretty awful decisions about how we treat other life and the resources of our one and only home.

This narcissism is understandable. All life behaves that way. What is difficult to understand is why, now that we know better, we cling so doggedly to this absurd concept of likeness to the supposed grand power of the universe. We appear unwilling to accept that the universe is so vast, our importance in it cannot even be measured mathematically. We appear unwilling to accept that we are a miniscule life form in a mediocre solar system, which exists in a galaxy of billions of other stars, which exists in a universe which has billions of other galaxies. We appear unwilling to accept that we have only one precious life in this universe, both individually and collectively, which must be treasured. We appear unwilling to realize that we cannot in any way control this universe, and cannot live forever. Until we accept those limitations, and our total dissimilarity to whatever great force may be behind this universe, we are not going to make very sound decisions about how we treat each other.

OUR PERSONAL GOD

We hold dearly to this belief that the force which controls all things in the universe is open to each of us personally. It gives us great comfort to believe that when we are in trouble, we can turn to this primary source, who or which will listen to us and help us through our grief and trouble. We are not quite sure how we could make it through life, if we did not have this source of solace and redirection. It makes all things possible, through our darkest hours. When we are in great doubt, we pray. When we hurt, we pray. When there is inconsolable loss, we pray. When we need to reach out to others, we all pray together. And after we have prayed, we almost always find some degree of peace. We still have pain or need, but it no longer seems as intense. We have found some type of equanimity, in some degree, allowing us to go on with life. How precious our prayer is to us, when we suffer through times of need. Our Lord seems to be quite distant, and far removed from menial human problems. But we think we can, without question, pray to the source of all things, and our prayers, we believe, will be heard by our God. We are sure that if we pray, some events will be altered by our God to benefit only us, as opposed to other life or objects. Our God is on our side, we believe, and our God loves us. According to our religions, our God is always listening for our prayers, so that He can direct us in the right path.

Football players on rival teams each pray to their same God that they will win this game, asking for intercession on their behalf. Soldiers in war, afraid that each day may be their last, pray with fervor and tears that their God will give them survival and victory. Those soldiers on the other side are also praying to their God, the same God, with tears and numbing fear, asking their God to intercede on their behalf. When the bombs fall, killing fathers, mothers and children, those remaining on the ground still alive raise their eyes to the sky and say, "Please, God, spare us!" When the captors threaten to behead, entire families fall to their knees, pleading with their God to turn the hands of the tormentors. When the earthquake hits, those who are running from the buildings are praying as they run, "Please, God, make it stop!" When the homeowners see the house next to theirs explode in the forest fire, feel the intense heat, and run in fear to their car, they are saying, "Please, God, show us a way out of here!" When the child is abandoned because her parents were killed by the marauders, she huddles in a corner, shivering and starving, saying over and over, "Please God, help me, help me!" Were it so simple.

There are multiple delusions derived from this belief in a personal God, who is on our side. One great delusion is to think that there is a force which manipulates the events of the universe, which will, at our request, step in to change things for our benefit. That's the wrong emphasis. It is not a matter of getting some outside force to make things different. It is a matter of our adapting to whatever challenges come before us, and making the best of those challenges that we can. The universe does not care, and has no personal interest in anything we do. It is certainly natural to pray with all our souls. What we can't expect is to receive succor from something, somewhere else. Most likely, that will not happen. It is entirely up to each of us to do what is necessary to make a better life, for ourselves and our companions in this journey, whenever our lives are challenged.

We get it terribly wrong when we think that it is a matter of our God favoring us over all other people or things. That's not the way it works. The only way we will survive is for all of us to work together on this planet. When we think there is a controlling force which manages all things and all life, which we can convince to act just for us, it becomes a matter of our group against all other humans, all other life, all other objects, all other natural disasters, all the rest of the universe. Historically, much of that fear has been valid. There has always been something or someone out there who is willing, on any whim, to take everything that is precious away from us, including our lives. We are in a fight for survival on this planet. That fight will rapidly come to an end not in our favor, however, unless we learn to respect all other life, and all our resources. What we cannot do is let each faction of our species believe that there is a God of all things who is in their favor and only in their favor. Unfortunately, this is precisely the narrow minded message that the dogmatic factions of our religions preach. They foster this concept of a personal God who will intercede especially on the behalf of a certain group possessing certain beliefs. That splintering of our effort is greatly harmful to human society. Unless all humans and all other life are included in this battle for survival, we will lose, and lose rather soon.

We have to understand that there is no personal God who will intercede on our behalf, at any time in our lives. We have to understand that there is no certain group, people, race, nation or religion that is favored by our Creator over any other people. We have to understand that when we pray, we lay ourselves open. We have to at those times set aside all our preconceived conclusions, all our greed, anger, jealousy, pride, physical and emotional pain, and ask ourselves what is right, what is the way out, what should we do with our life at this time. What would we want someone to do for us in this time of dire need? Then, during this time of laid bare self hypnosis, the answer comes. Our prayer has been answered, by us, reaching deep inside of us. Perhaps at these times we do place ourselves more in contact with all others, and with everything else in the universe, and momentarily lose our self-centeredness. If so, that is as it should be.

THE EARTH IS OURS

If we read it in the Bible, it has to be so, we think. There are fewer passages in the Bible we have taken more to heart than these early passages in the Book of Genesis, which command the human species to use whatever resources the earth possesses in any way that we wish.

Genesis 1: 20-30. And God said, "Let the waters swarm with fish, and other life. Let the skies be filled with birds of every kind."

So God created great sea creatures and every sort of fish and every kind of bird. And God saw that it was good.

And God said, "Let the earth bring forth every kind of animal – livestock, small animals and wildlife." And so it was. God made all sorts of wild animals, livestock, and small animals, each able to reproduce more of its own kind. And God saw that it was good.

The God said, "Let us make people in our image, to be like ourselves. They will be masters over all life – the fish in the sea, the birds in the sky, and all the livestock, wild animals, and small animals."

So God created people in his own image. God patterned them after himself: male and female he created them.

God blessed them and told them, "Multiply and fill the earth and subdue it. Be masters over the fish and birds and all the animals." And God said, "Look! I have given you the seed-bearing plants throughout the earth and all the fruit trees for your food. And I have given all the grasses and other green plants to the animals and birds for their food." And so it was. Then God looked over all he had made, and he saw that it was excellent in every way. This all happened on the sixth day.

We have certainly loved this command. We have consumed the resources of this planet earth with wild abandon. There has seemed to be no end to these riches, and we have reveled in mining them with glee. We have discovered deep deposits of coal, oil and natural gas, enough to heat billions of homes, even in the harshest of winters. We have found vast prairies of rich soil, producing bountiful crops of delicious fruits and vegetables. We have found great grasslands that support large herds of cattle. We have been able to produce great crops of grains, to raise large herds of pigs and billions of chickens. We have had the luxury of vast timberlands, which have given us wood for our houses and paper for our commerce. We have found precious metals and flashing diamonds, adding great value to our lives. We have discovered a bounty of mineral and plant substances which can be used as medicines. Where there are stable societies, we have eaten well, enjoyed great health, have had pretty, whole babies, have had the opportunity to grow and learn until late in life, have blossomed under an explosion of accumulated knowledge, and have extended our expected longevity from thirty to eighty years. This has been quite a marvelous ride, in spite of all the tragedies, wars, pestilences, earthquakes, tornados and hurricanes.

Now comes a rude awakening. We have been suddenly hit in the face with the realization that what the Bible told us has carried a rather stringent price. All of this largess has been on a contingency plan, and now we have to pay a hefty price for not taking care of it very well. Like all valuable property, it has to be nurtured and maintained. If it does not receive that respect and repair, it rots and falls down. The resources of our earth have resemblance to an old barn, which housed animals, held hay crops, protected equipment, and served as storage. Now our barn has cracks in the walls, and is starting to lean where some of the wood support is rotting away. It needs shoring beams, caulk and paint to continue to serve its purpose. We have to take care of it, or it will no longer be there to support us.

According to those who follow this depletion of our resources carefully, we are fast approaching a critical stage in that overuse, depletion and pollution. The ocean is no longer an endless bounty of food to be placed on our plates. Many of the largest fisheries in the northern Atlantic have collapsed. The rich topsoil of our most productive cropland is being depleted by inches every decade. About one half of all our virgin timberland has now been used, and it will not take long, considering the burgeoning world population, to deplete the rest. Our streams and rivers are so polluted that some of them catch on fire, and others sporadically kill millions of fish. Some of the largest predators in our oceans are so filled with mercury that they are no longer safe to eat. The land of Mesopotamia, described in Biblical times as a fertile crescent, is now so affected by salinization that it has completely lost that fertility. That process of polluted salinization of valuable cropland has progressed rapidly in India, Turkey and Australia. Our polar ice cap is melting – the earth's refrigeration system is disappearing rapidly. As the snow melt continues in our mountains, the water supplies for those arid farmlands and large cities that depend on that deep blanket of snow, are disappearing.

Our entire way of life is now deeply threatened because we believed that this biblical directive gave us free license. Well, we may be the top predators on this planet, and may be able to manipulate much of what happens here on our behalf, but we have been rotten stewards. Now, what we can expect in the near future, is to face shorter rather than longer life spans. We can expect to get more cancers and autoimmune diseases, which make us miserable and take our lives at an earlier age. We can expect to have poorer health, because all our food will be contaminated. We can expect to have more babies born with cleft lips, deformed arms, missing fingers, hydrocephalus, spina bifida, and mental deficiency. We can expect spells of crop failures and famine in pockets around the world. We can expect wars over water rights and mineral rights, fishing rights. It has, indeed, become time to pay the piper.

There are a few who think that this depletion and pollution of our resources is not so urgent, because we can find other resource on the moon, or establish a colony on Mars, so that our species will survive. That thinking is to my mind, fantasy land. The planet where we live is unique. There is no other planet like it we have found anywhere else in the universe. If there is such a planet, it is at this time unreachable. It is high time we realize that this biblical directive is not a command to use all the resources of the earth with wild abandon. It is a command to use those resources wisely and judiciously – or else gradually do ourselves in.

GOD IS GOOD

We seem to prefer religious concepts that we find comforting, rather than those that make sense. Our major religions had the opportunity to accept the common sense of Protagoras, but chose to ignore it. Instead, they chose to adopt an ideology which avers that there is a Grand Ruler of the entire universe who is totally beneficent, at least toward humans. They found the imaginative goodness God concepts of Socrates and Plato much more appealing for their religions. Besides, that idea of a totally good God fit in quite nicely with their other egocentric concepts. Being made in the image of a god, having a purpose here on earth, being able to communicate directly with this Grand Ruler, and having command over all the resources of the earth were nice companion pieces to this additional bit of egocentricity. If our God is totally good, and we are partially like this God, then we must be basically good creatures. All we have to do is hone that natural predilection of godlike goodness a bit more, in order to become godlike ourselves.

We have already addressed the major problems that this concept of a totally beneficent deity presents in our value systems, necessitating the additional creation of an evil persona, who can be blamed for all the bad things that happen to people. That conflict then leads us to a constant battle between a good god and a bad god, the end result of which, according to this theology, will be destruction of the entire earth and its inhabitants in an apocalyptic battle. As if this theology was not already far-fetched, additional really strange concepts have been layered on top, such as that all humans who have ever lived will come back to life at the time of that apocalypse in order to be judged for entry into a Heaven or dismissal to a Hell. Doubtless these concepts carried great meaning for those who formulated them, and gave them direction in their lives, but they no longer make any sense.

Moreover, this concept of a totally good deity is not at all necessary for a vibrantly alive religion. Confucianism does not believe in any deity at all, much less one that is totally good. The stability of human society and the achievement of individual morality are all that is important to this social order. Buddhism does not concern itself with a search for some intrinsic goodness, embedded somewhere in the universe. Buddhists concentrate on individual enlightenment, gradually lifting themselves away from the cares and pain of life, while still remaining completely a part of this life. For the Hindu, their God is everywhere and in all things, certainly not confined to an entity off to itself in a bin of goodness somewhere. For the American Indian, their Great Spirit was in all things, including the earth, land, water, animals and themselves. All these things were good, and all these things belonged together. There was no distant Goodness that had not yet been reached.

We can only partly blame Judaism for this totally good God concept. According to this faith, their God can do some pretty mean things, but always in an attempt to teach the Israelis a lesson. Their God can, according to Judaism, create great disasters directed toward people of their faith and other faiths, in order to punish those who mistreat Israelis, or punish the Israelis for not obeying His commands and laws. For the Israeli faithful, their God is all in all, really a good guy, but in an exclusive manner only. He is totally good only for Israelis, primarily because he will one day lead them to be the dominant nation over all nations on earth. This concept of a total Goodness which is directed only toward Judaism, then pales in comparison to that theology adopted by the Christian and Islamic faiths. In these faiths, their God is pictured as an elderly bearded wise-appearing gentleman who is dressed in a white robe, shining with light, surrounded by a dazzling aura, and radiating with purity. There is no greater Goodness in the entire universe, according to these two faiths, than that found in their God.

It is probably fair to ask the question, "Why does it matter?" "What is so wrong about having the concept of a God who is totally good?" "If people are trying to become good like the God that they worship, does this not lead each of us to lead better lives?" Not only is this an appropriate question, but the answer is probably yes. If each of us worships a God who, in our minds, wants each of us to be a good citizen, it is then likely that each person will make decisions about their reactions to other people, which show mercy and empathy. Those followers of Judaism, Christianity and Islam are clearly told that this is the way they are to behave.

There are multiple passages in the Old Testament where the God of the Jewish people tells them he expects them to be good, as He is good. He demands that they follow moral behavior, or else be punished. Isaiah, for example, who pulls no punches, makes it pretty clear how the god of Israel expects his people to behave.

Isaiah 58: 6–10. "No, the kind of fasting I want calls you to free those who are wrongly imprisoned and to stop oppressing those who work for you. Treat them fairly and

*give them what they earn. I want you to share your food
with the hungry and to welcome poor wanderers into your
homes. Give clothes to those who need them, and do not
hide from relatives who need your help."*

*"If you do these things, your salvation will come like the
dawn. Yes, your healing will come quickly. Your godliness
will lead you forward, and the glory of the Lord will protect
you from behind. Then when you call, the Lord will answer.
'Yes, I am here,' he will quickly reply."*

*"Stop oppressing the helpless and stop making false
accusations and spreading vicious rumors! Feed the hungry
and help those in trouble. Then your light will shine out
bright as day."*

In the New Testament Gospels, Jesus is constantly telling his disciples and his questioners that they must give to those in need. He tells his disciples to sell everything they have and give it to the poor. He tells a rich man he cannot get into Heaven until he gives up all his riches. He says that it is easier for a camel to go through the eye of a needle, than it is for a rich man to go to Heaven. He admonishes his disciples that they must always be humble.

*Luke 14: 12–13. Then he turned to his host. "When you
put on a luncheon or a dinner," he said,"don't invite your
friends, brothers, relatives, and rich neighbors. For they will
repay you by inviting you back. Instead, invite the poor, the
crippled, the lame and the blind. Then at the resurrection of
the godly, God will reward you for inviting those who could
not repay you."*

Muhammad, although he is consistently war–like toward anyone who does not believe his message, and although he preaches violence against those of other faiths, repeatedly instructs his followers that their God will not allow them into Muslim Heaven unless they show compassion for those other Muslims who are in need.

*Koran 2:177. Righteousness does not consist in whether you
face towards the East or the West. The righteous man is he
who believes in God and the Last Day, in the angels and the
Book and the prophets; who, though he loves it dearly, gives
away his wealth to kinsfolk, to orphans, to the destitute, to*

the traveler in need and to beggars, and for the redemption
of captives; who attends to his prayers and renders the alms
levy; who is true to his promises and steadfast in trial and
adversity and in times of war. Such are the true believers;
such are the God-fearing.

It's not the emphasis on a deity that is totally good, and who expects us to follow that example, that gets us into trouble. It's the other side of that coin, the bad side. At the time these concepts were formed of a totally good deity, there were not advanced mathematicians, astrologers with telescopes, or particle physicists there to give us their knowledge. There was no one there to tell us that the whole universe runs on balance, and that for every positive there has to be a negative. Yet the men and women who conceived of a totally good God knew very well that this just didn't explain everything. There was far too much evil in the world, in human terms, to not balance that total goodness out with some entity that was totally bad. There was no other way to explain all the suffering, pain, hunger, deprivation and sorrow that humans experienced. That necessitated the invention, in the human mind, of another powerful deity, who specialized in tempting, degrading, punishing and torturing humans. That invention, necessitated by the concept of a totally good God, has gotten us into a whole lot of trouble.

It would be okay if we used the concept of a truly bad power in the universe as a garbage dump, where we could put all the bad things we think of doing to other humans. If, whenever we had an evil thought, we could just throw it away into this bin of badness, get rid of it, and then get back to thinking good thoughts of compassion, cooperation and respect, we would all be better off than we are now. That, unfortunately, is not how we have used this concept of an Evil Persona. What we have done is to assume that if there is another human being who does not belong to our particular group of "good" people who worship a totally good God, that person must worship the really bad God, and must for that reason be evil. There is only one treatment that is appropriate, we think, for someone we have designated as evil. That person, religion, group or nation must be shunned, punished or killed for its evil ways. Only then, we think, will we have been faithful to our one, true, totally good God.

The human mayhem that has resulted from this concept of a

great God of total goodness, counterbalanced by the total evil of a great Satan, has been astonishing. What is even more disturbing about these concepts is that we have no evidence they exist. As far as we can tell, the universe has no value system. The evidence so far is overwhelming that the forces which control the universe are judged as good or evil only in human terms. Everything that we have learned about our universe tells us that it is completely impartial. The universe does not care. The only good or evil it contains are those value judgments which we give it. Why we persist in imagining these great good and bad deities, which lead us to kill each other, is a great question.

AN ETERNITY OF PLEASURE
AND
AN ETERNITY OF TORTURE

Although all of the previously discussed religious concepts, which are common to the religions of Abraham, have contributed greatly to our moral misdirections, it is difficult to find one of them that has been any more damaging to our moral compass than the concept of an afterlife, as it has been described in our religions. As with the other beliefs which are common to these three religions, perhaps thinking that there is some way we keep on living after our bodies decompose is not so bad, if we just left it at that. Quantum physics, after all, leaves room for other existences in other universes. There shouldn't be any harm in letting someone think that there is some other life, if it gives them comfort. The problems, once again, are the other ramifications of that belief. Our interpretation of what this means has been to think that this life has no value other than doing what each of us has to do to get to the next life. We also think that if, only a select few are chosen to live an eternity of pleasure, all others who do not adhere to that certain set of beliefs are going to be tortured for an eternity. This whole set of afterlife beliefs has fostered, for those reasons, an unending stream of mental and physical abuse of the human species, simply because these beliefs have served as a most convenient excuse for awful human behavior.

Our religions have taught us that this promised paradise is some-where else, and is not anywhere on this land that we know. We are told that this life, although ephemeral, is used as a measuring stick to determine if we deserve to be given an eternity of peace and happiness – or not. We are admonished to live by the laws of our particular religion, so that we may achieve this great reward, after our earthly life. We live our lives a bit intimidated by this threat that maybe we won't make it to this promised land. There are, our religions tell us, rather severe punishments if we do not live within these confines of our religious prisons, whatever that particular religion may define as that prison. Exactly where this paradise is, remains quite a mystery. It has to be somewhere, because we are told that a select few of us are going there. All the other humans, that being the majority of all those who have ever lived, will, because they have failed to fully comply with that faith, not get to this place, but will instead be tortured for an eternity. We are encouraged to regard our current lives as rather meaningless, other than holding these religious beliefs. As a matter of fact, we are sometimes encouraged to throw our lives away early in order to get to that judgment day sooner. We are sometimes led to commit torture, since that is what is going to happen to infidels anyway. For those who believe, based on this myth, that this life is meaningless, and/or believe it is acceptable to torture infidels, we have a great argument ahead of us.

Confucius believed in Heaven – sort of. He is quoted as saying, "There are three things of which the superior man stands in awe. He stands in awe of the ordinance of Heaven. He stands in awe of great men. He stands in awe of the words of sages." I am not sure exactly what concepts were in the mind of Confucius when he spoke of Heaven, but believe that he was probably expressing awe at the great power, mystery and vastness of the universe. We can share that same wonderment, should the universe be labeled with this term. Confucius wisely carried that deep reverence no further. He gave no guarantee of an afterlife. He believed in reverence toward parents and the elderly, study, enlightenment, and expressions of loyalty, courage and wisdom. He taught these values to his students. His later students emphasized that there was not an anthropomorphic God, and that Heaven helps those who help themselves to be moral. Government exists for the good of the people, they said, and not for the good of the ruler. The people have the right to receive good government, and to revolt if that government is not good. Confucianism is a social order that got it right, in my opinion, as opposed to our Abrahamic religions, whose emphasis on an afterlife of great pleasure has gotten it all wrong.

Buddhism also places no emphasis on an afterlife. The Buddha taught that each individual should spend his or her life in contemplation and study, gradually evolving in stages, until a final stage is reached of complete detachment from the cares and concerns of life. This enlightened state of Nirvana could, we suppose, in some sense be called a Heaven, since it is a state of peace. Only when this enlightened state is achieved does that individual achieve freedom from the unending rebirth into lives of want, desire and pain. Yet, in the Buddhist religion, it is simply a state of mind, and not a place. Furthermore, the enlightened one, once that state is achieved, is obliged to re-enter the market place, and teach all others how to reach this state of divine enlightenment. Although Buddhism teaches detachment for the miseries of want and desire, it also emphasizes full involvement in this life, and not some mysterious realm that only exists after death.

Hinduism also lays no emphasis on an afterlife of opulent pleasure. The Hindu religion believes that there is a Heaven and a Hell, but these are only temporary way stations in an endless cycle of birth, death and rebirth. It is a highly egalitarian religion, believing that all life forms are manifestations of their God. This allows them to remain Hindu while embracing all other religions in any form. Hinduism contains every form of worship, including fetishism, mysticism, advanced theology, female deities, animal worship, all of which it considers appropriate. It believes in a noble class, vegetarianism, devotion to duty, acquisition of knowledge, and devotion to a personal High God. It is, in a sense, a fatalistic religion, since all good and bad things in this life can be attributed to events that occurred in past lives. There are nowhere, however, streets of gold, harps of gold, and angels singing on high.

Judaism believes in Heaven – at least in one sense. It is mentioned as a reward for those who have obeyed their God's laws. Heaven is not emphasized in any part of Judaism, however. There is only one major emphasis in this religion. The one and only true God has chosen the Jewish people, and only the Jewish people, as his people If they, as a people, emulate their God, obey that covenant and follow their God's laws and directions in all ways, they will be rewarded as becoming above all other people. If they fail to follow their God's commands in any way, they will be severely punished. If they are compliant with their God in every way, they will be given domination over all people in the entire world, until the end of the world. This is their self-appointed Heaven. It is a Heaven on earth, and not an ethereal pleasure palace, achievable only after death.

Then come Christianity and Islam. Both of these religions have an eschatology that emphasizes a Day of Judgment and damnation for all those who have not professed complete adherence to the particular set of myths for that religion. Although each of those two religions uses a different hero figure who sits in judgment on that final apocalyptic day, each of these religions stresses the great torture for all beings, living and dead, who did not strictly follow their certain set of beliefs. Humans who were not willing to profess unreserved adherence to those beliefs during this life deserve, according to those religions, to be punished, maimed or killed for their infidelity. Only those who fully complied with the mythology of these religions will be granted, according to them, opulent wealth, food, drink and all pleasures for an eternity. We must make it clear that these great rewards are promised by these religions for complete obedience to their mythology, and not primarily for morality. For these select few, who declared complete loyalty to the tenets of that religion, Heaven exists somewhere, on a cloud or in an oasis. All other humans, that being the vast majority of all humans who have ever lived, will be, according to these religions, condemned to pain for an eternity. These religions carry this ethical apostasy to its grand conclusion. If the most evil person in the entire world commits to Jesus as the savior, the only son of God, or truly commits to Muhammad as the last and greatest prophet, that person will be given this epicurean pleasure for an eternity. If the most loving, gracious, compassionate and empathetic man or woman in the world does not commit to their particular mythology, that person will be burned in Hell forever.

Although these religions like to hide behind a cloak of morality, it is obvious their primary goal is complete allegiance from and complete control of their followers. The result of that primary goal is rabid intolerance for all those people who do not share their particular stories. That emphasis on complete allegiance to these religions has been devastating for human societies. Although the great majority of those who are committed to these religions believe they are doing so to become moral and compassionate, they nevertheless, because of this intolerance, passively allow and support the violent actions of the true believers in those religions. Rapes, murders, invasions, bombings, beheadings, torture and destruction are all passively permitted by the followers of these religions, because their religion says that non-believers deserve that kind of punishment. A great part of that passive depravity is fostered by the belief in an afterlife, which rewards only those true believers. What will it take to stop this long time pattern of self-suicide? Realizing that we have only one brief life to live in this universe, and only this one chance to show mercy toward other humans, should do it. Until that time, our paradise-elsewhere-at-some-time-in-the future concepts, with mandatory punishment for infidels, have placed many of our societies in a Hell here on earth. It is a bit maddening to see this damaging concept still pursued with a vengeance by these religions – simply because we are the ones that allow this self-destructive behavior to continue.

COMMENT

We can pretty safely assume that Abraham would take great umbrage, or express outright anger, at being accused of fathering the seven most deadly sins of those religions that have been attributed to him. He was, after all, only the demanding patriarch of a nomadic Arabic tribe, and really not intent on starting even one, much less three, world-wide religions. All he knew is that his tribe believed they had obtained a covenant from their God, who was extremely jealous, and demanded complete loyalty from them. Whenever his people did not demonstrate complete obedience to Him, this God struck out in anger at this tribe, and caused multiple disasters to fall upon them, as a means of telling them to mend their ways. If they did not show full allegiance to this God and obey all the laws which the oral traditions of that tribe said this God demanded, they would pay dearly, according to their belief. Abraham and his tribe used those self-centered concepts they had available to them, in an effort to understand how they should deal with this God. They did the best they could with what they had. There is no blame involved here. It is simply a recognition that everything in the human experience has evolved. Our bodies, our minds, our tools, our knowledge, our societal organization and our God concepts have all evolved. Those concepts we have just examined were a natural expression of awe at the universe and wonder at our place in this world. They put that awe and wonder in human terms in order to understand it better. These personal God concepts were the best they had to work with at that time.

For these reasons, I offer my apologies to Abraham, and hasten to add that I don't think any of this moral misdirection is his fault. It's just a statement of fact; these concepts became solidified at that time, around the inception of the Hebrew religion, and became adopted by those two additional religions that followed on its coattail, as they added their own moral pitfalls. If there is any fault to assign, we should lay that fault directly on our own backs. We are the ones who still think of this mythology as factual. We are the ones who swallow these fables hook, line and sinker, proclaiming them to be the Holy Words of the one and only true God. The blame is ours, for not letting our minds and our understanding expand. Nor should we shout angry words about these religious concepts, proclaiming them to be primitive mutterings which should be abandoned. They are a rich part of our history, and deserve to be continued as colorful parts of our past. Each of them, standing on its own, can be used for comfort and guidance in our lives. If we believe that these egocentric religious concepts of immense human power and of life after death are absolutely true, however, the ramifications of these beliefs allow us to make greatly immoral decisions in our societies.

FRACTURED MARRIAGES

We are all familiar with the story that if you blindfold six people, then ask them to describe an elephant by feel, each of them will have dramatically different descriptions of that animal, depending on whether they are describing the tail, leg, side, trunk, ears or head. None of them will even come close to an adequate description of this creature. Although this may be an inadequate analogy, it does make the point that there are many different ways of thinking about this terribly dysfunctional relationship between our religions and our morals.

There is one additional manner we can look at these same problems of moral misdirection. Early in my analysis of this failure of our religions to lead us in paths of righteousness, I thought of those failures as marriages which have gone bad. Each of our religions claims to be a guide for the future of the human race. Each of them has succeeded in some ways, and in other ways has failed miserably to do so. Where did these marriages go wrong? As we explore this significant failure of our religions to guide us into loving and compassionate societies, I am hoping it will help to look at this poor performance from this somewhat different angle, one that is familiar to all of us. I will apologize in advance for the redundancies that this additional alternative examination creates, but will attempt to keep them at a minimum.

It has seemed to be such a great marriage, for all of these religions. We have this deep in the gut awe at the vastness, complexity, savagery and beauty of the universe. Some of that is eloquently expressed in the Bible, as we have seen in some of those passages quoted from The Book of Psalms, and the Book of Job. That biblical wonder has not diminished over time. Even though we now understand so much more about our universe, its structures and its physics, we find even more aspects of it which amaze us. Some galaxies are forming, some are fading, some are exploding, and others are shrinking into super dense black holes, which eat up all stars and matter next to them. There is no end to the wonderment we have about our startling and bizarre living place. This neighborhood, although quite tame as compared to other structures in the universe, has so far had no end of its own surprises and mysteries. Europa, one of Saturn's moons, may have a deep ocean of water. Others of Saturn's moons may have seas of methane. Jupiter appears to have a deep sea of liquid hydrogen. It seems there is no end to the surprises our solar system and our universe have in store for us. It is no wonder that we struggle to understand all of this, and constantly search for ways we can fit in peaceably with this sustaining but treacherous world.

Juxtaposed next to that wonder is our recognition that life is indeed very precious for each of us, and that further, the greatest expression and prolongation of our precious lives can be obtained when we work together to achieve our goals. We keep searching for those rules of conduct, or morals, that will give each of us the best chance of fulfilling our potential. We pretty much understand that this is not an easy task and that there are not simple solutions. We will have to make a continued effort to achieve stable and nurturing societies. We understand that this will take group effort, in which we will need constant encouragement and redirection. Some organization that emphasizes those ways we can lead more peaceful lives seems almost mandatory, if we are going to give communal human living our best shot.

The merger of these two needs in our religions then becomes a natural. Combine this deep respect for this creation, however that may have occurred, with our continued search for better ways of living together, and you have the two major emphases of our religions. Each of our religions uses their own unique mythological construction of that reverence, and joins it with a strong morality program, providing a one stop shop for our most basic social needs. Like the onset of many of our marriages, it has seemed like a perfect union. The terrible problem with those marriages, in our current religions, has been that each of those two wedding partners has carried some pretty awful baggage with them into that union.

The contents of this book are pretty much an exploration of exactly what that awful baggage has been, and what it has done to these marriages along the way. I had originally intended to label these as dysfunctional marriages, but now think that is being too kind. The kind of mayhem our religions have incited in our world today can only be the result of fractured marriages. When deep reverence for all creation, deep humility at our smallness in this vast creation, and deep respect for other life produces bombs, tortures and beheadings, some, if not all of this marriage contract, has not been followed. We need to examine how this great failure of our institutions which emphasize combined reverence and moral standards, better known as our religions, has occurred.

This discussion has so far tried to present, by known examples, how each of those religions has shown great immorality in human society. It has tried to clearly define exactly what we are talking about when we speak of morals, ethics, fairness and justice. In addition, it has explored those basic beliefs of our religions which lead us to highly deviant behavior. When looked at from this angle, the failures of human conduct I see, stemming from this misuse of our religious marriages, show themselves at least in these categories: we cloak our greed in religious garb; we are blind to the bipolarity of our religions; we promote the intolerance of other faiths; we don't see the incompatibilities in our morality and our mythology; there is an omnipotence problem; punishment of infidels is fostered.

HUMAN GREED IN RELIGIOUS GARB

Human greed seems to have no boundary. There is a large segment of the human population that seems to be determined to take whatever they can, from whomever they can, for as long as they can. Some of that may not entirely be their fault, in the sense that those who commit these selfish acts may not be genetically programmed to know any better. Part of our evolution has not been just physical changes in our larynx so that we can speak, develop verbal and written language; becoming bipedal so that our hands become tools; or the burgeoning size of our brains, which become twice their size every 1.5 million years. That evolution has also included, by natural selection, those members of our society who are more empathetic, more cooperative, more loving, because those are the attributes that foster longer life and health for our species. The more members of any society who sense that need to work together, the better chance that society has of survival. It is, however, still a bell-shaped curve. There are members of our society, better known under the psychiatric diagnosis of psychopaths, who are unable to recognize it is better to cooperate with and respect others. There are many others who are semi-psychopaths, by virtue of genetics or inadequate social discipline. The result is a whole army of humans who have no interest in satisfying anything other than their own personal greed at that particular moment in time. Our courts and jails are full of these people, and many of them are still on the loose, working anywhere from back alleys to swank corporate offices.

Many of these people are really smart, and always looking for ways they can get what they want, and not get blamed for it. Each of these self-interested individuals looks for any way they can convince others they should support a particular bit of robbery, and feel that it was the right thing to do. There are a lot of techniques that work well in this regard, but there is one technique that always works really well. I would submit that one of the most effective ways of committing larceny, while gaining the support of those who will help you to carry out that selfish act, and getting them to do so with fervor, is to place it under the banner of a religion with a righteous cause. You get to take what you want, no matter how much violence is involved in committing that criminal act, and yet all your colleagues in that crime feel really good about themselves for having helped with this large scale aggrandizement.

Such was the situation late in the eleventh century. Europe had sustained a population growth stemming from moderate prosperity. Young sons of the nobility were more adventurous, seeking their own fortunes and land. There was no longer room in their own feudal states. Middle class and peasants were also involved in that expansion. Forests were being cleared, markets were being established, and borders expanded. The Normans conquered England, and the Italians were challenging the Muslim dominance of the southern and eastern Mediterranean. The Muslim world was also more aggressive. Turks had expanded southward, capturing Antioch in 1085, and had extended their trade north into Armenia. The Christian and Islamic worlds were about to clash over property and trade.

There was also a religious resurgence at that time, as the Popes assumed a more active role in the societies of Europe. There was abundant energy not only for the expansion of trade and acquisition of land, but also for religious expression. Pilgrimage to a Holy Shrine was emphasized. The need for that pilgrimage was urgent, in the minds of the priests, because there was a widespread belief at that time that the end of the world was near. Access to make a pilgrimage to the Holy City was either difficult or impossible, because those lands and Jerusalem were in Muslim hands. Moreover, Muslim expansion threatened the Eastern cousins of the European Christians. European Christians now felt that they should help those Eastern cousins. Pope Urban II, speaking at the council of Clermont in 1095, emphasized the plight of the Eastern Christians, who had experienced desecration of shrines and molestation of pilgrims. He urged Christians to use their warlike expansionist energy in a Holy War, instead of against each other. The perfect storm of commercial greed combined with religious fervor was about to begin.

The response to that call to arms from European Christians was unexpected and overwhelming. The Crusades began in waves. Early unorganized bands of crusaders were repulsed or killed, but four large armies of crusaders were being organized, each leaving at a different time. The battle cry was, "God wills it." All of the crusaders were urged to wear a cross, as if it would protect them from harm, and as if it validated this invasion of foreign lands with religious rectitude. The eventual target was the Holy City of Jerusalem. Defeating the infidels was, they believed with their hearts and souls, an act that would be most pleasing to their God. The original call to make this a pilgrimage for nothing more than complete expression of their religion had already been subverted to planned violence directed toward anyone else who did not share their belief. Even before they left home, those crusaders were intent on killing any human who professed a different faith than that of Christianity. Even recognizing such, the intensity of the violence soon to be expressed was overwhelming.

In 1097, Western crusaders, joined by Byzantines, captured Nicea. They proceeded from there across the mountains, where they were met by a force of Turks. They defeated the Turks in open warfare, then proceeded to Antioch. Antioch was surrounded by high walls, forcing a long and difficult siege. Finally, in the spring, the crusaders gained access to one section of the high wall through an act of treachery by one of the Antioch commanders. As the crusaders entered the city, they massacred the entire Muslim population. The siege of Jerusalem followed in 1099. After siege towers had been erected, one section of the walls was breached, one of the gates opened, and the crusaders rushed into the Holy City. They proceeded to massacre all Muslims, men, women and children, and massacred all Jews. It was a complete slaughter born of great hatred, fully justified in the eyes of the murderers because it was a "Holy Cause," The vengeful murderers felt no guilt, because in their minds they were fulfilling the command of their deity: "God willed it."

The only reason for emphasizing the depravity of these crusades is because they are still sugar coated in the minds of Christians today. They are thought of as poorly organized treks in which many of the Christians, pursuing a Holy Cause, died before reaching the Holy Land. The complete massacre of all men, women, children and animals in those cities taken by the crusaders is seldom mentioned. The fact that these crusades began as much for economic greed, as for religious aggrandizement, is almost never cited. They were simply, in the minds of gentle Christians today, an overexpression of religious fervor which happened at some time in the past, which has little bearing on the practice of their religion today.

Well, that lesson does still apply to our world today, and that lesson has not yet been learned. We still hide our motives of greed and jealousy behind religious banners, in order to justify cruel acts. Muslim nations see progressive invasion of their lands by American, British and European businesses, primarily seeking oil. When they resist that aggrandizement, they see, for example, one of their governments overthrown (Iran), and replaced by a ruler who abides by Western interests. They fear being overcome by these imperialists, who live by different standards and believe in a different religion. They feel obliged to strike back at these foreign invaders, who threaten their way of life, and do so with religious fervor. In the case of Iran, they revolted against that puppet government, and took their country back, under their religious rule. Other Muslims attacked embassies and ships in an effort to show these invaders they are not welcome. The one particular site all

Muslims have hated has been the World Trade Center Towers, because these represent all those economic and religious threats to their countries. When the planes strike, we hear reports of Muslims rejoicing, because the Great Satan has been taught a lesson. Even many of those who are peace loving, we are told, acquiesce with this action. The fascinating aspect of this event, sadly, is that our American leaders appear to have been clueless so far as to why this calamity occurred. They have seemed oblivious to the aggrandizement and disrespect America had shown toward Muslim nations for many preceding years. Rather than realizing that these violent acts were a strident call for understanding, they chose to declare a war against evil, rather than accepting that a great part of the blame is ours.

Even more use of religious banners to disguise economic desire soon followed. Our Christian president and his powerful, business executive Vice-president, happened to be oil men. They were deeply concerned that America would lose its access to cheap oil, a commodity on which this nation runs. They were greatly fearful that these terrorist attacks against the United States would rapidly spread, involving multiple Arab countries, and our access to oil. Those fears were probably justified, but were not the reasons given to us for the invasion of Iraq. Once again, a religious cloak covered fear and commercial greed. We were told that this was a battle against a universal evil. That sold, even to our cantankerous congressmen and women. America was soon involved in a long and bloody, bankrupting war, sure to leave lasting scars on this nation and on Iraq.

I don't think there is a complete answer to this problem, other than time and further evolution of human empathy. What we can do is to be acutely aware that most, if not all of the religious causes present today, which resort to violence to achieve their aims, cannot, in any reasonable way, be morally justified. The real motives are jealousy, greed and fear, covered with religious garb, in an attempt to disguise their true origin. What we can do is to protest such hypocrisy with vigor, whenever we see it, using whatever democratic process there is to voice our objection. If those in power still don't listen, then we need to speak more loudly. Sometimes marches, demonstrations, and perhaps civil disobedience, are in order. No religious precept is an adequate justification for violent aggression of humans against each other. We should always speak against disguising our fear and greed in religious garb.

RELIGIOUS BIPOLARITY

There is a psychiatric human disease which is in some ways similar to this religious disease. It used to be called a manic-depressive disorder, characterized by severe mood swings that go from euphoria to deep depression. Some of those episodes might last months or years, expressed as prolonged excitement about life, or prolonged despair about life. Neither of those is entirely healthy. Of course it is normal to be enthusiastic about new findings, new adventures and new loves in our lives. Extreme constant excitement, however, leads to excesses of behavior which are damaging to both that person and his or her companions. Common sense and planning for the future, hallmarks of a mature individual, are not expressed. Others who are sucked into this giddy phase also suffer the consequences when poor planning produces bad results. It becomes the equivalent of a speeding drunk passing other cars going up a hill, with a car full of other people. The risk for injury and even death becomes much greater.

The gloom of a depression is just as damaging. It is difficult to make any proper decision, plan any day or event, show care and concern, when you can't even think about getting through your own day. And of course, this is also normal at times in our lives. The loss of a loved one, whether father, mother, husband or lover, is a pall over every moment. The grief is at those times overwhelming. For there to not be recovery over time, however, is not normal. It becomes a heavy load that keeps us from living a worthwhile life. When the black cloud over our heads never goes away, it is time to treat the disease with counseling and medicine, in order to reestablish a moderation of behavior. The goal is never to eliminate happiness and sadness, which are normal and learning parts of our lives. The goal is always to put those emotions on a more even keel, so that each can be used in rational and productive ways.

Our major religions, in a similar manner, have a striking bipolar disorder. In their case, one pole is really good, and the other is really bad. This is the way they began, and they have not as yet been able to temper or get rid of their immoral pole. The denial of this bipolarity in those devoted to these religions is rather striking. Each of these religions has a marvelous pole of moral admonishments, designed to create stable and compassionate societies. Each of those religions has its devotees to those standards, who spend their days seeking ways to conform to these moral requirements. The other end of this religious staff, however, has a pole of deep intolerance for all those humans who do not share their particular mythology. That pole also has its devotees, who advocate bombs, bullets and suicides to express their beliefs. This is not a hidden agenda in these religions. Both these disparate goals are announced repetitively, stressed with great emotion, and sometimes brought into full juxtaposition, without any recognition that these two divergent views are totally incompatible. You can't preach compassion and at the same time preach violence toward all other humans who have a different faith, without being a great hypocrite. Kindness, followed with a bomb, simply leaves us with a destructive hole in our society. That light has apparently not yet dawned in Judaism, Christianity and Islam.

Each of these religions has practiced what it preaches. There are outpourings of aid from religious groups for the victims of earthquakes, Tsunamis and hurricanes. There are large scale relief efforts on an ongoing basis, from religious groups, who attempt to provide life for refugees in squalid camps, and sustenance for populations suffering from famine. Every disaster fosters a reaction from those churches who want to help in any way they can. It is indeed a blessing to have religious societies that care deeply about other societies that are far removed from them. Our world would be in an ever greater mess were it not for this outpour of concern for other humans. They put "Love your neighbor" into practice, and our world is a better place for them.

Coexisting with that morality, however, in those same religions, are militarist commanders who order invasions, killings and destruction at will, presidents who preach hatred against other countries, and true believers who blow themselves up with as many others they can, as an expression of their religion. The galling part of this antisocial behavior is that it is fully accepted by most of those who preach compassion. Each of those disparate poles recognizes the other pole in their religion, but each appears unwilling to accept their incompatibility. Each segment believes that these two parts of their religion belong together, and should work together for their common goal of domination over all other religions. Our religions have so far been unable to understand that these two poles negate their value to society. There can be no cure for this deep seated bipolar religious disease, until its devotees realize that compassion and intolerance are diametrically opposed.

This bipolarity is not a new phenomenon, wherein modern day followers have forgotten how to apply the teachings of their religious prophets. This dual emphasis on compassion and intolerance has existed from the very beginning of all these religions. None of their founders saw the incompatibility in these opposite emphases, and none of their followers now see that disease. They are simply carrying out the demands of their religions precisely the way in which they were established by those seers who began them. When Moses came down from the mountain top for the second time, carrying the Ten Commandments on two stone tablets, those morals were supposed to be the law for the people of Israel. Yet when Moses, immediately upon his return, saw revelry and worship of another God, he erupted in white hot anger. The other intolerant pole was immediately expressed; he called for his priests, and ordered a massacre.

> *Exodus 32: 27–29. He told them, "This is what the Lord, the God of Israel says; Strap on your swords! Go back and forth from one end of the camp to the other, killing even your brothers, friends, and neighbors." The Levites obeyed Moses, and about three thousand people died that day.*

> *Then Moses told the Levites, "Today you have been ordained for the service of the Lord, for you obeyed him even though it meant killing your own sons and brothers. Because of this, he will now give you a great blessing."*

This juxtaposed morality and violent intolerance, perpetrated by this founder of that religion, demonstrates a bipolar disorder of great substance. How killing your sons and brothers, friends and neighbors can be called a great blessing, is quite appalling.

Jesus was not a whole lot better. He gave us three magnificent leaps in moral understanding, and did not directly order anyone put to death. Yet out of the other side of his tongue, he prescribed violent death and predicted torture for those who did not accept his egocentric message.

> *Matthew 11: 21–23. "What horrors await you, Korazin and Bethsaida! For if the miracles I did in you had been done in wicked Tyre and Sidon, their people would have sat in deep*

*repentance long ago, clothed in sackcloth and throwing
ashes on their heads to show their remorse."*

*"I assure you, Tyre and Sidon will be better off on the
judgment day than you! And you people of Capernaum, will
you be exalted to heaven? No, you will be brought down to
the place of the dead."*

*Matthew 13: 40–42. "Just as the weeds are separated out
and burned, so it will be at the end of the world. I, the Son
of Man, will send my angels, and they will remove from my
Kingdom everything that causes sin and all who do evil, and
they will throw them into the furnace and burn them. There
will be weeping and gnashing of teeth."*

Muhammad, the founder of Islam, is the epitome of this religious
bipolarity. He carries the fractured dichotomy of Moses and the dire
judgments of Jesus even a step further. Muhammad commands that
all Muslims must show great mercy for all other believers, and at the
same time, carry out uninhibited punishment on all people who are
infidels of his faith. For Moses, this combined morality and violence
happens in an angry uninhibited response. For Jesus, these are promises of torture. For Muhammad, these are commands. He does not, in
the slightest, comprehend the clash of these two opposite dictums. If
compassion is to be shown only for Muslims, and all others of other
faith are to be killed, the result must be war with all other religions.
Although these commands have been variously expressed in the history of Islam, the substrate for violent response, when the Muslim
faith is challenged, is a clear command, from the Prophet who claimed
that he spoke the true words of the only true God of the universe,
Allah.

It is impossible for this startlingly dyssynchronous social code to
serve as the basis for a human ethic. Yet, as an example, this dual
emphasis on compassion and violent intolerance was the exact
foundation, which was used to begin the religion of Islam. At that
particular point in history, there was a political vacuum in the Arabian
peninsula. Both Persia and the Christian Byzantine Empire were weak
from constant fighting in the North. The southern Arab states, which
had been in part invaded by Christianity coming from Abyssinia, no
longer had support from the Byzantine empire. There was no politi-

cal pressure from either the north or the south. All the Arab tribes were fighting with each other, all of them trying to gain ascendancy. Many were rather weary of this constant warfare, and were looking for someone who could unite them. Like much of history, timing is everything. Muhammad was the right person at the right time, with the right message to capture the imagination of the Arab tribes.

Muhammad's father died before he was born. That left his management, by Arab tradition, in the hands of his grandfather, 'Abd al-Muttalib. His grandfather, one of the less influential Meccan traders, had his hands full dealing with the wealthiest traders, who no longer appeared interested in following Arab customs. Those wealthy traders had no interest in contributing to the needy members of that society. They had become rather imperious, believing that they could get whatever they wanted without cooperating with the rest of the tribe. Whether 'Abd al-Muttalib simply had his hands full, or wanted his grandson to grow up with a different set of values than those that prevailed in Mecca at that time, is not clear. What is clear is that Muhammad was sent to the desert as a baby, to be raised by a wet nurse in one of the nomadic Arab tribes.

Muhammad, during his formative early years, was a displaced, dispossessed desert orphan. The lessons he learned from that desert tribe were that those who had more, gave to those who had less. He learned that everyone contributed whatever they could, so that the whole tribe could survive. All tribesmen cooperated with and supported each other. He learned that it was their tribe against all other tribes, and that you had to fight for survival. He learned that there was a God, who was in control of all things, who brought the nurturing rain, turning the seared land lush green, brought the soothing cool of the night, and brought the scorching heat of the day. These lessons were burned into his brain in the desert heat, and they never left him.

Following his marriage to the wealthy widow Khadijah, and return to Mecca as a respected trader, Muhammad found that these values were not being honored in that trading center. There were idols in the Holy Kabah, the site of the sacred stone. No one took responsibility for the poor, and the wealthiest cared little for anyone else but themselves. There was no unity of these people, and no unity of purpose. The charismatic, deeply imprinted desert orphan, who knew in his heart that all of society had to be one, was unable to tolerate this irreverence. This lack of direction nearly drove him crazy. He often went to a cave just outside of Mecca, where he spent his sleepless worried nights in agitated thought. Then one particularly fitful night, sometimes toward dawn, he had a vivid dream. In that dream, the angel Gabriel, dressed in radiant garb, spoke to him, telling him that he, Muhammad, was the messenger of God. Gabriel commanded him to recite those words of the one and only God, which came to him in trance-like states, to other people, who were desperately in need of these messages.

Following his vivid dream, the distraught Muhammad began his ministry in 613 CE, with the encouragement of his greatly supportive wife, Khadijah. It was a cautious and tentative beginning, but he soon had a group of over 100 who gathered with Muhammad weekly to hear these recitations from the one and only true God, Allah. Soon, the wealthy traders took notice. They did not like the increasing influence of this latest prophet, and suspected that he would not be satisfied until he had a great deal more. That premonition was entirely correct. As Muhammad's ministry rapidly grew, and his influence in Mecca rapidly grew, the harassment from the established traders also increased. This upstart seemed impervious to their offers and threats. Placing piles of stool at his doorstep did not stop him. An offer of marriage to the daughter of one of the wealthiest traders was quickly rejected. Soon, there were death threats, gradually escalating in intensity. In 619 CE, two of his greatest protectors, his wife, Khadijah, and his uncle, Abu Talib, head of the Hashim clan, both died. Muhammad knew that if he stayed in Mecca, he would be killed. He planned ahead, sending many of his staunch supporters to the welcoming city of Medina. Late at night, he slipped out a back door, and using little known paths, arrived in Medina on September 24, 622. This was the *hijrah*, the migration, which began the independent religion of Islam.

Muhammad was welcomed in Medina as the last and greatest prophet, who would arbitrate their disputes, settle their differences, and bring all the warring fractious Arab tribes together. Both poles of this muscular, dually compassionate and warring religion, were immediately expressed. All members of the tribe were to be treated as brothers. Everyone was to provide care for other Muslims in need. Everyone had to show their devotion to the one and only god, Allah, in prayer, each day. At the same time, Muhammad led raids on Meccan caravans, killing the men, looting the goods, and taking women and children as slaves. When Jewish traders in Medina were suspected of tipping off some of the caravans in advance, they were ousted from their stalls in the market place, and later killed. Their women and children were also taken as concubines and slaves. Battles ensued with Meccan armies, in 624 and 625, without a decisive victory on either side. In 627, Mecca sent an army of ten thousand to defeat this renegade once and for all. Muhammad wisely had the crops harvested early, and had a deep trench dug to prevent horses from crossing. After two days of indecisive battle, an act of God occurred. A violent storm came through on the third day, creating frightened warriors and animals. The Meccan army melted away. Muhammad was hailed as the favored and victorious messenger of their God.

Muhammad did not waste time neglecting his military advantage. Letters were sent to surrounding heads of states, inviting them to embrace the new religion of Islam, or suffer invasion. Those Arabs who were dissident were killed. All the other Arab tribes rapidly found it to be to their advantage to pledge allegiance to this demanding new religion, or else be eliminated. Mecca was overcome without resistance in 629. Noncompliant Syria was invaded in 630, with an army of 30,000 men. The inception of Islam was a military campaign, full of all the violence a war contains. For those who professed allegiance to this new and exacting mythology, Islam produced sweet rewards. Communities became brotherhoods, with the single purpose of helping each other and expressing their devotion to their God. There was a flowering of literature, art, learning, scientific achievement and accumulation of knowledge everywhere the Muslim world dominated. The influence of Islam, under this flowering of societies, spread from the Arabian peninsula throughout the Near East, Northern Africa and Southern Europe. Their pole of mercy was expressed with vigor during the next several centuries of Islam. That all came to an end with the appalling horror of the Christian crusades. Once the hornet's nest had been poked, the poles reversed. The resulting protests of Muslims against Jewish and Christian invasions of their lands have been angry and violent, in defense of their beloved religion.

This incompatible bipolarity of love and hostility in our religions has never been fully appreciated by them, even though that divisive emphasis immediately hits you in the face, as soon as any of their beliefs or messages are cited. Muslims are not alone in their militancy.

Onward, Christian soldiers

Onward as to war,

With the cross of Jesus

Going on before.

Christ the Royal Master,

Leads against the foe.

Forward into battle,

See his banners go!

I would submit to you that these are messages of hostility and domination, and not messages of fairness and justice There are those devotees of these religions who, at one pole, choose to think of their religion as entirely merciful and just. They say, "These other acts are not our religion; our religion is one of love," apparently not aware that an act of love, if it is immediately followed by an act of destruction, has lost all its value. Then there are the majority members of that religion, who tend to think of their religion as compassionate, but who are well aware of violent acts committed by some of its members on behalf of that religion. These violent acts they dismiss as flaws of exuberance. They produce no vigorous, condemning protest against these hateful acts, apparently unable to comprehend that peaceful acts, accompanied by acts of war, negate. And at the violent pole, there are those members of these religions who constantly plan terror, invasion and domination. Unfortunately, this pole has a fairly devoted army of supporters, who, when destructive acts are committed, applaud.

Our married religions appear to be blind to their own faults and sins, a good part of which is to remain fully blind to their polar incompatibilities.

INTOLERANCE OF OTHER RELIGIONS

Intolerance is fully embedded into our religions. In essence, no religion currently exists without containing this pole of intolerance for other faiths. A core piece of any religion is belief in a deity of some type, and an accompanying legend of mythology which outlines the relationship of humans to that particular deity. Each religion believes that its system of thought is the true description of the relationship of humans to their God, and that all other religions don't have that description quite right. Each of them, in defense of their faith, speaks disparagingly of all other religious systems, not only to ward off criticisms of their faith, but also to proselytize new members to their faith. Most of the time, in these religions, cooler heads prevail, recognizing that they pursue common goals of reverence for the creation, and love of neighbor. Unfortunately, each of these religions also has true believer hot-heads, who are determined to force their beliefs on all other humans, or make them pay dearly for their apostasy.

Some may be quick to respond that there are several religions which are quite tolerant of other mythology. Confucianism, for example, makes no exception for other religions as part of its faith. That statement about Confucianism is quite correct, but it is not completely correct to classify this philosophy as a religion. It does not contain belief in a deity. It is a social order of the highest caliber, emphasizing industriousness, felicity, respect for elders, accumulation of wisdom, and full self-expression. You may say that Hinduism is a religion which, although it has its own belief system, fully accepts all other gods and religious thought, in an all-inclusive club. That also would be true, but conveniently does not mention that there are some violent sects within Hinduism, which have been at war with other Hindu sects and other religions. Sikhism, for example, began as a separatist religion in the fifteenth century, devoted to monotheism rather than polytheism. After significant oppression from Hindu majorities, and frequent martyrdom of their gurus by both Muslims and Hindus, this sect became militarized. It was constantly battling neighboring provinces, eventually controlling most of Northern India, as far west as Afghanistan. Those Sikh occupied territories were purposely split in half by the partition of Muslim Pakistan away from Hindu India in 1947. Most of those Sikhs settled in the northern Punjab state of India, but still remained a thorn in the side of the central Indian government. Prime Minister Indira Gandhi authorized military force against Sikh agitators in 1984, leading to the destruction of their Holy Temple. She paid for that action with her life, becoming assassinated by her Sikh bodyguards.

Or you could be a Tamil Tiger, a splinter group of mostly Hindus seeking independence for the northern section of Sri Lanka. This group has lived up to its aggressive name. They championed the use of surface-to-air missiles, rocket propelled grenades, and perfected the suicide bomb jacket. They were famous for encouraging the use of women as suicide bombers. Each of the fighters wore a necklace with a cyanide suicide capsule in it, to be taken if they were captured. They were specialists in terrorism, setting an example for terrorist organizations everywhere else to follow.

There appears to be no exception. So far, every organization that can be identified as a religion has had, as part of its entity, an extremist intolerant pole, dedicated to domination or separation, using whatever violent means are necessary to achieve their aims.

THE DARK AGES

The term "Dark Ages" was coined by the Italian scholar Petrarch in 1330 to describe what he saw as a void of Latin based church literature in the first several centuries following the fall of the Roman Empire. The term gradually came to mean something a lot more, referring to a period of constant warfare, no major urbanization, little building, few noteworthy achievements, and a great paucity of written history. It began when the Roman Emperor Augustulus was defeated by the barbarian Odoacer in 476, and continued until the Norman conquest of England in 1066. In general terms, it has applied to the centuries 400 to 1000, representing a period in human history when civilization was in decline. The term has lately fallen in disfavor amongst historians, for several reasons, although the lack of human progress at that time in European lands is not questioned.

Scholars of our era point out that this term excludes certain advances that were made in European countries at that time, and certainly does not include the great advances made by the Muslim community at that same time. At this time when Europe was in decline, Islam was still in expansion. Scholars in Europe who were being persecuted for not adhering strictly to church doctrine, as demanded by the Popes, found themselves welcome in Constantinople and other Muslim Universities. Studies of mathematics, medicine and science prospered; as a result there was significant accumulation of knowledge south of the Mediterranean. Much of the Muslim expansion occurred at the expense of a fallen Roman Empire, but was not overly violent. Camel mounted soldiers brought the thrust of Islam to northern Africa, the southern states of Europe, and the Near East, as well as the entire Arabian Peninsula. The reason for this flowering of science and literature under Islam was the majority expression of their brotherhood side, once those lands had been conquered. Had this religion chosen to express its violent extremist side at that time in history, the scope of the Dark Ages would have been rather immense.

Most English scholars now refer to this entire period of human history as the Middle Ages. They prefer to designate that approximate time from the fall of the Roman Empire to the Norman conquest of England in 1066 as the Early Middle Ages, and refer to those centuries that followed, up to the death of King Richard III at the battle of Bosworth, in 1485, as the Late Middle Ages. If this designation is accepted, the Late Middle Ages were full of human activity and achievements, much different than the void that existed in the Early Middle Ages. During these several centuries, many of the great English castles were built, as well as the Tower of London. The misdirected Christian crusades had their inception, eventually changing forever the relationship of Christianity to Islam, and fostering the defensive violence of Islamist extremists. Knighthood was in full form, featuring mounted iron clad hero warriors, who were quite busy, at least by rumor, slaying dragons and rescuing fair damsels. The Magna Carta was forced on King John by a group of his barons, in order to limit the power of the king and protect their privileges, That document was signed by him on June 15, 1215, giving rights to Freemen, respecting certain legal procedures, and guaranteeing that the rule of the king could be bound by law. It allowed for the first time, appeal against unlawful imprisonment. Portions of that document later served as a model for portions of the American Constitution.

There is considerable waffling amongst these historians as to exactly what brought on the Dark Ages, and whether or not that is even a correct designation. Perhaps those thoughts and perceptions are correct. Barbara Walker, however, has little doubt as to what caused the Dark Ages of Europe. She states that there is ample evidence this period of great inhibition in human civilization was caused by the intolerance of the Christian church. The clergy felt that any knowledge which challenged the beliefs of the church was evil, and that, therefore, the spread of knowledge was evil. They outwardly expressed their opinions that the more the population was kept in ignorance, the more they would be devoted to the church. Goddess worship was forbidden, large volumes of books were burned, libraries were destroyed, schools were destroyed, the studies of philosophy, mathematics, medicine, and geography were abolished, any opposition to church doctrine was punished by the death penalty, and no book reading was allowed unless approved by the bishops. Even reading the Bible, if it was not an authorized version, was punishable by burning at the stake. The result was an oppressive, stifling, regimented life of ignorance for the majority of the population. Religious intolerance was reaching its full expression, and human civilization paid a dear price for this depraved control, brought upon the entire population by clergy who lived in opulence. The Dark Ages, it appears, occurred mostly because of the intolerance of the Christian Church.

THE INQUISITIONS

That full and most egregious expression of religious intolerance came in the form of the church mandated inquisitions, beginning in the twelfth century and extending well into the nineteenth century. There is no more galling lesson in the corruption of absolute power, human cruelty and avarice, than in these religiously based, church directed schemes of human degradation. The church, as the recognized religion of the state, had the full power of civil government behind them for any action they wished to take against someone who was, in their opinion, a heretic, or in other words, someone who threatened the flow of cash to the church hierarchy. Various splinter groups, such as Cathars, and Waldensians, challenged the doctrines of the church on Original Sin, Heaven and Hell, Virgin Birth, Resurrection from the Dead, and supported direct communication with their God. None of this was tolerated. Beginning in the twelfth century, a series of Papal Bulls authorized the use of inquisitors to search for and punish these heretics. These inquisitors had virtually unlimited power; they had at their disposal lawyers, deputies, police and notaries. That unlimited power became a scourge on the entire population over the next eight centuries.

The original terms of the Papal Bulls cited a search for offenders who practiced sorcery, witchcraft, alchemy, devil worship, or who practiced adultery. The penalties that were cited for punishment of these church designated sins included recitation of prayers, fasting, almsgiving, flogging, wearing a yellow cross, imprisonment, and confiscation of property. Although a few of the inquisitors may have been more lenient, the great majority were not. This whole inquisition scheme rapidly deteriorated into a giant extortion racket, flagrant disregard for property rights, consummate greed, and great torture, mostly of women. Those who did not pay to avoid being accused of heresy, were accused on most any presumption. Once accused, that person's property was immediately seized by the church, before there was any hearing, and that person thrown in jail. There, he was tortured until he confessed his heresy, and was then turned over to the state for punishment, which usually consisted of hanging or burning, and sometimes both.

While in prison, that prisoner was ordered to pay for his own food or starve, pay for his own torture, and pay fines for his heresy. The families of those prisoners, now bereft of livelihood and dwellings, became destitute. The hearings for those prisoners were an apostasy of justice. None of those accused were allowed to have a lawyer, none could call witnesses on their behalf, all witnesses against them were concealed, the testimony of children was accepted, none was allowed to see the charges against them, and all were found guilty. If anyone attempted to speak on their behalf, that person was also accused of heresy, and suffered the same fate.

As if all this were not as depraved as human behavior can become, women had it even worse. Women, accused of witchcraft, were a favorite target of the Inquisitors. Their tortures were even more gruesome, the breasts and genitalia favorite targets for burning, pinching and penetration. Rape was the favorite form of torture, often used with abandon, and available to any male who obtained permission to visit that prisoner. Once that torture obtained the confession demanded, it was publicly announced. The executions were held publicly and the population required to watch them, so that all could see what happened to those who questioned the authority of the church. Any who chose not to watch were also accused of heresy. The screams of those who were burning to death filled the air, and the acrid stench placed a pall over those towns that never left. Some towns were completely wiped off the map, because all the women had been accused of witchcraft, tortured, and burned at the stake.

There were four major inquisitions, although all overlapped to some degree: the Medieval, Spanish, Portuguese and Papal. Of all those, the Spanish Inquisition was the most degenerate. It was begun late in the fifteenth century by the Catholic Kings of Spain, who felt that their religion was being threatened. Following the crusades in Palestine, large cadres of both Jews and Muslims fled, many of them settling in Spain. By the fifteenth century, both those enclaves were flourishing, much to the dismay of the Catholic hierarchy. Once the requests from the Spanish King had been made, Papal permission was quickly given to appoint a Grand Inquisitor. The first Grand Inquisitor, Tomas de Tourquemada, became known as the epitome of false accusation, torture until a confession is obtained, then public execution by burning at the stake. This practice was especially designed to convince both Jews and Muslims to recant their faith before they received a similar fate. Nor were Protestants excluded. They too were the target of the harsh inquisitors. Those that tried to escape to Portugal soon became the target of rabid inquisitions in that country. This Catholic scourge upon the Spanish population continued into the nineteenth century, lingering particularly in the Spanish colonies, where members of the native population were tortured into accepting Christianity as their religion. Over a span of two centuries, England falsely accused, tortured and murdered 30,000 women, who were convicted of being witches. The slaughter was even greater in Europe. On some occasions, hundreds of women were burned at the stake in a single day.

GALILEO GALELEI

Galileo Galelei was born in 1564, the son of a musician, He entered the University of Pisa in 1581 in order to study medicine. While there in the cathedral, he noticed a lamp swinging, and noted that it took the same amount of time for the lamp to complete its swing, regardless of the distance of the swing. This led him to believe that a pendulum could be constructed to tell time, a discovery that he promoted later in life. He was rapidly drawn to mathematics, rather than medicine, and made remarkable discoveries in that field. He accepted the position of Chair of Mathematics at the University of Padua in 1592, a position he held for eighteen years. His observations on the uniformly accelerated motion of falling bodies and the parabolic curve of thrown bodies were later used by Newton to formulate the Laws of Motion. Upon learning of the invention of the telescope, he rapidly modified it to increase the power of magnification from a factor of 2 to a factor of 32. With this telescope, he discovered that the Milky Way consisted of multitudes of stars, that Jupiter had moons, the sun had spots, discovered the phases of Venus and the Rings of Saturn. His observations led him to support the Copernican theory that the Earth was not the center of the universe, but was instead a planet revolving around the sun. He was the father of scientific measurement and the scientific experiment.

The factual observations of Galileo were not well accepted by the church authorities at his time, however. The church was interested in suppressing any knowledge that might interfere with their authority. The Pope took great umbrage at this pronouncement that the earth was not the center of the universe. The church hierarchy could not tolerate the thought that any scientific theory conflicted with their interpretation of the Bible, which placed them at the center of the universe and in command of the universe. This was blasphemous heresy, which had to be squashed. The ecclesiastical authorities demanded that Galileo denounce the theories of Copernicus, and sentenced him to house arrest for the next seven years. The official decree banned Galileo from any further publication of observations or mathematical calculations. Galileo was allowed a reprieve for two years to publish a book comparing the Ptolemaic and Copernican theories of planetary motion. Perhaps he saved himself from being imprisoned, tortured, and burned at the stake by this publication, *Dialogue Concerning the Two Chief World Systems – Ptolemaic and Copernican*. Because this book did not clearly denounce the Copernican theory of planetary motion, however, he was once again scathingly reprimanded, placed in house arrest, and spent the last eight years of his life confined to his home. Fortunately, he was able to communicate with other scholars as well as his students, and continued to produce brilliant scientific discoveries up to the time of his death in 1642.

This deepest of sins was not in those labeled as heretics, but in the church itself. There were only two realistic goals of the inquisitions, neither of which had anything to do with human value. They were designed purely to keep the population under subjugation, and increase the wealth of the church elite. The means they chose to achieve those goals was to blatantly display intolerance for any other belief, regardless of the immense human suffering that intolerance brought. In this effort, they were magnificently successful. Please, let none of us doubt that organized religion has a deep-seated innate flaw, that being a variously expressed, but often glaring intolerance, of other humans who do not share their particular faith. If each religion believes that only they have the right concepts about their God, life and death, then all other religions, according to them, have it wrong, and are bad. The price human society has had to pay for this religious intolerance has been grave.

IGNORED RELIGIOUS FLAWS

This marriage of reverence for the Divine, and our human morality systems, which we find in our religions, has over time shown some terrible characteristics. Only after these two have lived together for a while have these weaknesses in each become apparent. What seemed like perfect matches in the beginning did not show their incompatibilities for a while, but gradually the flaws in their personalities became quite apparent, and domestic violence began. Neither our morality systems, nor our religious beliefs, are exactly what they appeared to be when those religions began. The degree to which their guidance flaws are ignored is, to me, highly illogical. We don't understand that we lie to ourselves about how moral we are. We don't see that our morals are not solid and unwavering. We don't appreciate that we are far removed from developing a universal ethic. We don't comprehend that our religious mythologies often get in the way of developing valid systems of conduct. We are blind to the bigamy of our one and only personal God. We eagerly accept fantastic promises of eternal life from our religions, even though those promises defy what we now know about our existence and our universe.

I recently lied to myself about my weight. It was the most natural thing in the world to do, and rather humiliating to find that I had willingly duped myself about my own health. Last year, some of my labs came back abnormal. There was some protein in the urine, sugar was mildly elevated, and LDL was up by a few points. I began to run regularly and also stopped eating breakfast and lunch. After my weight came down to a normal BMI, I began to have a brief snack for lunch, consisting of an apple or orange. After a while, that got added to with some peanut butter and a cookie. I was quite happy with myself for meeting this challenge successfully, eschewing the normal meal pleasures that others enjoyed, for at least part of the day. When my pants started getting tight, I paid little attention. When my bathroom scales showed a higher weight than that I wanted, I simply rocked forward a bit, which produced lower readings by 5 to 10 pounds. When my scales showed even greater weight, I thought maybe they were just inaccurate. I continued to be rather proud of my ability to meet this challenge, and demonstrate self-control.

The scales at the doctor's office were unforgiving however, I was not only twenty pounds overweight, but my labs were worse. I had given myself the answers that I wanted to have, rather than accepting the clear evidence otherwise. I wanted to feel good about myself, and feel that I had kept my body healthy. I lied to myself with great ease, in an effort to keep my self-esteem. That ploy worked really well, until reality struck. Much more stringent dietary control and exercise would be necessary, for a long time, if I wanted to stay healthy for a while longer.

Similarly, we appear to be blind to our own moral ineptitudes. We continue to think that we are a highly moral nation, driven by principles of democracy which place our morals above those of any other nations. Yet that is not the way we have behaved. We failed to see the grave immorality of invading Korea and Vietnam. We fail to see that it is wrong to jail foreign enemy combatants without charge, and without representation, without trial. We fail to see that it is wrong to torture those same combatants. We fail to see that it is wrong to invade a foreign country without just cause. We fail to see that it is wrong to want only Christian elected officials, only Christian Supreme Courts, and only Christian prayers in our schools, courthouses and senatorial chambers. Israel fails to see that it was wrong for them to have invaded Palestinian lands, and have usurped that land for their own purposes. Muslims fail to see that it is wrong to bomb embassies, trade centers and market places. We all lie to ourselves every day, telling ourselves that we are moral, when we are, in fact, committing highly immoral acts. This self-deception is a major defect in our application of our own moral values, which lay embedded in our religions.

We are also quite blind to the fact that our morals are not solid, not constant, not fixed. We tend to think of our values as being the right values for all of us, all of the time. We tend to think that our values should be the same values for other people, in other societies. We simply don't stay aware that what we consider right today is not what we considered right in the previous generation, and is quite a bit different from what we considered right in the previous century. We don't constantly remind ourselves that every society lives in different circumstances, with different needs, and that what is right for other societies is not necessarily what is right for us. We don't remain fully aware that the moral system for each society is fluid and has been so for all of time. Morality is a quite shifty woman. She will change her personality to fit the needs of each society, and never stays the same, from one time to the next and one place to the next.

We remain blind, for the most part, to the fact that our morals are inadequate rules of conduct for all situations. Our rules of conduct are still a work under construction. Our morals fail us in times of war and in those acts of judgment after wars. They fail us in times of high stress, when lives are in danger. They fail us when our loved ones are threatened, or when precious possessions are threatened. There are, without doubt, acts of great courage and compassion in these times of high stress. There are also a lot of us who fail miserably at those times. A socially isolated man walks into an exercise gym, primarily targeting the best looking bodies, killing three women, wounding nine, then killing himself. A mentally deranged student opens fire on his college campus, killing many, then killing himself. Most every week in our local news, it seems, a jealous, angry husband has shot and killed his wife, then shot and killed himself in remorse.

We seem blind to the fact that our religions contain mythology systems, which are not necessarily tied to any certain set of values dictating what is right and wrong. We tend to think of our religions as being set in stone, such that you can't have that particular mythology without that particular set of social values. It just isn't so. Jesus could have given us these remarkable lessons about love of his God and love of neighbor, but not preached anything about an apocalypse, a life after death, a judgment day, and an eternal torture for all those who did not believe in his Divinity. Muhammad could have demanded that all Muslims show compassion and not demanded that all infidels should be killed. Confucius was able to teach a remarkable moral system and awe for the creation of the universe, without adding deity mythology to that moral system. Not only do we not need religious mythology to develop sound human morality, but we often do a better job of figuring out what human behavior is most productive, when we don't have religious myths to lead us astray.

This God of our religions is a bigamous, treacherous husband. If it is the same God, he is married to all these different religions, telling each of them what they want to hear, even though those promises he gives to each religion then puts them in direct conflict with those other religions to whom he is also married. It is almost as if He loves to make his women fight over Him. He tells the Jews that he will make them the dominant nation over all nations. He tells the Christians that only those who believe in Jesus will rule heaven and earth. He tells the Muslims that theirs is the only true religion. It is difficult to understand why we do not see that this cacophony of arguing voices, each speaking to their same God, is telling us something important. A personal loving God of all people will teach them to respect each other, not send them out to kill each other.

It is terrible easy for any of us to make fantastic promises, if there is never any proof needed to substantiate those claims. Especially if those promises are things that most any human would find very dear, it becomes almost a done deal. Our religions demand our money, time, effort, attention, and sometimes our lives. In exchange for these rather heavy demands, they make a fabulous promise: an eternal life without pain or suffering, and with great pleasure. What is there not to like about living forever in peace and happiness? This empty promise is too good to be true, but accepted wholeheartedly by devoted followers in the millions. Even though there is no evidence anywhere that any meaningful life exists in any form or fashion after death, and even though these imaginative promises defy all known human experience and all physical laws, multiple millions of humans accept this premise without doubt. Our religions never have to worry about proving their imaginary promises, because not one of us will ever know, or come back to tell us otherwise. Everything we know tells us otherwise; coagulated proteins never revert back to their original living state. A fried egg becomes a food source and not a chicken. Our deaths, as best we can determine, are quite final for our individual selves. Our memory will linger, sometimes quite vividly, in the minds of those who knew us. Whatever good or bad influence we have had on others will carry on after us. Some of our atoms will be put to use again to form other life. Our individual selves, however, come and go. All we can do is treasure that life while we have it – and that particularly means not giving it away for false promises.

Hamlet had a much more rational evaluation of the dark void after death.

> *To die, to sleep; perchance to dream – aye, there's the rub.*
>
> *For in that sleep of death what dreams may come,*
>
> *When we have shuffled off this mortal coil,*
>
> *Must give us pause; there's the respect*
>
> *That makes calamity of so long life;*
>
> *For who would bear the whips and scorns of time,*
>
> *The oppressor's wrong, the proud man's contumely,*
>
> *The pangs of despised love, the law's delay,*
>
> *The insolence of office, and the spurns*
>
> *That patient merit of the unworthy takes,*
>
> *When he himself might his quietus make*
>
> *With a bare bodkin? Who would fardels bear,*
>
> *To grunt and sweat under a weary life,*
>
> *But that the dread of something after death –*
>
> *That undiscovered country, from whose bourn*
>
> *No traveler returns – puzzles the will,*
>
> *And makes us rather bear those ills we have,*
>
> *Than fly to other that we know not of.*
>
> *Thus conscience doth make cowards of us all;*
>
> *And thus the native hue of resolution*

Is sicklied o'er with the pale cast of thought;

And enterprises of great pith and moment,

With this regard, their currents turn awry,

And lose the name of action.

How long it will take the human species to overcome this griev-ous error of expecting a life eternal that does not exist, is not clear. At least it fits in well with those other aspects of our religions in which rational thought is disregarded. We lie to ourselves about being moral, when we are not. We don't appreciate that our morals change from group to group and time to time. We do not understand that we are not yet even close to being ethical. We can't, for some reason, see that our religious concepts are myths, and not facts. We seem to be blind to the bigamy of our God, if the myths of each separate religion are true.

THE OMNIPOTENCE DELUSION

We have learned quite a lot since those times when men and women were drawing deity figures on cave walls. We have learned quite a lot since our ancestors were throwing various living sacrifices into fires in order to please their gods, those sacrifices including first born human infants as well as animals. All of our study now tells us that this vast universe runs randomly, governed only by laws of chance, without a planned outcome. We can see no grand program for this universe, and in particular, can see no planned goal for the human race. We find that we are outliers in this universe of chance. We are able to discern physical laws of order only in so far as they describe the interaction of large bodies. The base of the universe, in every way we look at it, consists of disorder and random interaction. We can detect nowhere that there is any force which is directing events on our behalf, and most certainly find no evidence there is any force which has a personal interest in our welfare. As far as we can tell, it is our species against all forces in the universe, which sustain us, but equally seek to eliminate us in any way possible. We do not have any outside help, to the best of our knowledge, in this quest for human survival.

In spite of this knowledge about our universe and our place in it, multiple millions of humans still cling to these God concepts that were born at a time in our history of great ignorance. The great misfortune is that these ancient religious concepts teach us we are nearly divine, almost totally good, extremely powerful, in control of the earth, if not the entire universe, and are going to live forever. This delusion of domination totally belies the reality of our condition on this planet. As best we can tell, we are highly insignificant life forms on a remote planet in a vast universe, have no power over this universe, have no plan for our future other than eventual elimination, and are completely mortal. When we base our right and wrong decisions on this delusion of domination and power, we make incorrect decisions. The correct decisions, if we are to persevere, will be made only if they are based on our insignificance, our dependence, our weakness, and our ephemeral existence. That means we all have to respect each other and work together in order to survive the longest possible time, and have to include all of life in that humble respect. Our religions, unfortunately, have taught us otherwise.

THE PUNISHMENT PHASE

It is not bad enough that we continue to hold these archaic God concepts close to our bosoms, and use them to make deconstructive decisions about our lives. We compound that error by adding an additional dimension preached by our religions, which gets all of us into a whole lot of trouble. We believe that if there is some other human who does not share our particular mythology, that human deserves to be punished. It is probably okay to have religious beliefs that don't jibe with what our scientists tell us about our world, as long as these beliefs are used for personal life meaning, and not used as tools to treat other humans with disdain. Unfortunately, that is not what is happening in our religions today. None of our religions have learned that other religious beliefs have just as much value to those others who hold their own faith dear. None of them has learned to say, consistently, "Perhaps your religion is just as valuable to you as my religion is to me." None of them has learned how to rejoice that other humans have found other systems of thought that give them guidance and emotional sustenance in their lives.

Why this emphasis on punishment of infidels remains such a powerful part of our religions is not entirely clear. Part of this terrible admonition is understandable in the sense that this is exactly what the founders of each of our religions taught. Hebrews massacred all people in all the cities of Canaan that they conquered, because they were not members of their tribe and their faith. Moses ordered that all members of his own tribe be massacred if they did not adhere to his faith. The early Christian church, once it had become the recognized religion of the Roman Empire, burned and looted all the shrines to Mithra in the Roman Empire. They followed that intolerance with massive book burnings and destruction of libraries, in order to suppress any other religious thought, and as a result, caused the Dark Ages. Those individuals who professed other belief were not just shunned. They were imprisoned, tortured and burned at the stake. Muslims bomb embassies, trade centers and market places, in an effort to punish the unbelievers, because this is what their prophet, Muhammad, told them they should do.

Perhaps we could understand this selectivity and rage at other faiths, when all religions were struggling to make their stand and survive against other belief systems. It is hard to understand, however, why we don't show some maturity, and realize that all human concepts need to evolve with new discoveries, or they lose their meaning. It seems pretty clear that some of what our religious founders taught was greatly immoral. Our failure to appreciate that there are these parts of our religions which lead to immoral destruction of our societies does not make a whole lot of sense. These beliefs are so clearly self destructive, it seems obvious that they should be recognized as false doctrine, and abandoned. Jews can strive to be Holy, just as their God is Holy, without helping human society one whit, as long as they continue to demand obeisance from the rest of the world as to their self-acclaimed superior status, and attack their neighbors. Christians can proclaim love of neighbor all they want; it does no good if they demand that the rest of the human species accept Jesus as a divinity on earth, or go to Hell for an eternity. Muslims can emphasize the compassion of their religion all they want; it does no good if they send a young female into a market place strapped with bombs. No amount of compassion is of value if it is always accompanied by violence toward other faiths.

This is, I think, probably another example of human fear of the unfamiliar, greed, jealousy and intolerance, dressed in religious garb. We would have otherwise abandoned this self-destructive creed a long time ago. It is difficult to find a better excuse for our base behavior than religious dogma, however. If "God wills it", whatever cruel act it may be, that act becomes justified in the mind of the perpetrator of that crime. Hate appears to be a powerful motivator of the human psyche. If we have something or someone to hate and strike at, we give our life meaning. We seem to cling to this really bad directive of our religions because it is a most useful tool for those of us who carry envy, hatred, and a burning desire for vengeance. If we sense that we have been wronged by a group with a different religious faith, the fire of retaliation burns in our souls. That group must be punished for their apostasy. The only way they can escape the terrible fate that awaits them, we think, is for them to become one of our brothers.

> *Koran 2:90. God's curse be upon the infidels! Evil is that for which they have bartered away their souls. To deny God's own revelations, grudging that He should reveal His bounty to whom He chooses from among His servants! They have incurred God's most inexorable wrath. Ignominious punishment awaits the unbelievers.*

> *Koran 2: 161. I am the Relenting one, the Merciful. But the infidels who die unbelievers shall incur the curse of God, the angels, and all mankind. Under it they shall remain forever; their punishment shall not be mitigated, nor shall they be reprieved.*

> *Koran 2:191. Slay them wherever you find them. Drive them out of the places from which they drove you. Idolatry is more grievous than bloodshed. But do not fight them within the precincts of the Holy Mosque unless they attack you there: if they attack you put them to the sword. Thus shall the unbelievers be rewarded; but if they desist, God is forgiving and merciful.*

No reasonable marriage survives this degree of intolerance. Marriage is a bond of mutual respect. No amount of respect for our creation and/or compassion, in any of our religions, gets us ahead in our human societies, as long as that empathy is accompanied by violent intolerance. Our religions are in need of depth counseling, if not a divorce. Those morals emphasized by our religions are falling on the floor in a dead heap, shot to death by a jealous husband who believes in punishment. I personally believe that human morality must be divorced from this religious mythology of vindictiveness, for this marriage to survive. We, as a human species, need this marriage of reverence for our creation, and love of our neighbors, in order to reach that fulfillment which each of us seeks. Yet our religious marriages will not survive in any way which provides moral service for human society, in my opinion, until we go through marital counseling in enough depth to convince us to give up our religious exclusivity, and our religious punishment of all others.

THE CASE FOR RELIGIONS

This afternoon, after working on the outline for this chapter, I went out on the back deck for a while to think about the content, before putting words and ideas together. The dogwood tree straight ahead showed tear drop brush strokes of light and dark green, but was just starting to show a little bit of pink in the berries, promising an auburn show in the fall. The surprise lilies underneath, which had come up last week, showed a stand of light purple clustered flowers, proudly displaying their colors. Down the path, the gazebo beckoned, asking me to come, sit in the swing for a while and look back up at the world in contemplation. The fire pot in the back yard asked when I would come, build a fire in the evening, and sit in grampa's back yard swing, in fireside contemplation, to think over life and swat mosquitoes. In the back of the yard, you could see where the tornado had come through ten years ago, laying down three adult trees off to the right, into our yard, where it had torn off the tops of the trees in the middle, but where it had spared the tough locust trees to the far left, which now reached 100 feet into the sky. Off to the right, the butterfly bushes were in full bloom, showing drooping splashes of purple, violet, white, blue and pink, swaying over silver green leaves below, which wavered in the breeze. Their invited guests fluttered and buzzed from one color to the other. On occasion the breeze would shift, bringing me an ethereal scent from their showy display. Straight ahead, the copse of trees in front of the shed showed lush dark green, both vines and trees reaching up to the sky and hanging, in symbiosis. Intermittently more potent breezes rustled their swaying branches. Off to the left, the apple and pear trees showed spots of green and pink, promising a fall harvest for pies and jams. A soft breeze wafted across my face, warm, comforting and gentle. Up in the sky, the clouds were wisps and fluffs of cotton, always changing, sailing to somewhere else to visit other lands and other watchers. There were a number of crisscrossing jet trails, expanding white scud marks from planes that had slid through the sky, leaving their trail behind them. A new trail appeared, close white trails from two tail jets, blue hot holes, spewing beautiful white debris behind a tiny silver mosquito, sometimes silhouetted by the sun. Two hawks drifted by, tilting, waving, riding the wind, looking for meals on the ground. The sky was a glowing pale blue, seemingly endless in depth. The grass was a light green even carpet, covered by dappled sunlight. The ruby-throated hummingbird stopped briefly at the feeder, tilted her head to show her iridescent color, then flitted off, looking for another snack somewhere else. The cats came to visit underneath, then hopped up beside me, requesting a petting purring séance before drifting away to show their independence. Down on the patio, the wood furniture asked when it would again have seated suitors, sharing drinks over a tete-a-tete, full of deep gazes.

Yesterday evening, the eight point buck came up into the yard, entering from the back woods stage right. He grazed up into the yard, pausing frequently to eye me suspiciously. Had I made any sudden move, he would have snorted at me in disgust then run away, angrily flipping me the white of his tail. He moseyed over nonchalantly to the pear tree. After a long pause of eye to eye contact, he raised up on his hind legs and snagged a few pears from the lower branches. Having obtained his dessert at that station, he ambled over to the apple trees, looking for fallen fruit, then sauntered out stage left. This morning, the doe appeared with her two fawns. One of them is bigger than the other, and I suspect they may be male and female. They are both losing their spots now and are rapidly gaining weight. Both will be young adults in a few months. Mother grazed across the yard, stopping at the shed to relieve the kiwi branches that projected out too far of their leaves. After they left, a young bunny came across the yard from behind the shed. She stopped at the gooseberry bushes, grazing for a few minutes, then suddenly bolted, as if the starting gun had fired and the race was on. As dusk approached, the male cardinal perched at the top of the telephone pole to produce his serenade:

Where is it? Where is it? Birdie,birdie,birdie,birdie.

Where is it? Where is it? Birdie,birdie,birdie,birdie.

Some of his friends, who join in that evening serenade, were there with their unique songs, as they called for their mates. Their songs were echoed, as they talked to each other, pairing for the night: This was the chorus of the evening:

Feed your neighbor! Feed your neighbor!

Preacher, preacher! Quit,quit. Do it, do it, do it, do it!

Twirrrrl it! Twirrrrl it!

Cheaper,cheaper, cheaper,cheaper!

There was sound, sight, color, touch, smell, motion, lush growth, gentle warmth, and everything was vitally alive. I thought, "Thank you, God. Thank you for letting me be here to enjoy this beautiful place. I don't know how you did it, to produce all these marvelous forms of life, all woven together in a magnificent scheme where each has its place. I bend my knees in humble reverence before the greatness of your creation. What a precious gift you have given us, to be alive in the midst of all this wonder. I am in awe of your greatness. Whatever I can do to preserve this marvelous creation for all others to enjoy is what I must do. Your power and majesty exceed my imagination. I am, until the day I die, your worshiping, abjectly obedient servant. Words fail me when I try to describe the magnitude of this, your creation, and the depth of my gratitude for you allowing me to enjoy your creation for this brief time. Praise you, my Lord. Praise you for this creation. Praise you for your grace, to allow us to exist in your world."

Judging from my own feelings, and judging from what I have heard expressed by others, there seems no doubt to me that there is a great need for us to express our reverence to this Lord of this creation, whatever that might be. There is an innate need for each of us to express that reverence and gratitude for our existence, each in our own way. There is a great need for all religions, and a great need for all religions to respect each other. Each serves its believers as an avenue of expression for our most heartfelt thanks, which come from somewhere deep in our souls. Without our religions, we would be rather lost, unable to express our wonderment, unable to express fully our yearning to feel communion with and union with the Divine, whatever that may be. The respect of our religions for each other is the part that has been missing.

COMMUNION WITH THE DIVINE

Our need for religion is not just a matter of reverence. There are times in our lives when each of us has the sensation that time has stood still, for just a little while. The pleasure of that event is so intense, it seems as if, for a time, we are momentarily in contact with some other realm, and the memory glows with us forever. Some may equate this intense pleasure only with moments of sexual climax, but that is, in my estimation, far too limiting. Certainly, for most of us, those are special times in our lives, when we have fully shared ourselves with someone we love. Yet I have found the same type of intense pleasure at other special times in my life, from sight, from sound, and from moments of fulfillment. When we have gone down to the mountains of Tennessee, I have stood, with loved ones, on the top of the mountain, with my mouth hanging open, completely awed by the endless progression of forested hills, a creation of wonder and praise. I have watched the birth of our best friend's child, with chills running down my spine. These deep treasures are the wellspring of a life which has known its God.

These special moments have also happened to me several times a year in the concert hall, particularly when there is a guest artist doing a familiar melodic concerto. The music ripples and flows. Startling contrapuntals weave in and out of each other, suddenly falling away to reveal a single instrument lyric of great beauty. Themes that I know from memory are played against each other, varying in intensity and rhythm, thrown from one set of instruments to another, like flashing bright colors which are tossed and turned like a hologram, taking different shapes as they bounce around the concert hall. The artist's fingers fly with unbelievable speed and accuracy, lifting a flood of entrancing sounds off the keys. There is a caesurian pregnant pause, carrying anticipation and tension in its quietude, followed by tunes tossed back and forth, filled with questions, answers, arguments, restated but still recognizable themes, and a rhythm which becomes driving and ferocious, as all of the notes, themes and colors come together in a glorious climax. That cacophony of orchestrated sound assaults my brain and fills my soul. My hair stands on end. Goose bumps appear and I tingle all over. Time stands still for a moment, as my autonomic nervous system goes into overdrive, and I sense touching everything, in a few moments of rapture. What these moments are, I do not know, but am fully aware that at those moments, I feel in communion with the entire universe, or with the Divine.

We go through our lives almost as if we were searching for these special moments to treasure forever. These are the stuff from which religion is born, because at these times, we feel as if we are a part of the grand mystery, in harmony with all other things that exist. There is an aura of peace and fulfillment which comes at no other time, and cannot easily be described by any words. Some will say that these are moments of mystical communion with the Divine. Some will say that these episodes are nothing more than a temporary loss of autonomic motor neuron control. Some will say that these are the times when their God speaks to them directly in their lives. Some will say that it is nice for you to feel good every now and then, but the sooner you get back to reality, the better. I will confess my inability to understand fully these moments of mystical union and temporary body paralysis, but know that each of them has made me feel very religious, and believe that this experience is not different than that felt by others.

We don't really know very well yet how to describe the emotions going on deep inside us by using words and language. We have only been at this language business for seven thousand years, and are still struggling to know how to say what we feel. "I wish I could describe it to you." "Let me see, how can I say this; it is hard for me to put it into words." "Um, um, I don't know what to say." When we have difficulty describing even the simplest of events, it is clear that we have even a harder time trying to explain something that is such a special emotional moment. I have done my best above to describe some of these to you, but still feel tongue-tied about relating what those moments were actually like. They were other-worldly and religious. They were each so deeply felt they became a part of my soul.

We are such an egocentric species. I have heard the opinion expressed many times that we are such advanced creatures, we are the only ones who can achieve these moments of rapture that bring us momentarily at one with the music of the spheres. I would most sincerely beg to differ. I have an outside front door cat, who hangs around waiting for me to appear. When I sit down in one of the front benches, she rubs my legs repeatedly, purring and looking up, walking back and forth as if in a figure of eight choreographed dance, ending in a ballet leap up beside me. She stands there for minutes, while being petted, the purring getting louder. Very cautiously, one paw at a time, she climbs up on my lap over several minutes, then curls, always facing to the right. She slowly sinks down, as if the air in her was deflating, then rests her chin on my arm. She purrs very loudly, and drools on my arm, with the same autonomic response as if she was about to catch a bird. Her eyes slowly close, her tail stops twitching, and she falls into a motionless purring trance for several minutes. If this is not cat bliss, I don't know what it might be. If there is any change in the slow petting rhythm, or a sudden noise, the séance is over. Her eyes open and the tail begins to twitch, then she is gone. I have no doubt, however, that my cat also knows moments of rapture. I have no doubt that all advanced animal forms have their moments of bliss, when they achieve their mystical unity with the universe. I also have no doubt that all advanced animal forms have their moments of great sorrow, when they are overcome with grief at the loss of a loved one. I have no doubt that advanced animal life, in this sense, also has its moments of deep religious emotion.

All animals, including humans, lead a quite egocentric life. We are all looking for sustenance, security, shelter, sexual gratification, self fulfillment, and ways we can maintain these needs for the longest period of time. Along the way, we take great pleasure in a lot of special moments. We love a tight game, and the thrill if our team wins. We take great pleasure in social teasing and sharing our concerns with our friends. We are sometimes entranced by beautiful scenes of nature, and sometimes overcome when we witness a truly loving act of one animal or human for another. We rejoice when a goal, which we have worked for, for many years, has finally been achieved. We treasure those moments of revelation, when an understanding comes that was previously hidden, revealing an entirely greater and more complete world. Some of this stuff is so special for us, it is life changing, and temporarily overwhelming. When we feel deep gratitude for our world, and our life, or when we have moments of rapture, we find ourselves in a state of humble gratitude. For want of a better description, this is what humans have called a religious experience.

RELATIVITY

It appears that we live in such a fixed world. Houses, rocks and streets are for us, very solid objects. If we stumble and fall against something, it certainly hurts, testifying to its solidity. My furniture, dishes, plates and utensils are, to me, quite solid. My furniture holds me up and my plates hold food quite well. Even though other people and animals move, they are quite touchable when near, and very real. The floors underneath us keep us from falling. The fuselage of an airplane zooms us along at a speed of several hundred miles an hour, while preventing us from falling some thirty thousand feet. Hills, lakes and streams may alter their appearance from season to season, but they are always there, when we look. Books can be held in my hands, and contain messages for me from some other mind. My washer and dryer are real enough to clean my clothes. My bed holds me up at night and the blankets keep me warm. The grass in the yard is real enough to require mowing, and my trees bear real fruit. Bee stings hurt, knives cut, ice numbs and fire burns. Run two cars together and the impact shows how solid they were before that collision. When we hit our thumb with a hammer, we are quite aware how solid that little piece of iron is. Our world, in which we live, consists of fixed, firm objects, as far as we can tell. It seems pretty absurd to think that any of it could be anything else.

There is a tremendous catch to the solidity and reality with which we sense our world, however. Our scientists tell us that nothing is as it seems. They say that everything we experience is force on force, a matter of mass/momentum/energy against mass/momentum/energy, occurring in a precise area of space/time, in which both space and time are never separate, but always joined. You can never isolate one from the other. Nothing, they say, is ever the same at one spot in space, at one time, as it is a split second later. They tell us that everything is expanding, as if in an accelerating explosion. Everything is flying apart in random directions, they say, with no end of that explosion in sight. They tell us that the solidity that we sense is simply our brain's interpretation of whatever else is out there, after the photons of light that reflect off those objects have been flipped over by our brains to produce an upright image of those other forces and electromagnetic wave colors. They tell us that eyes are not the only way that animals can see. Bats, they say, see with their ears, platypi see with their snouts, and dolphins see with their radar bulbs, just as if they had built in radar screens. Sightless creatures living in caves see with their tentacles and their hairs. Our scientists tell us that everything is in constant motion, whirling, tilting, rotating, and flying apart. They say that you cannot observe the full nature of anything in a static state, because if you stop its motion, you change the characteristics of that observed particle. Nothing, they tell us, is fixed anywhere; everything, they say, is relative and inconstant. They tell us that all these seemingly solid objects we appreciate in the universe, including suns, planets, moons, asteroids, comets, and objects that exist on all these bodies, represent less than ten percent of the mass of the universe. So far, they have no clear idea what comprises the other ninety percent of the mass of the universe, and for want of a better term, have called it dark energy. All of our physicists are looking for that realm where ninety percent of our universe exists, and right now, have no good clue as to where that mass/energy may be.

That part of the universe we know about, our little ten percent, is also quite a mystery. None of our brightest minds can clearly reconcile the fact that all their measurements tell us that this is a universe which runs purely on chance and random action, with the other fact that we are able to develop very precise laws of physics, which tell us exactly how anything is going to behave. Using these laws of physics, we have been able to perform amazing feats, such as send a several hundred pound package through space for several months, and then have it land, unharmed, on a specific spot on the next planet in our solar system, millions of miles away. How in the world did they do that? How in the world can that precision be reconciled with a universe that runs purely on chaos? How in the world did our nuclear physicists figure out how they could manipulate mass sufficiently to build an atomic bomb, with the power to destroy our planet in a matter of minutes? Why in the world is there a set of observations that describe the action and reaction of atomic particles, and an entirely different set of laws which governs the action and reaction of large objects in our universe?

The next, and most obvious question, as far as this book is concerned, is to ask what difference it makes. What does it matter, as far as our religions are concerned, whether our universe runs purely on the statistics of chance, or on specific laws of physics, or for that matter, on quite a bit of both? One could say that if everything is relative, everything uncertain, and everything happening by chance, this leaves no room for the belief that there is a superpower which created this entire universe a few thousand years ago, just for us, made us to look like Him, and has a definite plan for our future. If the entire universe runs on chance, that means that we also, as a species, occurred entirely by chance, without design and without purpose. On the other hand, others will say that since there are such precise laws of physics, which allow us to do almost godlike things in our world, there must be some force behind it which has organized this universe for a purpose. Most humans have great difficulty understanding how a universe, which has such exact laws of behavior governing those parts of it we can see and measure, could have just assembled itself, without some design having occurred to make it so.

The answer, as far as I am concerned, is that it doesn't matter at all whether this is a universe of chance, or a universe of precise physical laws, or both. I would be willing to bet that, as long as the human species survives, there will be a great need for religious expression. There will always be awe at the vastness, mystery and strangeness of the universe, and there will always be episodes of rapture, which make us, momentarily, feel at one with all life and all matter. I would be willing to bet that in one hundred years, if our species and planet have survived, we will have made discoveries and achieved understanding of our universe which to us today would be totally astonishing. I would be willing to bet that regardless of what fantastic leaps of knowledge we have gained at that time, there will still be great mysteries about how the universe works, awe at its vastness and strangeness, and exciting avenues of exploration in an attempt to understand even more about its properties. I would be willing to bet that, as long as the human species survives, there will be wonder at how little we know, and eagerness to discover more about our universe. Although our drive to discover more, learn more, and understand more is a good part of what makes life worthwhile, there is not, as far as we can tell, an end to this human quest; nor will there be an end for our need to express reverence, humility and gratitude. Another name for this great reverence, humility and gratitude, is religion, for which, as far as I can tell, the human species will always have need.

OUR UNIVERSE AGAINST US

It has taken us a while to understand that we live in a cocoon. We have a planet which is not so close to our energy source that all forms of life have been burned and desiccated, nor are we so far away that the temperature is too cold to sustain life. We are on a planet which is just the right distance away from our energy source to have water on its surface in liquid form. Water, as far as we know, is necessary in some form to sustain life. We have a rotating iron core in this planet, which produces a magnetic shield, and that keeps the electromagnetic storm from the sun from stripping away all life with deadly radiation. That magnetic shield also permits the development of an atmosphere, containing oxygen, which is necessary for our phosphorylating metabolism. We have frozen poles, which serve as an air conditioning system for the planet, moderating those extremes of temperature found in the equatorial areas. We know that if any one of us were exposed to the radiation of the sun outside this protective cocoon, we would be dead in four minutes, much less dead because of oxygen deficiency. This is, as far as the human species is concerned, a very special place. Some would say that is because their God put us here. Others would say that we live here because this is, so far, the only place we know where our particular form of life can exist.

It is not entirely a safe place, however. We have a historical record of planetary disasters that have eliminated most forms of life on this planet, on multiple occasions. Most of those have, as far as we can tell, been the direct or indirect result of asteroid impacts, which darken the atmosphere for decades, and produce suffocation from lack of light and heat. Both plant and animal life have changed dramatically with each of these impacts. We also have a lot of other threatening disasters from time to time. Massive volcanic eruptions can also cause crop failures and dramatic climatic changes, leading to wide spread famine. We are subject to tsunamis, hurricanes, tornadoes, droughts and deadly plagues. We are aware that there are multiple organisms which are developing resistance to our drugs, with the great risk that any one of them may emerge in a highly virulent form, wiping out large segments of our population. It is pretty clear that, although this planet is nurturing and sustaining in a most bountiful way, it is also the source of multiple severe threats to our continued survival.

Our universe isn't helping much either. Right now, it presents a constant threat of some hitherto unknown heavenly body suddenly appearing in the sky on a direct collision course with our planet, the expected result being our sudden demise. Long term, about all we can look forward to is a slowly dying sun, which gradually expands until it engulfs us in an all consuming conflagration. Our galaxy appears to be in the process of swallowing those billions of suns it contains, including ours, into a dense void at the center, called a black hole. Before that happens, however, this galaxy may be torn to pieces, since it appears to be on a collision course with the Andromeda galaxy, our closest galactic neighbor. Although all of this will take a long time, the message is, from all the evidence we have been able to muster, that the universe does not care about us, and would just as soon do whatever it does without having the human species around. The message is, that there is not, as far as we can tell, any force or power which will intervene to prevent any of these natural disasters from occurring.

This message, that the universe does not care about us, and will find a way, sooner or later, to eliminate us, is not reconcilable with what our religions are telling us about our universe. What our religions say is that this universe was begun by a Great Power, which did so with a purpose and a plan, and did so specifically with humans as part of that plan. Our religions tell us that we are like our God, and if we play it right, will live forever. In brief, our religions say that we are powerful, partially in command of the entire universe, and have the opportunity for immortality. This philosophy contrasts dramatically with that our scientific community has given us. If what they tell us is true about suns, galaxies and the evolution of life, we are, as a species, insignificant, constantly at peril, and completely mortal. Our eventual goal, they say, is not a glorious immortality, but a total demise as a form of life.

This is a pretty bitter pill for many humans to swallow, particularly after having spent most of our lives being told otherwise by our admired pastors, who have given us messages of grandeur along with messages of morality. It all gets mixed up in our heads, and many of us struggle to understand how any kind of moral life is worthwhile if it is not tied to some scheme fostered by a Great Power and with a great purpose. Why does it matter what any of us do or how we behave, if it is not for some glorious future purpose? Why should we struggle to be good people when others cheat us, rob us, shoot at us, and treat us like dirt? There is no point, we will say, in trying to lead a moral life, if it is not to be a part of our God's grand plan for the human race. Even life itself, we will say, has little meaning if it is not part of a wonderful plot to achieve greatness for the human race. This is not a message which helps us to lead a better life, we will say; it is a defeatist attitude, a message of doom.

It must be quite apparent to those of you who are reading this book that my inclination is to accept what our best scientific minds are telling us about suns, moons, planets, galaxies, evolution of life, and the laws of probability. Not only do I find it liberating to know that we are not powerful, immortal creatures, I also find that it gives me exactly the opposite message from that expressed above. What this knowledge tells me is that each of our lives is very precious, to be guarded and nurtured in any way we can do so. Each of our lives is a one-time deal, to be savored and guided to its greatest possible fulfillment. No life should be thrown away to satisfy the demands of a strident mythology. Each life should be deeply respected. No life should be taken unless it is to support other life. This knowledge, that the universe sustains us, but is also callously impartial, leads me to believe that the only way we can survive, for the longest time as a species, is for all of us to work together in empathy and morality.

If we kill other humans because it is part of our mythology, our religious God's grand plan, we are simply committing suicide as a species. Human survival requires exactly the opposite. Knowledge of our mortality and insignificance, and our need to seek each other's support, should lead us indeed to be very religious; to be reverently thankful for our creation, and respectful of all life. We should, in other words, love the God of our vast and mysterious universe, and love our neighbor.

ONE WORLD

The best evidence we have is that life began on earth about four billion years ago. Plant species evolved by natural selection for over three billion years, but there were no animals for those billions of years. The first evidence we have of advanced animal life is found from about six hundred million years ago, during the Cambrian explosion. That animal life also evolved by natural selection, producing our common ancestor about five million years ago. Hominids, the predecessors of humans, were found about four million years ago. Homo erectus, the forerunner of our species, was found to exist one and a half million years ago. Homo sapiens did not appear until four hundred thousand years ago. Although there is still controversy about where the first Homo sapiens appeared, the current bet is that this origin was in Africa, at a time when the land consisted of vast savannahs. Rather suddenly, by planetary time, this species migrated out of Africa some forty thousand years ago and colonized the rest of our planet. Humans now exist on every continent of this world, and on some of them, in great number.

During the last forty thousand years, as each pocket of civilization has developed, a great deal of ethnicity has also developed, as each of the pockets has developed their own color, stature and religious belief, as has best suited them. We have had sporadic rulers, who wished to conquer all other civilizations, but for the most part each of these different areas of our world has developed its own unique characteristics. By 8,000 BC, great city-states began to develop, each wielding great power in its own region. Commerce rapidly developed between these centers of political power, and trade of goods was common. Yet each of these areas remained its own civilization, each with its own set of rules, laws, punishments and rewards. Each developed its own religion, with conflicting concepts about exactly how humans should lead their lives, significantly conflicting beliefs about their God and the ways humans should express reverence towards their God. As each of these pockets of civilization has prospered and grown, each of their religions has also prospered and grown, giving us a rich history of religious diversity.

As each of these civilizations has grown in population and expanded, there has been an increasing friction as they have come in direct contact with each other. Whereas each of these conflicts used to be a local matter, not of much concern to all other civilizations, that isolation has now ended. It seems as if there is constant battle, with one sect, or group, always violently attacking other ethnic groups, and most of the time using their religions as an excuse for their violence against each other. And now, all the rest of us are greatly affected by this violence no matter where it may occur, because we have, within the space of a few thousand years, become one world.

One of the basic reasons why any human conflict, anywhere on our globe, now affects all of us rather dramatically, began about one million years ago. Human speech began. Up to that time, we will suppose that hominids communicated rather well with grunts, guttural shows of emotion and gestures, but they did not have the capability of forming multiple words which could be reformed in different arrangements to convey multiple different messages. That required a series of anatomic changes which are found only in the human species. The larynx deepened, allowing the lungs to be used as a bellows, the vocal cords as vibrators and the pharynx as a resonator. The mouth was freed from food gathering as our ancestors became fully bipedal, allowing the lips, teeth and tongue to be used as articulators. Unilateral brain dominance occurred, with an isolated speech center on one side, a change found only in humans. These anatomic variations created a remarkable change in human life. Ideas could now be exchanged freely and accumulated knowledge transmitted from one generation to another. Certain members of each tribe became wise ones or priests, entrusted with this dissemination of that collected knowledge to the young of that tribe.

A second revolution in human communication appeared about 5500 BCE. Written language appeared. At first it was only pictorial. Certain symbols were used to represent a hand, foot, spear, animal, tree, or other known object. Some languages today, such as Chinese, are still mostly pictorial, using a complex symbol to represent an entire word. By 3000 BCE, these symbols had become simplified to the point they could be collected together in syllables, so that different groupings of symbols represented different sounds. Much of the meaning of these early words was understood by the culture of that day, but those words were logo-syllabic, without vowels that allow precise definition. That represents significant difficulty when we attempt to interpret some of those logo-syllabic writings today. Greek civilization, in a stroke of genius, developed letters which were both vowels and consonants, allowing the formation of words in an almost unlimited manner, each of which could be designated as having a specific meaning. Now both the expresser and the recipient of those words could understand more precisely what was meant by that word. We not only had spoken transmissible language; we now had language which could be stored, and with it, knowledge stored.

A third revolution in human communication occurred in 1439. The printing press was invented. Up until this time, written language was laboriously reproduced by scribes, who sometimes left out pieces, or added their own little touches. The transmission of this stored knowledge was pretty much confined to the learned few, who could read and write. The vast majority of the population remained illiterate and ignorant. This fell to the advantage of the church, which could claim as part of its power over the population, this reservoir of human knowledge, available only to these privileged priestly few. That all changed, when the written word was available to all that could read. The pressure to become literate became immense, and the dissemination of knowledge led to an explosion of civilian power. Protestant sects formed, announced by flyers posted on church doors, which listed the grievances of the revolting faithful. The rights of kings were under challenge everywhere.

We are currently undergoing a fourth revolution of human communication, with telecommunication and computer access almost instantly available around the world. My auto mechanic communicates daily with his wife, who is in Thailand. She is serving in a mission field, trying to keep teen age girls from being sold into the sex trade by their families. We are all potentially in contact with all others on this planet, so that none of us is isolated, unless there is political and economic suppression to prevent us from doing so. We have become one world. All nations have borders which abut those boundaries of other nations. All ethnic groups are constantly juxtaposed against other ethnic groups. All moral systems are brought face to face against the moral systems of other cultures. All religions find themselves constantly arguing with other religions about who is most right about their God's will and His directions for the human species.

The fact that we are all now one world means that our religions must change, or we are all in a lot of trouble. None of them should allow the conservative elements of their religion to preach intolerance and violence towards others who believe differently than they. The fact that we are all now one world also means that there is an even greater need for us all to be deeply religious: to be humbly grateful for our lives, and deeply respectful of all other lives.

BORN AGAIN

There are particular segments of the Christian faith that place great emphasis on being "born again." This is particularly true of fundamentalist denominations, which carry this as one of the major tenets of their creed. This concept has significant value. It is intended as a recommitment of each person, once he or she has become of sufficient age to fully understand their choices in life. At that time they become able to make their own decisions about what is important and what is not, as to whether they are willing to commit to leading a moral life. That means, to these denominations, committing to Jesus as their savior, one who serves as an example of those actions all of us should make in order to be a person of high integrity. This creed has had various expressions, such as the fairly recent popular wrist bands carrying the letters, WWJD. These were understood to stand for "What would Jesus do?" Everything those persons wearing these wrist bands did in their lives was supposed to reflect this moral standard, and every action affecting other humans supposed to be done with this guide in mind. Born again Christians were absolutely delighted when one of their own was elected president of the United States of America. Such a person, they thought, would surely make the right decisions as to national policy, because he always had this moral guide behind him to tell him what to do. It would make him superior to any other person as to what would be the wisest directions in which to take our country. Their support of this president was, I believe, most well intended.

Unfortunately, most of the presidential decisions made by this person who was thinking as a "born again" Christian proved to be morally incorrect, in my opinion. I think it may be important to examine the reasons for this disappointing failure. The problem, as I see it, is that a lot of baggage comes along with believing in Jesus as a moral guide for our human actions. This phrase carries a lot more content to it than just a simple bit of faith. It means for one, as currently defined by the Christian church, believing that Jesus was the Christ, a Divinity on earth. It means believing that this historical person was part of a mysterious three in one Divinity, in which he was one part, one part some sort of universal mysterious Spirit, and the third part, the Supreme Creator of the entire universe. This, in itself, is enough to stretch my credulity beyond the breaking point. There is, however, a great deal more. It means believing that Jesus was able to walk on water, bring dead people back to life, create wine and food whenever he chose to do so, control the weather, make fish appear whenever he chose, cause a herd of animals to run over a cliff to their death and drive demons out of human souls. The gravity of these fanciful myths weighs heavily, when we have not in our own experience found any evidence that any one person of any description, is ever exempt from the physical laws of the universe.

A mind set which is convinced that there are miracles, that there was the God of all creation on earth, and that furthermore, since it accepts that Divinity, has that God on its side, is doomed to make grievous errors. This philosophy is pre-programmed to believe that, since it has the good God on its side, the other side, whatever it may be, has to represent some form of evil. Once you accept the first premise of being on the side of right, the second premise of fighting evil becomes almost mandatory. Once you see your opponents as evil people, all forms of invasion, bombing regardless of civilian deaths, torture, imprisonment without cause, disregard of civil rights and disdain for other religious belief, becomes a natural response. Such disregard for the rights of others and the virtues of other religions stems from this staunch belief in Jesus as the savior, mostly because this belief carries this incredibly irrational baggage with it. That weighty baggage veers a mind trying to find moral decisions into exactly the opposite immoral direction.

These segments of the Christian religion wish us to believe that none of us can lead the life of an adult human, with moral and ethical behavior, unless we have taken this additional step in our lives, to be "born again," as far as our commitment to our faith is concerned. Only then, according to this religious belief, will each of us have reached our full potential as human beings. Only then, they say, will we feel at peace with ourselves and others. Only those, they believe, who have professed that Jesus was the Christ, who was the savior of mankind, will be able to make moral and correct decisions, with their God on their side, and live in peace for an eternity. Unfortunately, for the reasons cited above, what happens when humans become radical in promoting this myth, or similar myths, is to enter a dark prison, with imposing walls that keep us from seeing the rest of the world. We cannot see, when locked into this prison, that there is a great world out there, full of diversity in appearance and diversity of thought. We do not understand, when locked into this prison of religious dogma, that other religions, no matter how strange they may seem to others who do not have that faith, have great meaning and value for their faithful. We do not see that the end to slavery is to allow freedom of expression, be it political or religious. We do not see that it is immoral to punish anyone in any way, for having a different religious faith than that we hold.

I don't mind at all the concept of being born again. In some ways, it makes a lot of sense. Those studies of our ability to understand the long term effects of those actions we take today have been quite clear. They tell us that we don't develop the capability to understand those long term ramifications of what we do until after the age of 25. If, at a time in our lives when we are capable of understanding what a certain commitment at this time will mean long term, we pledge allegiance to a certain cause, that pledge to me carries a great deal more meaning than a commitment that was done without thought. If the only devotion we have, is to causes that have been indoctrinated into us from the time we could understand language, I do not believe that these carry the same value. In that sense, we should all be born again, over and over, many times. We should continue to study, think, and grow in our knowledge all our lives. When we reach a new level of understanding from that knowledge, it is a great joy. We are born again, into a world of different meaning and broader horizons. As far as our religions are concerned, it would to me be a great new born again awakening, if we could all understand that neither the dogma of our dominant religions, nor the strident cries of atheists, are an adequate basis for understanding where humans are and how we should lead our lives.

Most of this book has been about the need for our religions to be born again also. If they are to serve those people who are devoted to their particular interpretation of life, they will have to release themselves from the dogma of the past. If they wish to believe in a certain mythology, which gives them direction in life, they should have that right. What none of our religions has the right to do, however, is to insist that only their belief system is correct, without regard for the beliefs of anyone else. They particularly do not have the right to punish some other human in any way, because that human does not have their certain belief. The punishment phase of our religions must be abandoned for these religions to continue to serve the human species, in a world which has become one world. As our religions now exist, they are incompatible, by virtue of their emphasis on the punishment of unbelievers, with any form of democracy. Democracy can only exist if there is tolerance for all beliefs. Democracy will not survive, unless our religions are born again, into belief systems which accept all other religious conviction as equally valid.

NEITHER ATHEISM NOR RELIGIOUS DOGMA

Those minds who founded our democracy were keenly aware that they could not let any religion become wedded to this new democracy, or it would fail. There was pressure to do otherwise. There were several attempts by members of the Continental congress to place Christian wording into the constitution, or to place Christianity in a place of prominence in this new government. Those attempts were greatly resisted by Thomas Jefferson, John Adams, George Washington and Thomas Paine. Thomas Jefferson, for example, in his comments on the attempts to refer to Jesus as the Christ, and the source of civil liberty, states that this amendment was:

> ...rejected by the great majority, in proof that they meant
> to comprehend, within the mantle of its protection, the
> Jew, and the Gentile, the Christian and Mohammedan, the
> Hindoo and Infidel of every denomination.

We are extremely grateful to these persons who recognized the need to tolerate all religions, and not let any certain one religion become imbued with the power to suppress all other religions. We wonder why we have lost our way, of late, and why there has been such an emphasis to declare this a Christian nation, founded on Christian values. During my radio interviews concerning my last book, *The Religious Subversion of Democracy*, this point was often raised. When I produced the actual quotes from Adams, Paine, Jefferson and Washington, in proof that they did indeed think of Christianity as a worthless religion, there was usually this countering argument: "Was not this country founded by men and women who were seeking escape from religious persecution, and does this not mean that this country was indeed founded by Christians seeking religious freedom?" My response has been so far to indicate that once these Christians found their religious freedom, they did not want anyone else to have their own freedom. They have been opposed to all other forms of religious expression in this country. Unless it is Christian, in some form, it is no good, in their opinion. At that point, the radio host or caller, after a slight pause, chooses to go to another question, rather than debate this item, which is difficult to call any other way. Christianity has not been beneficent towards other religions.

This is not to speak in total condemnation of Christianity, Islam, Judaism, or any other religion which claims direct access to the source of all creation. It is certainly not to speak in opposition to those moral lessons which each of these religions has brought to the table, to give all of us direction in how to lead lives that will produce healthy and happy communities. It is to speak against those parts of these faiths which express intolerance for other faiths, and particularly speaks against those parts of our religious faith which preach punishment for all humans who happen to have a different belief. As they now exist, none of our established religions provides us with that type of emotional experience that will lead us to respect and desire to work with all other life on this planet, so that we can all jointly survive.

We can also say that atheism, now preached with much greater bravado, gives us no better answer. Not only does organized religion, because of its intransigent intolerance, leave me quite cold as to a proper guide for my life, but atheism leaves me even colder. I am well aware that each of these writers advocating atheism has extremely valid points. Each of them also sees that our organized religions are leading us astray, and that the dogma our religions ask their followers to swallow whole does not make sense with our current understanding of our universe and our current understanding of human behavior.

Most of the books they have produced are extremely well-written and contain many valid arguments. For all the reasons which we have already listed in our discussions of religious faith, none of these intelligent gentlemen see that we can make any claim for a Divine Creator who made this world for a purpose, made humans in his image, and who has a glorious plan for the human race. I think that these points are quite correct. I have learned from each of those authors whose recent books I have read, including Richard Dawkin's *The God Delusion, Critiques of God*, edited by Peter A. Angeles, David Mills' *Atheist Universe*, Sam Harris' *The End of Faith*, George H Smith's *Atheism. The Case Against God*, and Christopher Hitchens' *God is not Great*. There are, I am sure, many more good books on the fallacies of our current religions out there to be sampled. Perhaps none of them, however, have made these points about our organized religions better than the dean of modern atheism, Bertrand Russell. The following quotes are taken from his book, *Why I am not a Christian.*

> *"You find as you look around the world that every single bit of progress in humane feeling, every improvement in the criminal law, every step toward the diminution of war, every step toward better treatment of the colored races, or every mitigation of slavery, has been consistently opposed by the organized churches of the world. I say quite deliberately that the Christian religion as organized in its churches, has been and still is the principle enemy of moral progress in the world."*

> *"Religion prevents our children from having a rational education; religion prevents us from removing the fundamental causes of war; religion prevents us from teaching the ethic of scientific co-operation in place of the old fierce doctrines of sin and punishment. It is possible that mankind is on the threshold of a golden age; but, if so, it will be necessary first to slay the dragon that guards the door, and this dragon is religion."*

> *"Let it be said with the utmost simplicity and directness: there is nothing bad in sex, and the conventional attitude in this matter is morbid. I believe that no other one evil in our society is so patent a source of human misery, since not only does it directly cause a long train of evils but it inhibits*

that kindliness and human affection that might lead men to remedy the other remedial evils, economical, political and racial, by which humanity is tortured."

"In the meantime, it would be well if men and women could remember, in sexual relations, in marriage, and in divorce, to practice the ordinary virtues of tolerance, kindness, truthfulness and justice."

"The whole contention that Christianity has had an elevating moral influence can only be maintained by wholesale ignoring or falsification of the historical evidence."

"I would invite any Christian to accompany me to the children's ward of a hospital, to watch the suffering that is there being endured, and then to persist in the assertion that these children are so morally abandoned as to deserve what they are suffering. In order to bring himself to say this, a man must destroy in himself all feelings of mercy and compassion. He must, in short, make himself as cruel as the God in whom he believes."

All of which leads us back to the origin of this chapter. At least to me, this pungent negativism, as expressed by Bertrand Russell, and in great detail by those other authors who speak in support of atheism, leaves me quite wanting, even though I believe in what they say, as far as they go. If also the tenets of our organized religions are leading us badly astray, what is left? Why has the human species almost demanded religious expression as soon as this life form existed? What are we looking for that we don't find expressed at all in atheistic thought, and find expressed in a highly contorted fashion by our organized religions? Why do we, in spite of all this misdirection and negativism we get from our religions, and from our intellects, still wish to fall on our knees in submission, gratitude and humble service to our God?

The great unknown is, in and of itself, at least for me, a cause to live my life in great awe and reverence. When I add to that my humble regard for the vagaries of chance, I find myself deeply religious every day. There is, in these two great unknowns, a God that is all around us, in everything that we do, in every decision that we make, in every action that we take. This God has been a part of every atomic, chemical and matter reaction in the universe, since the beginning of time. This God, for want of a better description or better term, is called the God of Chance and Vast Mystery. As best we can tell, we are unplanned life forms, who are totally insignificant parts of the universe, and highly mortal. We have one life chance to do whatever we do right, and leave something of value after us. There is, for these reasons, at least for me, a God, but it is a God who does not plan, does not direct, does not care, does not judge and does not interfere.

Religious fanatics, who practice human intolerance and violence based on myths of superiority and immortality, are certainly wrong, in my opinion. Atheist nihilists, who fail to appreciate that we should treat the vastness and mysteries of the universe with great awe and reverence, and who fail to appreciate that we all have deeply religious experiences, are also, in my opinion, very wrong. Human intuition is far more correct than religious dogma, and far more correct than those who fail to respect the great unknown. There is, to my mind, an all-pervasive God. There is a reason why religions are an innate part of human conception and human history. There is indeed, a Lord of the Dance; or perhaps we should say, there is indeed a Lord of the Chance and Vast Mysteries.

RELIGION AND GOVERNMENT

We are so greatly indebted to our founders, who saw clearly that every religion has a deeply ingrained grave intolerance for all other faiths. It was quite obvious to them that they could have no one religion wedded to our new government without poisoning that equality which they sought. Democracy cannot exist unless there is tolerance for all faiths and all beliefs. Our nation's founders had considerable pressure on them to do otherwise, but were able to resist those demands, and establish a government based on the premise that all men are created equal. We have yet, in this discussion, to explore in depth the inconsistencies of such a premise, but can express our great admiration for the morals contained therein. All men and women should have equal opportunity. All men and women should have freedom of faith. No person should be punished in any way for their religious belief. If there is equal opportunity, and freedom of faith, only then does democracy exist.

This democratic creed is obviously still a work in progress. It took us a long time to realize that this equal opportunity extended to women as well as men. It was not until the twentieth century that we were willing to accept, as a nation, that this freedom of opportunity extended to blacks as well as whites. We are still not sure how our Indian Nation should become assimilated into the rest of this nation. We are currently going through gyrations and seizures, trying to understand that homosexuality is a normal part of the human population, whereas that segment of our population should have received their democratically deserved rights long ago. Our failure to adhere to our democratic ideal in these major areas is not the totality of our failure.

We have found that our congressional representatives have become the tools of business interests and lobbyists, and that they have been doing what is best for those business elite rather than what is best for their constituents. We have seen, because of this betrayal of our trust, the rich get richer and the poor get poorer, as the middle class is being squeezed out of existence. We have seen, under Christian conservative government officials, the appearance of faith based initiatives, which have been a weakly disguised attempt to wed Christianity to our government, but exclude all other faiths. We have seen, under those same Christian conservatives, judges fired without cause, citizens secretly jailed without cause and without representation, computer, bank and tax records accessed without warrant, phones tapped without warrant, and worst of all, the callous justification of torture. Our government, which claims equality, is far from that, and remains under intense attack to take away that equality. We have a lot of work to do to regain our democratic moral sanity.

Although we are immensely grateful for a government which espouses equality, and immensely grateful that our founders saw it was necessary to exclude religions from our government in order to establish that tolerance for all, we have paid a rather hefty price for that exclusion. What we achieved was a marvelous goal: freedom from the punishment phase of our religions. No one is to be chastised, dispossessed, jailed, tortured or killed because of their religious belief. This has allowed a great flowering of religious faith in our country, contributing to the great health of our society. How wonderful it is to have a society where, for the most part, all of us can worship in the way which most sustains us and provides guidance for our lives. We are greatly blessed in this regard.

We lost something really important with that exclusion, however. We pushed away the other pole of our religions also, the moral pole. We succeeded in gaining religious freedom but also threw out the moral compass that our religions provide. The significant unwillingness of our religions to provide moral guidance for our government has been a societal defect. There has been a great void in the attempt of our religions to prevent moral malfeasance in our commanders. They say that morality is their mission, but they make almost no protest when our government rips away our civil liberties, and make no protest against war.

It is easy to think that our religions should have very little to do with our government or our economy. Religion, after all, concerns itself mostly with our reverence for our Creator and our system of morals. Our religions promote, or at least are supposed to promote, those values which we have previously discussed as essential elements of a moral life: love of our God, and love of neighbor. In order to do so, they have many times felt more comfortable staying at arm's length away from the dirty business of politics and international intrigue. As a matter of fact, they are required by the law of this country, in order to maintain their tax-exempt status, to not side with any particular business interest or politician. Our religions, for the most part, accept this category of bystander very well. This lack of involvement in the affairs of our country allows them to concentrate on their mission at hand; offering the reward of eternal life and superiority to those who wish to confess to a certain form of mythology. It appears that our religions have, as far as morality is concerned, usually embraced the matter of distancing themselves from our government and our economic decisions, in order that they may carry out their own, different, mission.

For our religions to not become involved in the bureaucracy of the government is one thing, which I think we should all find highly desirable. For our religions to not make any moral judgment as to those decisions our government makes is, to my mind, a great deficit. If our religions choose to make no protest about those foolish acts our government commits, the moral silence becomes most disturbing. If the morality of our society rests entirely with our churches, then we are getting little or no guidance from them for our government. Our churches have stood silently by, making no moral pronouncement, while other nations have been declared totally evil, and our civil liberties have been stripped away. Our religious faithful often make no moral judgment while other nations declare war, and make no value judgments as to who should be killing whom. They only concentrate on whether those who remain, after all the killing has been done, accept the Christian religious mythology or not. They do not seem to mind if those inhabitants of another nation, who strongly oppose Christianity, have had their demise hastened a bit.

These damaging statements concerning the moral lassitude in our religions may be a bit harsh, but their long standing absent moral guidance in our government is deeply troubling. Perhaps an example of this vacuum of morality, presented in further detail, will serve to bring this particular point home a bit more cogently.

During World War I, Iran was the site of foreign intrigues, national bankruptcy, a national famine and constant political turmoil. All of that came temporarily to a halt when a Cossack Persian military officer, Reza Khan, took control of all the military forces in that country, in 1921. After becoming named war minister, then minister of defense, he deposed the reigning Shah, and transferred all the central power of that country to himself, in 1925. The reign of Shah Reza Pahlavi (his imperial name) proved to be beneficial. He instituted reforms both in education and in the judicial realm, particularly lessening the influence of conservative religious groups on the life of the country. Women were no longer required to wear the restrictive clothing demanded before that time, and the divorce laws were changed in the favor of women. He sought to find ways to free Iran from foreign influence, and was successful in negotiating better terms with the Anglo-Iranian Oil Company, which was firmly entrenched in the Iranian oil fields. The nation's first railroad was begun in 1938.

There was significant resistance to the efforts of Shah Reza Pahlavi to free the country from foreign intervention, however, much of it coming from the Anglo-Iranian Oil Company, which would later become known as British Petroleum. The Soviets weren't happy either, and with the advent of World War II, they had an excuse. Iran was invaded by combined British and Soviet troops, the excuse being given that it would assure the safe passage of American goods to Soviet troops through Iran. The Shah was forced to abdicate and leave the country. In his absence, the Allied forces named his son, Mohammed Reza Pahlavi, as the shah, after making sure that he, as their puppet, would be friendly to the Allied forces as well as, perhaps more importantly, to Allied business interests. Mohammed Reza Pahlavi was more than willing to do so. During the war, Allied forces were able to dictate what terms of cooperation they wished from the Iranians, in all categories. This colonization of Iran, however, did not sit well with the Iranian people.

Iranians, with good cause, found this continued foreign meddling in the affairs of their country to be troubling, if not galling. In 1946, the Soviet Union and a communist regime in Azerbaijan were removed from power. In 1951, the prime minister of Iran, Mohammed

Mossadegh, nationalized the oil industry. The British response was immediate and drastic. None of this was about justice. It was all about oil. The British established an economic blockade, and convinced their American colleagues that an independent Iran might align with Russian business interests, cutting off American oil supplies. American intelligence was full of purported threats from the Soviets, as the cold war was rapidly heating up. The CIA did not need much convincing. They enlisted one of their favorites, Major General Herman Norman Schwarzkopf, to take care of this problem for them.

Schwarzkopf was the father of H. Norman Schwarzkopf, Jr., who later became the American commander in the Persian Gulf War. Schwarzkopf, Sr. was an imposing figure in his own right. He served with distinction as a part of the American Expeditionary Forces in Europe during World War I. During the occupation, following the war, he served as Provost Marshal, where he showed organizational skills and deft management, in part due to his fluency in German. When he returned to the United States, he organized the newly formed New Jersey State Police, forming troops to battle gambling rings in the New York City area, and moonshiners in the southern part of the state. He was narrator of the radio program Gang Busters, before re-entering the army in 1940. It was Schwarzkopf who had organized the Iranian police after the Allied invasion which deposed Shah Reza Pahlavi in 1941. Now, in 1953, he was being asked again to interfere with the rightful affairs of a foreign country, without just moral cause. It was to guarantee that there would be a flow of Iranian oil to American shores, regardless of how right or wrong that might be. There was no motivation of justice. It was all about avarice and oil.

Schwarzkopf convinced the deposed shah, Mohammad Reza Pahlavi, that he could bring him back to power, using the security forces he had previously trained in that country. A coup was formed, under the direct guidance of the CIA, and under the direct supervision of Schwarzkopf. The democratically elected and popular regime of Iran was overthrown. Mohammad Reza Pahlavi was placed in power as the Shah of Iran, in 1953. Mohammad Mossadegh, the duly elected Prime Minister of Iran, was placed in prison until he died in 1967. All the oil fields were placed back in the hands of American and British companies. There was a rapid westernization of the country. Muslim establishments were removed from religious power, and for many, much of their land was taken in order to redistribute that land to cultivators. At first, that significant change to a more capitalistic economic system was sullenly accepted, but it rapidly began to wear. There was the sense that too many changes had been made in agriculture and industry; there was revulsion for the libertine excesses of those in power. Iranians were keenly aware of the hypocrisy involved when a country priding itself on its democracy elects to depose a democratically elected government, just to get access to the oil it contains. There was revolt against the brutal tactics of the secret police, organized by Schwarzkopf, who murdered, tortured and imprisoned protestors. When the Ayatollah Khomenei offered freedom from this tyranny, the people of Iran welcomed a return to an Islamic state, albeit a restrictive one.

This was the setting in 1979, when the Islamic revolt was underway, that the American embassy in Iran was occupied by Iranian students, as previously described. This embassy was a special target for the hatred of Iranians, because it was the very spot from where the coup overthrowing their democratically elected government in 1953 had been directed, by this CIA designee of the United States, Schwarzkopf. It was considered a nest of spies, and served as a physical reminder of the hypocrisy of the United States. At the beginning, 64 hostages were taken, some of them being released early. The remaining 53 were held for the next two months. Iranians rejoiced at this showing of patriotism for their country. The Republic's first president, Abolhassan Bani-Sadr, who opposed the holding of the embassy, was forced to flee to France, together with opposition leader Massoud Rajavi.

The United States president at that time was Jimmy Carter, who has since his presidency distinguished himself as a moralist and humanitarian. I have not been able to find any statement by him that one of the reasons for his reluctance to act in a military way against the hostage situation in Iran was because he was fully aware of the immorality of United States action during the preceding 26 years, in deposing the democratically elected government of Iran. My bet is, although there is no public evidence of such, Mr. Carter found the actions of his government, prior to his ascension to the presidency, to be unjust toward the people of Iran. My bet is that he understood why there was such anger directed toward the United States, and was seeking to find the best way to end this crisis without making that anger even worse. My estimation is that his decision to continue nego-tiation with Iran until that crisis was overcome, was by all odds the best decision to make, and one that I would have also made.

That approach which Carter chose to make in this situation, however, did not sit well with the American public. He was roundly criticized as being weak and ineffective, effeminate, indecisive and unresponsive to the needs of American citizens abroad. That per-ception of Carter as a weak president in time of need is probably the reason why he lost the election in 1980. American citizens wanted someone as their commander in chief who would react with power when our country was threatened, both here and abroad. The public reaction to this hostage situation was to "hate the bastards" who had done this to American citizens, even though the motive behind this occupation of the American Embassy was an effort by those Iranians to patriotically serve the people of Iran. The only American under-standing of this occupation was that it was illegal, and a transgression against international law. There was no attempt by any American diplomat to help the American public understand the vile extent of our government's complete disregard for the sovereign affairs of the nation of Iran. There was certainly not any attempt by our moral-ist churches to help the citizenry understand why there was hatred directed against the United States, coming from Islamic countries. There was no attempt to love your neighbor.

I have at no time, heard any pastor, or read any statement coming from the religiously faithful, that there is a reason why an American flight is flown into the ocean by a Muslim copilot, after the pilot has left the cockpit, purposefully committing suicide and killing all passen-gers on board. I have heard none of them offer a reason why Muslims pull a boat up to an American naval ship and explode a big hole in it, killing sailors inside. I have not heard of any priest, pastor or rabbi who has offered a reason why American embassies are bombed, or why Muslims blew up a truck in the basement garage of the World Trade Center. It took Muslims flying airplanes into the world trade center towers for anyone to ask why anyone would want to take their own lives and 2500 others with them, in an act of great violence. The enor-mity of this, what is to us an absolutely evil act, has finally caused a few people to ask why. It is actually pretty simple. Muslims of the Middle East consider the United States of America the Great Satan, against whom they should act in any effective way they can, in order to protect their way of life and their religion. They do so in a very misdirected manner, but not without provocation. The United States of America has amply shown its disdain for their nation, their religion, and their way of life.

It is not just Christianity that is to blame, of course. It is also Judaism and Islam, both of whom have neglected to apply their own rules of compassion to their far neighbors. Our morals do us little good if they are not fully expressed. It would seem that our religions are experts in professing themselves to be moral, but not making any attempt to fully behave that way. Instead, they show their profound intolerance for humans who hold other faiths dear, which is, without mincing words, an expression of immorality. Our religions are, in a most major way, directly opposed to those grand ideals which are expressed in the Declaration of Independence of the United States of America.

FEAR AND NUCLEAR WAR

Religious intolerance is indeed, a fertile ground for our elected officials. As long as we have ease of life, and the respect of others, it is difficult to get us riled. All of us, however, are well aware that, quite frequently in life, we have lost something precious to us because of the aggression of some other human. It does not take a whole lot to arouse that fear within us that something else very precious to us is about to be taken away, and we can be convinced to do some pretty awful things to other humans, as a preemptive strike, before we lose anything more. Any leader, who has his or her own personal cause, based on jealousy, greed or personal vendetta, finds this religious intolerance, deeply embedded in the belief system of the majority of his or her constituents, a most convenient substrate to bend to his or her own purpose. In particular, if that message of fear is aimed at the true believers of any religion, the result is almost certain. There will be bombing, invasion, destruction and torture soon to follow.

Our human history of violence toward others of our own kind has been pretty frightening. As soon as a more destructive weapon of war has been conceived, it has been widely used, in short order. As soon as long sharp swords became available, they became the weapons of choice over spears. As soon as bows and arrows became perfected, everybody wanted them in order to kill each other. As soon as guns were manufactured, all warriors were putting them to use in their battles. It was for good reason. Those that had advanced weaponry were victorious in their aggrandizement, as Jared Diamond has fully outlined in his book, *Guns, Germs and Steel*. As soon as cannon were available, they were being dragged to every battlefield. As soon as airplane bombs were created, millions of people met their death in a rain of terror from the sky. Current technology allows that bombing to be very precise, using laser guided systems. It can even be done from thousands of miles away, using satellite systems and drones. All the operator of that bomb sees is a flash on a screen, as if it were simply a video game. He or she does not have to witness the horror on the ground that they have caused. As soon as an atomic bomb became available, it was put to use in war, causing millions of deaths, mutilations and late cancer deaths.

Our recent history of violence toward each other has been accelerated, if anything. In an article in the *National Geographic* in January of 2006, Lewis M. Simon states the last 100 years has been the century of mass murder. He states that more than fifty million people have been murdered during this time frame. From 1915 to 1923, Ottoman Turks slaughtered up to 1.5 million Armenians. In the mid-century, the Nazis liquidated six million Jews, three million soviet prisoners of war, two million Poles, and forty thousand other "undesirables". Mao Zedong killed thirty million Chinese, and the Soviet government murdered twenty million of its own people. In the 1970s the communist Khmer Rouge killed 1.7 million of their fellow Cambodians, in order to establish their regime. Saddam Hussein's Baath party killed 100 thousand Kurds in the 1980s and l990s. Rwanda's Hutu led military wiped out 800 thousand members of the Tutsi minority in the 1990s. Now there is continuing genocide in the Darfur region of Sudan. Simon states that "In sheer numbers, these and other killings make the twentieth century the bloodiest period in human history."

These lessons are not lost on those leaders of our nations that already have nuclear capability. All of them are opposed to any other nations also developing the capability to produce atomic bombs. It is seldom you find so many nations in complete agreement on any topic, but on this one, there is unanimity, amongst those who are nuclear powers. All of them are opposed to the nuclear program which is well underway in North Korea, and all of them are opposed to the nuclear program begun in Iran. What they see, and rather correctly, is that we have become one world, with the competing religions of the world each committed to persuading all other humans to accede to their particular point of view, or else eliminate them. Given this religious animosity, given the history of cruelty of humans toward other humans in the past century, and given the awful destructive power of nuclear weaponry, It seems that all it will take is for enough nations to develop atomic bombs, before one of them, in a fit of anger, be it for religious or other reason, pushes their atomic bomb button, to be followed in a few minutes by all others pushing their own buttons of self destruction. Perhaps the biblical prophecy of an apocalypse ending the world as we know it, is entirely correct, and coming soon to the planet on which we live.

These objections to the nuclear program in Iran, however, have been a bed of perfidy and double standards. According to nuclear experts, the reasons Iran says it needs to develop nuclear power make some sense. Its oil supplies will not last forever. It will need power generating capability beyond that time when they no longer have a copious supply of oil and natural gas to supply their energy needs. Furthermore, it makes no sense to use up those oil reserves early, then have no way of generating the power necessary to drive its economy. Now is the time for Iran to develop nuclear power plants, in order to conserve their natural resources as long as possible, as well as plan for the future.

There are three nations who have chosen to not sign the international Nuclear Proliferation Treaty, in which those signees promise to not further extend their nuclear bomb capabilities. Those three nations are Israel, India and Pakistan, yet none of them is being chastised for not agreeing to suspend all further atomic weaponry research. As a matter of fact, the United States provided India with additional nuclear expertise, in exchange for its no vote against Iran in the United Nations. This agreement was in direct violation of the Nuclear Proliferation Treaty, duly signed by the United States. If we look as this can of worms purely from the aspect of a disinterested observer, it would seem that the stand of the United States against

Iran is pure hypocrisy. Granted, there is the fear that any of the nations of the world will misuse, at any moment, its weapons of mass destruction, but to deny any sovereign nation the right to pursue the means of guaranteeing its long term survival, seems like the modern day version of the dog in the manger, on a grand scale.

The greatest threat to some sort of conflagration which could lead to the next world war or a nuclear holocaust may not come at all from North Korea or from Iran, but from one of those nations which already has an arsenal of atomic bombs. That nation would be one of those three which refused to sign the international Nuclear Proliferation Treaty, Israel. Israel has throughout this confrontation with Iran remained the most vocal against any further development of nuclear capability by Iran. In June, 2008, the Prime Minister of Israel, Shaul Mofaz, stated his belief that Iran was involved in uranium enrichment which would lead to the development of an atomic bomb. In an interview, he stated baldly that "If Iran persists in developing nuclear weapons, we will attack it." Although the official stance of Israeli officials is that there is a very low probability of Iran either developing an atomic bomb, much the less using it against them, it is clear that there is an element of the Israeli command that believes quite differently. When they hear the Iranian president, Ahmadinejad, calling for the destruction of Israel, and they see a developing Iranian nuclear program, their worst fears leap to the fore. The misfortune of all this is that Israel is famous for preemptive strikes against its neighbors, which it considers enemies. It has bombed Iran in the past. If it does so again, at this time in history, all hell may break loose, in a conflagration of religious and ethnic hatred. The nations of the world have a lot to fear, but may have a greater threat from a fearful Israel than any other nation.

CHRISTIANITY VERSUS DEMOCRACY

John Ashcroft was the son of a minister. His father served as the president of several Christian colleges, fully imbued with religious conservatism, which he imparted to his son. John served as the governor of Missouri from 1984 to 1992, his governorship being most noted for his tough on crime stance. He served as the United States senator from Missouri from 1994 to 2000, where he was most noted for being a friend of the pharmaceutical companies. He was appointed as United States Attorney General in 2000, where he was a staunch supporter of the Patriot Act. In fact, he proposed a further extension of that act, which would have stripped civil liberties away from ordinary citizens, allowing wire tapping without warrant and unlimited access to every citizen's personal financial, email and medical record. In 2002, Ashcroft proposed a program called Operation TIPS, which would require all government employees to spy on each other, and report any suspicious behavior to law enforcement agencies. It was, in other words, an attempt to create a police state, in which any dissent would immediately brand the utterer as an enemy of the state, presumed guilty and judged without knowledge of that charge. Fortunately, this proposal was not passed into law. The Patriot Act was, in and of itself, a great travesty of civil liberty, and did not need any further extension of its onerous intrusion into the private affairs of our citizens, and especially, their right to dissent.

Mr. Ashcroft was a good man, and a dedicated public servant. The reasons why such an outstanding citizen, such a religious and such a supposedly moral man would so staunchly be in favor of ripping the civil liberties of our citizens away from us, must give us some pause. At first blush, we do not expect an upright and religious man to be against those key elements of our democracy which make it so precious. The clue as to why John Ashcroft was blatantly in favor of a police state, and not a free democracy, probably lies with his conservative religious philosophy, duly imparted to him by his parents. He is quoted as saying, in a college speech during his tenure as Attorney General, "This country has only one King, and his name is Jesus Christ." The implications of that statement are rather chilling. His main source for all the decisions that he made, while supposedly serving all the citizens of this country, was to serve his Christian King. This religious king is the same king who preached that all who do not believe in him as a divinity will be tortured in hell for an eternity. Torture for all who do not comply becomes sort of a built in philosophy, applied whenever it can be expressed. For John Ashcroft, suppression and punishment of all who do not comply with a certain philosophy was apparently a natural extension of his religious faith.

John Ashcroft was certainly not alone. The Christian Taliban has been hard at work in the United States of America, attempting to win converts to its message of intolerance, using television ministries and megachurches, where there is blaring brass, large screen televisions, thrilling organ music, and excited choirs singing the praises of their religion. The rapt audience is told, by a flamboyant minister, dressed in colorful robes, that this is a Christian nation, based on Christian values, and that we cannot rest until all elected officials are Christians, making their decisions based on Christian values. The members of that congregation leave wide-eyed after each of these services, dedicated to converting all the rest of the nation to their Christian cause. The great misfortune of this well-meaning, but greatly misdirected effort is that, when they are successful, what they get is an official like Mr. Ashcroft, who believes in suppression of civil liberties, and punishment of all who choose to be dissident in any way. What the faithful of these conservative churches do not understand is that their efforts foster values which are in direct contradiction to those of our cherished democracy, and that our democracy is an expression of morality in action.

Our statements of faith have a wonderful ring to them. They just sound right. We all know that Christianity is a religion which promotes a high standard of morals. We all know that we should be more moral persons in our lives. We all know that we should be patriotic towards our country, which has nourished us in so many ways, and protected us from harm. Being Christian, being moral and being a patriotic American all seem to naturally fall together as if they rightly belonged, like peas in a pod. Not only do these statements of patriotism, morality and religious faith fall together so nicely, they are voiced with such emotion and enthusiasm, we find it hard to believe that they do not rightly belong together in every way. We get chills when Lee Greenwood sings "I'm proud to be an American." As far as the American public is concerned, this trilogy is sacred, and should be supported in every way. To them, America, Christianity and morals are an inseparable Trinity, showing only separate manifestations of the same entity. They rightly belong together just as, to them, the Father, Son and Holy Ghost of their religion belong together.

The great misfortune of this welded trinity is that Christianity, in its current form, cannot be attached to high morality, and certainly cannot be attached to democracy, without corrupting its companions, like a bad apple in a bag. It is easy for Christian zealots to think of their religion as highly moral, and a force for moral authority. There is that element in each of the religions of Abraham. Each of them teaches the Golden Rule in some form. Each of them admonishes its followers to be humble and compassionate toward their neighbors, the elderly, neglected children, poor, dispossessed, crippled and ill. Each of them deserves praise for these emphases on morals. That's not the whole story, however. I am sad for saying so, but believe that it is impossible to be a complete Christian, and be highly moral. The reason for that fault is that a major part of the Christian creed, as it now exists, is total intolerance for any who do not accept Jesus as the Divine One. All who do not profess devotion to Jesus as the Christ, a divinity on earth, are, according to this religion, going to be tortured in Hell for an eternity. There is, in other words, as a dominating key of this creed, bigotry towards all who are not Christian. That belief, if it is held and practiced, is in direct opposition to the golden rule of democracy, that golden rule being tolerance for all creeds. Christianity and democracy can coexist, and greatly support each other. They cannot be joined, or democracy ceases to exist.

Under the recent Christian leadership this country, this golden standard of democracy, tolerance for all, was callously circumvented in many different ways. What we got instead was a denial of our civil liberties. Federal judges were fired for supporting those civil liberties. Citizens were thrown in secret jails and tortured without charges, and without representation. They were denied access to a fair trial, and human torture considered moral. Federal money was given to Christian organizations for social programs, but denied to Muslims, Hindus and Buddhists. America was placed at war without just cause, in my opinion. The human cost of this tragic misdirection has so far been over four thousand soldiers killed, almost a million wounded for life, and the loss of over three million Iraqi lives. This leadership was not democratic; it was undemocratic, and never deserved our patriotic or church support. Economically, it has led our country to the brink of bankruptcy. This type of leadership will always deserve our patriotic moral dissent, as vigorously as we can make it.

My emails are an interesting window on the minds of my friends. I would not claim that my email friends are by any means a full representation of the conscience of the American public at large, but they certainly tell me what makes their wheels turn, and what, to them, is important to send on to me and their other friends. Judging from those messages, which my friends have selected out of many other messages as those most deserving of further broadcast, there is a marvelous support of our troops who are serving in foreign countries. That, to me, is certainly well deserved. Any young person who is willing to serve their country and put their lives on the line for the rest of us deserves all the support and praise we can give them. My emails tell me that the black/white issue does not matter too much anymore. There are not even any jokes about disparities between black and white cultures. About the closest we come is an occasional reference to generally accepted differences, such as white men can't jump like blacks can. I love this change; it is so healthy to fully accept whatever diversity exists between men and women of different colors. My emails tell me there is a significant resentment against illegal aliens, Hispanics in particular, and most specifically, Mexicans. If these messages are any indication, a significant segment of the American public is completely in favor of rounding all of our illegal aliens up, of any description, from any other country, and sending all of them back where they came from, post haste. Various programs which have been proposed for assimilating those aliens into our country have been derided with exclamation points all over the place. Fear that illegal aliens would be given health care coverage under the proposed changes in health care insurance, raised a storm of protest in town hall meetings.

The most disturbing email messages that I receive concern Muslims. I am fully aware that, throughout this book, I have taken pains to express those messages of hatred and violence which are embedded throughout the Koran, pointed toward all humans who are infidels, or in other words, all those who do not profess belief in Muhammad as the last and greatest prophet of the human species. The reason for that emphasis has been an attempt to help those who do not understand their great antipathy, exactly what the basis has been for those Muslim extremists who demonstrate their hatred toward the United States. I do not believe, however, that the Muslim religion is any more onerous than Christianity, which tells its followers that all who do not follow their creeds are going to be tortured for an eternity. The vast majority of Christians and Muslims, in my opinion, are peace loving people, who go about their lives practicing those moral aspects of their religions and demonstrating empathy for their neighbors. I deem it a tragedy when all Muslims are grouped together as evil people. In these email messages, Muslims are castigated in about every way imaginable, including appearance, mannerisms, faith and clothing. I cringe whenever one of these messages arrives. It is not Muslims we should hate, or any other people we should hate. The practice we should hate is the extremism of Judaism, Christianity, Islam, Hinduism, Buddhism and all religions, which emphasizes the violent intolerance of their religions, and not the compassion of their religions. The extremists of all these religions are enemies of democracy. They are greatly aided by those members of our churches who remain stone silent, voicing no protest when our government acts immorally.

CYRUS AND CIVIL LIBERTIES

We have not, as a species, always lived in times when extremist religious hatred has been allowed to dominate our group interactions. There have been a few eras of great moral enlightenment, when civil liberties have been advanced, resulting in a flowering of that civilization in arts, literature, music and science. When civil liberties become an established part of any government, the economic growth of that civilization has been immense. There is no doubt, at least from an historical account, that if we wish to prosper as a species, we will have to emphasize civil freedom. There are several wonderful examples of that flowering of civilization in the past, under the guidance of enlightened minds. The first of these that immediately comes to mind is the regime of Cyrus the Great, of Persia.

Cyrus the Great was one in a series of Cyrus rulers of Persia. He was born in about 585 BCE as the grandson of the King of Media, Astyages. According to legend, Astyages had a dream that at some time in the future, Cyrus would overthrow him, to become the ruler in his place. Astyages ordered the death of his grandson for that reason. His chief adviser, however, who was entrusted to carry out this murder, instead gave this child to a shepherd to raise. As Cyrus grew, it became obvious to all that he had exceptional qualities. Astyages became aware that Cyrus was still alive, when this child reached the age of ten.

He was persuaded to let Cyrus live, however, because it was clear that Cyrus was becoming an outstanding young man. Astyages later paid dearly for not carrying through with his original intent to murder this potential rival. Cyrus and his army defeated the army of Astyages in 550 BCE, and Cyrus became the ruler of the incipient Persian Empire.

It is not entirely clear how much of this story is true, and how much of it is legend. It follows the same pattern of many epic tales. The baby or young person of immense value is condemned to death by an oppressive ruler, who is able to forecast the future. This hero or heroine is saved, because the designee for killing that young person can't bring him or herself to murder such a valuable person. That young hero or heroine then returns triumphantly when he or she reaches adulthood, usually revolting against an evil ruler, that ruler often being a father or mother. There are many similar examples of childhood exile and later return as a dominant ruler, including Moses as a baby in a basket in the river, Muhammad exiled to the desert as an infant, Sleeping Beauty, Snow White, and Oedipus Rex.

Regardless of how he got there, Cyrus did not waste time after becoming the ruler of the Median territory. He proceeded, in rapid order, to conquer Lydia, Ionia and Babylonia. After conquering Babylonia, he freed the Jews, in 539 BCE, and additionally gave them money to rebuild their temple after they had returned to their homeland. He then turned to the East, also conquering most of Central Asia. By this time, he had extended the Achaemenid Empire to include all lands from the Mediterranean Sea to the Indus River. He established the world's first superpower, which included what is today Iraq, Pakistan, Afghanistan, Turkmenistan, Uzbekistan, Tajikistan, Turkey, Jordan, Cyprus, Syria, Lebanon, Israel, Egypt, and the Caucasus region.

Establishing this first great world empire was in itself remarkable. What is more remarkable, however, is how Cyrus ruled over this empire. The evidence is that he did not force any certain belief system or religious dogma on his subjects. He borrowed from the customs of those who were now his subjects, took the best of what they had to offer, and assimilated those advances into the Persian Empire he had created. This attitude of tolerance and civil liberties is found in the Cyrus cylinder, a corncob shaped clay body which has inscribed upon it the first Charter of Human Rights. This cuneiform message calls for religious and ethnic freedom, bans slavery and oppression of any kind, and bans the taking of property by force or without compensation. It offers all the member states the right to subject themselves to Cyrus' reign, or not. He shaped the culture and civilization that he had established with freedom of speech, freedom of religion, freedom from suppression, right of property, and respect for ethnicity. The result, even after his death, was a flowering of the Persian Empire, extending even further in size, for many ensuing centuries, in a civilization of peace and prosperity. Cyrus got it right, two thousand years before the Magna Carta was written.

Cyrus is the Latin translation for the Persian name Kurash. The fiery evangelist, David Koresh, considered this, his name, to be prophetic. He was dyslexic, could not read well, and did poorly in school, but by age 13, could quote the New Testament from memory. He joined the Branch Davidians in 1983, and soon married their leader, Lois Roden, even though he was in his twenties and she was then in her late sixties. Upon her death in 1986, he assumed leadership of the Branch Davidians. He believed that he was the modern day Cyrus, who would lead the Jews and Christians to freedom from their captivity. He also preached an apocalyptic end to the earth, and believed that he would become a martyr in this mission, the same as Jesus. He had an additional mission of his own, however. He claimed 140 wives, specializing in young girls down to the age of eleven, impregnating fifteen of those teens and preteens, in addition to impregnating many of the older women who were also his wives. The flamboyant life style of Mr. Koresh attracted the attention of the Texas authorities, particularly those who were in charge of child endangerment policies. When he refused to change his lifestyle in any way, twenty one children were removed from the Branch Davidian compound and placed in protective custody before that compound was placed under siege by the FBI. After 51 days of intermittent negotiations, Attorney General Janet Reno ordered an attack on the compound. Whether caused by the attackers or set inside the compound, the entire settlement was suddenly consumed by a fiery conflagration. Koresh and seventy-six Davidians were burned to death. Seventeen of those who died were children under the age of twelve.

The only reason to place the modern day Cyrus, David Koresh, in juxtaposition to Cyrus the Great of 539 BCE, is to highlight the difference is their approach to religion. Cyrus the Great will always have the admiration of the human species for showing that freedom from and freedom of religion is necessary to have civil liberties. Only civil liberties produce a vibrantly alive and prosperous society. The approach of David Koresh, on the other hand, was to believe in religious imprisonment. The result of that religious imprisonment was an apocalyptic, burning end to their world. This is the end we can always expect when there is an emphasis on religious suppression and intolerance, rather than religious tolerance and religious freedom.

JEFFERSON, RELIGION AND EQUALITY

Thomas Jefferson was born in 1743, the third of eight children born to Peter Jefferson, a self-educated planter and surveyor of Welch descent, and Jane Randolph Jefferson, whose ancestors were landed English gentry. The greatest gift his parents gave to him was not the 5000 acres he inherited at the time of his father's death, but their insistence that he obtain a formal education. Jefferson entered the college of William and Mary in 1760, where he became a protégé of Professor William Small, lawyer George Wythe and the lieutenant governor of the colony of Virginia, Francis Fauqier. He proved to be an apt student with a keen mind and a penchant for language. He was competent in Latin, Greek, Spanish, Italian, Gaelic, Ossian, and fluent in French. While in school, he is reported to have said that John Locke, Francis Bacon and Sir Isaac Newton were the three greatest men that had ever lived. He greatly enjoyed the lavish parties of Governor Fauquier, where he was a favorite, often asked to play his violin, and where he developed a taste for culture and fine wine. He graduated with honors from William and Mary in 1762, studied law under George Wythe for 5 years, and was admitted to the Virginia Bar in 1767.

Jefferson was tall and angular in appearance, stood about 6'2", and was straight backed. He was somewhat reserved in conversation, because he had a lisp. Because of that speech impediment, he did not favor debate or any form of public speaking, but instead, with his penchant for language, spent long hours in his study polishing what message needed to be said, using language that was fluent, concise and powerful. His capacity for stirring language became widely known with the publication of his first major essay while a member of the House of Burgess, *A Summary View of the Rights of British America,* published in 1774. The Virginia House was at that time hot in debate about their grievances with the British authority, but not prepared for Jefferson's conclusion that Britain had no authority over the American colonies. It became clear that Jefferson was a radical, by their standards, but within a few years, they were willing to accept this point of view.

By June of 1776, that decision to break with Great Britain had become a dominant consensus amongst those members of the Second Continental Congress. Jefferson, appointed as a representative to that Congress by the Colony of Virginia, was asked to serve on the committee which was given the task of forming an appropriate document which would voice their concerns in a manner to which they could all agree. At that time, these appointments to this committee were considered little more than busy work, of little importance. Other members of that committee, including Benjamin Franklin and John Adams, themselves no novices at expressing themselves eloquently in writing, nevertheless recognized the superior talent of Jefferson in producing language which would stir all the other members of the congress. He was asked to compose something which they could present to the Congress at large. The document that Jefferson produced was altered a fair degree once it had been presented to the Continental Congress. About one fourth of it was thrown out, for one reason or another. That document that remains, however, has since rung down through the ages. It was a masterfully eloquent piece of literature, which not only served as the declaration of a new country, but also served as the model for the constitution of that new country. It began this way.

> *When, in the course of human events, it becomes necessary for one people to dissolve the political bands which have connected them to another, and to assume, among the Powers of the earth, the separate and equal station to which the Laws of Nature and Nature's God entitle them, a decent respect to the opinions of mankind requires that they should declare the causes which impel them to the separation.*
>
> *We hold these truths to be self-evident, that all men are created equal, that they are endowed by their Creator with*

*certain inalienable Rights, that among these are Life, Liberty
and the Pursuit of Happiness – That to secure these rights,
Governments are instituted among Men, deriving their just
powers from the consent of the governed – That whenever
any Form of Government becomes destructive of these ends,
it is the Right of the People to alter or to abolish it, and to
institute new Government, laying its foundation on such
principles and organizing its powers in such form, as to them
shall seem most likely to affect their Safety and Happiness.*

I believe we are all stirred by these words, and I readily admit that
I also feel personally uplifted by them. It excites us just to think of the
basic truth of that statement, *all men are created equal.* It serves as
the basis for all good government, in the sense that none of us is born
into more right or advantage than anyone else. There is no race, no
size, no color, no inherited wealth that makes any one of us more valuable than any other person. According to Jefferson, none of us should
be superior to any other human.

*"Because Sir Isaac Newton was superior to others in
understanding, he was not therefore the lord of the
property or person of others."*

We think of this statement of equality as one of the bedrock
principles on which this country is founded, and one of the guiding principles on which all of our law should be based. The forms of
democracy that have been instituted have been established to provide equal opportunity for all. Slavery has been abolished because
of adherence to this belief. Civil liberties and rights of due process
have been established because of this belief. The single proud pillar of
democracy, which is tolerance for all people of all beliefs and faiths, is
settled on this foundation of equality. This is indeed a stirring message,
which will continue to ring down through more ages to come.

After this first blush of excitement about the wisdom and passion
of Thomas Jefferson, however, I become personally quite disturbed
with a series of very troubling thoughts about these rights, so eloquently stated in the Declaration of Independence. I beg your great
forgiveness for saying so, but the bald fact to me is that none of these
statements about these rights with which we are born has the least
chance of being true. The statement that all men are born equal, first

of all, leaves all women out of the equation, and secondly, must be utterly false in most other ways. The concept that we are born with a divine right to live, to be free and to be happy does not at all agree with what we know about ourselves and our universe. The Declaration of Independence of the United States of America seems to be in the same category as our religious myths. All of them are full of grand promise, assuring us of a great purpose for our lives, but none of them, as far as we can tell, have the slightest bit of truth to them, if they are based on this false assumption of divine right. The best evidence we have is that the universe created each of us to be unique, different and therefore quite unequal. None of us, as far as we know, has any right of any kind given to us by the universe, or given by any force in the universe, and all of us are completely mortal.

This statement of human equality is, in and of itself, rather absurd. Thomas Jefferson compounds that mistaken statement of divinely ordained equality by clearly not including women. He believed that women had no right to vote, and no place in life other than in the home. He disliked, in particular, the discussions emanating from women about politics, was offended when questioned by an intelligent woman, and treated any opinion expressed by a woman with disdain. He was also of the opinion that blacks were inferior to whites in mind and body, a grievous error of assessment. Thomas Jefferson, in other words, did not at all believe in the equality of humans, even though we love that phrase in our Declaration of Independence, and love that it was part of our country being born free and unencumbered to any other nation.

> *"The appointment of a woman to office is an innovation for which the public is not prepared, nor am I."*

> *"I advance it therefore, as a suspicion only, that the blacks, whether a distinct race, or made distinct by time and temperament, are inferior to the whites in the endowments of both body and mind."*

It would be hypercritical for us to label Thomas Jefferson as a flaming hypocrite, because he declared certain things and fully believed other things. He was a product of his time. Almost no one at that time was agitating for a woman's right to vote and hold office. No one else was of the opinion that there was an equality of the races. What we can hold him accountable for is his belief that all white men are born with divine rights of equality, freedom and happiness. The best knowledge we have been able to accumulate says exactly the opposite. We were not born, any of us, with any plan or scheme in mind by any force or power of any description. To the best of our ability to discern, our lives are simply a beautiful gift, with no divinity or rights about them. Most certainly, none of us are equal. We are each unique, individual, with different talents, unique immune systems that fight off any invasion by foreign cells of any other origin, human or otherwise, and none of us is exactly the same as any other person. The claim that all humans are born equal is quite bizarre, even though it stirs our emotions.

Right to life is such a ringing phrase. Just to think that, no matter what happens to us, we have an inborn right, given to us by our God, to be here, and to grow. The immediate question that comes to mind is, why did Thomas Jefferson believe that each of us is given, by our Creator, at the time of our birth, this inviolable right to live? For Jefferson, this was not just a matter of empathy, compassion or utilitarianism; it was a completely imbedded, inseparable, inalienable right which every human possesses, as much as his or her breath or heart beat. No one was born without being born with this absolute and undeniable right to life. To understand why Jefferson had this belief, we have to understand his life and education. He received a classical education, which means that he studied the true classics. He is said to have studied Plato in the original Latin, and, after having done so, expressed the opinion that Plato had very little important to say. There is one concept of Socrates and Plato, however, that must have come through loud and strong. Jefferson believed that there was an innate Goodness in the universe, and that humans were a part of it.

Thomas Jefferson described himself as a deist, that is to say, one who believes that there is a God, who began this universe, but after beginning it, has not interfered with how it is run. We would have to say that Jefferson's religious belief was not the same as that of Aristotle, who described the God or Force that began the universe as an "Unmoved Mover." His belief was also not the same as those deists who simply refer to whatever began the universe as a Force, of which nothing more is known in any way. With the Declaration of Independence as proof, we would have to say that Jefferson, although he claimed himself to be a deist, was a deist who believed in a God who was supremely good, and who put humans here as part of a grand plan for the human race, hence giving those humans an inalienable right to life. The shadows of Socrates have once again cast their long penumbra on our civilization, not just in our religions, who mistakenly believe that there is a God that is totally good, but also in the form of that stirring document, the Declaration of Independence, which declares that all humans have a God-given right to life. As far as we can tell, such is not at all the case. None of us has a divine right to be alive. For each of us, life is a precious gift, to be cherished every minute until it is gone; it is certainly, as best we can tell, not something that is owed to us by anyone.

Do all humans have a right to be free, as given to them by their creator, to not be subject to restrictions, laws, governances, rules and regulations? That hardly seems logical, but it was an important word for Jefferson. He was opposed to any form of tyranny over human life, and in fact believed that the Christian church was one such form of human tyranny. His belief in divine right included human freedom, as is aptly demonstrated by all of his writings.

> "I have recently been examining all the known superstitions of the world, and do not find in our particular superstition (Christianity) one redeeming feature. They are all alike, founded upon fables and mythologies."

> "Christianity is the most perverted system that ever shone on men. The authors of the gospels were unlettered and ignorant men and the teachings of Jesus have come to us mutilated, misstated and unintelligible."

> "History, I believe, furnishes no example of a priest-ridden people maintaining a free civil government. This marks the lowest grade of ignorance of which their civil as well as religious leaders will always avail themselves for their own purposes."

> "I have sworn upon the altar of God eternal hostility against every form of tyranny over the mind of man."

None of us, of course, has full liberty. Those in our society who do what they want whenever they want are chased down by the police, thrown in jail, and brought before a judge, who sentences them to assorted onerous punishments. We are all members of our societies, which exact rather strict guidelines against us, in order for us to have a modicum of freedom about our actions every day. For Jefferson to have said that we are all at liberty, and have that liberty given to us by a divine right, does not make any sense at all. Our societies do not function smoothly unless there is restriction of many aspects of our behavior. Had he not couched this statement with an attestation of divine right, and had he added a few words to state that we all had the right of liberty from tyranny, then it would have made great sense.

According to Jefferson, the great Creator of the universe put humans here for a purpose, and declared that each of us had the right to seek happiness. Few of us would protest that all living creatures, humans and animals alike, wish to achieve comfort and a complete life. Once we get here, all of us spends the rest of our time, while we are here, looking for ways to attain and maintain satisfaction in life. We can't help it; it is just us. The pursuit of happiness, or, as a better term, fulfillment, is part of all life. To understand that the drive for fulfillment is a normal part of life, is one thing. To declare that this drive to seek comfort, mature, and procreate is an absolute divinely decreed right that all of us possess, is quite another matter, and as far as we can tell, quite false.

I beg your indulgence to stay with me a little longer on this topic, because, in spite of all my criticisms, there is a reason why this piece of literature stirs our souls. My only point has been that all the evidence we have about our universe and our place in it as a species, tells us that we are not here as part of a grand plan, and not here for a specific purpose. We are not here as puppets, guided every step of the way by a master puppeteer, who interferes in order to guide us properly with our lives. The only guidance we have is that those of us who are able to best fit into our environment are selected to survive, while others, who do not fit as well, do not survive as long. We do not have any evidence that equality, life, liberty and the pursuit of happiness are divinely ordained. This document, based as it is on divine provenance, happens to be quite wrong. Religion does not serve as an adequate base for these noble values. If we are willing to say, however, that there is a great *moral* need for these values, then they happen to be superb guides for human behavior, They are a further definition of the admonishment of Jesus to love your God with all your heart, mind and soul, and to love your neighbor, both near and far, as yourself. The Declaration of Independence then becomes a brilliant practical expression of these biblical moral creeds, which can lead us to a human ethic.

The command of Jesus to love our neighbors, including our near neighbors, our far neighbors and even those far neighbors who hate us, serves to excite us, but then tends to fall flat. We all agree with this wonderful teaching, but then don't quite understand what this means in our daily work and our relations with other nations of the world. We do not have to wonder any longer. Thomas Jefferson put it into stirring words, which ring true for every action we take affecting our neighbors of any description. I consider the Declaration of Independence of the United States of America to be one of the central struts in our social march toward building a universal ethic. That understanding of what it takes for all of us to live together peaceably began in the Old Testament, as wandering tribesmen were advised to show compassion for those of other tribes. Our knowledge of that behavior needed to allow us to all achieve our goals was immensely increased with the wisdom of Isaiah, who taught compassion, rather than vengeance. It continued in the civil liberties championed by Cyrus, and took a great leap forward with the teachings of Jesus. Morality became better defined with the Magna Carta, and then received full definition in this Declaration of Independence. This morality necessary for stable societies has now been internationally recognized with the Universal Declaration of Human Rights.

> *Article 18: Everyone has the right to freedom of thought, conscience and religion; this right includes the freedom to change his religion or belief, and freedom, either alone or in community with others and in public or private, to manifest his religion or belief in teaching, practice, worship and observance.*

What does it mean when we are commanded to love our neighbors, both near, far and even those neighbors who show hostility? It means that we treat each of those neighbors as our equal. We understand that each of our neighbors has just as much right to life as we have. It means that we must show respect for that neighbor, so that he or she can be free from tyranny. It means that we should encourage each of our neighbors to find their own fulfillment in life, and not stand in their way. As a religious document, the Declaration of Independence is a frightful failure. As a document of high morality, it is a marvelous message.

Bereft of the fallacious and misleading concept of divine right, and recognizing that the human species consists of all men *and* women, *this* is how the Declaration of Independence of the United States of America should have been written. Perhaps it is not quite as stirring, but now it becomes a vibrant moral guide, which puts the teachings of Jesus into a marvelously practical social form, deserving our full devotion.

> *We hold these* truths *to be self-evident, that all humans are created unequal, but that they are equally endowed by their Creator with certain unalienable needs, that among these are Life, Liberty and the Pursuit of Happiness – That to secure these needs, Governments are instituted among Humans, deriving their just powers from the consent of the governed – That whenever any Form of Government becomes destructive of these ends, it is the Right of the People to alter or to abolish it, and to institute new Government, laying its foundation on such principles and organizing its powers in such form as to them shall seem most likely to affect their Safety and Happiness.*

Thomas Jefferson was born on April 13, 1743, and died on July 4, 1826, as did his good friend, John Adams, who also died on that same day. He served as Governor of Virginia, Ambassador to France, Secretary of State, Vice President of the United States, and as President, from 1801 to 1809. He was a scientist, architect, ornithologist, horticulturist, archeologist and inventor. He invented the swivel chair, a rotating book stand, and automatic doors. After the Library of Congress had been burned by the British, he donated his private library in order to start the Library of Congress. He was the founder of the University of Virginia, designing the campus and its buildings. He is the author of the phrase, "separation of church and state." As president, he was responsible for the Louisiana Purchase, doubling the size of the United States of America, even though it is doubtful he had the authority to make that purchase.

Jefferson opposed slavery throughout his career, but kept all of his slaves until his death. His first wife, Martha Wayles Skelton, died after the birth of their sixth child. Only two of those children survived. He was deeply grieved by her death, finding solace only in his work on the growing disputes with Great Britain. When he was appointed as Ambassador to France, however, in 1785, he took his two children with him, as well as two of his slaves to serve as their companions, James and Sally Hemings. Sally Hemings was a quadroon, who was the half sister of Jefferson's deceased wife, Martha. He began an intimate relationship with Sally while in France, which continued up to the time of his death. Six children were produced from that union, four of whom survived, Beverly, Harriet, Madison and Eston. Beverly and Harriet married into white society. Madison and Eston moved to Chillicothe, Ohio, with their families, where Madison remained identified as a black man. Eston later moved to Wisconsin with his family, where he passed into white society. Jefferson gave his two sons with Sally their freedom when they reached the age of 21, and Sally was given her freedom after the death of Jefferson, by his daughter.

The Declaration of Independence, of the United States of America, stands as a document of human freedom which will continue to ring down through the ages. It was a succinct and stirring statement of what moral attributes are needed to produce a stable and productive society. It was formed by a master word craftsman, who stands as a giant amongst the human race. It is a document for the ages, not because it is religiously correct, but because the moral values it proclaims are universal and timeless.

FREEDOM FROM RELIGION

The higher the degree of morality, the healthier and the more prosperous whatever society we wish to examine will be. One of the keys as to the health of any society will be the degree to which each human of sound mind is included as a citizen. Past societies, and many present societies, have been rife with layers of status, so that only a privileged few are allowed to govern, or prosper. Many people have been excluded from their personal pursuit of happiness because of their birth, or their language, or their color. One part of a moral, or healthy society, therefore, is the degree to which all its members are

MORALS, ETHICS AND RELIGIONS

able to make their vote count, or, in other words, to be equal in opportunity. A vital additional key to a healthy society is the degree to which
they value life. Is all life considered precious in that society? If life is
considered a commodity to be used as others see fit for their own
advantage, all the rest of that society suffers. Each life must be treated
with reverent respect. Another key to a healthy society is the degree
to which its members have unfettered civil liberties. How free are
they to speak their mind without reprisal? If, every time we speak our
minds in protest, we receive a tax audit, find our computers accessed,
and find our phone lines tapped, we soon learn to keep our mouths
shut, as a matter of self protection, and allow our leaders to proceed
with actions which we know to be quite foolish. The degree to which
we encourage each of our members to be all that they can be is also a
major indicator of the morality and health of that society. If we do not
lead each of our children to develop, as much as possible, all their talents, then that great untapped reservoir of human potential remains
unexpressed. In other words, the health of any society can be measured by the degree to which it addresses each of its citizens according
to the marvelous principles of the Declaration of Independence: does
it declare each of them equal in opportunity, does it treat each life
as precious, does it allow the greatest degree of civil liberties possible without anarchy, and does it foster each citizen to develop his or
her fulfillment? If it does these things, it is vibrantly alive, prosperous,
healthy and moral.

I would like to add one more category to this grading system as
to the morality, or health, of any society. Maybe, in and of itself, it is
in some ways just as important as those categories above. That additional, and in my mind, quite important indicator of the moral health
of any society consists of a single question: how much does it stress
freedom *from* religion? We are greatly indebted to the foresight of our
founders in making sure our new government was not tied to any specific religion, and most specifically, not to Christianity. They knew that
this freedom could not be maintained if any one religion became tied
to this new government, because if it was, all other religions would be
suppressed. They knew that this new democracy would not survive
unless it had its own freedom from the exclusivity demands of any one
religion. We are further indebted to Thomas Jefferson for impressing
upon all of us that great need to always maintain the separation of

church and state, both for the health of our democracy and for the health of our religions.

The point we usually miss in all of this talk about religious freedom is that this freedom cannot be maintained unless there is also freedom *from* religion. Democracy insists that all points of view must be heard and appreciated, all given equal weight, then let the majority decide by lawful vote what policy should be established. Our religions state the opposite. Each of them states that their own point of view, or mythology, is the only one that is correct, and that all other humans who don't agree should be punished. That narrow-minded philosophy cannot be part of a philosophy which asks that all voices be heard, and given equal importance. For any one of our religions to be compatible with our democracy, they would all have to change their attitude toward each other drastically. Each of our religions would have to say and mean these things: "Your stories are as good as our stories. We respect your mythologies and ask you to do the same for us. Each of us should take comfort in each other's faiths, rather than fight about them. We are at all times willing to share what is Holy to us with what is Holy to you. We need to emphasize our common morals, and not demand allegiance to our separate mythologies, when we deal with you."

Our religions are nowhere close. They are still killing each other using the excuse of their separate mythologies, and all the rest of us are getting caught in the middle. Until our religions change their ways drastically, and are willing to forgo their demands of exclusivity, their punishment of all who are other believers, we all need our freedom *from* religions. A moral society does not exist without freedom from religions.

This does not mean, however, that our religions should remain silent when they see our government commit immoral acts. Their protest, when they see our government treat other humans with intolerance, hatred and greed, should be strident. Unless our religions express this morality which they preach, that morality is of no use to them, to us, or anyone else.

INDIVIDUAL MORAL EFFORTS

Whether we are accustomed to thinking of ourselves in this way or not, the human species lives by herd instincts, just the same as if we were a herd of buffalo on the prairie, or a herd of zebras on the savannah. We have established and accepted behavior in that herd, and any member who does not behave in that accepted manner is either chastised or chased out. Human morality is a major part of that herd behavior. Each group, sect, clan or nation has its own customs and morality, spheres of which overlap. No one group has accepted rules of behavior, or morals, the same as any other. Those morals for all groups are not only unique to that particular group, in some way, but also change over time. We know that our morals are a fluid and dynamic system which keeps shifting, but all moral systems are a form of human group behavior, Perhaps they could be classified as the group conscience for whatever particular cohesive gathering of humans exists. This discussion has tried to bring more accurate definitions of those values. What we have addressed so far has been how these group values have changed and grown over time. We have looked at those major milestones in these moral systems, all of that discussion couched in terms of various groups, be it religions or nations.

We would be remiss, however, to not spend specific time looking at individual efforts to improve the morality of our societies. Although we may have group behavior, which gets passed into laws and enforced with varying severity of punishment, it is, after all, the individual application of those moral codes that matters. There has not been any advancement in morality without some individual seeing inequality, seeing disregard for life, seeing undue suppression and loss of opportunity, and then doing something about it. Those who have addressed these flaws in our moral codes have often paid dearly for bucking the system, suffering both mental and physical abuse, if not death, at the hands of those with vested interests. Each of us, however, must live within our own conscience, and if our conscience tells us that there is immorality in our society, then we are obliged to speak against that immorality. Greater morality of any group does not occur unless there is some individual who is willing to pay whatever price it takes to correct that wrong.

Some of these individuals and their great moral contributions to our societies in the past have already been discussed, and don't require further comment. Isaiah, Cyrus and Jefferson have been presented in some detail. Quite a few others, however, contributed greatly to our societal health. It may be very helpful to look at some of these lives more completely, to understand how they also contributed greatly to our societies. This is not meant to be a comprehensive list. I know there are many other lives that contributed significantly to the morality of our societies. I believe that each of us contributes in his or her own way to the equality and stability of our societies. This is only a set of examples, choosing those who have impressed me the most as to their contributions to our society – or our mistaken impressions as to their contributions. These people have shown us, each with their own effort, how each of us can help create loving, compassionate societies, where everyone grows and reaches greater knowledge, with greater expression; where everyone can lead a healthy life, enjoy reasonable freedom, and pursue their own fulfillment. These are some of the people who have brought us to a more complete expression of the Declaration of Independence of the United States of America.

JOHN LOCKE

John Locke (1632–1704) was born the son of a country lawyer of modest means. He entered Christ Church in Oxford in 1652, obtaining a B.A. degree in 1656 and an M.A. degree in 1658. The curriculum of that college was quite traditional, including grammar, moral philosophy, geometry and Greek. He found all of those courses unappealing, and as soon as he was able, devoted his attention to the study of science and medicine, topics which held much greater challenge to his intellect. He taught undergraduate courses for four years, and then went to Germany as part of a diplomatic mission in 1665. Upon his return, he rejected offers to continue diplomatic posts, and an offer to enter the ministry, but instead studied and wrote about those matters of his greatest interest: science, morals, society and politics. Much of that work was unpublished at that time.

In 1667, he accepted a position as the personal physician for Lord Ashley, the Earl of Shaftesbury, for whom he was not only a medical but a personal advisor. England was in the throes of change at that time, and Locke stood for the same values as his employer, even though there were many who were greatly opposed to these values. Both John Locke and Lord Ashley wanted a constitutional monarchy, civil liberty, religious liberty and the economic expansion of England, goals which only later became realized. While serving Lord Ashley, Locke spent four years studying metaphysics and epistemology in France, from 1675–1679, at the Gassendi school, where hedonism (pleasure as good) and corpuscular (atomic) physics were stressed. When Lord Ashley fell from favor, Locke became an exile to Holland from 1683 to 1688, which was, rather than a punishment, a sojourn he greatly enjoyed. Upon his return to England, he was appointed as a member of the Commission of Appeals, and as a commissioner in the Board of Trade and Plantations. He retired to the country in 1691, making only occasional trips to London because of his asthma.

Retirement was not by any means the end of John Locke. He was perhaps more influential at this time than any other time during his life. He remained the intellectual leader of the Whigs, all of the young leaders of that party coming to him for his advice. As a result of their efforts and his advice, most all the things for which he stood became a reality before his death. England became a constitutional monarchy, its parliament in control of the country. Greater civil liberties were obtained through the courts of law, greater religious tolerance was obtained, and freedom of the press was obtained by repeal of the odious "Act for the Regulation of Printing." There was now, for the first time, great freedom of thought and expression in Britain.

Law of Nature was published in 1663.

The Reasonableness of Christianity was published in 1695, calling for less dogmatism in religion.

A Letter Concerning Toleration was published in 1689, containing the following clearly stated concepts:

1. No person has such complete wisdom and knowledge that he or she can dictate the form of religion that another person should possess.

2. Each person is a moral being, created by and responsible only to God, and therefore free of intolerable human constraint.

3. No law that is contrary to the will of the individual is capable of receiving more than outward conformity.

Two treatises on Government was published in 1690. It states that government is a trust established between the government and those governed. The purpose of that government is to protect each person's life and property. Each person has the right to withdraw from that government if it fails to meet its obligations.

Does any of this sound familiar to you? Did you wonder why Thomas Jefferson called John Locke one of the greatest men to have ever lived? These same concepts became embedded in the brain of a master wordsmith from Virginia, who succinctly expressed them in a document called the Declaration of Independence of the United States of America. John Locke speaks through the pen of Thomas Jefferson. According to this belief system, every individual is a divinely inspired person, responsible only to his God, with the right to obtain his own happiness, with the right to his own religion, and the right to revolt against an oppressive government. Although these concepts were expressed in terms of an ill-perceived divinity, that divinity of these concepts is not as important as the morality they express, and that morality is vitally important. We owe a lot to John Locke, because of the high morality of his beliefs, which became branded into the mind of Thomas Jefferson.

THOMAS PAINE

Thomas Paine was born in England in 1737. His father was a Quaker and his mother an Anglican. He received a rather sparse education as a child, perhaps the equivalent of a grade school education in the United States. At the age of 13, he became an apprentice to his father as a corset maker. As an older teen, he became, for a brief time, a privateer, serving on a ship sanctioned by the English government to prey on other ships at sea, capture them and their cargo. His first wife, Mary Lambert, died in childbirth in 1760. In 1761 he became an auxiliary officer in the army, and in 1762 was appointed as an excise officer, at a salary of L50 per year. His job was to collect the taxes due on imported tobacco and alcohol, and make sure there was not untaxed contraband shipped into the country. He applied to become an ordained minister in the Church of England in 1766, and did some preaching at that time. In 1767, he briefly became a schoolteacher. In 1772, he registered complaints about the excise office, publishing his first treatise, *The Case of the Officers of Excise*. He outlined the causes of worker discontent, which included poor wages and graft. For his efforts, he was fired in 1774. At that same time, his father-in-law's tobacco shop, where he also worked, failed. Paine sold all his household possessions in order to avoid being placed in prison, as a pauper, and separated from his second wife, moving to London.

So far, the life of Thomas Paine had been quite inglorious. His two marriages, for different reasons, had failed, his business had failed, and he had been labeled as a complainer. He had failed to hold any job for any length of time, and had no direction in his life. He was soon to find that compass, however. As luck would have it, he was introduced to Benjamin Franklin, who was in London at that time, in 1774. Apparently Franklin saw something in this young man that others had not, and advised him to seek his fortunes in America. He also gave Paine a letter of introduction and recommendation. Paine was quite impressed with Franklin, and considering his failures in life so far, decided to take that sage advice. He barely made the trip over. All the occupants of the ship got typhoid fever. Thomas Paine was extremely ill, had to be taken off the ship by Franklin's personal physician, and nursed back to health over the next six weeks. Within the next year, he became a citizen of Pennsylvania, and was afterwards appointed editor of the Pennsylvania Magazine. At this point, the ideas of Thomas Paine were soon to be heard everywhere, and have not stopped since.

African Slavery in America, published under a pseudonym in 1775, bitterly opposed the slave trade that had become established in America. *Common Sense*, a title suggested by Benjamin Franklin, came off the press in January, 1776. More than any other publication, it set the stage for the Declaration of Independence, ratified with fervor later that year. It sold 500,000 copies almost immediately, an amount almost unheard of at that time, for which Paine refused to receive any payment. *The American Crisis* papers were published from 1776 to 1783, as the new nation prepared for war. George Washington had parts of the first Crisis paper read to his troops in order to inspire them to fight, after the bitter Valley Forge winter. In 1780, *Public Good* called for a national convention, outlining the means by which delegates should be chosen, citing the need for a national constitution.

In 1781, Paine recognized that the American troops had reached the limits of their endurance, because of their lack of pay and lack of supplies. He took $500 of his own salary to start a fund for the soldier's cause. He instigated a trip to France, accompanied by Col. John Laurens, where they met with the King of France. They were able to secure a gift of six million dollars from France, and a loan of ten million dollars, as well as ammunition and supplies. Without that additional support that they brought back with them, it is doubtful that the fledgling revolution of the Americans would have been successful. Thomas Paine not only supplied the ideology for the American Revolution, but supplied part of the monetary means for it to succeed as well.

The constitutional convention, which had been proposed by Paine to replace the articles of confederation, was finally held in Philadelphia in 1787. Paine was not there for this particular step of the new democracy. He had gone to England to get financial backing for a bridge project, and soon became completely involved in the developing French revolution. *The Rights of Man, Part I,* 1791, *and The Rights of Man, Part II,* 1792, outlined the reasons why he believed that the French revolution was brewing, which included arbitrary government, poverty, illiteracy, unemployment and war. The social corrections which he recommended to overcome these societal evils were astonishingly foresighted. He called for popular education, relief of the poor, pensions for elderly people, and public works for the unemployed, all to be financed by a progressive income tax. These ideas were far too radical for the wealthy and elite of Britain. His books were banned, the publisher jailed, and Paine was indicted for treason. He escaped to France, but was sentenced in absentia. This English repulsion and punishment did not stop his publications and ideas from circulating widely in France, however, where he was initially considered a hero.

Thomas Paine did not endear himself to the French for long. He was entirely in favor of abolishing the monarchy, but opposed the execution of King Louis XVI. He spoke against the other excesses of the radical French revolutionaries, and soon became to them persona non grata. He was jailed for speaking his mind against that capital punishment, from 1793 to 1794. While in jail, he wrote *The Age of Reason, Part I,* which was published in 1794, and followed it with *The Age of Reason, Part II*, which was published in 1797. In these pamphlets, Paine attempted to clarify his religious views. He made it clear that he strongly believed in a God, but not the same one as that espoused by organized religion. For his efforts to establish himself as a deist believer, Paine was labeled, for the rest of his life, as an atheist nonbeliever. His last pamphlet, *Agrarian Justice*, published in 1797, called for reform in the inequities of land ownership, which only served to create more enemies for him in France and England.

Upon his return to America in 1802, Paine found his contributions to the origin of this country unrecognized and unappreciated. He never accepted any monetary payment for any of his services to this new country, but had at one point petitioned the state of New York for some property. After considerable resistance, he had been given land in New Rochelle, New York. He was buried on that land in 1809. Ten years after his death, an English journalist, William Corbett, exhumed his bones with the announced purpose of giving Thomas Paine a proper burial on English soil. For the next twenty years, Corbett never got around to providing that heroic burial, and the location of Thomas Paine's remains is now unknown. There have been various reports of his skull or hand bones being in the possession of secretive collectors.

Let's let Thomas Paine speak for himself. These are the words that inspired the freezing army of George Washington in 1778, at Valley Forge. They were undernourished, poorly clothed, often living on flour and water, suffering from typhoid, jaundice and pneumonia, when they were rejuvenated by these words:

*These are the times that try men's souls. The summer soldier
and the sunshine patriot will, in this crisis, shrink from the
service of their country, but he that stands it now, deserves
the praise of man and woman. Tyranny, like hell, is not
easily conquered, yet we have this consolation with us, that
the harder the conflict, the more glorious the triumph. What
we obtain too cheap, we esteem too lightly: it is dearness
only that give everything its value.*

When there was great discontent and great argument in the
American colonies about what action they should take against
England to redress their grievances, there was this voice in Common
Sense, in 1776:

*In England a king hath little more to do than make war and
give away places, which in plain terms, is to impoverish the
nation and set it together by the ears. A pretty business
indeed for a man to be allowed eight hundred thousand
Sterling a year for, and worshiped into the bargain! Of more
worth is one honest man to society, and in the sight of God,
than all the crowned ruffians that ever lived.*

*Society in every state is a blessing, but government even in
its best state is nothing but a necessary evil.*

*Government by kings...was the most prosperous invention
the Devil ever set forth on foot for the promotion of idolatry.*

From the Age of Reason, here are his religious views:

*The opinions I have advanced... are the effect of the most
clear and long established convictions that the Bible and
the Testament are impositions upon the world, that the
fall of man, the account of Jesus Christ being the son of
God, and of his dying to appease the wrath of God, and of
salvation, by that strange means, are all fabulous inventions,
dishonorable to the wisdom and power of the Almighty,
that the only true religion is Deism, by which I then meant
and mean now, the belief of one God, and an imitation of
his moral character, or the practice of what are called moral
virtues – and that it was upon this only (so far as religion
is concerned) that I rested all my hopes and happiness
hereafter. So I say now – and so help me God.*

*I do not believe in the creed professed by the Jewish
Church, by the Roman Church, by the Greek Church, by the
Turkish Church, by the Protestant Church, nor by any church
that I know of. My own mind is my own church.*

*All national institutions of churches, whether Jewish,
Christian or Turkish, appear to me to be no other than
human inventions, set up to terrify and enslave mankind,
and monopolize power and profit.*

Thomas Paine received a British patent for the design of a single span iron bridge, developed a smokeless candle, and worked with inventor John Fitch in developing the steam engine. He was a deist, as were all those other great minds who developed our Declaration of Independence and Constitution. They all knew that for democracy to survive, it must be tied to no religion. Their minds were all playing against each other during this crucial birth of our country. The mastermind of all that interplay of ideology was Thomas Paine. Without his expressive vision and without his material support, it is unlikely that this country would exist, and certainly would not exist with the marvelous freedoms which it espouses.

We are indebted to Thomas Paine for the freedoms that we have in this country. Yet, to my mind, it was not his political ideology or his revolutionary spirit that we should praise the most. We should reserve our greatest praise for the morals which he brought us. It is the age old problem. We all believe in the Golden Rule, but get completely lost when we try to figure out how to apply love of our neighbor to our daily lives. Well, this particular founder mastermind was a superb pragmatist. He may have based his morals on the mistaken concept that there is only one God, who is totally good, but the practical morality he derived from that belief was impeccable. Long before anyone else preached these things with fervor and conviction, and at a time when such views got him branded as a criminal and thrown in jail, Thomas Paine told us that these are the ways we practice the Golden Rule in a just society: we educate all our children, we provide a minimum wage, we give pensions to the elderly, we form public works for the unemployed, we give relief to the poor, we encourage land ownership by the people, and not just a few wealthy, and we finance all of this with a graduated tax system. Everything he stood for has come to be. What a man. What a marvelous human being.

BENJAMIN FRANKLIN

He was born in Boston in 1706, the tenth of seventeen children. His mother, Abriah Folger, was a Puritan (one of her later relatives established the Folger coffee company). His father, Josiah, later converted to Puritanism. This religion derived its name from an attempt to "purify" the Anglican Church. They emphasized that their ministers should preach rather than perform rituals, that each person should, through Bible study, establish their own relationship with their God, and that each congregation should be self-governing. These values of independence, self improvement, and pragmatism rather than ritual would become the mainstay of his philosophy, the matters of which he spoke in his publications, and the touchstone from which he drew his approach to life both in the developing American colonies, as well as in his diplomacy abroad. His search for practical solutions led him to be an inventor of particular note.

Young Ben's formal education was minimal. He had two years, which was enough for him to learn to read and write. He was fortunately a voracious reader, and continued to learn throughout life because he never stopped reading. At age twelve he was apprenticed to his brother James, who was a printer. James began a weekly periodical, The *New England Courant*, in 1722. It was a weekly newspaper which sought opinions from readers, and published their essays on life. Young Ben thought that he could do better than most of those contributors to this periodical, and sent in a series of fourteen satires under the pseudonym of Mrs. Silence Dogwood. When James found out that his younger brother had pulled one over on him, he was angry, and also was in financial trouble. Some of these satires had raised the ire of the local authorities, and James was forbidden to further publish *The Courant*. In an effort to avoid his financial obligations, he moved to make his younger brother, Franklin, the nominal publisher of *The Courant*. The two argued over James' financial manipulations, and Ben walked out. He could not find work in Boston, so he went to Philadelphia looking for a job. He not only found a job in Philadelphia as a printer, but found a career.

In 1724, he was urged by the governor of Pennsylvania, William Keith, to set up his own printing business, and go to England to find financial backing as well as publishing connections. Keith promised him letters of recommendation for this venture. Franklin sailed for England but once there, found those promised letters of support to be absent. He again found work as a printer, and came to enjoy London social life with enthusiasm. That enthusiasm waned rapidly, however, as he got homesick, and wanted to return to America. When he got an offer, in 1726, from Thomas Denham, a gentleman who had become his friend on the voyage to England, he accepted, and sailed back to Philadelphia to become a clerk in Denham's store, which specialized in the West Indies trade. These were rather wild times for young Ben Franklin. He admits in his autobiography that he had a very strong sexual drive, and often frequented the company of "low women." With one of them, he had a son, William. Ben Franklin decided it was time to seek more stability in his life, and return to the values of his parents. He did not like the direction in which he was heading.

When he had first arrived in Philadelphia, he had established a relationship with Deborah Read, the daughter of the rooming house owner. While he was away in England, she had become married, in a not very propitious manner. Her husband had left her, running off with the dowry. She was now abandoned, and by bigamy law, unable to remarry. That social status did not deter young Ben, who was still fond of Deborah. They established a common law marriage in 1730, which, by all accounts, was a loving relationship, lasting until her death in 1774. Deborah graciously agreed to take William into their home, and raise him as their child. They also had two additional children, a son who died at age four of a streptococcal infection, and a daughter, Sarah. From this point on, if Ben Franklin had any wild liaisons, they were kept very discreet. He sought to purify his life, and practice the morals that he taught in his writing, stemming from his religion.

Success soon followed for Benjamin Franklin. He established his own printing company with a partner, and then became sole proprietor. After the publication of *A Modest Inquiry into the Nature and Necessity of a Paper Currency*, in 1729, his company became the printer for Philadelphia currency, the official printers for the colonies of New Jersey, Delaware and Maryland, and established ties with printing companies in the West Indies, New York and the Carolinas. *The Pennsylvania Gazette* was begun in 1729, and circulated widely in New England. Beginning in 1732, under the pseudonym of Richard Saunders, he published *Poor Richard's Almanac* for the next twenty five years, dispersing moral advice and practical solutions to both household and social problems. Some of those values preached by poor Richard had revolutionary flavor, although perhaps hidden. In addition to encouraging thrift, hard work, community spirit and education, poor Richard also emphasized self-governing institutions, religious freedom and opposition to authoritarianism. Ben Franklin's Puritan religious values were never far away.

Benjamin Franklin was the Postmaster of Philadelphia from 1737 to 1753. He became deputy Postmaster General for the colonies in 1753. *Experiments and Observations on Electricity* was published in 1751. Some of the terms he used in describing his experiments are still in use today, including positive, negative, conductivity and battery. He published a call for a central government of the colonies under the title of *Plan of Union*, which was adopted by the Albany council in 1754, but thoroughly rejected by King Richard's advisors, who found it quite objectionable. In the middle of all these other activities, Ben Franklin was inventing. He created the stove that still bears his name, invented the lightning rod, bifocal eyeglasses, a carriage odometer, a rotating drum musical instrument called the glass armonica, a flexible urinary catheter and in addition, charted the Gulf Stream.

The Seven Year War, or the French and Indian War, ended in 1763, and Canada was ceded to Britain from France by the Treaty of Paris. England could now turn its attention toward the American colonies, which were showing significant signs of unrest. The French and Indian war had been costly; the national debt of England had doubled during that time. There seemed to be a simple solution. The troops which had been used for that war could be maintained for the protection of the American colonies, if a tax were applied to pay for their continued existence on that continent. The result was the Stamp Act of 1765, a tax proposed on all printed material, which would have to carry a stamp showing that payment had been made for that material to be printed. Although the British parliament thought that this was a very reasonable thing to do, the colonists sensed that something else was afoot, and that the real reason for the Stamp Act was to use those troops to stamp out resistance in the colonies. Although Ben Franklin had spoken in opposition to the Stamp Act, as had most other colonists, he eventually acceded to that demand, and hired an officer to regulate those collections. He underestimated the vehemence of the resistance that was rapidly accelerating against this Act, which all of the colonists found odious. All of the colonists agreed that only they should be able to determine what taxes should be levied for their protection. All appointed tax collectors were threatened, all resigned or did not carry out their duties, and the tax was never collected to any degree. Benjamin Franklin rather promptly did an about face, and soon found himself representing multiple colonies before the British House of Commons in defense of the colonies right to determine their own taxes. It was at that time that he changed the life of Thomas Paine, and, as a result, all of our lives, for the better.

Following the Declaration of Independence in 1776, Benjamin Franklin was the head of a commission which was dispatched to France seeking economic support for the American cause. The result of that plea was to secure a lot of help; not only did France contribute large sums of money, but some 12,000 troops and 32,000 French sailors fought for the American cause. It is almost certain that the War of Independence would not have been successful, or that our nation would not exist in the form that it now exists, without this major support from France, secured through the persuasive power of that alter ego of Richard Saunders, Benjamin Franklin.

Toward the end of his life, he developed a large stone in his urinary bladder, which made travel difficult, because he had constant lower abdominal pain. In spite of that pain, he attended the Constitutional Convention in 1787, and contributed significantly to the formation of the Constitution of the United States of America. Franklin's proposals for an Executive branch committee, and a single Legislative branch, were not accepted, as various compromises were reached amongst those representatives. Franklin then graciously agreed to vote for acceptance of the constitution, as formed, by acclimation. Franklin was bedridden for the last years of his life, in constant pain, and dependent on narcotic for control of that pain. He died in 1790, at the age of 84.

Benjamin Franklin was perhaps the most religious of all our nation's founders. He believed that his God was in support of the American Revolution, and was the source of all good things that occurred in the life of a human. He was without doubt also a deist, as were all of those who were the most instrumental in establishing our country. All of them, including Franklin, saw no value in the dogma, rhetoric and ritual of organized religion. None of them believed in a Virgin Birth, a God on Earth, a Trinitarian deity, Resurrection after Death, Original Sin, priestly intercession, or any of the trappings of organized religion. Franklin, however, was a champion of all religions, showing support for Anglicans, Presbyterians, Quakers and Catholics alike.

Benjamin Franklin was particularly under the hypnotic spell of Socrates, believing that his god was an Absolute Good, and the source of all morality and virtue in human life. He did not see the fallacy of that theology, necessitating the creation of an evil Devil God to explain all the horror and misery of human life. He did not see that you cannot have a total goodness without having a total badness, neither of which makes any sense in a universe which has no moral or value system. It seems pointless to berate this issue further, however, or to point fingers at Benjamin Franklin for not understanding what we are now only slowly coming to understand very well: that morals are a human invention only. What is important, if we are to understand Benjamin Franklin, is that he was never far from his childhood Puritan religion. His list of virtues, one of which, it is said, he attempted to emphasize every day, reads like a Boy Scout manual: charity, community, spirit, honesty, temperance, frugality, sincerity, justice, tranquility, cleanliness, humility. They all derived from his religion, which also led him to preach hard work, equality and indignity against injustice. He established the Leather Apron Club in Philadelphia in 1727, to discuss morals, politics, and government. The need of the Leather Apron Club for knowledge led to the creation of the Public Library of Philadelphia. They agitated for, until established, a paid police force and a volunteer fire department in Philadelphia. Franklin was responsible for creating the Academy of Philadelphia in 1751, which became the University of Pennsylvania. He freed his slaves in 1785, and fought doggedly against any injustice.

Benjamin Franklin was a giant among human moralists. He intuitively knew the pragmatic ways in which each of us can show our love for our neighbor, and taught those virtues throughout his life. The social programs and practical morals of the United States of America are based, in large part, on the immense wisdom of Benjamin Franklin.

ABRAHAM LINCOLN

Abraham Lincoln was born in a log cabin in Hardin County, Kentucky in 1809. His father, Thomas, is described as a sturdy farmer and a sometime carpenter, who was illiterate, but a great story teller. He often kept the neighbors regaled with tales well into the night. Young Abe is said to have sneaked out of bed at night to listen to those stories, then to have recited them to his friends the next day in acts of great mimicry. His mother, Nancy Hanks, is described as being thin, stoop shouldered, and deeply religious. Later in his life, when embroiled in the taxing stresses of the civil war, Lincoln also became quite religious, expressing his belief that all his actions were simply an expression of the will of his God, with Lincoln as the agent of that God. It seems likely that this shield of determinism came from the Calvinistic beliefs of his mother.

The family moved first to Indiana and then to Illinois. Abraham helped to raise the crops and tend to the animals. Early in life, he developed an antipathy against hunting and fishing. He did not like the killing of animals, even when done so for food. For that same reason, he determined that he would find some life work other than farming. Strangely enough, this antipathy toward killing, which seems to have been a natural expression of his psychology, did not deter Abraham Lincoln from, later in life, actively promoting the death of soldiers on the battle field. Suffice it to say that we all have large areas of hypocrisy in our lives.

His mother died when he was nine, but fortunately, his father's second wife was a woman who was loving and energetic, raising her children and those of Thomas as if they were all her own. She was particularly fond of Abraham. Both she and Thomas encouraged him to read, and by the time he became a young adult, he could write and do simple mathematics. By this time he had become lanky and muscular, expert at wrestling and handling an axe. He is described as being moody but good natured, with a high twanging voice and a long plodding stride. Young Abe was trying to find his direction in life. He was temporarily many things, including a rail splitter, flat bottom boatman to New Orleans and back, surveyor, storekeeper, postmaster and volunteer militiaman. None of these vocations appealed to him for very long; he saw a lot of things that he thought needed to be changed, and decided to find a way to correct them. He began running for the Illinois legislature until he was elected to that body. He studied law voraciously, and in 1836 passed the Illinois bar exam. In order to find enough business in that profession, he moved to Springfield, Illinois, the state capitol, and after several other partnerships, set up a long enduring practice with William H. Herndon. His initial practice was the equivalent of the modern day ambulance chaser. He often traveled hundreds of miles with the court on its circuit to pick up criminal and theft cases, for which the awards were often small. It was not until he became a corporate lawyer, representing the Illinois Central Railroad, that his practice began to prosper.

Lincoln served in the Illinois legislature from 1834 to 1840, and served one term in the United States congress from 1847 to 1849. He supported Zachary Taylor for president in 1848, and expected a high ranking government post as payment for his efforts. When he was instead offered the governorship of the Oregon territory, he did not accept, since it would have taken him completely away from his valuable law practice in Springfield. Disappointed and discouraged, he dropped out of politics until the Senate campaign of 1854. It was the issue of slavery that drew him back into the rough world of politics.

Lincoln had previously expressed his opinion that slavery was unjust, and violated the Constitution of the United States, but he was not an abolitionist. Similar to Thomas Jefferson, he was opposed to slavery, but did not feel that it should be attacked directly. During his one appointment to congress, he had proposed a bill that would have freed the slaves in the District of Columbia, and compensated their owners for their losses. The catch was that this bill was to take effect only if approved by the free white voters of the district. It did not have a chance; both the slaveholders and the abolitionists were offended by this wavering assault on slavery. The issue that raised Lincoln's attention for the senate race of 1854 was a proposal by Stephen Douglas to allow slavery in the entire area of the Louisiana Purchase, according to the wishes of the population of those territories. Lincoln was opposed, believing that the western territories should be kept open as a place where slaves could go who had been granted their freedom. The Lincoln-Douglas debates did not win him the election, but they did attract the attention of the abolitionists, and Lincoln became a viable presidential candidate for the campaign of 1960. By skillfully avoiding controversy from that point on until the election, Lincoln was nominated on the third ballot of the Republican convention. In the following presidential election, he was elected on the first ballot of the Electoral College, because the rest of the field was so divided.

As soon as the election of 1860 was over, a bill was introduced in congress that would allow slavery to exist forever in those states that had already adopted it, and would allow the western territories to be divided into free and slave states. Lincoln didn't have a problem with the first part of this proposal. He initially believed that slavery would die a natural death if not confronted, and that military confrontation should be avoided. What he did not accept was the proposal to extend slavery into the western territories. When this proposal was not accepted, six southern states seceded, and were later followed by Virginia, North Carolina, Tennessee and Arkansas. The border states of Missouri, Kentucky, Delaware and Maryland did not secede, but were wavering. Lincoln negotiated furiously with them, guaranteeing that he would not interfere with slavery in those states, because he badly needed their support. He did this while jailing 18,000 secessionist rebels in those states, who were held in federal prisons without charge or right of due process.

What Lincoln wanted for the federal government was exactly the same as his failed proposal for the District of Columbia. He wanted to free the slaves, compensate their owners, and deport those slaves to other land or countries after their freedom. This plan still did not please anyone. No slaveholders wanted to lose their slaves, and no blacks wanted to be deported. The abolitionists were offended that this was, according to Lincoln's plan, to be a gradual process. In his assessment of this impending civil war, it appears that Lincoln greatly underestimated the support he might expect from those in the South who might want to preserve the Union, greatly underestimated the support he would get from the border states, and greatly underestimated the determination of the abolitionists to end slavery now. While this conflict was all about slavery, Lincoln didn't see it clearly. He initially thought that he could evade the slavery issue by simply not being the aggressor. Unfortunately, he was also completely fixed on preserving the Union, whatever the cost of that effort might be, and this incorrigible decision may have been a grave error. With this stance of Abraham Lincoln, the American Civil War was inevitable. The

resulting destruction and cost in human life from the civil war was horrendous. Some 600,000 soldiers were killed, another 400,000 maimed
for life, and the financial cost some fifteen billion dollars, a staggering
amount in that day.

> *"My paramount objective in this struggle is to preserve the*
> *Union, and is not either to save or destroy slavery. If I could*
> *save the Union by not freeing any slaves I would do it; and*
> *if I could save it by freeing all slaves I would do it; and if I*
> *could save it by freeing some and leaving others alone, I*
> *would also do that."*

The Emancipation Proclamation, therefore, occurring during the
civil war, was not an act of great enlightenment or magnanimity. It
was a calculated political act. The war effort had faltered. Greater support was needed both at home and abroad. Lincoln also had another
need; he needed more troops. He envisioned developing an army
of trained and well equipped blacks, who would bring the war to a
rapid conclusion once they began fighting on the Union side. This
Proclamation, first issued in 1862, and finalized in 1863, did not bring
him the troops that he wanted, but did have the political effect that
he needed. Support for the war rallied in the North, and the European
countries now allied themselves with the North. Some 200,000 slaves
in the North gained their freedom, but those in the South and the
Border States were not affected.

The Gettysburg Address was also a calculated political move, as
much as it was a statement of belief. Although the battle of Gettysburg
had turned the war in favor of the North, there was great dissatisfac-
tion at the number of soldiers killed and the length of the war. The
policy of Ulysses S. Grant, fully supported and encouraged by Lincoln,
was a war of attrition. Neither Grant nor Lincoln cared how many soldiers got killed as long as at least an equal number of Confederate
soldiers were also killed. Lincoln knew that eventually the manpower
for the Confederacy would give out before that of the Union, since
they had a two to one population advantage. Costly battles were quite
acceptable to him as long as Confederate soldiers were being killed
at the same rate. Although that assessment was correct, it provided
for a grim and gruesome conflict. At that time in the war, the political climate at home had deteriorated. The governor of Pennsylvania,
Andrew Gregg Curtin, told Lincoln that if the election were to be held

in 1863, he was sure that they would lose. There was growing pressure from a group of Democrats, called the Copperheads, to seek a peaceful end to the war by negotiating with the Southern states. Lincoln knew that he had to present a call to action which would rejuvenate the war effort, or else he would lose the election in 1864, and possibly lose the war also. This speech was not as much a dedication of a graveyard as it was a calculated patriotic call to action. It eventually worked. Several weeks later, after newspaper editors read the Gettysburg address, and cogitated over what it said, there was a groundswell of praise for these lofty words. The effect was electric in a northern divided nation, which was war weary. The carryover effect was sufficient to provide enough further support to win the war, and carry Lincoln to election in 1864. Lincoln had craftily used his divine right beliefs for political gain.

The background to the Battle of Gettysburg is that General Robert E. Lee had just defeated General Joseph Hooker at Chancelorsville, Virginia, in May of 1863. Lee felt that he had to push this advantage. If he could at this time mount an attack that would carry the Union far into the North, and as an ultimate goal, capture Washington, D.C., he would probably win this war for the South. Such an incursion would rally European nations to their cause, and provide further economic support for their side in this internal struggle. This was the crucial time, in the thinking of Lee, that he had to make his move. The rebel army gradually advanced until by late June, 1863, they had reached land south of Gettysburg, Pennsylvania, where there were hills, a cemetery, an orchard, and open fields. Scouts were sent ahead into town to determine what the situation was that lay ahead. When they did so, they saw a few Union soldiers, and knew that the Union forces were not far ahead.

The Union, now under the command of General George G. Meade, was not dumb. They recognized the importance of Gettysburg as a road center, and also were aware that if they did not make a stand here, the rest of the North was an open target. They also determined that this was the spot where they had to make a stand. They did have a few advantages, which probably made all the difference in the world, although they are seldom quoted. They had several thousand more soldiers, and those soldiers had just been issued Spencer repeating carbine rifles. These advantages did not give them a great deal of confidence, but they were well aware it was now or never if they expected to win this conflict. All told, including both the Rebels and the Union, there were about 160,000 soldiers gathered on those fields for that battle, which began on July 1, 1863.

During the initial phases of that battle, on the first day, neither side could claim an advantage. The hill, the cemetery and the orchard were captured and recaptured, with heavy losses on both sides. By the second day, Lee believed that he had to make a charge, or else he could not win against greater numbers. The Confederacy Army of Northern Virginia made a strong charge toward the center of the Union Army line. They succeeded in pushing forward far beyond the front of that line of defense, but then found that the Union Army had simply given, but not retreated. The soldiers of the South found themselves facing a withering fire from the front and both sides. Their losses were great, leading to the issue of a retreat back to the original battle lines for that day. It was clear that they would have to try to fight another day, once the gravity of their losses became apparent. The Confederate Army could have easily been defeated at that point, but that advantage was not pushed by General Meade. Under the cover of a heavy rain on July 3, 1863, the Confederate Army retreated, leaving behind them only a few isolated skirmishes. The loss of life on both sides was dramatic, about 20,000 for each. The abandoned battle ground was covered with about 7500 bodies, and several thousand horses. It was Pennsylvania, in the summer, hot and humid. The smell of rotting flesh filled the air for miles around.

This mess presented the some 2400 citizens of Gettysburg with a significant problem, as to how to bury the dead in a dignified manner, and do so fairly rapidly. It was not feasible in time for them to attempt contact with the families of the deceased, and ask them to bear those expenses. A young Gettysburg attorney, David Wills, submitted a request to the governor of Pennsylvania, requesting funds from the states for the purchase of a national burial ground. That request was granted, and the town purchased seventeen acres at a price of $2,476.87. Initial plans were to hold a dedication ceremony on October 23, 1863, but the renowned speaker they wished to give the oration for that ceremony, Edward Everett, replied that this did not give him enough time to prepare an adequate address for such an august occasion. The ceremony was then reset for November 19, 1863. As an afterthought, the president of the United States, Abraham

Lincoln, was asked seventeen days before that event to give a few appropriate remarks at the end of those ceremonies.

Approximately 15,000 people were said to have been in attendance at that solemn event. Only half the dead had been buried, and the smell of death still lingered in the air. The program consisted of band music, prayer, more band music, and then the eloquent oration by Edward Everett, which lasted for two hours. A new hymn, composed for this occasion, was then sung, after which the President of the United States arose to speak. His remarks were so brief, the photographers did not have time to set up their cameras, and no pictures were obtained of Lincoln giving that speech. He is said to have spoken in a high voice, with a Kentucky drawl, but those in the crowd stated later that they could hear every word. They were still numb from the two hour preceding oration. When Lincoln sat down, there was no applause for a long time, just silence, then a few scattered hand claps. Lincoln himself is said to have remarked to his body guard, as he sat down, that this speech would not scour, a reference to the mark a plow makes in the ground, or, in other words, was a failure. The initial remarks in newspapers were condemnatory. It was not until several weeks later, as other newspaper editors of the North reflected on those words, that this speech became lauded, and a rallying cry for the abolitionists. The Gettysburg address served the political purpose that Lincoln wanted. The troops and supplies needed to win this civil war now became available, and he was able to win the election of 1864.

> *"Four score and seven years ago our fathers brought forth on this continent a new nation, conceived in Liberty, and dedicated to the proposition that all men are created equal.*
>
> *Now we are engaged in a great civil war, testing whether that nation, or any nation, so conceived and so dedicated, can long endure. We are met on a great battlefield of that war. We have come to dedicate a portion of that field, as a final resting place for those who here gave their lives that that nation might live. It is altogether fitting and proper that we should do this.*
>
> *But in a larger sense, we can not dedicate – we can not consecrate – we can not hallow – this ground. The brave men, living and dead, who struggled here, have consecrated*

it, far above our poor power to add or detract. The world
will little note, nor long remember what we say here, but
it can never forget what they did here. It is for us the living,
rather, to be dedicated here to the unfinished work which
they who fought here have thus far so nobly advanced.
It is rather for us to be here dedicated to the great task
remaining before us – that from these honored dead we
take increased devotion to that cause for which they gave
the last full measure of devotion – that we here highly
resolve that these dead shall not have died in vain – that
this nation, under God, shall have a new birth of freedom –
and that government of the people, by the people, for the
people, shall not perish from the earth."

Although Lincoln was a Calvinist, who believed that all of the efforts of men were directed by his God, and that everything he did personally was determined by that God, it was not just the Bible that was his inspiration for the actions that he took. His Bible, stemming from the ideology of John Locke, was also the Declaration of Independence, which declared that all men, because of their divinity, must be free and equal. Following the dictates of that document, to his mind, gave him the moral authority to insist that any peace with the South must primarily contain the elements of restoration of the Union, as well as the freedom of slaves. He believed that he would not be following the dictates of his God, unless he insisted on that preservation of the Union. When he met with the commissioners of the South at Hampton Roads in February, 1865, and made these demands, even though he promised liberal pardons, those commissioners found these contingencies unacceptable, and the war dragged on, with the further loss of human life and destruction of the South. When General Robert E. Lee surrendered the remainder of his decimated forces to Ulysses S. Grant at the Appomattox Court House on April 9, 1865, the American Civil War was officially over. Five days later, President Abraham Lincoln was shot at Ford's Theater in Washington, D.C. on April 14, 1865, and died the following day.

During the rather brief tenure of Abraham Lincoln, the shape of the Federal Government changed dramatically. He believed the government should obtain from the people the financing necessary to provide programs for them they could not individually provide for themselves:

> *"The legitimate object of government is to do for a community of people whatever they need to have done, but cannot do at all, or cannot do so well for themselves in their separate and individual capacities."*

In keeping with that philosophy, during his presidency, most of the programs he had promoted while a member of the Illinois legislature became federal programs, and a few others besides. A national banking system was established, a protective tariff created, funds appropriated for the construction of a railroad from the East to the West coast, and the federal income tax was established. Prior to his time, Thanksgiving had been a regional holiday. He decreed that the entire nation would give thanks for its existence on the last day of November each year.

What moral judgments we should pass on Abraham Lincoln during these difficult and trying times becomes a thorny question. During the last seven score years, he has been lauded as the Great Emancipator, and one of, if not the greatest, of our presidents. These lofty accolades are given not just because he freed the slaves, and because of his futuristic domestic programs. He also proved to be a military genius. The plan he had for winning the war, providing pressure on the South at multiple points of attack, in a war of attrition, proved to be the correct strategy. Once he found a general who would follow that costly plan of attrition, Ulysses S. Grant, the North began to win this civil war. On several occasions, when something else was needed to gain support for the Northern cause, he found a way to rejuvenate the support of the population. Both the Emancipation Proclamation and the Gettysburg address, for example, were calculated political maneuvers to gather financial support and supply more troops. He was gracious to Negroes everywhere, inviting them to the White House, where all proclaimed him to be completely free of bias or racism. He was honest and straightforward in his negotiations, never derogatory, and based his aims on the glowing morality expressed in the Declaration of Independence. For upholding those morals, and ending slavery, he justly deserves great praise.

There is also just criticism that should be made, however. If, as he has clearly stated in his own words, his aim was to preserve the Union as an example to the rest of the world of glorious democracy and freedom, one has to ask why it was necessary to preserve the Union to achieve that laudable goal. It seems that the shining example of freedom and democracy could have been more clearly met by freeing all of the slaves in the North and prohibiting all slavery in the new expansion territories to the West. The South would have been isolated from the North, as well as from the most wealthy European nations, who opposed slavery. The slaves who wished to escape would have found ready refuge in the North and the West. It is likely that slavery would have died in the South from external pressure and attrition over the next 25 years. Which was morally better? Was it better to have allowed several hundred thousand slaves to suffer the deprivations of humiliation and degradation for another quarter of a century, because he allowed the South to secede? Or were the decisions that were made better, causing the callous loss of one million lives, destruction of the economy of the South for the next quarter century, a crippling debt, and war wounds which have not yet fully healed?

My opinion, although it may be highly unpopular, is that the incorrect moral decision was made. Honest Abe had it within his power to eliminate all slavery in the North and the West, and find ways to end slavery in the South without the horrendous loss of human life that he promulgated. His eagerness to kill rebellious Indians in the Santee Dakota Indian uprising in Minnesota is greatly troubling. His willingness to sacrifice as many Union soldiers as was needed to win a war of his own making is deeply disturbing. I believe it is the errant symptom of an otherwise moral man, who was misdirected by his Calvinistic deterministic religion to sacrifice human life in order to meet an artificial goal. His religion led him to make an historic moral blunder. This is not meant to be hypercritical. Probably none of us could have anywhere approached the skill he demonstrated in guiding our country during that awful time in our history. As all of us, he did the best he could with the knowledge that he had at that time – but with hindsight we see that he could have done better. My estimation is that long term history will still hold Abraham Lincoln in high moral esteem, because he ended slavery, even though his reasons for doing so were political rather than moral. My estimation is also that long term history will find great moral fault with Abraham Lincoln. He did not understand that human life is a one-time only precious gift, and that the cost of hold-ing recalcitrant states together in an unwilling union was not worth that morbid cost in human life. Long term history will recognize that the American civil war was not necessary. Abraham Lincoln could have achieved the same goals of freedom and democracy without sacrificing 600,000 precious lives, morbidly maiming 400,000 other lives, depriving several million other lives of their pursuit of happi-ness, and without destruction of the South. We can blame Calvinism, deeply rooted in Abraham Lincoln from his childhood, for leading him to believe that he was the agent of a God who controlled all events on this earth, had a plan for all humans, and who had placed him, Abraham Lincoln, here on earth as His personal agent, to keep a few states from seceding from this newly formed democracy. This was a grievous moral error, derived from his conservative religion, for which this entire nation has paid dearly. I am not sure this hor-rendous war was not an act of immorality more damaging than any of the good things he accomplished for this country.

MAHATMA GANDHI

Mohandas Karamchand Gandhi was born in 1869. He would not be known as the Mah-Atma (great soul) until later in his life. His father was poorly educated but served capably as the Prime Minister of the small Indian state of Porbander in British India, a state also ruled by princes. His father found himself constantly negotiating with recalci-trant princes, suffering peasantry, and demanding British overseers. Gandhi's mother, Putibai, was a devout Jainist. This religion has as its core belief, *akimsa*, a doctrine of non-injury to all living creatures. This doctrine would be most easily understood by us as pacifism, although it extends to both human and animal life. This religion believes that man's nature is perfect, but is spoiled by *karma*, that accumulation of property, desires and life burdens which weighs us all down. The way to escape from this oppressive burden, and to achieve a state of bliss and unending knowledge, is by asceticism. That asceticism includes fasting, vegetarianism, lonely meditation, atonement for sins by ser-vice to humanity, and renunciation of the ego. Violence in thought precedes physical injury, and must be avoided. This religion believes that all humans are equal. It seems clear where Gandhi got the traits for which he would later become famous. He got his administrative skills from his father, and got his pacifism, asceticism and demands for equality from his mother. He would need all of those skills to overcome the injustices which were soon to face him.

Gandhi had a rather inauspicious start in life. At his primary school, there was not a chalkboard. The children learned the alphabet by writing the letters in the dirt with their fingers. His performance later in school was far from laudatory: "good at English, fair in arithmetic, weak in geography, conduct very good, bad handwriting." As a teen, he went through a rebellious phase, although it was brief. In rapid succession, he became an atheist, smoked, did petty thievery, and ate meat. After each of those sins of his religion, he did not return to them. Given his druthers, he would have studied medicine, but was instead sent to study law, so he could qualify for a government office, following the footsteps of his father. For that purpose, he was sent to England, promising his mother before he left that he would not eat meat and would not have sex with women. His vegetarianism was initially quite a problem in England, until he found a vegetarian group which was moralistic and idealistic. Members included George Bernard Shaw and Edward Carpenter. He found kindred minds and mental stimulation in that group, while completing his law studies in England. Upon return to India, he found no decent job opportunities. In order to have work, he accepted a clerical position with a firm in Natal, South Africa. His conversion to social activism and civil disobedience, using pacifist methods, was about to begin.

Nothing went right upon his arrival in South Africa in 1893. Even though he held a first class ticket, he was thrown out of the first class train couch in order to make room for a European. On the stagecoach, he did not make room for a European passenger. The stage couch driver beat him up and forced him to ride on the foot board. When he went to court wearing a turban, he was asked to remove it. When he refused, he was commanded to leave the court. Rather than cower against these racist insults, he was moved to defend his Indian dignity. He founded the Natal Indian Congress, which began to expose the discrimination practiced by Britain against the people of their Indian colonies. Soon the rest of the world, as it became aware of these practices, became critical of England and its South African rulers. None of this made Gandhi very popular. He was attacked by a mob in 1896 and almost hung, escaping with his life only through the efforts of the wife of the police superintendent. He did not carry a grudge. He declined to press charges against those who had assaulted him. When the Boer war began, he organized a volunteer Indian Ambulance Corps to carry injured British soldiers. His belief was that in spite of the indignities to which they had been subjected, they were nevertheless Indian subjects of Britain and should support the British in their cause. He also thought that this display of loyalty would help the Indian population gain their independence.

To the contrary, the opposite result occurred. The government formed after that conflict was purely Boer/British, leaving the Indians further suppressed than before. That discrimination seemed to arrive at a culmination in 1906, when a tax registration in South Africa was required for Indians only. This was more than the Indian population could tolerate. Gandhi organized mass protests, insisting that they would all be non-violent on the part of the protestors. The South African response was brutal. Indians were jailed, beaten and shot freely, but in spite of that cruelty, refused to submit to this indignity. The severity of treatment against the Indian population, as it became known to the rest of the world, was roundly condemned by all other nations, and by much of the other population in South Africa. Even though those cruel methods successfully quelled these rebellions, General Smuts was eventually required to reach an agreement with Gandhi as to the treatment of Indian subjects. The methods of passive resistance by which entire nations can be made to change had been born, and were never far away from him for the rest of his life.

Back in India, he founded the Indian National Congress, which became the tool by which these techniques of protest and resistance were used. Although it began first as a series of reactions against odious British policies, it soon became clear to Gandhi that the ultimate goal should be Indian independence. He established a commune where they grew their own vegetables, and lived sparsely without dependence on outside supply. His home became a common meeting ground for young and old protestors, his sparse table always open, creating much strain on his faithful wife, but no one was ever turned away. Planning sessions at that commune led to mass responses by the Indians. Legislatures, schools, courts and offices were boycotted

whenever the enforcement of government policies became unacceptable. The government response was harsh. Thousands of Indians were
beaten, killed and jailed, and as the years progressed, at least 60,000
were imprisoned. Gandhi was jailed, and may have stayed there for a
much longer time, but developed appendicitis, leading to his release
in 1924. By 1930, a truce was called to have a negotiation session in
London, which produced no results. Even more stern repression was
applied by the British police. While in prison in 1932, however, Gandhi
was able, though a fast of 21 days, to obtain a form of status for the
untouchables. Indian independence continued to elude the Indians. In
frustration, various schisms appeared in the Indian National Congress,
some of which wanted a more aggressive form of protest. This was
not tolerable for Gandhi, who resigned to promote communes and
cottage industries among the poor, teaching them spinning, weaving,
and other forms of self-reliance.

The outbreak of World War II added another dimension to this
conflict between England and their Indian colonies. Britain desperately needed the support of the Indian population in this war, a
directive which was greatly resisted by the Indian National Congress.
It did not make sense to them to fight a war for the independence
of England unless they were also to be granted their own independence. The British response was draconian. The entire Indian
National Congress was jailed, in an attempt to eliminate this unre-
pentant source of domestic resistance, once and for all. That ploy
certainly did not work for Britain. Under Gandhi, the massive protests continued by the Indian population until the Labor Party came
to power in England in 1945. Following prolonged negotiations, in
which England was greatly afraid of conflict between the Muslim
and Hindu populations, the Indian National Congress finally agreed
to the establishment of two independent states, Pakistan and India.
This was a crushing disappointment for Gandhi, who wanted India
to remain whole. The resulting disruption and migration of entire
communities was horrendous. Gandhi did what he could to serve
the people during this fractious time. He admonished those who
showed prejudice, comforted those in sorrow, and provided means
of rehabilitation for refugees. The result was that he was no one
group's favorite. Hindus and Muslims both criticized his aid to any on
the other side; the wealthy felt that he favored taking their posses-

sions away, and the poor felt that he was not doing enough. He was the target of criticism from his own party, who felt that he hindered them in the separation of the British Indian colonies into two separate states. Throughout the years, there had been many attempts on his life. Finally, a young Hindu fanatic achieved, on January 30, 1948, what other fanatics had failed to do in the past. Gandhi was shot and killed while on his way to evening prayers.

The death of the Mahatma was not the end of his ideology. It was more a new beginning. Among his ideological children we can include the Dalai Lama, Lech Walesa, Martin Luther King, Jr., Cesar Chavez, Desmond Tutu and Nelson Mandela. There have been in addition, a whole host of admirers, greatly influenced in their own thoughts and actions, by the thoughts and actions of this singular man. Perhaps in some degree, we are all gradually learning from his example that non-violent resistance, negotiation and compromise are better than war, even though we have to worry that recent events tell us some have learned otherwise. There are apparently many who have not yet learned this lesson, the warlike attitude of the United States of America and the violent tactics of Islamic extremists both being a case in point.

There is, in my mind, one major criticism of the ideology of the Mahatma Gandhi. It has been not his religious views, which favored no certain religious faith. He felt that all religions had great value in their stress upon compassion, but that all of them had been overcome with ritual and hypocrisy, an assessment with which I would heartily agree. He did not comment on the great bipolarity of our religions, but he understood very clearly that all religions were damaging to society when they interfered with the free access of any one individual to his or her God. When asked if he was a Hindu or not, he replied that he was a Hindu, but also a Christian, Muslim and Jew.

Another criticism, which I also consider minor, is that Gandhi seemed to have an unrealistic appraisal of the needs of society, insisting that all communities should be self-ruled and self supporting, without a central government. While that utopian ideal is greatly to be wished, it does not appear to answer the needs of large populations as they deal with each other, and as such, appears quite unrealistic for large segments of our population, at this stage in the development of the human species. These parts of his belief system do not bother me much. I can accept them as reasonable parts of his system of faith, and accept that perhaps we have allowed ourselves to be governed too much.

I also consider it quite inappropriate that Gandhi was criticized for his opposition to the creation of the state of Israel, when that land was taken away from those Palestinians who called it their home. He had great sympathy for the Jewish cause, and great empathy for their ages-long persecution, but found no way that this egregious land grab could be justified, on any religious or other grounds. He was quite right, in my opinion. Judged in any moral sense, this invasion and occupation of homes and land that belonged to others, in the name of a religion driven by mythology, was a crime against humanity. Those who criticized Gandhi for his opposition to this crime simply showed their bigotry and intolerance. I believe that he was right and that they were wrong.

> "My sympathies are all with the Jews. I have known them intimately in South Africa. Some of them became life-long companions. Through these friends I came to learn much of their age-long persecution. They have been the untouchables of Christianity...But my sympathy does not blind me to the requirements of justice. The cry for the national home for the Jews does not make much appeal to me. The sanction for it is sought in the Bible and the tenacity with which the Jews have hankered after return to Palestine. Why should they not, like other peoples of the earth, make that country their home where they are born and where they earn their livelihood? Palestine belongs to the Arabs in the same sense that England belongs to the English, or France to the French. It is wrong and inhuman to impose the Jews on the Arabs. What is going on in Palestine today cannot be justified by any moral code of conduct."

There is one part of Gandhi's ideology, however, which I do not find acceptable, if not odious, and have the temerity to believe almost everyone else should also find it unacceptable. It is this: sometimes his deep commitment to pacifism slips dangerously over into unpalatable passivism. In relation to the threatened invasion of Britain by the Nazi army, Gandhi had this advice for the English people:

> "I would like you to lay down the arms you have as being

*useless for saving you or society. You will invite Herr
Hitler and Signor Mussolini to take what they want of the
countries you call your possessions. If these gentlemen
choose to occupy your homes, you will vacate them. If they
do not give you free passage out, you will allow yourselves,
man, woman and child, to be slaughtered, but you will
refuse to owe allegiance to them."*

He had these comments on the extermination of Jews by the Nazis:

*"Hitler killed five million Jews. It is the greatest crime of our
time. But the Jews should have offered themselves to the
butcher's knife. They should have thrown themselves into
the sea from cliffs...It would have aroused the world and
the people of Germany...As it is, they succumbed anyway in
their millions."*

When greatly criticized for these statements, Gandhi replied in
several writings, indicating he understood that Hitler and the Nazis
were a great threat to the world, and understood that if there were
ever any war that could be justified, it would be this one. He then
immediately followed this realization by stating that no war was ever
justified. He believed that he had demonstrated, in the Indian struggle for independence, that change in a society could be accomplished
through non-violent protest, rather than through violent resistance.

*"The tyrants of old never went so mad as Hitler seems to
have gone. And he is doing it with religious zeal. For he
is propounding a new religion of exclusive and militant
nationalism in the name of which any inhumanity becomes
an act of humanity to be rewarded here and hereafter.
The crime of an obviously mad but intrepid youth is being
visited upon his whole race with unbelievable ferocity. If
there ever could be a justifiable war in the name of and for
humanity, a war against Germany, to prevent the wanton
persecution of a whole race, would be justified. But I do not
believe in any war."*

While I find myself in agreement with the last quote above, I also
find revulsion for these directives which advise Jews and the English
to passively offer their lives for murder, or else commit suicide, when
faced with violent aggressors. There is, to me, a monstrous differ-

ence between passive submission, and passive resistance. Life is far too precious to simply offer to give it away. That, to me, is immoral. No life should be taken unless it is done in an effort to make some other life better. A complete lack of resistance simply encourages those who have gone mad with greed and power to commit more evil acts. Complete passivity has never worked. The protests which Gandhi organized in India for those people to become free of suppression were acts of passive resistance; they were not in any sense complete passivity. These acts only succeeded because those people actively supported their cause, and actively resisted an unjust government with boycott, voice, loss of job, incarceration and sometimes, loss of life. None of that loss of life, however, was of their own volition. All of it required that an act of violence be committed against them by the perpetrators of injustice. Perhaps Gandhi does not mean what he says. What he says in the above quotes is, however, in my opinion, immoral, because of its emphasis on passivity, and certainly not the way he practiced.

The only moral response that creates a change in society for the better, is called tit for tat, which we have already fully discussed. In the first encounter with another individual, always give them the benefit of the doubt. If however, they lie to you or cheat on you, resist any further attempt on their part to gain your cooperation, until such time as they have demonstrated to you a change in their ways. Many will deserve a second change to not abuse you. If, after a second chance, that other individual persists in taking advantage of you in an egregious way, there are no more chances. They will no longer at any time ever receive your cooperation. You will not be violent toward them, but you will never assist them again. In other words, everyone deserves a first chance to cooperate; many will deserve a second chance; none deserve a third chance. This approach fosters empathy and trust, and shuts the door on those who act only in self-interest. Society improves its morality only through tough love. None of us should continue to give to those who react to that giving with abuse.

If someone tries to take something away from me that is mine, that attempt should be resisted by me with everything that I have within my power, other than preemptive violence on my part. I find it impossible to believe that the world would have been a better place had Hitler been allowed to invade all lands he wished, and exterminate all those who displeased him. That is to me, highly illogical. It is just one more example of, even in Gandhi's great mind, a sound moral principle being carried to the extreme where it becomes immoral.

A poll was conducted last year among historians as to whom they considered to be the most influential person in all of human history. The winner, at least in the minds of these students of human history, was Muhammad, closely followed by Jesus, with the Buddha in a somewhat distant third. If the criterion of this contest was to decide only that person who was the most influential in human history, without regard for the goodness or badness of that influence, these scholars were probably quite correct. We should by no means confuse greatest political influence with the influence of morality, however. If the criterion of this contest would be to decide who was the most moral person of all recorded human history, both in terms of ideology and social action, then Mohandas Karamchand Gandhi wins hands down. No one else even comes close. He freed an entire nation without sacrificing any of the lives of those who enslaved and mistreated that nation. To be sure, both Muhammad and Jesus preached magnificent morals, which, if they are followed, are marvelous guides for the creation of a stable and loving society. Each of these self-proclaimed Prophets, however, also demanded an eternal torture, or death, on all those humans who did not, for some reason, agree with their particular mythology. The result of that demand for violent punishment of all those who have a different belief, has fostered a storm of cruel and unusual punishment, torture and death, since the inception of those religions. As our world has now become one world, those violent prophecies consume us all, and affect all nations of the earth. There is, in fact, grave doubt that Muhammad and Jesus have not done human societies much more harm than good, because of their total intolerance for other belief and other thought. Both these Prophets should grovel at the feet of the great soul, the Mahatma. The Buddha should praise him for demonstrating how one brings moral enlightenment back to the market place. Gandhi was the greatest of all human time (my apologies to Muhammad Ali).

MARTIN LUTHER KING, JR.

Michael King, Jr. was born on January 15, 1929, to Michael and Alberta Williams King, the second of three children. Both his father and grandfather were Baptist ministers. After a trip to Germany in 1934, his father was so impressed with the reforms of Martin Luther that he had his own name changed to Martin Luther, as well as that of his son, Michael. Young Martin Luther was a gifted child. He entered Morehouse College at age 15. Although the junior Martin would have preferred medicine or law, his father directed him to study divinity. He graduated with a Bachelor of Divinity degree in 1951, and received his PhD at Boston University in 1955. While in Boston, he met a girl from Alabama who was studying at the New England Conservatory of Music. Coretta Scott and Martin Luther King, Jr. were married in 1953 and subsequently had four children.

What happened next became a matter of the right man, at the right place and time, to create an upheaval in the organization of Southern society. King's first charge after graduating from seminary was the Dexter Avenue Baptist Church in Montgomery, Alabama. Civil rights unrest was already highly present in that town. Under that influence, a lady named Rosa Parks refused to give up her seat on the segregated bus system to a white passenger, in 1955. She was arrested and charged with violating the laws of that community. The Black protest was immediate and strong. They formed the Montgomery Improvement Association and elected this dynamic new pastor, Martin Luther King, Jr. as the leader of their organization. From the moment of his first speech to that group, they were all inspired to continue their struggle until they had achieved their right.

"We have no alternative but to protest. For many years we have shown an amazing patience. We have sometimes given our white brethren the feeling that we liked the way we were being treated. But we come here tonight to be saved from that patience that makes us patient with anything less than freedom and justice."

None of this was easy. There was constant strife and resentment against the black community for their subsequent boycott of the Montgomery bus system, which lasted 385 days. There was violence against many of those who were instrumental in that boycott. King's house was bombed, his family threatened, and he was arrested. The end result, however, was an end to segregation on the Montgomery bus system by order of the United States District Court, after which the boycott ended. One step on the road to freedom had been reached, but King was now galvanized. He knew there was much more to be done, and to extend that effort to a larger campus than the city of Montgomery, he formed the Southern Christian Leadership Conference.

By this time, India had won its independence from Britain using non-violent resistance to the ruling authorities. Although the Indians had paid a bloody and suffering price over several decades, they had achieved their goal without directing violence toward their oppressors. King was tremendously impressed. Encouraged and supported by the American Friends Service Committee, he visited India and followers of Gandhi in 1959. He was there warmly received, and counseled in the methods of non-violent protest to change the wrongs of a society. There was, at that point, no turning back for this dedicated and dynamic leader. If the black community in his country was to achieve their freedom, it would have to be done through the powerful tool of non-violent protest, and the time to do that protest was now. King was committed, somewhere in his soul, to find a way of bringing justice for his people, and equality for all people of the United States of America.

King found an immediate ally back home, Bayard Rustin. Rustin was one of the associated founders of the Southern Christian Leadership Council, a talented black civil rights activist who had studied the methods of non-violent protest at length, and who became King's closest advisor, as well as, at times, his personal counselor. It was a dicey relationship, which eventually ended in a separation, but not until after Rustin had organized the famous March on Washington in l963. The problems were that Rustin carried significant baggage with him. He was a former member of the American Communist Party, and probably one of the main reasons that J. Edgar Hoover soon targeted King, unjustly, for having Communist affiliations. The more heavily weighted baggage that Rustin carried was his overt homosexuality. It eventually led to his expulsion as an active member of the American Friends Service Committee actions, and forced him to become an outside player in the civil rights movement.

That was a minor tragedy. I personally had previously met Bayard

Rustin in 1951 while attending a Southern Christian Leadership conference in Columbia, South Carolina, organized by the American Friends
Service Committee. He was a fascinating, energetic man, deeply
devoted to the cause of civil rights and to the non-violent methods
of resisting injustice. He led several of our sessions, where we talked
about the tactics of civil unrest and the philosophies of A. J. Muste.
As eager idealistic students, we often gathered around for informal
sessions afterward while Rustin continued with his wisdom and enthusiasm, to teach us how to carry ourselves when we were involved in
the protests we were about to do. These were heady times for those
of us who were, at a young age, concerned about the morality of our
society and ways to bring justice to all members of our society. I subsequently rode on buses in the back seats, black section, expecting
to be arrested at the next bus stop. I participated in sit-in protests at
a segregated playground in Washington, D.C., expecting the police to
arrive at any moment to take us off to jail. I drank at the black water
fountain in the bus stops, wondering if I would be accosted for my
brazen action. We were all motivated to do whatever it took to create
a more just society.

I attended that conference in Columbia, South Carolina, with my
college roommate and best friend, Paul Williams. I am not sure how it
happened, and do not remember where I slept on those nights at that
conference, but do remember that somehow Paul wound up staying
with Bayard Rustin. I also remember that Paul seemed to behave a
bit differently after our first night there. That change in attitude continued afterwards when we returned to college. The reason for his
emotionally disturbed state did not become clear until later that year,
after we had written personal essays for our English Composition
class. Paul only told me briefly what he had described in his essay, but
enough for me to understand that he had been used by Bayard Rustin
in a way that he did not want, and altered by that encounter in a way
that changed him for the rest of his life. Paul had finally been able to
describe in detail those actions of his night with Rustin. Although being
able to vent his emotions from that time, in confidence, to his trusted
English professor, this release was not enough for him to ever recover
fully. He received an A+ on his paper and the immediate concern of
our great professor, Thomas A. Perry, although that grade was poor
compensation for the dramatic change it made in his life. Paul's report

back to the AFSC, after that conference, may have been the final blow which led them to separate permanently from Bayard Rustin.

In l960, King and his family moved to Atlanta, where he joined his father as co-pastor of the Ebenezer Baptist Church. Later that year he was arrested at a segregated lunch counter, along with 33 students. King was targeted for punishment; he was sentenced to the Reedville State Prison on the charge that he had violated his probation after a minor traffic citation given several months earlier. The national reaction was highly condemnatory. Not only were the charges against him egregiously incompatible with the sentence he was given, but there was great concern for his safety in any prison. Dwight D. Eisenhower, the sitting president, made no move to intervene. King was released from jail only through the efforts of a young presidential candidate from Massachusetts, John F. Kennedy. That release, occurring only a few months before the election, was the probable reason Kennedy was elected the President of the United States of America, in the tight election of 1960.

King did not stop after this threat to end his productive career. He organized more protests, sit-ins and marches, in some of which, police turned dogs and fire hoses on the demonstrators. In 1963, he was briefly jailed again, along with several hundred schoolchildren. The March on Washington, organized primarily by Bayard Rustin, occurred later that year. In front of more than 200,000 people, white and black, gathered together at the Lincoln Memorial, King delivered his "I have a dream" speech. The solidity of his faith, the power of his conviction, the soulful depth of his emotional commitment to the cause of equality for all people, and the ministerial vibrance of his voice resonated with all 200,000 who attended that day, resonated throughout our nation, and has since continued to resonate in our lives. We all knew, and still know, deep in our souls, that he was right. In 1964, the Civil Rights Act ended segregation in all public schools, in any public facilities, and in any place of employment. Although aided by several hundred thousand who had undergone personal injury, privation and great suffering to achieve that equality, it was one man who led the way, and bettered the morality of an entire nation in a monumental way. The greatest disciple of the Mahatma was a man of color, Martin Luther King, Jr.

Blacks, however, still did not have voting rights. A march was planned in Selma, Alabama, in March of 1965, to the state capitol, in order to dramatize this need. The president of the United States, Lyndon B. Johnson, urged King to not continue with the march, in order to avoid conflict with the police. King, in deference to Johnson, did not authorize that march, but it was carried out anyway by civil rights activists who were more impatient. The police turned the marchers away with nightsticks and tear gas. Two days later, King led another march toward the state capitol, using the same route. When confronted by the police at the Edmund Pettus Bridge, he knelt in prayer, asked his followers to do the same, and then turned them back to disperse. Whether because of the police brutality of Bloody Sunday, or because of King's non-violent march, the national reaction to those events led to the Voting Rights Act of l965, which established voting rights for blacks.

From 1965 to 1968, King continued his morality campaign, and continued to gather enemies. There were members of the Southern Christian Leadership Conference who were more militant, and seethed at the pacifist stand he had taken at the bridge in Selma. During marches organized in Chicago, to protest housing racial inequality, there was rather violent reaction by some of the bystanders. King was struck by a brick, but continued the march. He negotiated a settlement with Mayor Richard A. Daley, rather than expose his followers to further screaming, bottle-throwing, hostile crowds. He was strongly opposed to the Vietnam War, stating that the money that was being spent to kill Vietnamese should have been spent instead on eliminating poverty in the United States. Southern loyalists were particularly incensed at this apparent lack of fidelity to the United States. His planned march on Washington to protest the plight of the economically depressed was opposed by the more militant blacks, who felt that he was abandoning their cause to intercede on behalf of the poor. All of it shuddered to a halt when King was assassinated by James Earl Ray on April 4, 1968. His life ended, but his legacy has grown. This one man gave the United States of America a great leap in morality.

King's stances were, without exception, of the highest moral caliber. His recognition of the rights of the black population, opposition to segregation, support of voting rights, opposition to the Vietnamese War, recognition that we were actually fighting against equalitarian land reform in Northern Vietnam, support for the rights of the poor, support for equal housing rights, insistence on non-violent protest and resistance were all absolutely morally correct. His willingness to support those causes, with his life constantly at risk, is a tribute to his courage. He showed us all how we should love our neighbor, in the most practical of ways, that always said, all other people are my brothers and sisters. He falls closely behind Gandhi as one of the greatest moralists of all time, ahead of the Buddha, who preached separation from practical morality, and far ahead of both Jesus and Muhammad, both of whom insisted on the violent punishment of those who did not believe in them.

Lest we should glorify Mohandas Gandhi and Martin Luther King, Jr. too greatly, it should be made clear that they were both very human. Early in his career, Gandhi took a vow of chastity, after the birth of his children. He stated that he did so in order to devote all his attention and energy to the fight for freedom of his people. Gandhi did, however, have one strange habit. He particularly liked sleeping naked with naked women. He said that he did so in order to test his chastity vows. One would have to wonder, however, exactly what he did when he got an erection during the night, as all normal men do. That question remains unanswered. In the case of King, the answer is much clearer. J. Edgar Hoover, certain that the civil rights movement had been infiltrated by communists, persuaded Attorney General Robert F. Kennedy to give him telephone tap authorization. Those taps did not reveal that there was any communist influence on the actions of King, but did reveal that he had frequent extra-marital relationships, and saw one woman, not his wife, almost every day. This evidence was used in an attempt to blackmail him into quitting the civil rights movement, which King refused to do. That threat would have probably been carried further, except for his subsequent death, the circumstances of which are still not entirely clear.

In spite of this evidence that Martin Luther King, Jr. was very human, the legacy of morality he left behind in the United States of America was immense. Gandhi and King, in my opinion, stand head and shoulders above all other moralists in the history of the human race. This is not because they understood more than Cyrus, Locke, Paine, Franklin, and Jefferson – but because they saw exactly how to make love of your neighbor an integral part of our lives. They did not make the huge mistake of Jesus and Muhammad, as they are recorded, who hated all those who did not believe the same as they believed. Gandhi and King did not show intolerance. They demonstrated how, in the most practical of ways, to show love toward your neighbor, even if your neighbor was your enemy. May we all follow their example for the rest of our lives. It is obvious that politicians around the world have not yet learned these lessons of great humility.

OTHER LUMINARIES
MIXED MORALS

There is wonderful guidance from that prayer of Saint Francis of Assisi, "God grant me the courage to change those things that I can, the serenity to accept those things I cannot change, and the wisdom to know the difference." I thought there might be other significant moral lessons from his life. My review of his biography, however, gave me no other value lessons that were greatly pertinent to this discussion that I could impart to you. That was true of many of those other biographies that I read, describing people who, although they may have had great impact on the course of human history, contributed little, in my opinion, to the better behavior of their societies. There were some, however, who fell in between, if you will, in the honorable mention category. I would be remiss to not include some of these in this discussion of those persons whose individual efforts have contributed to the better behavior of their society and other societies to follow, even though each of them showed significant moral flaws in their character.

Francois-Marie Crouet (Voltaire) was born in 1694 and died in 1778. He was a consummate satirist, but also a playwright, poet, historian and scientist. He did everything well, with a sharp tongue that constantly got him in trouble. If there was any one person who was responsible for the French Revolution, it was Voltaire. He was on the run for most of his life because of his sarcastic criticisms of almost everyone else, was beaten up by the authorities, and spent some time in the Bastille because of his caustic tongue. The only stable time in his life was that spent in the chateau of Mme du Chatelet, who was a vibrant, intelligent woman, herself a scientist. They had a fifteen year grand relationship, feeding off each other's intellect, leading the

high life of society with gaming, regal parties, theater and other luxuries. He had his own sexual indiscretions during that heady time, but
then paid dearly for that unfaithfulness when Mme du Chatelet had
her own affair with the poet Saint-Lambert, and subsequently died in
childbirth in 1749. The love of his life, protectress and counselor was
gone. He continued to embrace life, but much of the joy was gone.

Voltaire continued to write plays, histories, scientific articles and
satires, alienating most everyone from time to time. He was banished
to England for a while, where he learned English and read Shakespeare,
which he considered rather brutal. He had to move frequently
because he had alienated someone, but attracted great crowds of
visitors wherever he went, and carried on a constant correspondence
with many of the great minds of Europe. He correctly opposed the
theory of spontaneous generation of life, called the intolerance of the
church infamy, favored material prosperity, praised benevolent rulers,
believed that all people should have equal rights, abhorred torture,
and demanded the liberation of serfs. He was a theist, but believed
that no church should be joined to the government. He was a consummate lover of luxury, and had great disdain for those who were less
intelligent. On the other hand, he saw clearly those moral steps that
would be needed to create a stable and supportive society. Most of
what this brilliant mind preached has later come to be.

Jean-Jacques Rousseau was born in 1712. His father was a watch-
maker and his mother was the niece of a Calvinist minister. When he
was ten years old, his father was forced into exile. Rousseau and his
brother were left in Geneva in the care of relatives. His teenage years,
in this state of limbo, were subsequently rather turbulent. He found
work temporarily as a clerk, read prohibited books whenever he could,
and was for a while a gang member. Through the help of the Catholic
Church, he escaped from Geneva in 1728, and found a protectress
in Savoy, Mme de Warens. Under pressure from the Catholic Church,
Rousseau converted to Catholicism in 1728, but could not bring himself to become a priest. Although much older, Mme de Warens soon
offered herself as his mistress, a relationship that lasted seven years.
It must have been good for both of them; Rousseau began to read
voraciously, and began to write. He produced poetry, a new method
of musical notation, an opera, a comedy, and papers on chemistry. He
began to be widely recognized, and then became famous after win-

ning the Dijon Academy Essay prize in 1750, wherein he attacked the tyranny of kings, the hypocrisy of the church, denounced luxury and called the arts corrupt. Controversy swirled about him for these defiant stances for the years to follow. He continued to defend himself for these beliefs, but found himself condemned by all interest groups in France. He was for a while exiled to Switzerland, then exiled to England. David Hume was his protector in England, but they also eventually argued, probably because of Jean-Jacques' paranoia, and Rousseau subsequently returned to France.

In 1740, he had begun a relationship with a chambermaid, Therese Levasseur, which continued up to the time of his death. They had several children, all of whom were sent to a foundling home. It was only later in life that he felt remorse for abandoning his children. Late in life, he wrote bad advice on methods of raising children and then married Therese in 1768. It was far too little, too late, in most all respects. He felt that all those who criticized his life style and his concepts were conspiring against him, slowly went mad, and died in 1778.

The one prominent and enduring theme of Rousseau was that material wealth and prosperity led to luxury and inequality. With that beginning supposition, he got a good bit of what follows right. In *The Social Contract,* he explored the ways by which one person can exert authority over another person, and still remain otherwise equal. Rousseau comes to the conclusion that only a contract which is freely accepted by all, in which everyone has something and no one has too much, will suffice to prevent inequality. The only sovereign portion of that contract is the people, who have the right to revoke that contract at any time. The private will of the wealthy should not at any time impinge on the freedom of any one person. There should be public education for all children. The costs of public properties should be met by taxes on the wealthy, on inheritances, and on luxuries.

The part Jean-Jacques Rousseau got wrong was his antipathy toward the arts and literature, those parts of our societies which are often the best that we have to offer. For his cry to produce a society which is equal in wealth and opportunity, however, a cry which reverberated in all those to follow him, we offer our deep gratitude.

George Washington was born February 22, 1732, in Virginia. He was the son of landed gentry, both on his father's and his mother's side. The family land had been given to them by King Henry the VIII.

George had an education that included Latin and English literature, as well as practical mathematics. By the time he was in his teens, he was experienced in tobacco growing, stock raising, and surveying. His father died when he was eleven, leaving him a ward of his half-brother, Lawrence. Lawrence married Ann Fairfax, a woman who is described as charming, graceful and cultured, coming from other prosperous landed gentry in Virginia. Ann Fairfax gave that sense of grace and culture to her half-son, George Washington.

Young Washington at first turned to surveying as a profession. With the aid of his family connections, he was appointed county surveyor in 1749. Much of that work was done in primitive conditions, where he learned to be resourceful and survive in a state of deprivation, and where he also developed a keen interest in developing lands to the West. All of that changed in 1751. His half-brother Lawrence died of tuberculosis, and the only other remaining heir, Lawrence's daughter, also died two months later. At age 20, George became the proprietor of one of the largest estates in Virginia, Mount Vernon. He proved to be a most capable manager. Although he sent to England for luxuries and equipment, and although he was subsequently away for years at a time, he gradually developed Mount Vernon into a self-sustaining community which had its own flour mill, blacksmith shop, brick kiln, fishery, carpenters, masons, coopers, weavers and shoe-maker. He rotated crops, bred cattle and took good care of his slaves. He provided them with clothing and medical care, and refused to sell them. In his will, he provided a clause that they would all be set free upon the death of his wife, Martha.

His military career began in 1751. He was drawn to a call to arms naturally. Several ancestors had been Indian fighters and officers in the British militia. His first action was on behalf of the British, who found the intrusions of the French into Ohio lands unacceptable. He was sent north to Fort le Beouf with a guide, interpreter and four men in 1753 to warn the French that they should end their expansion into that territory. The French reply was rather curt; Washington was told that he and the British should butt off; they considered these to be their lands. It was a perilous journey in the winter; Washington was nearly killed by Indian snipers, nearly drowned, and nearly froze to death after falling into the Ohio River. When Washington subsequently returned north with troops from the colony of Virginia, to fight the

French, he made a surprise attack on Fort Dusquesne, killing the commander and taking the rest as prisoners. This marked the beginning of the French and Indian War in 1754. The French retaliated in force. Washington and his army of 350 were forced to surrender, under siege by 700 French soldiers, after an all day fight. Washington was forced to sign a confession of surrender. His later return to that same battle area as an aide to the British General Edward Braddock also had a fatal result. He gave Braddock the wrong advice, telling him he should send part of his troops on to battle at Fort Duquesne while letting the supply wagons lag behind. Braddock was killed, Washington had bullet holes in his clothing, was nearly killed, and the British forces were defeated. Washington spent the next two years trying to hold a ragtag colonial army together through hard winters, with few supplies. He finally developed uncontrolled bloody diarrhea, and was forced to return to Mount Vernon. He did not participate further in the French and Indian War.

Washington was opposed to an American war for independence, but when the winds of revolution blew hot, he readily agreed to be the commander for all the colonial forces. He did whatever it took to bring discipline to the colonial army. He hanged a few deserters and had those who did not follow orders flogged. He had initial success taking over Boston, but was then soundly defeated at New York, with the loss of 5000 men. He garnered a victory at Trenton, New Jersey, but was then soundly defeated in Delaware by British forces. His meager army barely survived through the hard winter at Valley Forge, and it appeared that the American Revolution was all but lost. It was only through the efforts of Thomas Paine, who secured additional help from the French at this time, consisting of a gift of ten million dollars, a loan of sixteen million dollars, ammunition and clothing, that the tide turned in favor of the Revolutionaries. The American Revolutionary War ended with the capture of Cornwallis at Yorktown, in 1781.

The relationships between the united colonies of America were pretty rocky over the next five years. It was clear that they would either have to form a solid federal union or give this new independent union up altogether. When the Constitutional convention was called in 1787, Washington was unanimously appointed as its president, and presided over all the sessions. He said little, but wielded considerable influence on the candidates, outside the meeting hall, to reach the compromises necessary to form a constitution for the United States of America. At this point, he only wanted to retire to Mount Vernon to enjoy the good life: picnics, barbeques, fishing, fox hunting, puppet shows, dancing, cockfights, cards, entertaining guests, and developing his estate further. It just was not meant to be. As soon as the constitution was ratified, Washington was unanimously elected as the first president.

Washington, apparently by his own choice, proved to be a rather aloof president. He remained out of the fray as political wrangling mounted during his eight years in office. He chose to not become involved when the war broke out between France and England in 1793. He promoted religious liberty, favoring no certain religious group. While he took umbrage at the suggestion that he was holding office like a king, he certainly behaved that way, as judged by external appearance. He returned calls from no one and shook hands with no one. He rode in a six horse carriage with outriders and richly dressed lackeys. He wore a black velvet suit with a cocked hat and ostrich plume, yellow gloves, and a sword in a white scabbard. His manner was cold and reserved. Having said as much, there was still probably no better choice that could have been made for the first president of the United States of America. He kept the new country on an even keel during its first years of existence. Although pressured to seek a third term as president, George Washington had become greatly weary of serving his country by 1796, and refused to stay in office any longer. He retired to Mount Vernon in 1797, surviving for another 2 and one half years. After being exposed to winter cold all day in December 1999, he developed what sounds like an acute streptococcal pharyngitis. Instead of receiving antibiotics, he was bled four times and cantharides were placed on his throat. The expected result, as viewed by our hindsight, occurred; he died on December 14, 1999.

Henry Lee described Washington as being "first in war, first in peace, and first in the hearts of his countrymen." His death was mourned by the entire nation, as well as leading European figures. His importance in the development of our country was immense. On the other hand, it should be made clear that the war for American independence was not won mostly by the intrepid leadership of Washington. He made a number of tactical blunders during that war. It was well on its way to being lost, saved only by the efforts of Thomas Paine and initial efforts

of Benjamin Franklin, who obtained the assistance of France in turning the British away. His moral legacy was also extremely mixed. He
was a courageous leader, fair in his judgment, kind to his slaves, tolerant of all religions and a rock of strength for a burgeoning new country.
He was also a man who got a charge out of killing animals for sport,
a charge out of killing other humans in a power struggle, thought of
himself as some type of royalty, and prospered from the free labor of
his slaves. He was a great military and political leader. I would, however, take exception to the statement that George Washington was
first in peace; he was a warrior, and not a pacifist.

   Rolihlahla (to pull the branch of a tree, i.e., troublemaker)
Mandela was born in 1918 in South Africa. His great-grandfather was
king of the Thembu people, although by Thembu custom, his side of
the family was not able to ascend to the throne. His father was chief of
the town of Mvezo. Rolihlahla first attended an English school, where
the teacher gave him the English name of Nelson. When he was nine
years old, his father died of tuberculosis. After enrolling at Fort Hare
University for his college study, Mandela was expelled after one year
for participating in a student revolt against school policies. In that
interim, a marriage was arranged for him by his family guardian, who
had been appointed after his father's death. In order to escape that
undesired union, Mandela and his friend, Oliver Tambo, moved to
Johannesburg. Nelson worked there as a guard at a mine and also as
a clerk at a law firm. While in that firm, he completed his B.A. degree
at the University of South Africa, and his law studies at the University
of Witwatersrand.

   After the election of the Afrikaner National Party in 1948, which
supported racial segregation, Mandela began to participate in politics. He and Tambo, through their law firm, provided low cost legal aid
for blacks who needed attorney representation. He also participated
in non-violent resistance. In 1956, he and others were arrested and
charged with treason. His trial lasted five years, eventually ending in an
acquittal, but soured him on passive resistance. He began to coordinate
sabotage against government targets, organized militia and sought
funding as well as arms for these guerilla units. He lived on the run as
a designated terrorist, until captured, by means of a tip from the CIA.
He was convicted and subsequently imprisoned for twenty seven years.

   His imprisonment eventually accomplished more, perhaps, than he would have accomplished as a terrorist guerilla. International pressure gradually built over the years to free Mandela and end apartheid. In 1990, President F. W. de Klerk revoked the ban on the African National Congress and freed Nelson Mandela. After multiple party negotiations, the first elections were held in South Africa in 1994. Mandela was elected as the country's first black president. While serving as president, he played an important role in the negotiations between Libya and the United States over the men accused of bombing Pan AM Flight 103 over Lockerbie, Scotland. He promoted reconciliation rather than retribution as the country struggled toward integration. Mandela was criticized for not moving more swiftly against the growing AIDS epidemic in Africa, but served capably as the first president of a unified South Africa.

Nelson Mandela was both a terrorist and a pacifist. Fortunately, his pacifist intentions were greater than his violent bent.

> "During my lifetime I have dedicated myself to the struggle of the African people. I have fought against white domination, and I have fought against black domination. I have cherished the ideal of a free and democratic society in which all persons live together in harmony and with equal opportunities. It is an ideal which I hope to live for and to achieve. But if it needs be, it is an ideal for which I am prepared to die."

Agnes "Rosebud" Bojaxhiu was born in Macedonia, in 1910. As a child, she was greatly impressed with the stories of missionaries working in foreign lands. When eighteen years of age, she left home to join the Sisters of Loreto, and do missionary work. After one year of study learning English at the Abbey in Ireland, she was stationed in India, to teach school children at a convent. She took her vows as a nun in 1931, assuming at that time the name of Teresa, after the patron saint of missionaries. While she enjoyed her time with the children, she was greatly disturbed by the immense need of the poor in Calcutta. Not only was there abject poverty and rampant disease, but there were also sporadic Hindu and Muslim violent conflicts. In 1946, she received an inward call to leave the convent, live among the poor, and provide whatever assistance she could for them. The first years were extremely trying. She had to beg for subsistence and shelter. In 1950, however, she received Vatican permission to begin the order of the

Missionaries of Charity. Its purpose was to care for "the hungry, the naked, the crippled, the blind, the lepers, all those people who feel unwanted, unloved, uncared for throughout society, people who have become a burden to the society and are shunned by everyone." There were thirteen nuns in the original order. That order gradually developed, through charitable donations, to include thousands of nuns running orphanages, AIDS hospices, and charity centers worldwide, caring for refugees, the blind, disabled, aged, alcoholics, poor, homeless, and the victims of floods, epidemics and famines.

In 1952, Mother Teresa used an abandoned Hindu temple to create the Kalighat Home for the Dying, a free Hospice for the poor. Inhabitants were given free medical care and treated with dignity. Muslims received readings from the Koran, Hindus were given water from the Ganges, and Catholics received last rites. She soon thereafter opened a home for those who had leprosy, followed by several other houses for leprosy in Calcutta, providing medicine, bandages and food. In 1955, she opened the Numali Shishu Bhavan Children's Home for orphans and homeless youth. She soon attracted other volunteers and donations, allowing her order to establish orphanages, Hospices and leper houses throughout India, then throughout the world. This remarkable humanitarian effort, brought about by the singular efforts of this remarkably caring woman, followed a simple philosophy, as stated by this unrhymed poem, which hangs on the wall of the Shishu Bhavan Children's Home.

Give Anyway

People are unreasonable, illogical, and self-centered
Love them anyway

If you do good, people will accuse you of selfish, ulterior motives
Do good Anyway

If you are successful, you win false friends and true enemies
Succeed anyway

The good you do will be forgotten tomorrow

Do good anyway

Honesty and frankness make you vulnerable
Be honest and frank anyway

What you spent years building may be destroyed overnight
Build anyway

People really need help, but may attack you if you help them
Help people anyway

Give the world the best you have, and you'll get kicked in the teeth
Give the world the best you've got anyway

Mother Teresa's letters to her confessor show that, late in her career, she was greatly troubled by a lack of faith. I find that emotion completely understandable. My personal experience has been that, after so many years of trying to provide care for the disadvantaged, and finding that effort often unappreciated, a lack of faith in your mission is a natural phenomenon. I suspect that, although her intent was to provide compassionate care for all of her life, it became a matter of great question to her when she became roundly criticized from some quarters for trying to convert all those for whom she provided care, to Catholicism. She was also criticized for concentrating only on comfort care, and not addressing the root causes of the diseases for those she served. These criticisms seem hypocritical, although it is true that when she needed cardiac surgery, she went to a modern hospital in California, rather than to stay at home and receive comfort care. I would guess, however, that when she gave the world the best she had, even though she got many humanitarian awards for her remarkable work, but still got no praise from her Jesus and her God, she began to wonder if any of it was worthwhile.

Mother Teresa describes, in her letters to her confessor, Rev. Michael van der Peet, trying to speak to God, but having no answers come back. She describes praying to Jesus, but receiving no reply. She began to wonder if her God and her Jesus existed at all. Perhaps most damaging is the criticism of Christopher Hitchens, who says Mother Teresa told him directly she had not done any of her work to alleviate suffering and poverty, but had done it all in order to expand the number of Catholics in the world. "I am not a social worker. I don't do it for this reason. I do it for Christ. I do it for the church." In other words, a woman of great compassion and morality did everything she did, with angelic righteousness, but for the wrong goals. Her moral status in society is great, much the same as that of Abraham Lincoln, who freed the slaves for political, rather than primarily moral, reasons. Mother Teresa gave all of her remarkable love for her neighbors, in order to convert them to Catholicism.

Historians, in their judgments as to whom in human society has been great, and which of us has been unimportant, base that judgment on the amount of influence that particular person wields on human life after their death. It is a total package deal, which includes an increase or decrease in knowledge, enlightenment or suppression, destruction or building, depravity or morality. That is as it should be; it's just being realistic. There will always be human greed, anger, jealously, revenge, sexual perversion, hormone power struggles in the human experience. We should make due note of those influences on our lives whenever they happen, to whatever degree. On the other hand, I find revulsion for the degree to which violence and power struggles are not only emphasized in human history, but glorified. It is as if these wars, invasions and battles are examples we should all follow in directing our lives. I find it greatly disturbing that there is a vast library of violent video games which are vigorously promoted, and played incessantly by the young people of our latest generation. The lesson that each boy or girl gets from that game, is that killing and destruction are really fun things to do. It is no wonder that they then act out this lesson in real life, to the detriment of us all.

Although we should indeed be quite aware of those events in the past, good or bad, which have greatly influenced our lives, no matter how violent they may have been, I believe we are remiss if we do not place more emphasis on those persons in our past who have, by their individual effort, made all of our lives better. We make a big mistake if we equivocate, in our judgment of greatness, the overall influence that any one person has made on human society, with the advancement of morality, or what is right for human society. Greatness, in my opinion, should be reserved for those humans who have materially increased our knowledge, or who have shown us the practical moral ways we can and should love our neighbor. They have shown us how to become more at union with our universe, and how to bring the teachings of Jesus to the market place. If these are the criteria that are most important in judging greatness, Einstein and Gandhi top the list. All others fall somewhere beneath. Jesus and Muhammad lie near the bottom; both of them advocated violent intolerance for all those who did not share their mythology. We all continue to pay dearly for this immoral philosophy, as advocated by these Prophets, and as currently practiced by these religions of Abraham.

We must learn to live together as brothers, or perish together as fools.

-Martin Luther King, Jr.

REACHING A UNIVERSAL ETHIC

That's a goal that is a long way off for the human species, in my opinion. In order to complete this dissertation on human values, however, we are obliged to take a considered look at what it is going to take to reach an ethical human society, and what it is going to take to reach a universal ethic for all of life. In my estimation, those are two quite different things, although they follow closely on each other.

Each of us, during our lives, learns gradually what it is like to be on the other side, as other people treat us with disdain and disrespect, cheat us, rob us and hurt us. As we learn those lessons, we find that some of what it takes to be highly moral is difficult and painful, and entails personal loss on our part. We are bent to make decisions which are easy, or will profit us, rather than those decisions that are best for everyone. We then rationalize our poor decisions, in order to convince ourselves that what we are doing is right, regardless of what evidence exists to the contrary. We don't always ask ourselves if what we do is just for us, or is an act that will benefit others as well. Yet our experience has been that, whenever we deal with other humans on the basis of our greed, envy and revenge, we have a society that suffers and struggles. If we do not show reverence for life, do not love our neighbors, and do not demonstrate that love by giving to our neighbors, we do not have a society that will survive in health. Then all of us, as a result, suffer.

Achieving these moral goals is not an easy thing to do. We all often lack the courage to do unto others as we would have them do to us. How to bring these goals into reality becomes a great learning experience for us in our imperfect lives. I confess that there have

been many times when I know that I have not done all that I should
to express love for my neighbor. There is more that I could have done
while involved in the civil rights movement in the 1960s. There is
much more I could have done for my wives and children, rather than
spending most of my time at work. What was correct morally when
taking care of surgical emergencies, intensive care patients, terminally
ill patients and cancer patients often tried my soul. Perhaps review-
ing some of these moral quagmires which I have lived through during
my lifetime will help to highlight the dilemmas we all face in trying to
reach a human ethic.

THE KOREAN WAR

Europeans began to arrive on the Korean Peninsula in the
1600s. As trade became established, the first conflicts were between
Confucianism and Catholicism. Confucianism attached great importance to ancestor worship, which the Catholics considered a form of
idolatry. It was an uneasy and occasionally a nasty dispute. Sometimes,
Catholic missionaries were ferreted out and beheaded. The Koreans,
rightfully so, greatly distrusted these foreign invaders. That distrust
was not enough to keep Catholicism and other religions from making
inroads into the Korean culture. Other attempts by merchants from
abroad, including French and American ships, were repulsed well into
the 1800s. That resistance to foreigners wanting to take over Korean
commerce and their land did not last forever, however.

Japan long had cast its eye on Korea, both for military and economic purposes. They were finally able to convince Korea to sign a
pact of friendship and trade in 1876. That proved to be an opening
of the gates. This pact did not sit well with China, which also forced
Korea to sign a trade agreement with it, a pact which heavily favored
Chinese merchants. What followed next was almost a free-for-all.
Similar generous merchant pacts were soon signed with America,
Britain, Germany, Russia and France. Everyone who was not a Korean
wanted a piece of the pie, and none of it was advantageous for Korea.

The result of that exploitation was heavier demands on the peasantry and heavier taxes, which soon led to great poverty among the
farmers and the poor. The Tonghak revolution of that working class

followed, and was initially successful in disrupting government control and government demands. The Korean rulers turned to outside help to help them quell this rebellion. That request simply opened the flood gates even further for foreign domination. Both China and Japan responded to that request, and put down that rebellion, but then vied for control of Korea. Japan won that particular battle, and then took over complete control of the government of Korea. When they extended that control to the Liaotung Peninsula in Manchuria, however, that was more than the Russians could take. The Russo-Japanese War followed in 1904. Korea was forced to provide its land and resources for the Japanese to battle the Russians. Japan was victorious, and made Korea their protectorate; not long after, they annexed Korea as part of a greater Japan. The next several years were dismal for Korea. Japan basically attempted to obliterate Korean culture. They forced the Koreans to worship Shinto, dictated the teaching curriculum in the schools, changed the financial system, and placed Japanese in charge of businesses, while prohibiting Koreans from occupying managerial positions. Koreans were deprived of freedom of assembly and freedom of speech. Sporadic resistance was repeatedly defeated. An independence movement in 1919 resulted in the imprisonment of 40,000 Koreans and the death of 10,000 others. Large numbers of Koreans migrated to Manchuria, China and Hawaii.

The Japanese occupation of Korea did not stop until after World War II. As part of the Cairo agreement in 1943, America, Britain, China and Russia had promised that Korea would gain its independence "in due course." When Japan surrendered in 1945, it was to surrender all of its forces north of the 38th parallel to the Russians, and all those south of that parallel to the U.S. commander. This initially was simply a military expedient as part of the surrender process, but it soon became a more permanent process, as haggling continued over how to gradually allow Korean control. There were ideological disputes which could not be resolved, and were not amenable to compromise through the United Nations.

In 1950, North Korea, backed heavily by Russia with armament and training, invaded South Korea, advancing as far south as to capture Seoul. A counter-offensive under General Douglas MacArthur drove the North Koreans out of the south back to the Manchurian border. That successful military campaign only led to further conflict.

The Chinese then felt threatened, and intervened, driving the U. S. forces back below the 38ᵗʰ parallel. That level became the stalemate, and the chance of Korea becoming unified would be gone for a long time in the future. An armistice was finally signed in 1953. The loss of life was over four million, including thirty three thousand American soldiers. South Korea received over five billion dollars in American aid, and North Korea fell completely under communist domination.

I was drafted to participate in the Korean War early in 1953. We were told that this was a war to stop Communism from taking over all of Korea, and then spreading like some horrible disease throughout the Pacific Rim, eventually to reach our shores and take away our manner of life. I did not believe any of that propaganda. Most wars are fought for economic domination, and this one was no different. I had no desire to go off to a foreign land and shoot some other human so that American merchants would profit, and thought that any military action we took in Korea was immoral. I registered as a conscientious objector, fully expecting to be thrown in jail. I was eager to serve my country, but not in this way. Perhaps because of the ministers in my family, and perhaps because of the objections I presented to them, the draft board agreed to send me to alternative service for two years, rather than jail. Through the assistance of the American Friends Service Committee, I was assigned to the state supported Mental Health Institute of Independence, Iowa, as a psychiatric aide.

That assignment led to a career that up to that time had not remotely occurred to me. It was in other ways not an easy station. There were frequent hostile glares and frequent slights from some of the other employees, who had bravely served their time in Korea, and were greatly angered at seeing this coward, who, in their opinion, had refused to serve his country in its time of need. On multiple occasions, they offered to fight me and deliver that punishment which they believed I richly deserved. I believed that, most any day, I would be assaulted, but apparently those who were full of anger needed their jobs too much to carry out those assaults.

It was greed that led Japan to invade Korea and attempt to completely obliterate it as a nation over the first part of the twentieth century. It was greed that led Russia, China, France, Germany and America to economically invade Korea and rape its resources to their own advantage. It was greed that led Russia to invade from

North Korea into South Korea. It was the selfish desire of the U.S. for economic power and control, that led them to respond with armies, killing four million. It is continued economic greed, and ideology intolerance, that keeps the Korean people from becoming unified. All of this was immoral, and remains immoral. It was soon to be followed by the immorality of Viet Nam.

THE VIET NAM WAR

European penetration into Viet Nam began in the sixteenth century, first by the Portugese, then by Spanish, Italian and French missionaries. English and Dutch traders soon entered the fray to establish trading centers in Viet Nam. Most of that intrusion eventually failed, leaving only Portugal with a portal in that country. Missionaries were for the most part persecuted. Early attempts by France to establish an economic base in Viet Nam were repulsed, in both the eighteenth and nineteenth centuries. It was not until the 1860s that the French, simply because they had the use of modern weapons, were able to take control over South Viet Nam. Over the next twenty years, they extended their influence also over the Northern provinces. By 1900, Viet Nam had become a colony of France. The worst of colonial exploitation followed. Viet Nam became a rich source of rice, coal, rubber, textiles and raw material, all of which went to benefit France, and none of which benefited Viet Nam. Vietnamese farmers lost their land to large land owners, becoming landless tenants living at poverty levels. Only 15% of the population was literate. French inhabitants were given an education and health care. Vietnamese subjects were given neither. Civil liberties and a voice in the affairs of their own country were absent for the Vietnamese.

The expected result occurred. There was constant civil unrest, not reaching appreciable strength until the movement for national liberation beginning in the twentieth century. Those uprisings that occurred up to that time were sporadic and always viciously quelled by French forces. Attempts by the Vietnamese to enlist Japanese or Chinese help were unsuccessful. In 1925, however, an able-bodied seaman, who had spent time in Russia, France and China, returned to Viet Nam to establish the Vietnamese Communist Party. His name was Nguyen Ai

Quoc, who would become better known to the rest of the world as Ho Chi Minh.

During the 1930s, Ho Chi Minh laid his base. Legal fronts were established, recruits were obtained in all the villages, and extensively indoctrinated in guerilla warfare, as well as heavily armed. Their aim, first and foremost, was to obtain independence for Viet Nam. The French resisted these guerillas mightily. They still wanted their colony, and the exploitation that it afforded them. During World War II, Viet Nam was for several years under Japanese control, but then returned to the French. This did not stop the guerillas. Their insurgence increased, until the French, by now war weary, and unable to obtain support from other nations, agreed to a cease fire in 1954 that ceded everything north of the seventeenth parallel to the communist Viet Minh rebels, allowing France to stay south of that line.

The Hanoi regime in North Viet Nam now embarked on an ambitious scheme of industrialization, land reform and economic recovery. Conditions remained turbulent in South Viet Nam, however. Political fighting and coups prevented any return of stability. Communist sympathizers in the south registered an increasingly strident demand that the south and north parts of Viet Nam should be united. That demand was highly supported by North Viet Nam, which sent a steady flood of well trained and heavily armed resistance fighters into the south; these fighters were known as the Viet Cong.

At that point, this internal conflict became heavily Americanized. Up to that time, the number of American advisors in Viet Nam had been about 700. By 1963, that number had grown to 17,000. The propagandized reason for that heavy American involvement was again, an attempt to stop the spread of that nasty disease, caused communism, into all of Viet Nam, where it might fester, then spread, infecting all the rest of the world. Helicopters soon arrived, followed by troops, reaching 510,000 by 1968. Those troops were joined by some 600,000 Vietnamese, and a few thousand troops from Korea, Thailand, New Zealand and Australia. This large commitment of troops and armament did not succeed against the wily and determined Viet Cong guerillas. They fought, killed, and then disappeared. In frustration, the United States resorted to a wide spread campaign of destruction. The North was heavily bombed, thousands of acres of forest were sprayed with agent orange defoliant, destroying all vegetation and poisoning the land, and villages where some resistance was met were completely wiped out, killing all men, women and children. Incendiary bombs laid down explosive sheets of flame, which incinerated buildings and burned all inhabitants to death. It was hell on earth, wanton destruction and abject disregard for precious human life, all at the hands of a nation that prided itself on freedom and equal opportunity, where all people, they claimed, had the right to life, liberty, and the pursuit of happiness. It was apparent that this championship of life, liberty and the pursuit of happiness extended only to Americans, and at that, quite tenuously. The hypocrisy of those acts was immense.

The great immorality that these acts represented was increasingly sensed by the American population. Demonstrations against the Viet Nam War became increasingly more demanding and more strident. Not only was this a war which could not be won, but it was a war which was horribly destructive of human society. Our leaders finally saw the light. By 1973, all American troops were withdrawn from Viet Nam. By 1976, the Communist North had overcome the South, once again unifying Viet Nam. As an aftermath of the war, vast reaches of the northern and southern provinces had been destroyed, 57% of the population was left homeless, and at least 16% of the population had been killed or severely wounded. The residual moral scar on the United States of America was appalling; it was deep, broad and ugly, with a constant post-traumatic painful neuralgia, for the rest of the life of this country.

MISSIONS TO MEXICO

Over the last ten years, I have gone on three church missions to Mexico, accompanied by other members of the West Ohio Conference of the Methodist Church. Each of those trips was about a week long, each time with a group of about thirty wonderfully devoted people. Each was a unique educational experience, in its own way. There was a lot to be learned.

On the first, we flew out of Columbus headed for Houston and then McAllen, Texas. All of us were chattering and full of anticipation. The lady next to me, a lovely elderly lady who had worked on a Northern Ohio farm all of her life, started sucking on lozenges as soon as we were airborne. She soon was leaning her head back and closing her eyes, then became silent and pale. About an hour into the flight, she started vomiting into the bag provided in the pouch, in front of her seat. She filled that one up, and others were passed up or handed over for her to fill also. After three bags had been used and handed over to the stewardess, she leaned her head back for a few minutes, and then slumped over the fold-out table in front of her, unconscious. The stewardess rushed to get me their first aid kit, which on this large jet carrying 150 people, consisted of a blood pressure cuff, two syringes, a vial of adrenalin, a vial of Benadryl, and some bandage material. There were no other medical supplies of any kind on board or available on this craft, isolated in the sky. Her blood pressure was 88/58, and I could not elicit any abdominal tenderness. They patched me through in the cockpit to their medical control on the ground, who asked me to give her the Benadryl. I did so, thinking that this wasn't going to help at all. She needed intravenous fluids and a CT scan of her head as soon as possible. I asked if the plane could be diverted to land at the next available large airport, and was told that they would let me know. That didn't happen; we continued flying on to Houston, and I kept checking her pulse and blood pressure to make sure she was still alive. It was obvious that this airline was going to take its chances on this lady's survival, rather than bear the expense of an extra landing, disrupting the schedule of all 150 persons on board, and all the connecting flights. The airline made an economic decision, calculated against the possible loss of life.

When we landed in Houston, she was taken off on a stretcher, and I accompanied her to the hospital in the ambulance, along with her husband. She was soon after arrival taken to the CT scanner, where her study fortunately showed no tumor or bleed on her brain. She was given intravenous fluids, had her electrolytes checked until they returned to normal, and had no other abnormality that showed on her screening blood tests. By the next day, she was able to converse normally, was alert, and admitted that she had motion sickness, but thought that she could make the trip by not eating or drinking on the flight. Her attending physician told me that they planned to release her the next day, to travel back to Ohio by car when one of her relatives could come to pick them up. At that point, I flew on to McAllen and met the rest of the mission team there.

We spent our time on that mission building church pews, putting up playground equipment, and constructing an addition on to the back of the church. On the first day, while we were in the midst of our carpentry, I was asked to see a lady who was ill across the street. We walked in the mud over to their house, which was a plywood shack with no door in the doorway, no window in the two window spaces, a dirt floor, a single lumpy sofa, two bunk beds, and a shelf where there were some pots and pans. The inhabitants of that house were a man and woman, two young children, and a woman who sat on the lumpy sofa with uncontrollable constant seizures on the entire left side of her body. Her left face, arm and leg were twitching and jerking constantly. Her frightened face stared at me, begging for succor. The story was that her husband had left her, and that she had nowhere else to live. She had for that reason come to live here with her sister, her sister's husband and their children. These seizures had been going on for hours. She remained conscious and had use of her right arm and leg. Her pastor asked me what I thought. I told him that uncontrolled seizures on one side of the body usually indicated a brain lesion on the opposite side; she needed a CT scan of her head and seizure medicine. The pastor gave me a long hard look, and then said, "Señor, they have no money." He next did what they always did when there was no immediate solution to the problem. He gathered all of us around in a standing closely bunched circle, arms over arms, and we prayed.

Back at the work site, when we related the situation next door, hands went into pockets, and money began to appear. Soon we had over $100 dollars, which was donated to provide care for her. With that backing, the pastor took her to the hospital, where she did not receive a CT scan, but was given seizure medicine. That medicine provided her, we were told, with at least temporary relief. What happened after that, we never knew. When there is no health care insurance, life becomes hard.

On the second mission, we spent our time working under a boiling summer sun, putting up concrete wall as an upstairs addition to an existing church bottom floor. Long range plans called for, on future missions, the addition of a parsonage, and a small building which could be used as a health clinic. It was truly hot. We usually drank eight to ten bottles of water a day, and sometimes had to take breaks in the shade. On the third day, there was a loud explosion to our south. We looked up to see a tin roof twirling up one hundred feet into the sky, accompanied by other debris, all of which then came crashing down. We were not permitted to reach the site of that explosion, which was only a few blocks away. By afternoon, trucks full of soldiers appeared, headed for that site. The next day, we were advised that an illegal fireworks plant had blown up, destroying one block of shacks and badly damaging those in the next block. The blast made newspaper headlines, and the write up described how such dangerous cottage industries, all of them illegal, were common in Mexico, in an effort to generate income. Dense poverty does that to you.

In two days, we were allowed to visit that site. There was a deep hole in the ground where the blast had occurred. The surrounding land had been leveled bare, with no vegetation. The houses across the dirt road had holes in them where shrapnel had penetrated. No remains of the owner of that shop had been found. We again did what was always done when there was a disaster without a solution. We gathered around in a circle and prayed. Some of our group stayed to lay down concrete footers for one of the houses that had been completely leveled. The rest of us went back to our mission site, to complete our task. After the last concrete block of the new wall had been placed, on the last day of the mission, we also gathered around to pray.

On our third mission, we traveled well into Mexico in order to establish our base at the Methodist Church in Monterrey. The first thing that could not be missed, as soon as we cleared customs and traveled across the border, was the number of American manufacturing plants just across that border, all of them showing signs of being very busy. We were told that while the cost to those companies in America may have been $14 an hour for an employee, they could obtain a Mexican worker for that same price all day long, and throw in bus transportation as well as a free lunch. They had no trouble getting their full complement of employees, and all plants were highly profitable. Something seemed to be terribly wrong with that economic picture. Industrialists were prospering, but not those American workers who had lost their jobs. They and their families were suffering.

As we approached Monterrey in the evening, the appearance was hellish. The fires and smoke were belching from their refineries; the air was hot, heavy and sulfuric, in a haze of smog. I wondered what sort of terrible things lay ahead of us.

After our first night in, on a Saturday, we joined members of that church for their worship service the next morning. We were taken that afternoon to a downtown shopping mall to spend a few hours, before heading out to our work site the next day. The rest of the group went one way, on into the mall. For some reason, I turned to go back to the street. Something there looked familiar. Coming out into the sunlight, I looked across the street and was stunned. There was the hotel where we had stayed, when we had come to Monterrey to get our adopted daughter. There was the park where we had taken her in a stroller, after the Mexican consulate would not release her until further investigation had been done. I walked slowly through that hotel, in a daze. I slowly crossed the street and went over to that oasis park, surrounded by picturesque mountains, past the noisy folk festival, and slowly sank down at the fountain where we had sat years before, full of sorrow. All of the other memories came flooding back.

We had adopted her before birth. Her birth mother already had two children, was unmarried, and did not feel that she could support a third child. She chose us, from our descriptions and pictures, and from other options that she had, to be the parents of her baby. When her baby and our baby was three months of age, we were advised that all of the adoption papers had been completed, and went to Mexico to pick her up. Her nanny at the orphanage in Ensenada, who had cared for her over the last month, handed her over to us sadly, with the look of love coming from her heart, and with tears in her eyes. We then took a Mexican flight to Monterrey, to get final approval from the consulate of her birth state. As we got on that plane in Ensenada, ready to take off, one of the passengers two rows behind us, apparently quite frightened about this flight, began projectile vomiting pure blood. He was carted off the plane and all those seats had to be cleaned before we could depart. We noticed that there was no control tower at the airport in Ensenada. When the plane bounced down to a landing in Monterrey, there was a loud round of applause from all the passengers, as soon as it was clear that we were going to stay on the ground. They were greatly relieved to have survived that flight, and obviously knew a lot more about Mexican air travel than we had known. We were bunched into an open air taxi on our way to the hotel. Then it was my wife's turn. She began vomiting, forcing the driver to stop while she threw up. I was the object of long, searching stares from brown men, a tall white man with a freckled face, who was holding a brown Mexican baby, while his woman retched by the side of the road. That evening, in the hotel room, we fed her and played with her, until she started tongue thrusting, pulled her little blanket up over her head, and fell asleep. At that moment, I fell in love with my latest daughter. The bond was intense, and has not stopped since. We were heartbroken when the consulate in Monterrey would not clear her for adoption. We were not allowed to bring her home, and had to return her to the orphanage in Ensenada.

After three more months with hundreds of phone calls, a visit to the consulate in Detroit, and a camp-out in the state representative's office in Washington, D.C., we were able to go back to Ensenada to pick up our daughter and bring her home. She was six months of age, and it was on Valentine's Day in 1986. We were greatly fearful, until we made it through customs in Houston without being stopped. We took it as symbolic that there were colorful sunbows low in the sky all the way home from the Cleveland airport. She was sitting in a little bunny suit in the back seat, with a brown face and staring big black eyes, apparently aware at that tender age that a major change had occurred in her life.

The rest of our mission in Monterrey went well, in spite of my initial premonitions. We put in a water line, hung electrical fixtures, finished off the drywall for the walls and the ceilings, and put in doors. We turned a shell into a home for the pastor, who served three churches. After all the work had been completed, we again gathered in prayer, wishing the pastor and his family success in guiding his flocks. On the way back to our base, after that last day of work, something very touching occurred, at least for me. There were low sunbows in the sky all the way back to town, just the same as those we had on the day we first brought our adopted daughter home. Then something else unexpected happened. Before going straight back to our base, on the last day, we decided to visit a 400 year old monastery which sat nestled in the hills above Monterrey.

After several climbing twists and turns, we reached the parking area in the back, and then walked around to the front to look over the city. As dusk gradually settled, city lights blinked on down below in forms and patterns. Out front, the figure of Jesus stood with his arms stretched out over the city. Off to the west, the sunset cast an orange and magenta glow over the tops of sawtooth mountains. Over to the southwest, there was a brilliant vertical scarlet slash in the sky. I had seen colored jet trails before, but never before had seen such a deep scarlet slash in the sky, as if it were an exclamation point. As darkness fell, the monastery was bathed in yellow light on old stones and facades. On the steps of the monastery, a wedding party had gathered, with a beautiful bride and handsome groom posing there with their families. They were taking photos in this picturesque setting before it became too dark. Just then, a group of giggling young girls, about age 15, came around the corner, showing shiny satin purple dresses, white sashes, brown skin, red lips, flashing black eyes, and smiling white teeth. They were animated and happy, and beautiful, each in her own way. At that point, a great calm suddenly came over me. I had seen my adopted daughter's humble place of origin; I understood that her birth mother had given her up because she loved her. I understood the economic circumstances that led this woman to give up her baby, in hopes of giving her a better life. I saw who my youngest daughter was and where she was going in life. My circle had been completed. The feeling of peace, and knowledge of direction, was immense. It was a religious experience.

What I learned in our missions was, for one, that there is something very wrong with the organization of our American economy. The rich are getting richer, and the poor are getting poorer. The rich are becoming wealthier by feeding off the poor, a human failure that cannot continue in a moral society. I learned that you can live in a shack with a dirt floor, no windows and no doors, and still be a loving and caring person, who is clean most of the time, even though there are no shoes, no toilet, and no running water in the home. It appears that wealth feeds immorality, more than poverty feeds immorality. I learned that human love and bonding knows no boundaries of gender, distance, nationality, genetics, age, race or color. I learned that you do not feel whole until you have given of yourself for another person. Only then, does each of us know our God.

ANIMAL RIGHTS

Several decades ago, on a trip to the Cincinnati Zoo, we came up to a small glass cage where there was a large gorilla, out away from the others, where the crowds could get close to him. Children were gathered around, pointing, talking and gesturing. One of them put her finger up to the glass, and the gorilla responded by putting his finger up to the glass across from hers. She squealed with delight and laughed. Then the children moved on, and the gorilla swung his attention to me. He stared at me, and I stared at him. We locked eyes for a full minute, and I had the uncomfortable feeling that he was more in control than I. He knew that he was an individual who should be able to pursue his life, and had instead been put in this cage on display. He was asking why it had to be him, and why it couldn't instead be me that was locked into a cage. He stared me down, causing me to look away and walk away, feeling that he knew me better than I knew him. There was no doubt that he was a discerning creature with an analytical mind, a bit angry about his circumstance in life. He seemed to be asking me why I did not set him free. That experience, and my experience with my pets, who frequently give me more love than I give them, has convinced me that animals think, discern, plan, feel deeply, experience pain, and express great sorrow. To my mind, they deserve to have life, liberty, and the pursuit of happiness, as much as humans do.

That passage in Genesis, declaring that man shall have dominion over all living things, need not be repeated here. It was interpreted by the Jewish faith to mean that all these things in this world could be used in any way that humans saw fit. That belief was further compounded by their mistaken faith that they were god-like, or created in the image of the Creator of the entire universe. This meant to them and those who followed, that all other life and things were inferior to them, and therefore subject to their manipulation in any pleasurable way they pleased. These two greatly flawed concepts, in our millennia to follow, have led to an exploitation, rather than careful and respectful management, of the earth's resources. That exploitation and corruption has included not only mineral and plant resources, but also, all animal resources, many times in ways that are extremely cruel.

According to Descartes (1596–1650), the universe was mechanical. By his accounting, the mind was separate from the physical, mechanical body. Since animals, in his opinion, did not have the same sense of self-awareness, they were, in his mind, simply automatons. His appreciation of animals was pretty dismal.

"They can see, hear and touch, but they are not, in any sense,

conscious, and are unable to suffer or even feel pain."

The first known laws in England against animal cruelty were initially passed in Ireland in 1635. Farmers were told they could not pull the wool off sheep, and could not tie a plow to a horse's tail. The Puritans, who temporarily took control of England in the 1650s, took offense at those bloody sports which used animals. They correctly interpreted the passage in Genesis to mean that they should be responsible stewards of the earth's resources, and that this passage did not mean they were masters of all things. They passed laws prohibiting cock-throwing, dog fighting and bull baiting. Unfortunately, those laws they passed were later repealed under the English rule of Charles II.

John Locke (1632–1704) was a bit more enlightened. He understood that animals have feelings, and that cruelty toward them is, for that reason, morally wrong. His concern about the mistreatment of animals, however, was not because it was immoral to be cruel to a feeling animal. He didn't see that this fact, in and of itself, was a primary reason to oppose the mistreatment of animals. Locke was against animal cruelty because, rightfully so, he felt that it had a deleterious effect on the perpetrator of that crime. He at least got part of it right.

*"For the custom of tormenting and killing of beasts will, by
degrees, harden their hearts towards men."*

Jean-Jacques Rousseau (1712–1778) understood a bit more. He believed that animals did have self-awareness, or sentience. This meant that they should be treated with respect.

*"It appears, in fact, that if I am bound to do no injury to my
fellow creatures, this is less because they are rational than
because they are sentient beings; and this quality, being
common both to men and beasts, ought to entitle the
latter to at least the privilege of not being ill-treated by the
former."*

Immanuel Kant (1724–1804) was at least half blind, if not more so. He could not see that animals have any significant value, and did not believe that humans have any obligations to non-human life; both of these attitudes are, in my opinion, grievous errors. As did Locke, he at least understood that cruelty toward animals corrupts the perpetrator.

"Cruelty to animals is contrary to man's duty to himself,

because it deadens in him the feeling of sympathy for their
sufferings, and thus a natural tendency that is very useful to
morality in relation to other humans is weakened."

Jeremy Bentham (1748–1832), who was the founder of American Utilitarianism, got a whole lot closer to the real condition of animals, and the real reasons why we should be kind to them, as well as to each other. He not only understood that animals can reason, but more importantly, also understood that they can suffer.

"The French have already discovered that the blackness of
the skin is no reason a human being should be abandoned
without redress to the caprice of a tormentor…What else is
it that should trace the inseparable line? Is it the faculty of
reason, or perhaps the faculty of discourse? But a full grown
horse or dog, is beyond comparison a more rational as well
as a more conversable animal, than an infant of a day or a
week or even a month. But suppose the case were otherwise,
what would it avail? The question is not, Can they reason?
Nor, Can they talk? But, Can they suffer?"

During the 1800s, multiple attempts were made in England to introduce legislation against cruelty to animals. Most of these proposed laws were immediately laughed out of whatever legislative body received these requests. The first law to be passed in England declaring the mistreatment of animals to be illegal, in any sense, was the *Ill treatment of Horses and Cattle* bill, introduced by Colonel Richard Martin. When Colonel Martin brought the first case to trial himself, against a street fruit vendor who was consistently beating his donkey, the jury was falling asleep as he made his case. At that point, the good Colonel decided to bring the donkey in the courtroom to testify on his own behalf. When he demonstrated the extensive injuries that the donkey had sustained, the shocked jurors rather quickly rendered a guilty verdict. At this point, other laws against cruelty to animals soon followed, not only in England, but also in many European nations. Fostering this rapidly awakening awareness of the rights of animals was not the only good deed done by Colonel Martin for the benefit of animals. Under his direction, the Society for the Prevention of Cruelty to Animals was founded in 1824. The American wing of the SPCA was founded in 1860, near the onset of the American Civil War.

The German philosopher Schopenhauer (1788–1860) was also a champion of animal rights. He applauded the increasing amount of legislation which attempted to protect animals from mistreatment, and had a flirtation with vegetarianism, at least discussing that possibility, but could not quite get himself to accept that necessity. He stated that Europeans were

> "...awakening more and more to the sense that beasts have rights, in proportion as the strange notion is gradually overcome and outgrown, that the animal kingdom came into being solely for the benefit and pleasure of man."

Henry Salt, a professor at Eton University, finally understood correctly the true relationship of humans to animals, in 1894. Perhaps he did not fully understand the additional implications of what he said, but he certainly got the basic ideas right. We will never understand how we should behave toward animals, he says, as long as we think of ourselves as more moral, or of greater purpose, or of greater worth than those animals.

> "The notion of the life of an animal having 'no moral purpose' belongs to a class of ideas which cannot possibly be accepted by the advanced humanitarian thought of the present day – it is a purely arbitrary assumption, at variance with our best instincts, at variance with our best science, and absolutely fatal (if the subject be clearly thought out) to any full realization of animal's rights. If we are going to do justice to the lower races, we...must recognize the common bond of humanity that unites all living things in one universal brotherhood."

The rest of the world has been slow to follow this enlightenment, and we are certainly not there yet. During the twentieth century there were an increasing number of animals used for research, in all fields, including medical research, pharmaceutical companies, food and drug additives, military investigations, and others. Animals have had noxious drops placed into their eyes until they are blinded, burning pastes put on their backs until the skin sloughs, and monkeys have been bashed in the head while fully alert to record the damage to their brains. Surgeons have been carving up dogs, pigs and cattle in most any way imaginable. They have been taking out their hearts, lungs, livers, kidneys, and pancreases to see what it took to transplant those organs. The remains have been discarded. Not all of this, by any means, has been humane. There was a rapid growth of megafarms, restricting animals all of their life to small cages or pens, treating them only as sacrificial eating machines. Legislation requiring the respectful treatment of animals on farms has been slow in coming.

There has been a moderate degree of outrage against these immoral practices, with only limited success. There has been very little inroad against the deeply rooted practice of hunting for sport, treating animals as moving targets, as if they were pieces in a video game, of no intrinsic value. This is a multi-billion dollar industry, where schools empty for deer hunting season, and the newspapers always each year show pictures of proud hunters showing off their buck, or their tom, or their big fish, as if killing that life made them quite important and powerful. If all of it were used to donate to soup kitchens and the homeless, there might be some value in that hunting. As it stands now, a whole lot of that hunting is pretty disgusting, from a moral point of view. At least *The Animal Liberation Front*, an anti-hunting group, made enough inroads into that business to be labeled as a terrorist organization by the Department of Homeland Security. Under pressure from animal rights activists, many experimental programs for medicines, cosmetics and the military have been persuaded to use other methods than animal suffering to investigate their products or answer their questions.

One good response to this misuse of animals has been the rapid growth of human vegetarianism. This practice has blossomed, demonstrating that a healthy life can be obtained and probably a longer life by eliminating meat from the human diet. Vegetarians seek each other out, and frequently gravitate to fairly large communities where others are of like mind and menu. Their recipes are not only varied and healthy, but a good deal more interesting than a steady run of meat and potatoes. At current time, vegetarianism is a healthy choice, which is good for humans, and blunts the exploitation of animals. As the world's population grows further, vegetarianism may not only become the moral and humane choice, but also a matter of necessity. Since only ten percent of the value of our foods is preserved, when our vegetable resources are used to produce meat, this may well be a practice the world can no longer afford. We will need maximum use of our food resources in order to feed the burgeoning population of this world. The sooner we all adopt vegetarian practices, the better off both humans and animals will be, and the better we will preserve our sustaining home, the planet earth.

FINAL COMMENTS

Henry Sidgwick put it pretty well. He made it clear that we are all in this life trial together. *"The good of any one individual [man or animal] is of no more importance from the point of view... of the universe, than the good of any other."* The first basic point to make, in talking about human value systems, morals to any degree, or extending to ethics, is to understand that there is no basic Goodness in the universe. Socrates, even though he meant very well, was terribly wrong. Yet that concept has been carried over into our philosophies and in particular, into our dominant religions of today. It is depressing to see that the human species has labored under this false pretense for many millennia, and greatly frustrating to see that we have as yet been unable to break free from that heavy ball and chain. As long as we believe that there is a total Goodness in the universe, we also have to invent a total Badness in the universe – and both of those get us into a whole lot of trouble. We want to identify ourselves with the goodness part, and all the other guys with the badness part. Races, nations and other groups then use these good/evil concepts to excuse their violent conflicts. We must realize that the universe is indifferent about humans or any other life form. We can make rational decisions about our lives, other humans, and other life, only when we realize that the universe is neither good nor bad. We are, along with all other forms of life, in a fight for survival, in a universe which sustains us in our little cocoon; but it is also against us, and will, in due time, totally eliminate us, because it does not care, in any way.

We also have to understand that we are not made like the force which created the universe, are not being directed toward a planned goal by any force, are not in direct communion with some commander of the universe who intercedes on our behalf, are not immortal, and are most certainly not in command of all life. We are here because a certain life form began some four billion years ago, and because, through a process of natural selection, species evolved, and we evolved. When we think, under the misdirection of these religious myths, that we are godlike creatures, headed toward a grand destiny, and hold great power over all life and perhaps other parts of the universe, we make awful moral decisions. Only when we realize that we have just this one precious gift of life, after which our individual selves will be gone forever, are at the mercy of the universe, and must preserve all our resources with the most diligence, can we make moral decisions. Semi-divinity, great power, grand purpose and immortality don't get it. They are perhaps greatly comforting concepts which help us get through this cruel world; when used as rationalizations, they also lead us badly astray. We treat all other life with respect and our planet with care only when we realize the urgency of using our mortality wisely, and know we are at the mercy of this grand universe.

We have to understand clearly that morality is purely a human invention. We make those judgments as to what is good or bad on the basis of what gives each of us pain, pleasure, sustenance, shelter and survival. When larger groups are involved, morality gets messy, and it becomes a matter of what provides the greatest good for the greatest number. Extending that number to include all other humans has been a difficult task. We still live in a world which is full of jealousy, greed, revenge, selfishness and anger. Each group or nation continues to vie for an advantage against all other nations, in order to protect their particular form of society, or their particular misleading religious mythology. We have as yet been unwilling to recognize all other humans as our brothers and sisters, each of them with the same right to life, liberty and the pursuit of happiness as we possess. As a species, we have not yet been able to accept that none of us has more intrinsic righteousness, goodness or morality than any other person, or any other form of life.

There is a compelling reason why it is highly important that we, as a species, must greatly advance our morals, if we are to survive as a species. That particular reason is because, at this seminal time in our development, we have become one world, involving all of life. We are all joined together on one planet, so that any event in any area has an effect on all the rest of the planet and on all other life. We are no longer isolated in pockets, free to do whatever we want in our society. We are all neighbors. The Good Samaritan now lives in China, or some other land half way around the globe. The imperative of Jesus to love your

God *and* love your neighbor now becomes even more dire, and covers the complete planet. The directive to also love your enemy becomes not just a moral, but a necessity, if the human race is to survive. We cannot much longer continue to burn, bomb, destroy and behead each other, while raping and polluting our resources, without jeopardizing all of life.

The last point again returns to the language of precise definitions, which appear to be much more important to me than to any of the other authors who have addressed these issues. In my opinion, we cannot claim a universal human morality, or, as exists in my definitions, a Human Ethic, until we treat *all* humans of any gender, race, religion, color, intelligence or stature with equal respect, and with equal opportunity for life, liberty and the pursuit of happiness. In my opinion, we cannot claim a Universal Ethic, until we include in that respect, and in that morality, *all of life*, human and otherwise. I believe that human morality must take this one additional giant leap in its value systems, before it can call itself a totally ethical form of life.

There is much left to be done.

-February 15, 2010

A

I

R